From Temple to Meeting House

Religion and Society 16

GENERAL EDITORS
Leo Laeyendecker, *University of Leyden*
Jacques Waardenburg, *University of Utrecht*

MOUTON PUBLISHERS · THE HAGUE · PARIS · NEW YORK

From Temple to Meeting House
The Phenomenology and Theology of Places of Worship

HAROLD W. TURNER

University of Aberdeen

MOUTON PUBLISHERS · THE HAGUE · PARIS · NEW YORK

B
829.5
T87

ISBN: 90-279-7977-4
© 1979, Mouton Publishers, The Hague, The Netherlands
Typeset by Cédilles, Amsterdam
Printed in Great Britain

For two who embrace different aspects of this study

My Father, Herbert John Turner, 1883-1952
Who built houses well

and

My Son, David
Architect and urban designer

Preface

This work was never planned in the form it has finally assumed. It began under the stimulus of the Senior Seminar in the Department of Religion of the University of Nigeria in 1964-1965, with a simple thesis concerning the repeated failure of Christian places of worship to express the distinctiveness of their own religious tradition. Subsequent teaching at the University of Leicester provided the occasion for the development of phenomenological tools for the analysis of structures for worship in all religious traditions. By means of formalized phenomenological criteria we then sought to reveal the religious content of places of worship across the history of the three Semitic religions. In so doing we sought to avoid the type of study — exemplified in so many guidebooks to churches, mosques or synagogues — that merely catalogues historical data or else belongs to the history of architecture or of aesthetics.

Later, when at the University of Aberdeen, an inevitable logic carried the study forward into Christian theological comment on the results obtained in the earlier work, and finally into an attempt to explore the relationship between phenomenological and theological procedures. The study as a whole therefore resembles the Topsy of the popular saying.

It will be apparent that several changes of role occur in this work, as between the phenomenologist, the historian and the theologian. These 'hats' are mostly worn separately, but on occasion they appear together. It would have been laborious and pedantic to have specified the particular headgear being worn at each point in this study, and we hope readers will recognize this for themselves, assisted by the discussion in the last chapter of the interrelation of these roles. It is our own belief that most of this work could have been undertaken by one of any religious allegiance or of none, provided trouble had been taken to understand representative biblical and theological scholarship.

Over the years of the making many debts have been incurred. Acknowledgement is made firstly to the members of those enjoyable seminars at Nsukka, where Murray Ross (architect), Geoffrey Nutting (musician and lay theologian), Geoffrey Johnston (Protestant seminary historian) and Jerry Creedon (Catholic seminary lecturer in Old Testament) added much to the outlook of those of us in the Department. In Leicester my students contributed a stimulus of which they may have been unaware, and Dr. Joan Tooke (as she then was) of the College of Education encouraged me with her enthusiastic trials of my first drafts on her students. Mr. Peter F. Smith, architect, the Rev. John F. Butler, Methodist scholar, and Professor Marcel Simon of Strasbourg also reinforced the will to continue on lines with which they warmly sympathized. While at Aberdeen I have benefitted from professional criticisms of the Islamic material by Dr. Elizabeth Macfarquhar (as she then was) and by Dr. James Dickie whose own work on the liturgical history of mosques is eagerly awaited. Likewise Professor L. G. Geering of Wellington, New Zealand, provided keen critiques of the chapter on Judaism and especially of the final chapter. A special acknowledgement is due to the Very Rev. Dr. John M. Bates in New Zealand, lifelong tutor and mentor; his brief but penetrating comments on the conclusions drawn from the first twelve chapters quite changed the content of the theological material in Part III.

That this work has reached publication is largely due to the persistent support of Professor Jacques Waardenburg of the University of Utrecht, as an editor of the series 'Religion and Society' in which it appears. That it ever came into existence at all depends more than even I know upon Maude, who has had to live with it for fourteen years and whose typing skills finally helped to bring it to a conclusion.

Department of Religious Studies   Harold W. Turner
University of Aberdeen
Scotland

Contents

PART THREE: THEOLOGICAL SYNTHESIS

PART ONE

Phenomenological Analysis
The Sacred Place and Its Biblical Versions

1

Methods of Approach

The most enduring monuments surviving from the long history of mankind are those erected under religious compulsion for the worship of the gods and the well-being of the dead in some further existence. These span only the last few millennia of the human story, but earlier evidence for the use of unstructured places for special purposes comes from the ritual and burial caves, underground or on mountainside, of prehistoric men in Europe and elsewhere. Together these religious edifices and sacred places have withstood forest encroachment, desert exposure, natural decay, and the misfortunes of war and conquest, to bear their impressive witness to the nature of man as worshipper, lavishing his limited energies and resources on the laborious construction of religious sanctuaries, ritual centres, or burial places for his dead.

This is no merely historical phase, an infancy of mankind superseded in a maturing secular world. Despite the claims for the decline of religion in our time and most of all in areas where the Christian tradition has been strongest, it is possible that the present century has seen more buildings erected for worship than all previous centuries combined.

Winston Churchill's remark on the rebuilding of the House of Commons in its peculiar traditional form is well known: 'We shape our buildings, and afterwards our buildings shape us.' It is not surprising that the same sense of the importance of buildings as places designed for certain uses has resulted in the extensive modern discussion of the architecture of churches, and the founding of special agencies for the study of this subject.

1.1 DIFFERENT STARTING POINTS

The seriousness of this current discussion warrants an equally serious examination of its starting point and premises, and of the concepts with which it operates. The last occasion of a comparable discussion was in the forties and fifties of the nineteenth century, when the Gothic Revival inspired by Pugin, the Cambridge ecclesiologists, and later the Tractarians and Ruskin, changed the ecclesiastical landscape of Britain, the United States and much further afield, and left in the popular mind an image of what a church building should be like. The starting point for the ecclesiologists and Pugin was an idealized period of Christian history, the fourteenth century when Europe was regarded as having achieved a Christian civilization and culture, and when the Christian faith was both pure and influential. In church building the manifestation of this golden age was fourteenth century decorated Gothic architecture, which was therefore accepted by the Gothic revivalists as the normative or only truly Christian form. Their premises, their starting point and their dominant concepts are explicit and clear.

The recent discussion reveals strikingly different positions. While recognizing the great contribution made over a century ago to our historical knowledge of Gothic, the present movement has repudiated both the starting point and most of the concepts of the previous movement. Historical study of the building of churches has been carried back to their beginnings in the third and fourth centuries, and has given us a much fuller account of the many forms of subsequent development up to our own times. This information has been joined to the contributions of the biblical and theological movements of the present century that have clarified the understanding of the nature of the church as a worshipping community, and also the understanding of worship itself due to more adequate knowledge of the history of Christian liturgies. The efforts of the modern liturgical movement and of its associated studies in church architecture have been concentrated upon the assimilation of these new historical, biblical and theological insights into a growing ecumenical consensus as to the nature of Christian worship and of the building designed to accomodate it.

The position reached in the sixties may be seen from the titles of some of the books published in that decade: Hammond's *Liturgy and Architecture* (1960), Bieler's same title in French in 1961 translated as *Architecture in Worship* (1965), White's *Protestant Worship and Church Architecture* (1964), Debysts' *Modern Architecture and Christian Celebration* (1968), and what would seem to be the ultimate in this direction, Bruggink and Droppers' seven hundred pages on *Christ in Architecture* (1965) with its specific applications of a Reformed theology to the building of churches. Further titles could readily be added, as also the various publications of the Institute for the Study of Worship and Religious Architecture of the University of Birmingham and of the Department of Church Building and Architecture of the National Council of Churches of Christ in the U.S.A., and the Constitution on the Sacred Liturgy adopted by Vatican Council II in 1963. Despite some continuing differences the overall consensus is clear and remarkable, and the impression might be given that the liturgical movement has virtually arrived at its goals and that there remains only the application of its insights to the building and liturgical activities of the local churches.

It is our conviction that there is still considerable work to be done in seeking a proper understanding of what we here call 'the Christian version of the sacred place'. It is probably true that the historical outlines of Christian building are sufficiently clear for most purposes, and that the early and important period is well served by works such as Krautheimer's *Early Christian and Byzantine Architecture* (1965). It is true that gaps remain; little seems to be available as to the ideas and practices of the various sixteenth century groups covered by the term 'the radical Reformation'. It is, however, unlikely that further discoveries will require a major change in the historical perspectives now available.

It would appear to be in the biblical and theological fields that further discoveries may be made. By the 1960s a notable series of works had examined the biblical position concerning the interrelations of the place of worship, the religious community and the presence of God. We may mention Congar's *The Mystery of the Temple*, surveying both Testaments, Clements' *God and Temple* for the Old Testament, and for the New Testament Lohmeyer's *Lord of the Temple* and McKelvey's

The New Temple, together with Cole's smaller work of the same title, and Gaston's *No Stone on Another*. As background to these studies there is the work on temples of the Ancient Near East by the *Biblical Archeology* group, summed up in their *The Biblical Archeologist Reader*, and the valuable study of Gärtner, *The Temple and the Community in Qumran and the New Testament*. Davies' massive *The Gospel and the Land* added another basic dimension to the discussion. We shall have occasion to refer to many of these as this study progresses.[1]

1.2 NEED FOR A THEOLOGY OF SPACE

While advance in the biblical field is being well served it is possible that we are only at the beginning of some of the theological work necessary for further understanding of the place that provides the spatial setting for worship. This requires a theological exploration beyond doctrines of the church, its ministry, sacraments and worship, beyond even theological accounts of work, of matter, and of art that are involved in any theology of the church building. We need a theology of space itself, as a basic category or dimension of human existence with the most immediate relevance to a spatial structure such as a church. We have here an extensive lacuna in theological thought that becomes apparent when we consider the considerable attention given to the category of time, and therefore of history, as also to the philosophy of history. We have forgotten that history always has a geography, and that each is essential to the other; it is no accident that while historical studies of religion flourish the very concept of a geography of religion is almost unknown in most religious studies. And yet for Christians the incarnation was a spatial and geographical event as much as it was temporal and historical, and the Church itself exists likewise in both dimensions.

There is a sense in which the development of the historical interest and the ever-widening pursuit of historical enquiries is a modern development of the last two centuries. It may well be that we are now entering upon a parallel development of a new sense of space, a space-age in more ways than one. As our control over the spatial environment increases, and the pressures upon its use likewise increase in a crowded world, architecture and town and country planning become more space conscious. While on the one hand a travel speed that can take us around the surface of the earth in a day virtually eliminates the spatial distances within the world, and consequently the time dimension of travel, on the other hand the achievement of travel into outer space faces man with journeys to the remoter planets that could take a lifetime. The so-called conquest of space only reveals how firmly our human existence is embedded in both the spatial and temporal dimensions.

The need for theological understanding of the space used in worship is therefore only one of the reasons why a theology of space is becoming a practical necessity. We welcome recent signs of theological interest in this direction, of which we may mention two.[2] The first, Spindler's *Pour une Théologie de l'Espace*, raised the whole issue but is primarily a missiological exploration by one actively concerned in the Christian mission where geographical factors are more obviously important. The other, T. F. Torrance's *Space, Time and Incarnation*, approaches the question from the side of dogmatics, and asks whether the spatial concepts embodied in the creeds are merely symbolic and oblique ways of speaking about the nature of God, or possess a more direct and cognitive reference.

1.3 THE PHENOMENOLOGICAL APPROACH

It is our purpose in these pages to set some of the results of these studies in another perspective, that of the phenomenology and history of religions. The biblical records describe a great range of places of worship, and subsequent Christian and Jewish history reveals many further developments; these, together with the ideas and theories that gather around them, constitute an important section of the phenomena and the history to be studied by these wider disciplines. Unfortunately there has been a tendency for scholars working on the biblical and Judaeo-Christian materials to deny the relevance of these other disciplines or to ignore their results, while those engaged in phenomenological and general historical studies have been tempted to concentrate on the other main religious traditions and to leave the Judaeo-Christian field to its own specialists.[3] In this way all have suffered.

We are not suggesting that either kind of study can replace or absorb the other, and least of all do we mean that the biblical material must be forced into categories established in the examination of other religious traditions, or treated as necessarily only a particular form of the religions common to the Ancient Near East. This kind of reductionism is no longer possible after the intensive work done on the peculiar features of the biblical tradition. By the same token, if the categories, the analyses, and the structures of the phenomenology of religion are inadequate to encompass the biblical data then the phenomenological equipment must be extended until it can do justice, for its own purposes, to this as to other sections of the religious world. At the same time it must welcome the most complete and authentic interpretations that the biblical and theological studies of the Judaeo-Christian data can supply.

On the other hand these biblical and theological studies are dealing with something that remains a religious tradition, and only if we deny it the name of religion can we assert that there is nothing to be learnt from the categories, analyses, and structures employed in the study of other traditions. As J.F. Butler has put it, 'Christianity is entitled to its own norms; but it will understand its norms less well if it thinks of them in isolation'.[4] If there is a distinctive Christian version of the sacred place then this should never be clearer than when set in relation to the characteristic developments of other traditions in the wider religious world. A phenomenology of religion that is adequate and truly scientific can do nothing but reveal this situation and indeed give it formal recognition by extending its own equipment to include these new forms. If the Christian disciplines trust the phenomenological approach in this way then they themselves will be able to share in its discoveries of the vast range of forms and meanings in the whole spectrum of religion. This further knowledge should make the Christian disciplines more sensitive and alert to aspects, forms or nuances in their own field that might otherwise be missed, as well as clearer as to what is a truly new development or unique feature. In short, the more one has studied other religions the better equipped one is to study a particular religion; and when the religion studied is also that of one's own personal adherence it becomes vital to secure this wider perspective.

The validity or otherwise of the approach we here adopt will be seen in the course of the study that is to follow. We outline it at this stage as a declaration of intent, and to allay any fears such as those expressed by Professor J.G. Davies that use of the phenomenological starting point may lead to 'accepting an outlook simply because it is common to the majority of the world's religions'.[5] Insofar as they are all religions they must of course share some common outlook and be none the worse for that; insofar as there is a fear that phenomenology accepts some majority form and then regards this as a norm, the fear is based on a misunderstanding of the nature of this discipline. Its task is not to establish norms but to discover and interpret faithfully whatever norms there may be in the various religious traditions, and then to assist those traditions to compare their own norms with their empirical manifestations, and to relate both norms and manifestations to their equivalents in other major traditions. In this way phenomenology, like theology in other ways, is the handmaiden of the religious traditions themselves, and by no means the source of a new religion or the adjudicator between the religions.

1.4 PHENOMENOLOGICAL ANALYSIS OF SACRED SPACE

It so happens that the phenomenology of religion is now well equipped for the study of the religious use and understanding of space, and therefore of places of worship in their spatial reference. The spatial dimension has been recognized as an important category of religious existence and expression, and has been analysed to reveal its characteristic structures or forms, which we may outline briefly at this point. There is first the idea that all space is organized and orientated by the sacred place, itself regarded as the centre of man's life, the point of reference around which his world is built, or, as it is vividly put in a number of traditions, the navel of the earth. From this point men take their bearings and establish some system and meaning in human existence; at the sacred place life finds its centre of unity and ceases to be merely a chaotic flow of experiences.

This functioning as the ultimate centre for human affairs derives from a second characteristic structure found in the sacred place, its capacity to mirror or to represent on earth a more perfect and ultimate realm conceived as lying beyond the terrestrial domain. The detailed form of the sacred place is not given by the needs or imagination of men, but is provided by the gods so that it may serve as an earthly microcosm of the cosmic realm that is their abode. So much of human life is disordered and imperfect, but here is the one place amid the uncertainties and frailties of human existence that reflects or corresponds to the ordered strengths of the heavenly realms.

As a consequence of this correspondence the sacred place is the one place on earth fit for the gods to visit, where they may be encountered with certainty by men, and where the heavenly and earthly realms continue to intersect. Here men may bring their prayers and offerings, and here the divine powers and wisdom may be exercised for human welfare. The sacred place is therefore the meeting point between heaven and earth, and in its later developed forms, the house where the gods dwell when they deal with men.

A fourth characteristic form is the cult object, image or idol that symbolizes and embodies the divine presence at the sacred place. It may be almost anything – an unshaped stone, a wooden pole, an empty throne, an elaborate metal image. or even a mirror or a written document. Whatever it is represents the very complex notion implicit also in the two previous structures, that while the gods are really to be met at this place they cannot be contained in it, that while they are truly immanent in this sacred object they are just as truly transcendent and beyond it in their own proper realms. Indeed, this may be regarded as the basic endeavour of all sacred places, to guarantee the immanent presence of divine beings who by their very nature transcend all such places; and what is this but the basic problem of the relation of man to his gods?

Finally the spatial and the temporal categories are related through the myths that are associated with the sacred place, especially cosmogonic myths reciting the creation of the world and its beginnings from the sacred place itself as the navel of the earth. These myths reveal how it is in fact the centre, the microcosmic centre of the heavenly reality, and the meeting point between men and their transcendent gods.

These typical structures have been elucidated by studies directed mainly to the religions of primal societies (the 'archaic' religions), to the religions of antiquity, and to the living religions of the non-semitic traditions. Emerging from this range of religions we discover a general similarity of sacred place, both in physical structures and in interpretations; in its final or most developed forms we may call this the temple type or the *domus dei*, and we shall find that it serves as a basic tool in our later discussions and analyses of church buildings.

1.5 THE TWO MAIN TYPES DISCOVERED

Phenomenological studies have not yet made an equally intensive approach to the living religions within the Semitic tradition; here, at least on the face of it, a quite different type of place of worship appears – not a house for the god but a house for the people of the god, not a temple but a meeting-for-worship house where a rather different conception of the immanent presence of the transcendent deity is apparently in operation. The phenomenologist, having observed these new forms, will naturally ask whether the analyses and structures that have elucidated so much in his other studies will prove equally illuminating in the Semitic religions. It may be that unsuspected identities will emerge and the Semitic sacred places be discovered as special forms of the temple type; on the other hand points of difference may be clarified and confirmed and a new type systematically delineated. If few of the previous tools prove helpful then phenomenologists will have to develop new tools for the new data, and at all points they must endeavour to remain faithful to the most authentic interpretations and norms of the several Semitic traditions, and do justice to the differences between these traditions themselves.

It is our own conviction, to be supported by the pages to follow, that we do in fact find the sacred places of the world's religions falling into these two forms, the temple type and the meeting-house, and we shall use these as working concepts for the analysis of places of worship.

While the former can be called the *domus dei* the latter is appropriately called the *domus ecclesiae* only within the Christian tradition, and so we shall retain the term meeting-house in order to speak of the Semitic religions in general, and normally use their own terms of synagogue, church and mosque when dealing with them individually. We hope to demonstrate that even at the phenomenological and historical level the meeting-house type presents the authentic norm for the Christian tradition.

1.6 RELATION BETWEEN PHENOMENOLOGY AND THEOLOGY

While this study starts, as phenomenology must, from the human end, from sacred places in men's religions, sooner or later it comes across new forms which force it to recognize that they themselves contain another standpoint from which all that has gone before must be reviewed. This is a familiar development in the history of any science and should not be regarded as abnormal when it occurs in the sciences of religion. The phenomenological approach, once it has served this purpose, passes over into theological considerations which in turn are subject to further phenomenological study as data within a particular religious tradition. Phenomenology and theology, therefore, are each indispensible to and inseparable from the other and through their relationship each gains a new dimension which we shall examine more fully at the end of this work. The following pages are offered as a case study, exemplifying the relation between these religious disciplines in the one particular field of the place of worship.

2

The Sacred Place

The space in which human life is set is far from being homogeneous in our experience. Only in a world 'without form and void' could one space be the same as another, and then all space would be equally meaningless to us. Spaces, or the different places within space, have meaning and value only because of the different organization and content they contain, which mark them out from one another. Among the many differentiations those with the greatest meaning and value are distinguished from the more ordinary places through their association with supra-human powers or presences. This kind of place may be called magico-religious space where daemonic and mysterious powers are believed to operate. As these powers become differentiated into magic forces, evil or dangerous spirits, and divinities who sometimes at least may be benign, so these places themselves are likewise distinguished into sites appropriate for magic rites, evil places to be avoided at all costs, and sacred places where the gods may be approached.

2.1 THE SPATIAL REFERENCE IN RELIGIOUS LANGUAGE AND WORSHIP

The sacred place in a particular religious tradition or community is only the most obvious and concrete expression of the spatial element in religions. A metaphorical and symbolic use of spatial references pervades all language and not least religious language. As Ernst Cassirer has well expressed it,

> Often the terms coined by language for the expression of religious awe and veneration go back to a basic sensuous-spatial idea, the idea of shrinking back from a particular zone.... Wherever mythical thinking and mythical feeling endow a content with particular value...

13

this qualitative distinction tends to be represented in the image of spatial separation. Every mythically significant content, every circumstance of life that is raised out of the sphere of the indifferent and commonplace, forms its own ring of existence, a walled-in zone separated from its surroundings by fixed limits, and only in this separation does it achieve an individual religious form.[1]
Christian religious language provides examples at every turn. Examine the succession of spatial references in a prayer which might begin as follows: 'O God, the high and lofty One, dwelling in light inaccessible, before whom the angels veil their faces and fall down in adoration, behold thy servants assembled here and be present in our midst....' In the same service, the Creed will assert that God in the incarnation 'came down from heaven... was crucified, dead and buried... descended into hell... rose again... ascended into heaven... sitteth at the right hand of God the Father, from whence he shall come again....' Such language is entirely and inescapably characteristic of religions and needs study rather than apology.

Both the meeting between men and the gods, and the language men use to the gods and about them are inevitably involved in spatial references, so that in examining the sacred place of meeting we are dealing with a basic category of religion. That it is basic is indicated perhaps by the tremendous variety of spatial forms that the sacred place may adopt: stones singly or in circles, grottoes and groves, trees, pillars and mountains, springs, rivers and seas, altars, shrines and sanctuaries, temples, tabernacles, synagogues, churches, stupas and mosques, places of pilgrimage where divine actions have been recorded or holy men are buried, sacred cities and holy lands. It is not our purpose to attempt a detailed study of these myriad manifestations but rather to set forth the ideas, structures and functions most commonly found among them, to examine the variations in these features with a view to establishing a typology of sacred places, and in particular to delineate the two main types of temple and meeting-house.

2.2 THE EARLIEST SACRED PLACES

Both of these, however, are late developments in the history of religions. The first sacred places were quite independent of buildings or indeed of any human construction or artefact and were defined by some natural form that had come to possess religious significance, the stone or the tree, the cave, grove or hill where men had been specially aware of the presence of divinities. The first human contribution to the development of the sacred place arrives when these or other features are provided with a specially cleared or demarcated area, a precinct or τέμενος (temenos) bounded in some way by lines or stones, by hedges or walls, or by a ditch of non-defensive shape with its high bank on the outside. These elementary forms of demarcation are the ancestors of all later ways of distinguishing the sacred area from the ordinary world, whether it be the walls of the holy city that had profounder meanings than that of military defence, or the altar rails and chancel screens found in some Christian churches.

These are the most ancient known forms of man-made sanctuaries and they occur across all cultures and religions. Archaeology has shown this to be the form of the places of worship in Celtic Britain and in north-west Europe until well into Roman times, and it continued in pagan Saxon Britain after the Roman era in spite of the impressive example of the Roman temples. In the same manner Greek temples began as open-air sanctuaries where the place itself was holy as the abode of a divinity, Japanese shrines were merely a sacred precinct around a sacred object, and Polynesian sacred places were open spaces marked out by curbings or low stone walls with perhaps a platform and a line of vertical stones at one end. Similar forms have been found in the remains of Minoan, Mycenian, the Indus and many other civilizations, so that it was by no means confined to primal societies lacking the technology for more impressive structures. Such open-air sanctuaries reveal that the essentials of a sacred place for worship are location and spatial demarcation rather than buildings or other elaborations that come first to our own minds.

The very word 'temple' begins its history in the Greek verb τέμνω (temno) referring to the cutting or marking out of a special area of the heavens where divine signs might be seen, a kind of heavenly precinct as it were — in fact a τέμενος (temenos); then it is applied to the earthly image of this heavenly area, the corresponding place on earth where divine actions occur, omens are given, and sacrifices offered in a sacred precinct. When buildings came to be erected they were at first very small, merely a cover or shrine for the cult object through which the divinity was present. Other buildings within the precinct were entirely ancillary — shelters for the resident guardians of the sanctuary, for pilgrims or the sick who came for healing, storehouses for the accumulating gifts brought for the gods or for the materials required for sacrifices, huckster's stalls for the supply of the worshippers' wants whether of food or figurines. These were all utilitarian rather than religious buildings, and none served as a place of assembly or shelter for a congregation of worshippers. Only the shrine itself, protecting the sacred object of the god from careless intrusion by the outside world, could be regarded as a sacred building and then only in a derivative fashion; its later elaboration into a temple, a richly decorated or impressive palace-like structure fit for the residence of a god, must not be allowed to obscure this point.

2.3 THEIR DIVINE ORIGINS

If the essentials of a sacred place are location and a defined spatial extension, how does it originate? It might seem that certain natural phenomena are inherently suited for the purpose of arousing a sense of a divine presence, and inevitably become places of worship. For instance, the sacred grove in early Roman religion has been described for us:

How powerfully the dim light of a grove works upon the feelings of a religiously sensitive soul!... the slim lines and height of the trees, the mysterious gloom of the place, the wonder at the shadows, so thick and unbroken, calls forth in you a belief in divinity.[2]

We moderns confuse our aesthetic and emotional reaction with a religious reaction to natural phenomena, but this has not been typical in human history. Not every striking or mysterious object or place in nature possessed religious significance, but only those so designated by the gods. Thus in West Africa a place of this nature is accepted as sacred only after consultation with a diviner who reveals whether a divinity inhabits the place and wishes it dedicated to him. Some sign from the gods, some theophany or manifestation of divine power and presence at a certain place is the explanation of its sanctity. Otherwise we cannot explain why some apparently most suitable places are treated with indifference and others less striking are sanctified; why great effort may be expended in constructing a grotto-like sanctuary from large rocks when there is a most impressive and mysterious natural cave in the vicinity; or why such places may cease to be regarded as sacred.

To say that a place has been sanctified suggests that it is made sacred by human choice and an act or rite of consecration. This is a common misconception which is exposed as soon as careful examination is made of consecration rites whether in a primal society ritual or at the opening of a new church today. Then it will usually appear that the essence of the ritual lies in prayers to the divinity, either beseeching the god to come and consecrate this place by the divine presence or recognising that this has already been done by some sign or act. Indeed in most religious traditions, including the Christian in its earlier history, great pains have sometimes been taken in order to secure, or even to provoke, a sign from heaven as to where the sanctuary should be. It may be where the hammer the mason-monk throws into the air falls to earth, where a mysterious vision was seen on a hill-top, where a man was healed or a prayer answered, or where an animal specially driven out into the bush first lay down.

Neither natural nor human agency makes a place sacred, but only the action of the gods. Here the divine has been present in power, and here the gods continue to dwell or at least to visit men, so that this place is now a regular holy place of worship. Jacob at Bethel provides a classic example (Genesis 28). But even more significant is the attitude of the Israelites to the many ancient sanctuaries they inherited and retained from the Canaanites. For Israel these could only be legitimated by some theophany of their own god, Yahweh, and so we have a whole series of what Pederson has called 'consecration legends' describing the experiences not only of Jacob but also of Abraham at Shechem, Isaac at Beersheba, Jacob at Peniel, and others at Mahanaim, Gilgal, Mizpah in

Gilead, etc.. Of special interest is the account of Gideon at tha sanctuary of Ophrah where Judges 6:11:32 preserves two stories, the first clearly a consecration legend and the second exposing the nature of the pre-existing Baal-sanctuary.[3] In all cases the divine revelation has created the sanctuaries for Israel, and this is characteristic of religions in general.

That the consecration of a sacred place is essentially a divine act has been recently illustrated in Dr. Reymond's account of the consecration rites of an Egyptian temple:

> ... the ritual episodes are interpreted as mythical events in which the gods themselves enacted the consecration of the temple... when the temple was constructed.... They arrived at the site together with... the deities who were engaged in the creation of the temple. The first act to be performed then was the naming of the enclosing wall... to... define the main part of the enclosure.... Thereafter another ceremony was performed... the ceremony of giving the temple its names... an independent act which seems to be of prime importance... then the assembly of the gods performed a procession at which they sang hymns and recited spells of adoration. There followed an early Festival of Entering... opened by Tanen, who seems to have invited the god, the lord of the temple, to enter his sanctuary.... An act of adoration... was... performed thereafter by the lord of the temple.... Thereafter a procession seems to have been conducted along the four sides of the enclosure, the participants being the deities who were engaged in the construction of the temple.[4]

The mythical interpretation of the actual rites conducted by the Egyptians shows in vivid fashion how strongly men feel that the gods themselves are responsible for the sacred places where men worship.

2.4 THEIR FOUR FUNCTIONS

The functions of the place so designated as sacred have been outlined already in our brief account of the basic structures elucidated by phenomenological study; it acts as centre, as meeting-point, as microcosm, and as a transcendent-immanent presence. To each of these we must now give somewhat fuller attention.

2.4.1 THE SACRED PLACE AS CENTRE

All of us have had sufficient experience of being lost in a physical and spatial sense to know how devastating it can be. To have strayed from parents when a small child in a crowd, to be deposited in a strange city without map or language, to enter an informal social gathering as a complete stranger, to be lost in a pathless forest without sight of the sky, or blown out to sea on a dark night – imagination if not actual experience reveals how in such situations the loss of all points of reference threatens the total dissolution of one's world, and leads to panic. Parallel experiences in the psychological realm occur when a man retires from a busy life and says he suddenly feels 'lost', in a sudden emergency when we say we were 'at a loss to know what to do', and in the more serious situations where there is a pathological loss of any incentive to act, to go on living, or even to know one's own identity. In a somewhat different connection we speak of a person who is spiritually confused as a 'poor lost soul'.

These examples, which could be indefinitely extended, indicate how basic is some centre of reference for life as a person in what we call a 'world' – some organized system which supplies meaning and direction for our actions, some point from which we take our bearings and make sense of it all. Without this life is a senseless flux of events and degenerates into chaos. Value systems, world views, ideologies, philosophies of life as well as the more physical orientation to our material environment through sight, hearing, movement and memory are essential to existence as a man, and all of these imply some centre of reference.

Men have always known a good deal about the forms and structures of the physical and social world about them; they have had their bearings sufficiently to develop language, to create social organizations, to hunt, farm, and build. At the same time none of these forms or structures is regarded as an autonomous reality, self-perpetuative, self-explanatory, complete and lasting. Each is only too liable to collapse, to prove inadequate or to succumb to attack from hostile powers. All become completely reliable and receive the protection they need only when linked to or organized from some secure centre of power that is unassailable, permanent and immutable. Such a centre of reference is found in the sacred place where contact may be made with a much more real and solid world than that of everyday uncertain and changing experience. The transient and vulnerable affairs of men then have 'an anchor in the ultimate'. To the sanctuary all human needs may be brought, here every failure may be confessed, guidance sought in every problem and power invoked against every threat or danger. From this centre man can face his environment and find his way through life's hazards and problems.

As a concrete example that is all the more vivid in coming from a nomadic people, the Sioux Indians, we may quote the account of the establishment of a new altar as given by one of their holy men:

Thus ... Kablaya ... made the sacred place; first he scraped a round circle in the ground in front of him, and then ... he prayed.... A pinch of earth was offered above and to the ground and was then placed at the center of the sacred place. Another pinch of earth was offered to the west, north, east, and south and was placed at the west of the circle. In the same manner, earth was placed at the other three directions, and then it was spread evenly all around within the circle. This earth represents ... all that is in the universe. Upon this sacred place Kablaya then began to construct the altar. He first took up a stick, pointed it to the six directions, and then, bringing it down, he made a small circle at the center; and this we understand to be the home of *Wakan-Tanka*. Again, after pointing the stick in the six directions, Kablaya made a mark starting from the west and leading to the edge of the circle. In the same manner he drew a line from the east to the edge of the circle, from the north to the circle, and from the south to the circle. By constructing the altar in this manner, we see that everything leads into, or returns to, the center; and this center which is here, but which we know is really everywhere, is *Wakan-Tanka*.[5]

All directions of the spatial world and their contents were thus related to the one centre where the divine power was present. The Sioux 'world' had been re-established at their new camping site and human life could continue.

Typical of many other manifestations of the same idea was the temple of Apollo at Delphi where the sacred conical stone in the sanctuary was regarded as the centre of the earth. This centre is often identified with the point from which the creation of the world took place, and is represented equally at all the sacred places of a particular people. Thus 'the historical temple in Egypt is regarded as the direct descendant of the primeval temple that was erected on a low mound near the island on which the drama of creation commenced. ... Every cultus place took this myth of creation and adapted it to local needs, and thus every temple in Egypt appears to have claimed to be the original place of the creation of the earth.'[6] Hence it is that the sacred place is called the navel of the earth.

The same idea may persist even with a less parochial outlook. In certain Jewish traditions the Holy Land or Jerusalem itself is spoken of as the navel of the earth, the point from which all else unfolded at the creation. Another Jewish legend regards the site of the Jerusalem temple as the point where creation began and where the first ray of primeval light shone forth upon the whole world. This light continued to shine after the temple was built, and to let it out upon the world the windows were narrower on the inner side and widened towards the outer side, thus reversing the usual shape where light is to enter rather than leave the building. Therefore, 'the lighting of the great candelabra... may have represented the kindling anew of the cosmic light, at its proper place, the Temple, the centre and source of the light of the world'.[7]

Essentially the same idea of the need for an ultimate centre of reference is seen in the ways in which a territory newly occupied by a people must be made into a 'homeland', into 'our world', or a 'holy land'. Mere occupation by men is not sufficient. It must secure some relation to the gods through a ritual of possession or consecration as a sacred place. Then it is distinguished from all surrounding territories as 'our world' because given us by the gods and bound to them; only here do truly human beings live a proper human life, for beyond it lie strange chaotic lands peopled only by barbarians, sub-humans or ghosts without benefit of the divine centre established in our midst. Only we are 'the-men'; thus in one African area the people call themselves 'ba-ntu', (the people) and in another in Chile, 'mapuche' (the people of the land).

There are therefore manifold ways in which the sacred place serves as the special point in this world where men may share in the reality of the divine life with its vitality, power and order; it is the 'heart of the real', the centre of the world, the navel of the earth from which created life receives its vitality, its periodic renewal, its proper organization and its satisfying meaning.

2.4.2 THE SACRED PLACE AS MEETING POINT

Our account of the sacred place as centre has inevitably revealed its further function as point of communication between heaven and earth, the place where the gods have revealed themselves and where men go to meet with their divinities. The many physical forms and associated ideas that manifest this function may be grouped into those concerned with man's entrance into the sacred realm and those representing a connection between the divine and human spheres.

Of the 'entrance' phenomena we may begin with the significance of the threshold. The various means of demarcation of the sacred precinct that were mentioned above also indicate that this meeting point must be respected and protected, and that the worshippers themselves must be safeguarded from casual or inappropriate dealings with such a centre of power. They correspond therefore to the insulators and guard fences that contain the electric power and exclude casual entry at an electricity substation. There must be a particular place of entrance and to cross the threshold at this point is a momentous act for it marks the transition from the everyday natural order to the place of divine power and presence that lies beyond, within the precinct. In consequence, a host of religious practices are concerned in one way or another with the protection or the crossing of the threshold. The fetish or medicine bundle hanging over the entrance to a hut in a primitive village (where the house has its own meaning as a sacred place) has something in common with the sacred symbols carved at church doorways, or the small mezuzah cylinder on the doorpost of an orthodox Jewish house, to protect the entrance. Similar protection is given by the images of special gods of entrances such as Janus in Rome or Lakshmi in India, or by the fearsome daemonic images in other traditions. Purification rituals qualify the worshipper for entry, and so we have the various ablutions in an outer area, the washing-fountain in the courtyard of the mosque, the similar bowl outside an African prophet-healing church or the stoup of holy water just inside a Roman Catholic one; baptismal fonts and chambers were originally outside the main body of the church and still commonly adjoin the entrance. Many threshold rituals are now found only in vestigal or superstitious form, such as the removal of hat or of shoes, the carrying a bride over the threshold, or the removal of the dead by another and special corpsedoor as in Denmark. Behind all these forms there lies some sense of the seriousness of the entrance into a holy place.

A similar meaning inevitably attaches to gates and doors, both as physical objects and in metaphorical images. The word Babylon itself is literally 'gate of the gods', and when Jacob received the theophany at Bethel he exclaimed 'this is the gate of heaven'. Religious experience appropriates the same image and Luther feels himself 'to have gone through open doors to paradise', or the Muslim ecstatic prays 'O my Lord... open the door to me that I may attain thy presence'. In religious architecture the doorway and the doors themselves acquire much more than merely utilitarian significance, and this explains the various means adopted to stress their importnace and symbolic value: they are made much larger than physically required, multi-leaved, highly decorated, recessed in impressive porticoes, surrounded by statuary, or multiplied into a series of successive entrances as so often in India or Japan. Examples abound in the great religious buildings of all traditions, and not least in Christian churches, especially in the French and Italian cathedrals where Daniel-Rops can refer to 'those glorious doors at Florence which Michelangelo described as the Gates of Paradise'. Even the church itself can be called the 'gate of heaven' as is the Church of Puerto Coeli in Puerto Rico, with its peculiar facade containing one large plain doorway surmounted by a smaller one.

An exhaustive study of the triple combination of doors and arches in the facades of tombs and religious buildings in the Graeco-Roman world of antiquity has shown that from China to the West this form emerges without structural or functional necessity, unless it be the function of symbolizing the transition from the realm of the living to that of the dead, and from the realm of the human to that of the divine. The facade 'indicated that God had come to man, and that through its doorways man could go to God in mystical union, or into immortal life'.[8] The triple-arched cemetery entrance or the similar church facade marks the entrance to a sacred place for a meeting of momentous importance.

This place where other realms are met is also indicated by various forms representing a link or connection between the human and transhuman spheres, and usually set in a vertical dimension as ladders, poles and pillars, trees and hills. The traffic between heaven and earth figures in that classic experience of Jacob at Bethel, with the angels traversing the ladder of his dream. Other ladders, ropes, stairways, or trees that grow to reach the sky figure in the experiences of Muhammad, of the Christian saints, and of men in the religious traditions of all continents, and several of these forms may be physically expressed at sanctuaries where sacred trees and long flights of steps are not uncommon features.

More common are sacred wooden poles or stone pillars with the same symbolism of connection. It may be no more than the bamboo pole to which a white fowl is fastened at the top and left to die in an Igbo village as a way of carrying the sacrifice to the supreme god; it may be the sacred pole carried everywhere with the Achilpa in Australia as a 'cosmic axis' around which their life and changing territory are centred and which provides a constant point of communication with the heavens, as their myths explain in detail.[9] Free-standing pillars with no architectural use are common in temple complexes and 'suggest the archaic function of holding the firmament high to provide an ordered space between earth and sky wherein man could move'.[10] The finial or spire of a Buddhist stupa or Hindu temple was imagined to be the top of a pillar passing through the whole structure which supported it, and providing the 'moment of Release', the point of contact between the human and the divine. Similar sacred pillars and poles will be found in any modern translation of the accounts of religious practice in Canaan and Israel given in Judges 6:28, I Kings 14:23, and II Kings 10:26; 17:10.

The same symbolism is supplied by the sacred tree, although this is a most complex symbol, for the tree that grows along with man and about the same rate is a token of human life, and in its shedding of leaves and renewal is a sign of death and immortality, or if it be ever-green, of immortality alone. All these meanings cluster round the idea of communication between the two realms, wherein life comes to men from the gods and returns in the end to its source.

Mountains also have natural qualities that lend themselves to sym-bolic purposes associated with the sacred place as point of intercon-nection. Just as rising up is a symbol of life and lying down of death, so the life of the world was seen by the Egyptians as beginning when the first land rose above the primeval waters as a small hillock; this was the creative centre for the world from which all further land appeared, and the hill or mountain remains as the sacred replica of the beginnings. By its nature the mountain seems devoted to the gods, the creative powers, for normally neither vegetable, animal, nor human life can occupy its higher reaches but only the gods themselves, now hiding within the clouds that gather round its peaks, now manifesting them-selves in its uncanny silences or thunderous lightnings. Small wonder that a peak such as Mt. Kilimanjaro on the borders of Kenya and Tan-zania and lifting its snow-capped summit nearly twenty thousand feet to dominate the tropical landscape for fifty miles around should domi-nate also the myths of the Masai and be called 'the house of God'. It is the obvious point of connection between their world and the divine realm. Examples are familiar and endless, whether it be Olympus or Fujiyama, Sinai, Hermon, or Golgotha, and they can be discovered in such unsuspected places as the English names Weycock and Weedon, where the first syllable means holy and the second represents different terms for hill. Not all hills were holy, but all were potential locations for the theophany or sign that marked them out as links with the gods.

The mountain symbolism has also been applied to sacred places ir-respective of any such physical form in order to declare their purposes; thus the sacred black stone in the Ka'bah at Mecca has been regarded as the highest place on earth and facing the centre of heaven, while Jerusalem has been similarly described, apart altogether from the fact that it was also Mt. Zion. Indeed, in the Church of the Lord (Aladura) in West Africa its most distinctive festival is held annually on many local 'Mt. Taborars', and while these may be actual hills the central

Mt. Taborar at Ogere in Nigeria is no more than a large flat cleared area in the bush; on the other hand Shembe's Nazareth Church in Natal always holds its famous New Year festival on Mt. Nhlangakazi itself.

By the same token temple buildings and altars as sacred places have appropriated the mountain image along with its meanings. Every Egyptian temple was built on an artificial mound representing the primeval hillock, and the pyramids, which must be thought of as temple-tombs, repeat the theme. The Babylonian Ziggurats (meaning 'mountain peak') as vast earth mounds or artificial hills forming replicas of the cosmic mountain; the temple of Borobudur in Java where pilgrims climbed from terrace to terrace to the 'centre of the world' at the summit; the Toltec pyramid of the sun, at Tetihuacan in Mexico, reaching two hundred feet in height and the similar artificial temple-mountains of the Aztecs and the Maya; the altar in India representing the sacred mountain; and then the altar terrace, the addition of the shrine or stupa to the terrace, and finally the repetition of this terrace-and-shrine unit in diminishing tiers to form the Hindu temple — all these testify to the same function of the sacred place as the meeting point between heaven and earth. Even the different local names of Babylonian temple-towers prove to be variations on the same theme: 'the house (which is) the link of heaven and earth' or 'the mooring-post of heaven and earth'.

2.4.3 THE SACRED PLACE AS MICROCOSM OF THE HEAVENLY REALM

The third function that we distinguish for the sacred place arises inevitably in conjunction with the two we have discussed. If this delineated space is the creative centre whence the divine powers give reality and meaning to the world, and if it is the place where the gods come to meet with men, then it is part of the world which shares most fully in the heavenly realm and must be fit for the gods' presence. It is, as it were, a little piece of heaven on earth, or at least it corresponds to the heavenly original as an earthly replica, a mirror of its model or a microcosm of the cosmos as a whole. This theme of earth and heaven being corresponding realities, existing in mutual relationship, with the sanctuary as the particular point of connection and similarity, finds many expressions.

There is first not only the actual location of the sacred precinct which as we have seen requires divine indication but also the directional position, what is known as 'orientation' of the site or temple, where the very word itself derives from one of the commonest forms, a direction facing to the east. This is found in early stone circles with an entrance space towards the rising sun, or in Egyptian or Nabatean temples where the first rays on midsummer's day shone through the long courts or ante-chambers directly on to the sacred image or altar. The great majority of Celtic temples in Roman Britain show this eastern alignment, and the practice has been traditional in Christian churches with a suitably transformed symbolic meaning. Other temples, as in Greece and Rome, took their direction from the point of rising of other celestial bodies, while the Ka'bah at Mecca has its four corners directed to the four cardinal points of the sky. In all cases the intention is the same, to link the sacred place to its prototype in the heavens; it must face, as it were, the reality of which it is to be an earthly reflection.

Secondly, the sanctuary must manifest this reflection in its own proportions and shape. It has been claimed that the earliest known sacred buildings of the world are those found at Tell Arpachiya in Assyria where sacred precincts seem to have surrounded circular shrines with domed roofs that may be seven millennia old. So long as the cosmos was thought of as spherical the sacred place could be a hemispherical pit covered by a similarly shaped roof and these together represented the earth and the heavens united. If, as in early Egypt, the sky was believed to be supported by a circle of mountains around the world then their temples were also circular, but when the idea of four pillars emerged as sky-supports square temples with four corner posts were built in imitation. Likewise the Babylonian ziggurats on their square bases represented the earth as a square. The idea of a square earth with its four 'corners' was combined with the continuing view of the heavens as a hemisphere in temples that consisted of a square chamber covered by a dome, as at a temple at Ur in the first part of the third millennium, and in the characteristic churches of Eastern Christendom where the same symbolism was preserved.[11] The proportions also of the sacred place were sought not so much in the principles of utility or of aesthetics as in heavenly proportions revealed in astronomical observations or the mystical meanings of numbers, although these might also coincide with certain mathematical harmonies and issue in highly aesthetic results. The continuing fascination for some minds of the measurements of the Great Pyramid or the numbers in the Apocalypse of St. John as secret revelation is but a minor survival of an ancient concern that at the holy place man should erect 'a building in tune with the rhythms of the universe, and which was as a consequence, a kind of resonator of the sacred'.[12]

As the sacred place becomes elaborated with formal enclosures, shrine buildings and their cultic objects, and finally the whole complex of courts and entrances and temple buildings, it remains important that all such development should continue to be patterned on the heavenly model. As an early dwelling for divine beings the sanctuary is not designed according to human aesthetic or architectural principles, nor even according to the functional needs or the actual mechanics of the cult, but on the basis of revelation through dreams, oracles, the stars, or other media. The architect must seek for the plan the gods will reveal and not construct his own, even if the resulting structure be ugly or have no provision at all for cultic rites, which could be left to the open air. In the Old Testament both the Mosaic tabernacle (Exodus 25:8-9; 40) and the Solomonic temple (I Chronicles 28:10-13; 19; Wisdom of Solomon 9:8) are described as explicitly modelled on a revealed heavenly pattern, and the second temple also was given to Ezekiel in a vision. These are characteristic of accounts in other traditions, as in Babylon where the king Gudea was shown the plan for a temple by the goddess through a dream; after all, it would be for her presence and use rather than for her worshippers.

The same idea tends to extreme conservatism in religious buildings, for any repairs or rebuilding must adhere rigidly to the original divine design. This is still to be observed at the ancient shrine of the Japanese sun goddess, Amaterasu, who gave the oracle that determined the original wooden structure, which has been regularly replaced as an exact replica. An excellent illustration comes from the history recorded of the north Babylonian temple of Shamash the sun god in Shippar, which had been restored by Nebuchadnezzar. He had sought in vain for the cornerstone on which the original divine plan could be expected to be engraved, and then proceeded according to his own ideas. In consequence, only fortyfive years later the temple was again in ruins, but King Nabunaid thus warned would not rebuild until further search revealed the long-buried corner stone with its revealed designs. Only then did the work start 'so that the temple did not diverge an inch from the plan towards the outside or the inside'.[13]

Similarly, the Ka'aba has been rebuilt a number of times but never altered from its slightly irregular cubic form. This may well illustrate a further feature of the earthly replica, that it is recognized as only a copy within the human sphere and so incapable of absolute perfection. For example, in Hindu temple architecture

... certain architectural elements are slightly displaced with respect to the symmetry of the design. The geometrical symbolism of the building as a whole is not thereby obscured; on the contrary, it retains its character as principal form while avoiding confusion with the purely material form of the temple... (this) is equally valid in principle for every traditional art and craft, whatever may be its religious foundation. The surfaces and angles of a Romanesque church for example are always found to be inexact when strict measurements are applied to them, but the unity of the whole imposes itself all the more concisely. ... Most modern constructions on the contrary can show a purely 'additive' unity, while they present a regularity in their detail that is 'inhuman' – because it is apparently absolute – as if it were a question not of 'reproducing' the transcendent model using the means available to man, but of 'replacing' it by a sort of magic copy in complete conformity with it, which implies a Luciferian confusion between the material form and the ideal or 'abstract' form.[14]

This provides a new understanding of what we may mistake as the errors and crudities of earlier religious builders. For instance there is the very ancient Saxon church of St. Laurence at Bradford-on-Avon, perhaps dating from about the end of the seventh century. Its eastern orientation is some twentyseven degrees out of line, its chancel skewed some three degrees north of the line of the nave, and its entrance in the north porch two feet out of centre. Since it was all built at the one time these features are there by design, and are not the accidents of later extensions. Of course skewed chancels are common, and commonly interpreted as symbolizing the head of Christ falling sideways on the cross, where the whole ground plan is cruciform. But this church is not cruciform; may there not be another and much more ancient and profound symbolism behind such irregularities, recognizing the element of the contingent and the imperfect in all human affairs, and even in man's most faithfully constructed sacred places? This seems to be in the mind of a Jewish writer when he compares the earthly Jerusalem or its temple with the Heavenly Jerusalem: 'This building now in your midst is not that which is revealed with Me, that which was prepared beforehand from the time when I took counsel to make Paradise, and showed it to Adam before he sinned' (II Baruch 4:3-7).[15] Although heaven and earth are corresponding realities in their mutual relationship this correspondence is spoilt by the forces of evil, by time and decay, and the limits and imperfections of men, and even the sacred place contains within itself reminders of the very situation it exists to heal. Thus do earthly builders avoid any 'Luciferian confusion' between the human and the divine.

The same idea of an earthly microcosm of the heavenly reality is found in sacred places when these are conceived on the larger scale of the city or the whole of society. Just as the city wall has been regarded as the boundary protecting the sacred area so the whole city is a sanctuary, founded under divine instructions and with the proper rites. The Indian holy city of Benares was allegedly built by the god Siva; the plan of Nineveh was believed by Sennacherib to have been 'drawn in the celestial script'; Jerusalem has its heavenly prototype, the New Jerusalem as it will be when it comes to replace the earthly copy (Revelation 21:2, 10); Babylon is shown on one ancient map as the centre of a large circular territory bounded by a river and so indicates that it reflected the Sumerian idea of Paradise.

This principle applied to the whole social structure appeared in China where the imperial organization was a reflection of a similar system among the gods, where the 'Ancient One of the Jade' ruled over a heavenly court that was matched by the court at Pekin, and where lesser gods served as his ministers of state issuing their directives and making their reports with all the formalities and pedantries of the earthly counterpart. Javanese traditional society reveals the same correspondences:

The Javanese village community is ... a world unto itself, a microcosmos which is but the image of a similarly structured world around it, the macrocosmos of the feudal realm, of the heavens and stars of the spirit world. Microcosmos and macrocosmos obey the same laws: the affairs of men and the events of sky are both directed by elemental forces that recur over and over again.... Even in its outward structures the community of men conforms to cosmic precept: the partitions of the traditional Javanese house no less than the architectural plan of *kraton* (court) or urban square, of the concentric structure of temple shrine and monument, show the existence of the ancient classification system, the division according to the wind directions, each indicating an appropriate human function or ritualistic obligation.... In the traditional village the spot where the microcosmos and the macrocosmos *interact* is clearly marked: this is the shrine of the village spirit or deity who is the protector of the group.[16]

The chief manifestation of this principle in a Christian social context is probably to be found in the Eastern Roman Empire or Byzantium, where all social and political concerns took a religious form and the emperor was chosen by God (no matter by what means he had come to power) as the vice-regent of Christ; the earthly empire must in the end include the pagan territories to the north and the Muslim lands to the south and be invulnerable to human attack, for was it not the earthly form of the kingdom of God that was both universal and eternal?[17] Thus whether it be an empire or a smaller society, a city, a temple, or an open-air sanctuary each has sought in its own way to be a microcosm of the divine world.

2.4.4 THE SACRED PLACE AS IMMANENT-TRANSCENDENT PRESENCE

We indicated in our earlier outline that the fourth function of the sacred place is associated with the cult object that so often becomes a substantial iconic image of the divinity, or, in popular parlance, an idol. The latter term is almost universally misunderstood by Westerners who totally identify the physical image with the god who is believed to be confined within it, and then say that 'the heathen in his blindness bows down to wood and stone'. This is to reveal the poverty of Western thinking rather than that of 'the heathen', and to obscure the very purpose for which the image, and indeed the sacred place itself, exist. This purpose is to deal with the problem and seeming paradox in all religion, that while the gods are in all things earthly as their source and life, yet they are not equally in all things nor confined to this immanent existence. They also transcend the earthly sphere and have their proper home in an ideal and ultimate realm whose dimensions and nature are fitting for the gods. Varieties among religious outlooks such as pantheism or deism, can often be understood as but variations in the emphasis on these two contrasting modes of divine existence in relation to man, as immanent and as transcendent.

The very setting aside of a special sacred area or precinct is the first recognition that the gods are not equally present at all places, that their presence at the sanctuary transcends, as it were, their immanent presence elsewhere. Their presence in the holy place is indicated by the cult object and finally the shaped image, and this assures men that the divinity does visit them there and even dwell there, so that the image requires the daily ministrations of feeding and dressing and washing, entertaining and being taken in procession, that seem so naive to Western minds. A smile is the main reaction when we read of the idol being chained in the temple lest the god desert his people when the city is under military siege. No doubt the transcendent dimension can be obscured in religions, and men act in ways that would deny it, but not for long; much more characteristic is the sense that divinities without transcendent existence are of little use when they cannot bring transhuman or ultimate powers to bear on human problems.

This sense that the god cannot be identified with the image that assures of his immanence is revealed in the casual way that images are manufactured and sold like any other objects before they are ritually consecrated by and for the god, and in the way they are as readily replaced when decayed or accidentally destroyed. It is also obvious to the simplest worshippers that the same god who is adored through his many images in numerous temples scattered across the land cannot be confined to any of them and is equally to be found in them all. Each, and all of them together, are only microcosms of the heavenly dwelling that alone is adequate for such a transcendent being. This is clearly manifest in the Sioux priest's account of the making of an altar in the new camp, that we quoted above: 'We fixed in this place the centre of the world, and this centre, which in reality is everywhere, is the dwelling-place of the Great Spirit.' In like manner an ancient Egyptian text, after speaking of the ritual service of the material image, recognizes that 'there is no stream that suffereth itself to be confined: it bursteth the dyke by which it is confined'.[18] Just as there must be no 'Luciferian confusion' between the sacred building and its heavenly prototype so also the same danger was usually avoided with the image, and together they served to represent both the immanent real presence and the transcendent being of the gods.

It may be noted that we have used two terms for the presence of the god at the sacred place — as dwelling and as visiting. To our literal minds these seem to be mutually exclusive alternatives. On the contrary they represent the richness of the divine presence, manifest both through the regular dwelling in the sacred cult object filled with divine power, and through intermittent special theophanies when god visits men in vision, dream, miracle or other wonder. The sacred place which became a regular sanctuary on the basis of such a theophany in the first place, is revivified or reactivated, as it were, by further explicit divine manifestations, and so confirmed as the place where the god still dwelt. This combination of visiting and dwelling is but another indication that the god present at the sanctuary both transcends it and yet is immanent within it.[19]

The sacred place is therefore one of the most complex developments in human history, rich with meaning and of many functions, the centre of reference from which all else is orientated, understood, or valued and on which it should be patterned, the one ordered place in a disordered world, the source of life's meaning and the anchor that gives security, the rendezvous between the human and the divine where the two worlds intersect and the gods and men may meet. The fullest development of this sacred place is found in the temple complex, and further attention must now be directed to this form and then to its explicit manifestation in the successive temples at Jerusalem.

3

The Temple Type

While the essentials of a sacred place do not include any edifice, the most characteristic form of its fullest development is found in the temple-complex of buildings. The first step in this development occurs when some simple shelter is erected for the central cult object and produces what is best called a shrine. In the course of elaboration this is enlarged with ancillary chambers and enriched with decoration until it becomes a substantial structure better called a temple. The term shrine then remains for the earlier or smaller forms that may be multiplied within the temple complex, or else for the inner cell or sanctuary where the main cult object is probably to be found in the heart of the temple building itself. While not all religious traditions exhibit this development, and some remain content with the simplest of shrines or with none at all, and while there is considerable variety among the temples of the world, it is still possible to trace certain basic features across the various traditions and to speak of the temple-type of sacred place. These characteristics will appear if we consider the temple in the service of the four functions of holy places that we have now surveyed.

3.1 THE TEMPLE AS CENTRE

The very elaboration from simple shrine to magnificent temple in so many cultures, with the consequent absorption of energies and resources over long periods of time, indicates at once the position it occupied in the minds of its builders. The excellence and permanence of the materials, the care and skill in the building, and the subsequent respect for a sacred edifice, together in many cases with the nature of the site and the size of the structure have ensured that the temples of antiquity have survived better than most other buildings of their culture or even when all other structures have vanished entirely. Where great cities and palaces have left not a trace of their existence we still have pyramids and temple mounds, sanctuaries and altars as the sole legacy of a society that once was centred upon these remains.

Even when regarded only as cultural and technological achievements they must have stood at the centre of the society that produced them. This is confirmed wherever texts and other evidence reveal the part they played as civic and ceremonial or ritual centres for the whole community, and especially for the king who stood in various special relationships to the gods whether as earthly embodiment, as son, vice-regent or servant, with corresponding ritual duties. Around the temples liturgies and literatures developed, great festivals were held, and to their more obvious sacred functions were added those of community finance, legislation and administration. Something of the same central place in the community is to be seen in the great cathedrals of mediaeval France, and while many of their former functions now have other centres of reference a modern cathedral such as Coventry still endeavours to serve as spiritual centre, for the ultimate values of its community. During World War II wherever a temple, mosque or church survived, as did St. Paul's Cathedral amidst the devastated city area, it must have served many in the community as a rallying point for the spirit and source of meaning in a disordered world. Further signs of the temple functioning as centre will appear in the course of our discussion of the other associated functions of the sacred place.

3.2 THE TEMPLE AS MICROCOSM

We have already noted the cosmic source of the orientation, shapes and proportions applied to the holy place. A temple edifice obviously provides considerable scope for these and other references from the earthly construction of the heavenly or cosmic model, as when the five or seven stages or platforms incorporated in a temple-mound represent the planets, with the addition of sun and moon. The earliest and most lasting symbolism accepts the roof or ceiling as the sky or heavens, the floor as the earth and the space between as the human world. The roof may then have a circular opening, an oculos or window that marks the point of communication with the realm beyond; the ceiling may be painted with stars and planets as still today in a modern church; around the lower parts of the walls occur portrayals of the life of the earth in plant and animal forms, as in Egyptian temples; the space between may be shaped and orientated to indicate the four corners of the world. Even in the simpler architecture of a primal society these meanings appear, as in the description of the 'Big-House' of the Delaware Indians of North-America, where the house itself 'stands for the universe; its floor the earth, its four walls, the four quarters; its vault the sky-dome atop, where resides the Creator... the centre post is the staff of the Great Spirit with its foot upon the earth, with its pinnacle reaching to the hand of the Supreme Being sitting on his throne'.[1]

It is sometimes remarked that the exterior of temples may be much more ornate than their plain interiors. This has been explained on the analogy of a jewelled casket for some precious object, but a more cosmic symbolism has been suggested at least for Indian temples where this feature is so prominent: the dark interior occupied perhaps by a single image or symbol in the compact space of a single cell or shrine-room represents the ultimate unity of all things in the divine or absolute spirit, while the riot of images and forms on the exterior indicates the outward multiplicities of this world and the endless ways in which the divine acts in creation and in encounter with men. The hierarchies of the gods themselves may be reflected in the ordered grades of priests and attendants or the relative importance of different areas or shrines within the temple and its courts. For further illustration of this cosmic symbolism we shall await our examination of this theme in the temple at Jerusalem; it occurs again in those forms of Christian church building, such as the churches of Eastern Christendom and of the Gothic Revival, where such symbolism was a conscious feature.

3.3 THE TEMPLE AS MEETING POINT

In the wider sense as the central point of reference for all major affairs of a community the temple serves as meeting point between the whole structure of human life and the life of the divine realms. In the narrower sense of the more intimate personal needs of individuals it reveals the same function of a rendezvous between men and the gods. Here they make their vows and offer their prayers, seek divine healing or an oracle for guidance, or perhaps spend the night hopefully 'incubating' a dream bringing a message from the gods; here they present their thanksgivings and offerings to the priest, or the materials for the sacrifice he will offer on their behalf at the open-air altar or in some subsidiary hall, and here they join with their fellows in the rejoicings of the festivals; here they dedicate their children and ensure the continuing fertility of flock or farm or family; here too they endure vigils and fasts or make the pilgrimage through many stages of courts or stairs or ascents, terrace by terrace and ritual by ritual, in the spiritual journey that brings them ever closer to the divine realm. The very variety of the human response to the divine, of man's spiritual search for a world beyond the ephemeral life about him, and of the ways in which he senses the presence of the heavenly realm has provided a powerful incentive for the development of a temple complex of equal variety, catering for the great range of cultic actions through which some encounter with the gods is effected.

The particular aspects of the temple which express this meeting with the gods have illustrated our earlier remarks on this theme: the importance and elaboration of the entrance idea in portals and arches and facades, in courts, vestibules, and ante-chambers, and the symbolism of ascent to the heavens in terraces and flights of stairs, soaring pillars, pinnacles and towers, and in the mountain-like nature of the building or of its whole complex.

Even the buildings and courts themselves may be regarded as a permanent gift established in homage to the gods at the meeting point they have themselves designated; to revive the analogy of the casket richly ornate for the precious jewel it contains, the temple is elaborated not only for utilitarian reasons in coping with the religious needs of men, nor as an aesthetic or architectural spectacle, though this it may be also, but in the first place as an offering to the gods of the best that man has in materials and skills. Nothing is too good or too costly or too difficult, and whole empires have poured out their resources in a few temple complexes. When the central temple building is examined it is often remarkable how small is the usable space contained in its vast bulk and how little it has to do with the worshippers themselves – there may be no more than a tiny shrine set on a temple pyramid and entered only by one or two of the priesthood, as in the temples of the Maya; even the massive storied structures in India that might seem to contain a great space for worshippers or many cells for meditation prove to be for the greater part solid masonry with no purpose other than the glorification of God, and aim to be seen as such from the outside rather than used for religious activities inside. Although not all temples are necessarily large and some of the finest Greek ones were quite small, the same principles will usually be found to obtain. The temple itself is indeed a precious casket, a worthy place for the god to visit his people or dwell with them, and not, as we shall see, a place of meeting for the congregation of the people themselves.

3.4 THE TEMPLE AS IMMANENT-TRANSCENDENT PRESENCE

When the gods grant their presence to the temple as the appointed rendezvous with men it is usually regarded as their abode, a *domus dei.* This is equally true whether it be a simple structure of grass and poles called 'the hut of God' by an African people or an elaborate palace-like temple for the chief god of a great civilization. We may call it the house of God without entering into controversies as to whether it was a later idea in imitation of human or royal habitations, as is so commonly assumed without much evidence, or whether it was actually the first human construction from which palaces and then humbler houses later took their pattern, as Lord Raglan endeavoured to demonstrate.[2] We are encouraged to regard the term as appropriate when we observe the close similarities of form and structure between temple and house in so many cultures, even where one might least expect to find it, in a cave-

temple sculptured in imitation of a peasant's cottage, the cave of Su-
dana at Barabar in India. 'It is of rectangular form ... while ... the end of
the cave is occupied by a circular monument that is an exact imitation,
sculptured in stone, of a hut built of planks (the joints are perfectly re-
produced) with an overhanging thatched roof. We have thus a peasant's
hut preceded by a walled in garden. The great shrines of Amaterasu at
Ise represent exactly early Japanese wooden huts with thatched roofs,
and the Japanese word for shrine is literally, "honourable house".'[3]

While the ordinary term for house may be used of the divine abode,
where it is not called a palace, the fact that it is indeed a dwelling for
a god is not indicated by the usual means whereby a house reveals the
importance of its owner. These methods, as we have shown, do apply
to the whole temple complex and to the main temple building, but the
actual place reserved for the god alone, usually as some iconic image
or other symbol, may be invisible to the outer world or even to the
worshippers, some small dark cell or chamber in the inner depths of
the building or at the far limits of a series of courts or halls. In this
silent inner sanctuary or holy of holies the god dwells, and although
in some cases, as in Hindu temples or Buddhist halls, his worshippers
may approach and perform their cultic actions in his immediate presence, it is more common for them to no more than glimpse his image
from afar through the intervening spaces and structures, or to see him
on rare occasions when borne in procession at some great festival. This
small and remote cell for the god is what we find if we examine the
size and position and also the nature of the entrances to the god-room
as shown in the ground plans of the temples of Egypt and Greece and
Rome, of Babylon and Japan, and especially of the Hittites' five temples at Boghazköy.

The nature of the occupant as divine is further distinguished by various numinous effects associated with his chamber. The image may
be hidden in the shadows of an already darkened room, or alternatively
set in the midst of the only light allowed to enter, as at one of the
Hittite temples; it may be of immense size or fearsomely distorted as
compared with human beings; or it may be set in low buildings that
have narrowed down at the rear from magnificent approaches through
large entrances and courts. Thus the mystique of the divine is presented

and preserved, indicating at one and the same time that while the immanent presence is indeed here in this place it differs from all ordinary presence by retaining a transcendent existence that men can only suggest by these oblique methods. So overwhelming is the sense of the transcendence that at times the presence is indicated by an empty throne in the god-room. The same transcendent being of the god is also emphasized in all numinous phenomena interpreted as his special visit to the temple in a theophany, which as we saw above is not incompatible with the idea of this being his dwelling house.

This double emphasis on the immanence and transcendence of the divinity present at the holy place is further exhibited in the way the worshippers are so often excluded from the actual house of their god, just as subjects may be from the palace of the emperor. The main building is not for a congregation but for the residence and rituals of the god, and at the most will admit individuals and small groups for prayers and offerings. But in many traditions even this was not possible and the normal place for corporate worship was in the open-air precincts or the ancillary halls and porticos. Only two known Greek temples, the Telesterion great hall at Eleusis and the Sanctuary of the Bulls on the Island of Delos, could have accomodated a congregation; likewise the temples of the mystery cults such as those of Mithra differed from the normal plan in being designed to house the initiates, although these again were not large and the original from the Mithraeum at Carrawhurgh in Roman Britain could hold only twelve people.

The distinction whereby the special place of the gods stands over against the place of the people and so reminds worshippers of the transcendence of their divinities may be traced in Polynesian religious history. We have described the original open-air sanctuaries and the development of raised platforms with altars and cult objects at one end; then buildings appear — a food-store for the offerings, and a storehouse for ritual objects or, in the Society Islands, a god-house for the images and symbols. In New Zealand it seems that the open area for congregational assembly developed separately into the large marae space, with its own meeting-house for ordinary communal purposes, and the *tuahu* or specially religious place with highly charged spiritual power in the form of a small shrine, usually in a secluded spot outside the village.[4] Thus the transcendent nature of divinity has been emphasized while the presence immanent in the shrine and its objects is also secured.

The same combined emphasis upon immanence and transcendence lies behind the characteristic temple idea of graduated sanctity, of different degrees of holiness running from the life of the world outside through various stages to the absolute holiness of the inner shrine and the god himself. This accounts for many features in the development of the temple complex whereby these stages are both multiplied and expressed in physical form, as multiple entrances, a series of porticos, courts or halls, or of ascending ramps, stairs and terraces. Thus in southern India temples commonly have successive enclosures containing halls through which devotees proceed with appropriate exercises, each representing an initiation into or conquest of a new spiritual stage; in northern India a series of chambers between the outer entrance and the inner sanctuary each represent a different form of sacrifice or a stage in the spiritual ascent of the soul.[5] The Jerusalem temple in its final form exhibited this principle perhaps more vividly than anywhere else: from the outer court of the Gentiles one ascended up a flight of steps to and through the court of the women, and then up again to that of the men of Israel; past a barrier of some kind lay the altar and court of the priests, from whence steps led up into the porch of the temple proper, and then past curtains into the holy place; beyond this again and heavily curtained off lay the holy of holies entered only once a year by the high priest, the inner shrine where the very absence of an image emphasized the transcendent presence of Yahweh. The rituals themselves were distributed over this series of increasingly holy places, and there was a corresponding gradation of persons (according to their relation to the inner shrine) from the high priest, through the other priests to the levites and then to the nethinim and singers and porters, and so to the men of Israel, the women and the aliens.

The same concern appears in cruder fashion in modern times when the distinction is made between local Mormon churches and the temples which no Gentile and not every Mormon can enter; or in those Christian churches where there is a sense of the altar space being holier than the place of the choir, and the latter holier than the nave, so that a Pugin could burst into tears at the thought of a woman or an unbaptized child in the sanctuary; or where a preacher could be admitted to the pulpit but, through lack of episcopal ordination, be excluded from the chancel.

One result of the emphasis upon the transcendence of the divinity present in the house of god is seen in the impersonal and remote nature of much temple worship. The worshipper is conscious of the unsurmountable barriers between himself and the shrine. His only contact with the image of the god may be a fleeting glimpse through some opening or during a procession, or by water the priests have consecrated at the shrine being sprinkled upon him. As it has been expressed for a worshipper in Babylon, '... there was no room or time for the intense subtlety which links the individual to his god. No deeply spiritual bond could emerge.... The "house of God" was separated from the fostering soil of individual religious intensity....'[6] The more the temple sought to formalize the expressions of the transcendent-immanent presence the greater the cleavage between temple-worship and popular religion which turned to smaller more local and accessible shrines and sacred objects, or relied as with so many primal societies upon the gods of the domestic cult, the spirits of the shrine within the house or its courtyard. In a highly developed cultic system the temple and the domestic shrine would therefore represent the two poles between which it operated, although Assyrian temples seem to have been unusual in combining the intimacy and the mystery of the presence – the worshipper was invited to enter the divine abode itself where the image rested on a platform only partly partitioned from the main room.[7]

3.5 THE TEMPLE TYPE OR *DOMUS DEI*

It is now possible to use the term *domus dei* for the temple type towards which so many sacred places have developed, in distinction from the undeveloped sanctuary precincts or small local and domestic shrines. Not all temples exhibit the features of this form as early and explicitly as the temple of Herod in Jerusalem, but we may illustrate the extent to which it is a common form with examples from a contemporary temple in neighbouring Syria and from traditional China, and we may show how the same form is readily identified in the much simpler structures of primal societies in West Africa, and in a modern community in the United States.

3.6 EXAMPLES: SYRIA, CHINA, WEST AFRICA, UNITED STATES

For the Syrian example we take the temple to Atargatis at Hieropolis-Bambyke as described in the late second century A.D.:

As for the temple *it looks to the rising sun.* In appearance and in workmanship, it is like the temples which they build in Ionia: *the foundation rises from the earth to the space of two fathoms, and on this rests the temple.* The ascent to the temple is built of wood and not particularly wide; as you mount, even the great hall exhibits a wonderful spectacle and it is ornamented with golden doors.... But the temple within is not uniform. *A special sacred shrine is reared within it; the ascent to this likewise is not steep* nor is it fitted with doors, but is entirely open as you approach it. *The great temple is open to all; the sacred shrine to the priests alone* and not to all even of these, but only to those who are deemed nearest to the gods and who have charge of the entire administration of sacred rites. *In this shrine are placed the statues, one of which is Hera. the other Zeus,* though they call him by another name. Both of these are golden, both are sitting; Hera is supported by lions, Zeus is sitting on bulls....[8] [Italics in original.]

The Chinese temple is a less ambitious structure, being essentially a compound surrounded by a wall, and orientated on a north-south axis. In the south wall the main entrance is a triple-roofed gateway raised several steps, with heavy double-leaved doors for each gateway and painted guardian figures to repel evil spirits. The courtyard is surrounded by buildings each raised on an earthen platform and approached by stone steps, with the ancillary buildings at the sides and the main halls across the rear. Here the principal deity is enthroned in the chief room and lesser divinities as his attendants or in smaller rooms. Thus there is the *domus dei* in the shrine itself, the courtyard and other buildings for the worshippers and for many communal activities.[9]

The universality of these principles for the development of the sacred place is strikingly exhibited by an examination of the shrines in current or in recent use among the Igbo peoples of eastern Nigeria. In the Udi division of the Enugu province shrines devoted to the Alosi or nature spirits have been described for us.[10] Many West African shrines take the form of a cleared area in the bush marked by a mud wall or a hedge, and perhaps a tall tree or a dense grove behind the clearing. The Alosi clearing has three huts in it. The smallest is the actual dwelling of the alosi, and here only the priest may enter for dealing with the spirit. Outside this hut stands a stone pile as an altar for the reception of offerings, exactly as at the Jerusalem and so many other temples. The other huts are used for the reception of visitors while explaining their business to the priest or for preparing the food offerings. This is an example of the temple plan in its simplest form.

An Igbo scholar has given us the details of a slightly more developed form; those who are ritually unclean are excluded from the court within the walls, and this space has many functions — not only for sacrifices and prayers, but also for invitations and oath-taking, for refuge and immunity, for meetings and even markets. The main hut has two chambers, an outer space to be entered only by the male title-holders (a form of seniority and status) but perhaps no more than forty square feet, and an inner shrine which only the priest or the cult servants may enter to present the sacrifices or for other duties.[11]

A still more elaborate development occurs in the Iba house of the Onitsha province. Here the god's dwelling is a small casket of special shape and carving, not unlike the Hebrew ark, placed upon an altar. The iba house is built round this to provide accomodation for the ceremonies, and consists of an open-air central court with the altar at one end, and a further range of rooms designed for ordinary dwelling purposes lining each side of the court but not opening on to it directly. The term iba applies both to the court itself and to the whole house, for which the court provides an ordinary living area when worship is not in progress. 'The philosophical foundation on which the design of this building is housed', says the Igbo author (who we can assume had made no study of the *domus dei* or phenomenology of temples), 'states that man should build in the likeness of the house of God in order that God may come and dwell with man.... It is the endeavour to interpret the form of (the special casket) that has resulted in the character and style of the Iba.... The planning is based upon the concept of the essential unity between God and man, extended into family life.'[12]

The temple principle is exemplified still further in the secrecy connected with the sacred casket, whose contents are known only to those initiated into the cult. The inner court has no windows and only one door placed in the centre or a screen across its outer end, and guarded during the secret part of the service by youths who sit at this point and exclude children and usually also the women. The gradation of persons starts with the priest who sits behind the altar, and extends through the elders who sit in rows in descending order according to their ranks and ages, to the young men, the women and the children. At all important points this is remarkably similar to the standard temple plan.

Detailed accounts of the sanctuaries of other African peoples are rare, but fortunately the fast-decaying traditional temples of the Ashanti people in Ghana have benefitted from a recent detailed study by an architect. The basic pattern is the same as that of the domestic house and shows common features across the nine examples discovered. One enters an enclosed courtyard flanked by ancillary rooms and providing for various communal activities. There will be a room for the liturgical music from the drums, a kitchen for ceremonial meals, another room for singers or a woman's choir, and perhaps provision for visitors from a distance. At the far end and opposite the entrance there is the shrine room, raised above the level of the court, and more enclosed with screens or grills than the other rooms. This is the abode of the divinity and contains the sacred symbols or images on a raised platform, the major objects being along the right-hand side of the room and behind the screen wall so as to be out of the full view from the court; lesser divinities may have their symbols similarly placed on the left-hand side. This shrine is not to be entered by any save the priests and their attendants.[13] While this is a fairly basic stage of development it already shows the temple principle in course of application, and reveals the kinship between the great temples of the larger civilizations and these humbler examples from smaller primal societies.

As a final example representing a modern Western community we refer to the great granite temple of the Church of the Latter Day Saints at Salt Lake City, Utah. The plan for this was revealed in a dream to the then leader of the Mormons, Brigham Young, so establishing it as a divinely-given sanctuary. Although the public were admitted before its consecration, to show that it contained no fearsome secrets, it then became distinguished from Mormon chapels and tabernacles by being confined to those deemed ready to receive the mysteries of advanced religious teaching. In no sense is it a Mormon congregational meeting place. It is reserved for special functions which all seem to have some cosmic reference. In one chamber is the great copper tank where Mormons may be baptized for, and so united for all eternity with, deceased non-Mormon ancestors (hence the great concern with genealogies); here also is the marriage room where unions regarded as holding through all eternity are celebrated. The splendid classrooms are each devoted to consideration of one of the four great periods in cosmic history; the teaching and the murals help one to understand and meditate upon first, the primeval era, then the paradisal world of Eden, followed by the disordered world as we know it, and finally the perfected celestial realm. The increasing number of Mormon temples in other areas throughout the world show similar features which in their own peculiar way reveal some of the marks of the temple type and make the term entirely appropriate.

Whatever other versions of the sacred place we may yet encounter, here is the form it has taken in most of the earlier and some of the modern history of mankind, and across various races and cultures. We can therefore speak of this type in our further discussions as the temple form, the *domus dei*, or simply as the house of God, and we must now make a closer study of its occurences as the main sanctuary of the people of the Old Testament.

4

The Temple in Jerusalem

We have already suggested that the Jerusalem temple in its final form as developed by Herod provides one of the best examples of this type of sacred place. We must now examine not only its form and its history but also the very ambivalent attitudes towards it which appear in the records. Here we are at once confronted with the usual difficulties whereby the complex composition and history of the documents prevent us from accepting all statements and viewpoints as contemporary with the events they describe or necessarily belonging to those in whose mouths they are placed. While remaining aware of this hiatus between the event and its records it will not be necessary to attempt a full collation between the two. We shall endeavour to locate the physical development of the temple complex in its proper historical circumstances, but we shall not seek for the same exactness when discussing the attitudes to the temple that appeared during the millennium of its existence. It will be sufficient for our purposes to observe the great range of interpretations and comments to which it gave rise at some point or other in its history and to relate these to their particular period or source only insofar as this is significant for our enquiry. A further difficulty lies in the physical and religious relation between temple, Mt. Zion and Jerusalem, and the dual nature of the latter term as used for either the city itself or the community living in it; any term may overlap with the others or even be synonymous with them. We shall concentrate upon references to the temple itself, but passages referring primarily to Zion or to the city or community may also provide enlightenment.

4.1 THE RELIGIOUS INHERITANCE OF SOLOMON'S TEMPLE

Apart from the sanctuaries of the patriarchs and the tabernacle deriving from the Mosaic period, which we shall examine in the succeeding chapter, it is the temples of Canaan that provide the immediate background to Solomon's construction. The numerous Canaanite sanctuaries taken over with the land by the Israelite settlers consisted of stone altars, often on 'high places' reflecting the mountain theme, with sacred pillars, poles and groves, and in the more important places with a shrine building. These are clearly in the temple tradition, and the actual evolution of the building from a one-room stage at Megiddo and Jericho to a three-room form as at Beth-shan has been revealed by archaeology.[1]

The details of a smaller local sanctuary of the Canaanite type may be discovered in the story of the shrine that Micah erected in the Ephraim country (Judges 17-18) which seems to have contributed its main cult image to the important Israelite sanctuary at Shiloh just north of Jerusalem, where the ark of Yahweh had been housed at one period. This was based on an older Canaanite sanctuary, but we know nothing of its construction except that it seems to have been a permanent and fairly substantial shrine that could be called the temple of the Lord — literally the palace, i.e. house, of Yahweh (I Samuel 1:3; 3:3). Something of its importance emerges in the stories of Elkanah and Hannah, of Eli and his sons, of the apprenticeship of Samuel to the priest Eli, and the loss of the ark kept there (I Samuel 1-4). Its importance and its recognition as belonging to the temple tradition are further revealed when Jeremiah some four and a half centuries later could take the destruction of the temple at Shiloh (ca. 1050 B. C.) as a forewarning and example of what could happen to God's later temple at Jerusalem (Jeremiah 7:12-15).

Shiloh was probably only one of a number of such temples used in the worship of Israel and providing a background for Solomon's building. There is some evidence that one of these may have been in Jerusalem itself, a sanctuary of the Jebusite people which David maintained as the main place of worship after his capture of the city and its establishment as the capital, the place where after the death of Bathsheba's child he 'entered the house of the Lord and worshipped' (II Samuel 12:20). The antiquity and importance of this sanctuary may well reach back to the mysterious figure of Melchizedek, the priest-king of Jerusalem who is recorded as having blessed Abraham in the name of God Most High (Genesis 14:18-20), and who provides a parallel with later kings of Israel in Psalm 110:4. The fact that there is no reference to his sanctuary, and the emphasis on the profane threshing-ground of a private individual that David later bought as site for his new temple (as in II Samuel 24:18-20), were possibly 'deliberately meant to conceal the fact that the Temple of Jerusalem had been built on the site of a pagan sanctuary'.[2] This would then be a Jebusite temple of El-'Elyon, the high or sky god, where the Jebusite priest Zadok may have ministered in the time of David.

These possibilities apart, there is more certain evidence that Solomon's temple had a considerable inheritance of a similar kind through the site itself. This lay on the rocky spur occupied at its southern end by the ancient Jebusite fortified city of Jerusalem; to the north of this city, overlooking both city and the spring of Siloam that lay below the end of the spur, stood the fortress or stronghold of Zion that protected them both. It was in this area that Solomon built his palace and adjoining temple, an elevated expanse called Mount Zion. This was already a sacred hill in Jebusite tradition where it was identified with the same cosmic significance as that of the mysterious northern Mt. Zaphon of Canaanite mythology, the home of El-'Elyon. Similar meanings are attached to it, with the substitution of Yahweh for El-'Elyon, in the many subsequent Israelite references to Mt. Zion as God's holy hill where he dwells or whence he will bring blessing to his people or to all men (Psalms 14:7; 20:2; 132:13-15; Isaiah 2:2-4; 11:9). It would be strange indeed if the nature of the site as a traditional holy mountain made no contribution to Israel's understanding of its new sanctuary, and we can see the contribution in the process of being legitimized when Yahweh is said to have chosen Mt. Zion as his dwelling place; in this way its origin was transfered from mythology to historical event (e.g. Psalms 78:68; 132:13; Exodus 15:13-18).

Further enquiries as to the prior sanctity of the temple site focus upon the threshing-ground of Araunah which David purchased for the altar where sacrifices to stay the plague would be made (II Samuel 24). Threshing-floors already had long associations with religious rites, especially of a harvest nature, and it has been suggested that this was no exception, but was chosen by David for this very reason, a reason which later writers preferred to suppress.[3] Given the religious outlook of the times this is much more likely than any merely utilitarian considerations. There is, however, no evidence that David intended this as the site of the temple, although the Chronicler accepts it as such (I Chronicles 22:1; II Chronicles 3:1); nor is it possible to describe any specific relation between the threshing floor and Mt. Zion.

The remaining possibility of a prior religious tradition lies in the great outcrop of rock within the same general hilltop area that is now enshrined in the Muslim Dome of the Rock. It is a reasonable speculation that this was a Jebusite rock-altar, although all attempts to prove that this lay within the later Holy of Holies or under the great altar for burnt offerings have been inconclusive. What is clear is that the temple site was in an area already rich with religious associations, that the Jebusite term when applied to the whole hilltop as Mt. Zion must have brought some of these associations with it, and that these meanings were taken up into the religion of Israel in the concept of Zion that became so basic in its thought. By the same token we can understand how the term came to be applied to both city and community, as well as to the temple complex itself, while retaining a certain priority over all of these.

The situation resulting from the conquest of Jerusalem and its establishment as the new capital has been well described by Clements: '... Mount Zion had already come to be claimed as Yahweh's dwelling place... To have built a temple was quite naturally the next step which would have affirmed ... the divine foundation of the state and the sacred authority of the Davidic dynasty.' '... it can no longer be maintained that it became Yahweh's abode because the temple was built there. Rather the reverse was the case and the temple was built there because Mount Zion had become Yahweh's abode.'[4] This follows the usual order in the development of sanctuaries, as described above: first a place becomes sacred through a presence in numinous power, then a shrine or temple is erected upon it. In this case Solomon's temple inherited by one route or another a site of ancient sanctity, and many of the ideas that went with it.

It is well known how Solomon used Phoenician architects and artisans for the building of his temple, and this influence, together with those already described, account for its being so similar to others in the ancient world. Its general plan was that of a long narrow structure commencing with an impressive entrance porch in the shape of a broad room, followed by the 'holy place', a nave with the shape of a long room, and then the square 'Holy of Holies'. This three-chambered building faced the east, and outside its portals stood two large free-standing pillars whose exact significance has been much debated. Although no identical ground plan has been found elsewhere its form was entirely typical. Its magnificence was worthy of Solomon's empire, although like many other splendid temples it was modest in size since it served as a royal sanctuary attached to the palace and did not replace those scattered through older Israelite territory, at Hebron, Bethel and elsewhere.

The inheritance through site and design was further strengthened when Solomon expelled Abiathar, a priest of the Israelite tradition represented by Shiloh and Eli, and appointed a leading priest of the Jerusalem cult, Zadok a Jebusite, as high priest in the new temple. In this way the Jebusite temple tradition was influential in Solomon's temple from its beginnings. When we remember that sanctuaries were also built for the gods of Solomon's foreign wives, and doubtless like the temple close to the palace, and that other gods had their sacred places in Jerusalem right up till the exile, it becomes clear that this new temple was no novelty but rather another and splendid example of an ancient form of sanctuary. Its importance lay in its social and political significance in the new empire, and in the centralization some three centuries later, when it replaced all local sanctuaries and began to emerge as the central symbol of the life and religion of the Jews. However much the religion of Israel was a new departure that developed over against its religious environment, with a god radically distinct from the gods of the nations about her, it remains true that her main sanctuary shared in the traditions of these nations and matched the temples of their gods. The results of this tension between a religion and its sacred place will engage us at a later point, likewise the manner in which it was removed. But first we must attend to the ideas about the meaning and function of the Jerusalem temple that arose in the history of Israel and the Jews and that may be elucidated through the categories we set forth in the two preceding chapters. How far is our analysis of the sacred place reflected in the thought of those for whom Solomon's temple became their central sanctuary?

4.2 THE DIVINE SANCTION

We have already seen how sacred places derive not from inherent suitability nor from human choice but from some sign or action of the gods, some revelation that this is where their presence and power are to be met. Is this true of Solomon's temple, or was it merely the shrewd choice dictated by David's political needs or Solomon's famous wisdom? Congar recognizes the pattern of divine origins common 'in various oriental religions' but denies its occurrence in this case. He assimilates the origins of the temple to the beginnings of the Israelite monarchy and asserts that 'both originate in a purely human project', with David choosing the site and Solomon (or his architects) drawing the plan. Only afterwards did Yahweh intervene. 'Just as he ratified and blessed the institution of the monarchy which he had first refused to do ... so too he consecrates and ratifies the building of the temple although he had in a sense rejected ... the proposal that he should be provided with one.'[5] This view, whether or no it be true to the historical events, sets the origins of Israel's main temple over against the normal pattern in religions.

It is therefore all the more remarkable that later writers such as the Deuteronomist and the Chronicler, who might be expected to be far more aware of the importance of distinguishing Israel's religion from that of other peoples, reverse this attitude and relate various revelatory phenomena connected with the origins of the temple. Firstly, a dream is associated with the origins; in this case it is Nathan's dream that David should not proceed with the building, and this could be taken as an indirect divine warrant for Solomon to do so. We shall be examining Nathan's opposition later, but in II Samuel 7 we have an account of human initiative towards establishing a sacred place that is answered by divine revelation, albeit negative in verdict. Secondly, David is described as having received the plan of the temple 'by the spirit' and 'from the hand of Yahweh', before he passed it on to Solomon (I Chronicles 28: 11-19). All this is quite within the pattern found in the history of religions.

This pattern is further illustrated in other revelatory events. If, as the Chronicler believes, David's threshing floor altar was the site of the temple then its selection is associated with the angel theophany, and confirmed by the heavenly fire descending upon the altar (I Chronicles 21:15-26; II Samuel 24:16-17). Likewise in the Deuteronomist historian's account of the opening of the temple there are both the cloud theophany on the occasion itself and after the event Solomon's dream confirming its consecration to show that this was no merely human enterprise (I Kings 8:10-11; 9:2-3).

All this is congruent with the origins of temples in other religions, and this congruence is further manifest in the characteristic conservation of temple form through the Jerusalem temple's thousand years of chequered history. The basic pattern of Solomon's temple, the 'first' temple, was of a three-cell rectangular building entered up steps, with an altar in front of the entrance, and surrounded by a complex of courts which were shared with the palace buildings. After four centuries of existence without major change this temple was looted and destroyed by Nebuchadnezzar in 586 B.C.. Its first tentative successor is found in Ezekiel's elaborate vision of a restored and enlarged complex which was never built (Ezekiel 40-43). Here the main temple building faithfully reflects its predecessor in design and proportions, and the ancillary buildings and courts are considerably extended to produce a splendid precinct entirely within the temple tradition. A magnificent outer court was entered by flights of steps through elaborate gateways, and from this the priests could proceed further through stairways and gate-buildings into the inner court of the terraced altar and the temple building itself. It was still essentially Solomon's temple but its rising terraced courts and entrances made it even more clearly a mountain sanctuary appropriate for the sacred Mt. Zion.

The actual second temple, replacing Solomon's, was completed, probably on the same site, in 516 B.C.. There is little information about it except that it seems to have been a meagre replacement reflecting the straightened circumstances of the Jews returning from exile in Babylon. The important point for our purposes is that it followed the pattern of its predecessor in building and contents (except for the loss of the ark from the Holy of Holies) and in possession of an inner and an outer court, with altar for burnt offerings in the former. This temple suffered various desecrations and lootings by Greek and Roman conquerors but remained substantially intact and was even further decorated and strengthened in its surrounding court walls.

What is sometimes called the third temple was really the second one rebuilt and much extended into the grandiose complex that represented Herod the Great's endeavour to enhance his own prestige and humour the piety of the Jews. Great care was taken to preserve the nature and proportions of the main sanctuary as it was rebuilt by priest-masons, and the exterior of this and the other buildings was resplendent with gilding and white marble. The main extension consisted of a series of courts in the form of terraces each higher than the other and entered by numerous gateways; these we have already described in illustration of the idea of graded degrees of sanctity that marks the temple type (p. 41). As a divinely sanctioned *domus dei* the temple of Yahweh reveals the same conservation of its original form through two rebuildings in ten fitful centuries as is to be seen in the temples of other religions, and in its final development it exhibits the characteristic temple type as clearly as any sanctuary in the world.

4.3 THE FUNCTION AS CENTRE

In discussing the functions of sacred places as the centre for human existence we were able to use illustrations from Israel's life and religion, and especially the view of the temple as the source of primeval or cosmic light for the whole world (p. 21); elsewhere we alluded to the quite concrete ways in which a sanctuary has been central to the everyday life of a community (p. 35). To this the Jerusalem temple was no exception. Besides the specifically religious functions as the centre for prayers and sacrifices, and especially for the great seasonal festivals, there were many other aspects of the life not only of Jerusalem but of Israel as a whole that found their focus here. As the centre for festival and ritual it served also as the national conservatory of music; as an administrative centre it was involved in taxation, and as judicial centre it was equivalent to both a college of law and a supreme court, conserving, interpreting, transmitting and applying the laws; for individuals here was the great place of pilgrimage, in its later history attracting Jews from throughout the diaspora, and acting always as a place of asylum or refuge; as a literary and liturgical centre it was also a national archive, and from such deposits the Book of the Law that started a reformation was found.

Besides these functions in the day to day life of Israelite or Jew the temple occupied a central place in his hopes for the future not only of his own people but of all mankind. Ezekiel foresaw God's sanctuary set in their midst for ever as a witness to the nations; and the peoples gathered from the nations dwelling peacefully at the centre (literally 'navel') of the world (Ezekiel 5:5ff.; 37:26-28; 38:12; also Zechariah 14:9). The Gentiles of the world would come to Mt. Zion to learn of God and worship him together with his people Israel, and here would be the centre for the administration of divine justice and for international harmony. A splendid expression of this hope is found in Micah 4:1-2 and in Isaiah 2:1-4, while a later writer repeats the same theme of the temple as a 'house of prayer for all peoples', for 'I am coming to gather all nations and tongues; they shall come and see my glory ... on my holy mountain in Jerusalem' (Isaiah 56:7; 66:18, 20). The apocryphal and pseudepigraphical literature develops the theme still further as, for instance, in the Sibylline Oracles: 'Then again all the sons of the great God shall live quietly around the temple ... free from war shall they be in city and country' (3:702, 707).[6] Perhaps it was something of these ideas and hopes that survived in the mediaeval maps showing Jerusalem as the centre of the world long after the temple itself had been finally destroyed.

This hope that here creation would be renewed and perfected drew strength especially in the later centuries from the belief that this same sacred area was also the centre for the original creation of the world; what had begun on Mt. Zion would also be consummated there. One expression of this — the temple as source of cosmic light — has been examined; another already mentioned is the idea of the sanctuary as the navel of the world. This is but one example of the analogy men find between the forms and functions of their own bodies and the structures of the world in which they live. In this case just as the umbilical cord is the source of life for the embryo through the navel, around which it grows, so also the whole world starts and grows from the temple, or the temple on its Mt. Zion, as the first point of creation. As one midrash or literary expansion of the idea put it, later in the Christian era,

> God created the world like an embryo. Just as the embryo proceeds from the navel onwards, so God began to create the world proceeding from its navel onwards and from there it was spread out in different directions. Where is the navel? It is Jerusalem. The navel itself is the altar. And why is it called the Stone of Foundation? Because the world was established from it. (Bet ha-Midrash 5:63, 1ff.)[7]

This also introduces the belief that when the ark had vanished from the Holy of Holies its place was taken by a stone altar; it is possible that this was, or was believed to be, the natural outcrop of rock we have already noted as an ancient altar. Creation legends grew round one or other or both of these in expansion of the foundation stone spoken of in Isaiah 28:16. In this view:

> This rock ... the Stone of Foundation, was the first solid thing created, and was placed by God amidst the as yet boundless fluid of the primeval waters. Legend has it that just as the body of an embryo is built up ... from its navel, so God built up the earth concentrically around this Stone, the Navel of the Earth. And just as the ... embryo receives its nourishment from the navel, so the whole earth too receives the waters that nourish it from this Navel. The waters of the Deep crouch underneath the Foundation stone at a depth of a thousand cubits, and down to them reach the ... shafts, also created according to a legend in the days of creation. Thus when the libations flowed down from the bowls on the altar into the shafts, they finally reached the waters of the Deep and could so fulfil their mission.[8]

Here we have a whole complex of ideas linking actual structures and rituals in the temple with the creation and nourishment of the whole universe, but whether as navel or as foundation stone the temple and Mt. Zion occupy a position as centre of all things.

4.4 THE FUNCTION AS MICROCOSM

'Solomon's temple was ... the earthly representation of the heavenly abode.... "The temple was ... pictured as a microcosm of the world, the realm of the god." Numerous passages in the Old Testament support this view.'[9] Thus speaks one eminent biblical scholar, G. E. Wright. 'In the Bible there is very feeble support for these cosmic theories..., there is not a single text which suggests that the Temple itself ever had a cosmic significance.'[10] So speaks another, R. de Vaux. We are clearly on controversial ground. Could it be that the correspondence we have been tracing between the Jerusalem sanctuary and the temple type breaks down here at this very important feature? Or are de Vaux's interpretations affected by an unnecessary fear of cosmic symbolism?

The central conception involved is that the earthly sanctuary is a copy or reflection of a heavenly prototype or original which is the true and abiding home of the gods. It is true that there is not much explicit statement in this pattern. Psalm 78:69 which seems to say that the sanctuary was built like the heights of heaven is dismissed by de Vaux as meaning only that God's choice both of Mt. Zion and of David is definitive, and as enduring as the heavens. More to the point is Psalm 11: 4, where 'the Lord is in the holy temple' is placed in parallel and in contrast with 'the Lord whose throne is in the heavens'. Since the former temple seems to be that on Mt. Zion it is treated as 'the symbol and counterpart' of the heavenly sanctuary. This combination is common in the Psalms including some that are pre-exilic, as may be seen by examining Psalms 14:2 and 7, 20:2 and 6, 76:2 and 8, 80:1 and 14. While scarcely conclusive in itself this evidence is certainly congenial to Wright's view.

We may also refer to the prototype for the temple to be found, according to the Priestly writers, in the Mosaic tabernacle. In Exodus 25 Moses receives from Yahweh very detailed instructions for the plan of the tabernacle, and this is matched by the precise details for the reconstruction of the temple in the vision of Ezekiel. It is not stated, however, that the tabernacle represented Yahweh's heavenly abode, and in Ezekiel's theophany at the River Chebar he saw only the indirect reflection of the glory of Yahweh in a sheet of shining metal, and not the heavenly realm itself (Ezekiel 1:4). On the other hand it is a reasonable presumption that the details of these models were believed to derive from the divine abode.

What is more certain is that the shapes and proportions, especially those of Ezekiel's temple, are not the result of practical or aesthetic considerations but represent in their perfections and harmonies the very nature of heaven itself. The Holy of Holies throughout its history seems to have been a perfect cube with sides of twenty cubits, and the relation between the floor areas of this chamber and of the larger holy place and vestibule appears fixed in the ratio of 2:4:1, although Ezekiel's porch was slightly larger in proportion. In his accounts of the entrance to the Holy of Holies we find ratios of 2:6:3 between its various parts (41:3-4). The whole temple compound is four-square, with concentric inner and outer courts each entered by symmetrically placed gateways. These gateways were fifty cubits long and twentyfive broad, and the same proportions of 2:1 applied to the main temple building which externally was a hundred cubits long and fifty wide. In front of it was an open space of a hundred cubits each side, with the altar in the middle; the main central block of the altar if carried down to the base and including the horns at the top corners was another perfect cube of twelve cubits each side. All these symmetries, unities, and mathematical proportions are expressions of one basic idea, the perfections of the heavenly realm that must be thus reflected in the earthly *domus dei*. It is for this same reason that the shape and proportions of the temple itself were fixed for all time, and as we have seen were so carefully preserved throughout its history.

A temple with this cosmic reference in its basic design naturally supported further cosmic symbolisms in its details and furnishings. Firstly there is no doubt that all three temples faced the east, like so many counterparts elsewhere, and like the main gate and altar steps in Ezekiel's vision (43:2, 4, 17). In the first century A.D. Josephus was able to interpret the three main parts as corresponding to the three cosmic regions – the Holy of Holies to the heavens, the holy place to the earth, and the surrounding court to the sea or the lower regions; the latter was further represented in the huge bronze basin or 'sea' in the inner court (I Kings 7:23-26). There is no reason to believe that this was then a new idea, for a generation earlier Philo, another Jew who shared such cosmic interpretations, implied that they were common knowledge;[11] at the same time it is true that fuller application of cosmic ideas, down to the minutest details, occurs in the rabbinic writings of the next few centuries, one of which may be quoted:

The Tabernacle [i.e. temple] was made to correspond to the creation of the world. The two Cherubs over the Ark of the Covenant were made to correspond to the two holy names [of God: Yahweh and Elohim].... The eleven hangings of the Tabernacle were made to correspond to the highest heaven. The table was made to correspond to the earth. The two shewbreads were arranged to correspond to the fruit of the earth. 'In two rows, six in a row' [were set the twelve cakes] to correspond to the months of summer and winter. The laver was made to correspond to the sea and the candlestick ... to the lights [of heaven]. 'And he set up the pillars' ...Jachin and Boaz ... corresponding to ... the moon ... and ... to the sun.[12]

Before this, however, Josephus had already set forth no fewer than thirteen such correspondences and the question is whether these views stand early in a newly developing tradition or reach further back into Old Testament times.[13]

Those who support the position of de Vaux regard this cosmic symbolism as a post-biblical speculative and mystical development in sophisticated and possibly hellenized minds. It would then represent similar developments in the application of cosmic or other elaborate symbolism to Christian churches by the mediaeval French bishop William Durandus or the nineteenth century Cambridge Camden Society, sophisticated interpretations well beyond widespread popular acceptance. This view is strengthened by similar suggestions that Egyptian and Mesopotamian temples were at first utilitarian structures, platforms to keep the shrines above the floods, and that the later cosmic symbolisms had no influence on the daily rituals or the social function of the temples.[14]

We are not satisfied that the position was as simple as this. The small attention given these matters in the canonical books of the Old Testament may mean no more than an absence of interest on the part of writers and leaders, whose concerns and reforms lay in other fields. There is no necessary disjunction between utilitarian and symbolic ideas, and the fact that buildings meeting practical requirements were also so patient of cosmic interpretations and in ways so uniform across the world strongly suggests that such ideas were operative in their construction from the beginning. In the case of Israel's temple, of course, cosmic symbolism might have been only an inheritance from a pagan world that was uncomprehended or else quickly suppressed, but from all that we know of the long intermingling of Canaanite and other influences with the religion of Israel it is most unlikely that the temple would have been such an exception.

Clements, while recognizing with de Vaux that 'not all of these supposed symbolic references of features of the temple are convincing' asserts that 'the essential claim that the temple and its furnishings did possess a cosmic ... symbolism must be upheld'.[15] To the arguments we have presented above he adds considerations drawn from the undoubtedly mythological and cosmic interpretation of Mt. Zion, which as we have seen was either intimately connected or identified with the temple. While not every worshipper would be fully conscious of all the cosmic symbolism in detail, some sense of the temple as the earthly representation of the heavenly realms must have permeated the religious consciousness of Israel long before post-biblical writers worked the idea out in elaborate and somewhat artificial analogies. These writers were encouraged by a nostalgia for the temple that had already been destroyed and no longer remained as a visible check upon the pious imagination. But this was still a Jewish imagination that was neither pagan nor merely Hellenized but rooted in the traditions of Israel.

4.5 THE FUNCTION AS MEETING POINT

The various complexes of ideas that we have distinguished in terms of four functions overlap and support one another so that the temple as meeting place has been implicit in our considerations of its function as centre and as microcosm. This is apparent when we remember how the temple provided the great future meeting point for all the nations, and that the navel concept involves a connection between heaven and earth as well as the growth of the earth from this point. Similarly the temple as microcosm not only reflected the heavenly prototype but was that point on earth which came closest to the heavens, in distance as well as in design. In one Jewish mythical view the actual distance between heaven and earth, expressed in terms of the thickness of the firmament between them, was five hundred years. This meant a walking distance requiring five centuries which, if taken literally, represents some three and a half million miles. The temple, however, was conceived as being no more than a mere eighteen miles below its heavenly counterpart. This made it the highest spot on earth and relatively speaking in close contact with the heavens that it almost met in a physical sense.

This idea of the sanctuary as the highest spot on earth is contained in the image of the holy mountain and not least in that of Mt. Zion, which we have seen to be so deeply connected with the Jerusalem temple. Jerusalem itself was higher than the rest of the world in the minds of prophets and psalmists, and the temple itself rested on top of the highest mountain and so was the very entry into heaven (Isaiah 2:1-4). As Clements has pointed out, the emphasis upon the height of Zion found especially in Micah 4:1-2 and Isaiah 2:1-4 'cannot have arisen from the actual size of Mount Zion, but is due to the "mythological" notion that the divine dwelling place is higher than all other mountains'.[16] As we have seen, this same mountain theme found expression in the ascending steps at the many entrances to the courts, and in these terraced courts themselves, leading in and up to the main altar for burnt offerings. This again was built in terraced stages and the term used for the uppermost stage has been best interpreted as 'mountain of God'.

Rabbinic thought was fascinated by the rocky outcrop that formed the peak of the holy Mt. Zion, and regarded this as the point of connection not only with the world above but also with the lower world. These contained the primeval chaotic waters that could still arise to engulf the ordered created world but were prevented by this great rock which stopped the exit. At the same time these primeval deeps contained the sources of the waters necessary upon the earth for the welfare of all living creatures (Genesis 49:5; Deuteronomy 33:13; Psalm 33:7), and therefore also figured in Ezekiel's picture of the life-giving streams flowing from beneath his ideal temple (Ezekiel 47: 1-12).

This nether world was also the abode of the spirits of the dead, the place of Sheol and Paradise, so that the temple rock was the point of connection with the departed. In this way it stood at the centre and navel of the universe as the meeting point for its various spheres, the place of communication with both the lower worlds and the heavenly realms.

Apart from these later post-biblical developments among the rabbis there were other ancient biblical expressions of the idea of the temple as the place of meeting between man and Yahweh. We shall examine the predecessor of the temple, the tabernacle as the 'tent of meeting', in the next chapter, and here it is sufficient to point out that this seems to have been as much a rendezvous as a dwelling, a place where God came to visit men who sought him. After the suppression of the local sanctuaries and the centralization of worship the temple became the normal place to meet with Yahweh, and as the diaspora increased faithful Jews came on pilgrimage, going 'up to Jerusalem' and finally ascending the hill of the Lord to the temple where God descends to meet His people; nowhere else could men feel so close to Yahweh or bring their prayers and gifts and dedicate their children (as Jesus himself was dedicated) with more assurance of acceptance.

4.6 THE FUNCTION AS IMMANENT-TRANSCENDENT PRESENCE

It is apparent that the temple as a place of worship attempting to express both the immanence and the transcendence of the gods has been involved in our discussion of the two previous functions. As meeting point it brings the transcendent Yahweh to an immanent presence at one place in this world, and perhaps we can interpret the Jewish mythical account's quaint gap of eighteen miles between the heavenly and the earthly realms as an attempt at conserving the distinction between the divine and the human even while asserting their propinquity. Likewise the temple as microcosm represents the immanent presence of a Yahweh whose transcendent being requires a macrocosmic heavenly abode. The cosmic symbolism attaching to the temple stressed the transcendence of a universal god who had created the universe and was not tied to an earthly abode in Jerusalem even while it validated that same temple as a place fit for his dwelling in the midst of his people.

The Jerusalem temple also exhibited the usual signs of a *domus dei*, especially in being non-congregational as far as the main sanctuary was concerned, and in the emphasis upon a remote inner cell as the actual dwelling place of Yahweh. This Holy of Holies was a windowless chamber, numinous in its silence and darkness, instinct with the mysterious presence of Yahweh conveyed by the cult objects of cherubim and ark, and whatever replaced the ark at a later stage, communicating with the world only through the rare and careful entrance of the high priest. It has even been suggested that there may have been other God-cells in the temple side rooms or complex, for there is usually some basis of fact for a vision such as Ezekiel's wherein he saw the idolatrous elders of Israel each worshipping the image of his own god in the darkness of its cell or shrine (8:9-12).[17] However this may be there is no doubt that in physical form and popular interpretation the temple was a house for the immanent presence of Yahweh (I Kings 8:12-13).

The nature of the two main cult objects within the Holy of Holies is by no means clear, except that they mediate the real presence of Yahweh.[18] The ark especially seems to have been a kind of powerful 'extension' of the person of Yahweh, as is manifest throughout the stories of its wanderings before it was finally deposited in Solomon's temple (I Samuel 4:1-7:2; II Samuel 6:1-15). Here it was so important that the temple could be looked upon as the house of the ark, and that meant the dwelling place of Yahweh. There is a good deal of controversy as to exactly how ark and Yahweh were related in the temple. A common view has been that the ark was the throne of God, and that the absence of any image for the deity stressed the transcendence of the being who was also really present in this place, as well as marked the uniqueness of Israel's religion. On the contrary this would serve to place it more firmly in a wider tradition, for there were empty thrones in the temples of other gods in Phoenicia and Greece with exactly the same significance.

It is possible that the ark was originally related to Yahweh in other ways, especially as the box for tokens or records of the Sinai covenant, and that the imageless deity was regarded as enthroned in the space between the two cherubim, a Canaanite conception that some have traced to the winged sphinxes of Egypt (I Samuel 4:4; II Samuel 6:2). The ark is then not a throne but a support for the mercy-seat which the Priestly writers develop as a cover above the ark (Exodus 25:22), or even only a footstool (I Chronicles 28:2). This could explain how its loss somewhere before the building of the second temple does not seem to have been too serious a matter, and how Jeremiah could prophesy that the ark would be of no further consequence when all Jerusalem served as the throne for Yahweh's presence amid the nations gathered there (Jeremiah 3:16-17). The ark and the cherubim therefore had no importance in themselves as magical or inherently sacred objects, but in their different ways testified to the real presence of a god who was immanent and yet transcendent.

When examining the combined expression of immanence and transcendence in the various temple forms that reveal a graduated sanctity the Jerusalem temple was inevitably used as an example (p. 41). We were then referring to the final Herodian temple, and it has been pointed out that Solomon's temple probably had only one court peculiar to the building itself, and that even when an inner or 'higher' court appeared it was not yet the basis for separation between priests and people, for Baruch read Jeremiah's speeches there. After the building of the second temple there seems to have been priestly agitation for this distinction, but it is doubtful whether it was successful before the second century B.C.. Earlier Ezekiel had insisted on it, and it was consonant with the gradations among the priests according to their degrees of purification and their duties. When Herod's temple gave such extensive expression to graded sanctities it was therefore no new idea but the culmination of a long development in which holiness 'had its centre in the temple of Jerusalem in the holy of holies' and 'operated in a less and less intensified form as one withdrew further and further from the temple'.[19]

The dual dimensions of the divine presence are also expressed in the most extended commentary on the functions of the temple to be found in the Old Testament, the magnificent prayer of Solomon at the dedication (I Kings 8:12-53). If the splendid statements emphasizing the divine transcendence should be the contribution of a Deuteronomic historian added to more primitive accounts concerned with the mysterious presence immanent in cloud in the outer chamber and thick darkness in the holy of holies (vv. 10, 12), then the final combination of these two emphases exhibits the very point in question. In the one emphasis the temple has been built as God's dwelling place for ever (v. 13); in the other the highest heavens cannot contain Him, much less a building such as this (v. 27 and the repeated references to heaven throughout). This is consonant with the more profound interpretations in other nations, whether it be the Phoenician Baal who could not be confined to a single temple as his sole dwelling or the Egyptian Amon whose litany conceived him to be 'in every place where he desires to be ... in all his monuments ... and (all) lands'.

The tension between these two dimensions of God's presence appears in the question of I Kings 8:27 as to whether this transcendent God can really dwell with men on earth. The answer lies in the repeated assertion that Yahweh has 'placed His name there', and will assuredly meet all who seek Him and hear their prayers, indeed, His 'heart and His eyes will be there for all time' (9:13). This introduces a more sophisticated interpretation of presence through 'the divine Name', a kind of *alter ego*, by means of which He made Himself present to men, without ever leaving His heavenly dwelling place'.[20] This development of a name-presence is a Deuteronomic contribution that testifies again to the effort to hold the two emphases together in thought about the temple.

Allied with this form of the dual emphasis are the other conjunctions whereby Yahweh both dwells in His temple amidst His people and also visits them from His heavenly abode, is regularly present and yet also manifest in special theophanies from time to time. These dual modes of speech permeate much of the Old Testament and imply a constant 'fluctuation of perspective' in the effort to apprehend the fulness of man's relation with the divine. Doubtless some were able to maintain this dual perspective without strain, keeping company with the young Isaiah who went to the place of God's presence seeking consolation 'in the year that King Uzziah died' and encountered an overwhelming theophany in which he was called to the prophetic vocation (Isaiah 6). But in any religion these would be the minority and many would succumb to the tension by allowing one or other of the two dimensions to fade from their experience.

For many it was the sense of transcendence that diminished until Yahweh was reduced to an earthbound deity who could be taken for granted as inevitably present in his Jerusalem sanctuary, securing the safety and prosperity of his worshippers so long as the temple remained intact. As we have seen the very multiplicity of shrines in earlier Israel reminded men that Yahweh was not confined to any one of them, and it was the centralization of worship in the Jerusalem temple, coupled with the memory of the miraculous deliverance from Sennacherib's siege in 701 B.C. (II Kings 19), that gave a powerful impetus to this restricted view of a merely immanent deity, with a 'fixed and static presence'. Then 'Israel could feel itself so sure of the immanent presence of Yahweh that it forgot his transcendent lordship'.[21] It was this attitude that drove the prophets to threaten the destruction of the temple, and even though this unbelievable event occurred in 586 B.C. the attitude itself was not destroyed but survived in popular dependence upon the later sanctuary.

In more sophisticated quarters and in later centuries, among the Septuagint translators, in the Qumran community, among the writers of the apocrypha and pseudepigrapha and among the rabbis it was often the sense of God being really present in the temple at Jerusalem that tended to grow weaker and to be offset by various forms of emphasis upon the transcendence. The Septuagint replaced the Hebrew verb for 'dwell' where Deuteronomy used it to describe the placing of God's name in the temple by its own 'I will be invoked', and elsewhere the same verb gave place to another meaning, 'appeared' (Exodus 25:8; Deuteronomy 33:16); in each case the meaning was changed to stress the intermittent presence of Yahweh in a theophany.[22]

Among the more thoughtful and historically minded there was an understandable dissatisfaction with the second temple both on account of its poverty of structure and its chequered history. Some rabbis said that the presence of Yahweh had never returned to the sanctuary after the exile, or that it lacked five things, such as the ark, the urim and thummim, the fire from heaven, the Shekinah or presence, and the holy Spirit. Others, such as the Qumran community, felt that the desecration by Antiochus Epiphanes' heathen sacrifices upon the altar in 168 B.C. had never been removed, and the present temple and priesthood had not been restored to full holiness. In compensation for the deficiencies of the Jerusalem temple together with the continuing postponement of its promised glory as the centre for the worship of the world, the spiritually minded Qumran members and many writers among the non-canonical books developed a strong interest in the heavenly temple of God, and then identified this with the long-hoped-for new perfected temple in Jerusalem. The heavenly temple must therefore descend to earth when God once again returned to dwell amidst his people more intimately and clearly than ever before.[23] This disjunction of the two emphases might therefore be said to contain its own corrective, and to lead to a restored sense of the immanence of Yahweh in his own good time.

This completes our formal examination of the Jerusalem temple using the categories employed in the study of the sanctuaries of other religions. It is now clear that this temple also may be analysed and understood in these terms, and that the richness of its history enables it to make its own contribution to the elucidation of the temple type of sacred place. This further insight concerns especially the tensions and ambiguities, and the sense of its limitations and failures that appear in men's attitudes to the temple at Jerusalem, and these now demand fuller attention.

5

The Problem of the Jerusalem Temple

All great religious traditions have their internal sources of self-criticism and throw up their own reformers, but there can be no people in history who have examined their temples in the way that Israel and the Jews defended or opposed, reformed, reinterpreted or even discarded the sanctuary that stood as the centre and basis of their existence for more than millennium. The opposition that began with Nathan even before it was built continued through the canonical prophets and reached a new intensity in Stephen near the end of its history, and was still being voiced by the Jew Trypho after it had been finally destroyed. Nor was it confined to more thoughtful individuals: there were the Rechabites who would not build houses for themselves, much less a house for Yahweh, and in later centuries there were groups such as the Essenes and Ebionites, together with the Qumran community in some of its thinking, who maintained the same opposition. These criticisms could not be dismissed as the attitudes of cultural reactionaries like the Rechabites, and so possibly only sociological or psychological in origin, for they are shared by some of the greatest Old Testament figures and the most spiritually minded sections of the community; clearly they came from the resources of Israel's religion itself.

Over against this critical tradition stands the equally impressive loyalty and devotion to the temple, manifest at times even in these same critics themselves. Only this loyalty and a sense of the temple as really mediating the presence of Yahweh to his people can account for the persistence with which the repeated destruction or defilement of the sanctuary was faced. If we include the Shiloh sanctuary destroyed by the Philistines there were four such disasters in eleven centuries, and even today there are some who would replace the Herodian temple now that the new state of Israel for the first time makes this conceivable.

68

There is no better mirror of this devotion to the temple than the Psalter — read the lovely Psalm 84, where the writer's spirit longs and pines for the courts of the Lord's dwelling place and would rather spend a single day there than a thousand anywhere else (see also Psalms 23:6; 27:4; 65:4; 122:1-4; 134, etc.). It is this piety which is still manifest in the parents of Jesus, in his own practice, and in that of his disciples and of the early church.

5.1 AMBIVALENT ATTITUDES: CRITICISM AND SUPPORT

Apart from the prophet Nathan whom we shall consider separately, it is clear that the most severe criticism of the temple comes from the canonical prophets or is found in the Deuteronomic histories, and so derives from the Levitical priests. It cannot therefore be identified with the supposed inevitable opposition between the charismatic prophet concerned to speak for a dynamic Yahweh, and the professional priest conserving the cultic rites at the sanctuary where dwelt a static and almost passive deity. At the same time one can say that the prophets were the more explicit and frequent exponents of the critical tradition, although at times they could show a devotion to the temple equal to that of any cultic official.

The burden of these criticisms lies not so much in the nature of the temple itself as in the attitudes men adopted towards it and the foreign practices that were allowed within its precincts. The presence of Yahweh was primarily to be found in the life and history of Israel and was not tied to any particular place, not even the temple. Indeed, his real dwelling was in the heavens (Hosea 5:15; Deuteronomy 26:15) and if men persisted in merely formal worship corrupted by alien practices and dissociated from moral obedience and social justice then God may withdraw his presence from their temple or even destroy it altogether. He reminds Israel that he had already done this to Shiloh (Jeremiah 7: 1-15). A similar warning is placed by the Deuteronomist at the opening of the Jerusalem temple, which would be destroyed and left in ruins that would witness to Israel's unfaithfulness if her people strayed from the covenant obedience (I Kings 9:3-9). The same principle appears in the later Qumran criticism of any temple cultus that ignores the primary demands of justice and righteousness, in this case as formulated in the Law.

The book of Deuteronomy has its own peculiar ways of avoiding emphasis upon the temple itself. As we have seen, it describes Yahweh's presence there as the 'placing of his Name'; but although this formula occurs one way or another some twenty times the place itself is never specified—neither as Zion nor Jerusalem nor as the temple, even though this is clearly what is intended. This stands in contrast to Old Testament writers who use these very names as a benediction in themselves, and is part of the campaign to purge Israel's worship of all Canaanite ideas of a god who dwelt permanently in an earthly shrine. After all, those behind the Deuteronomic book recalled these ideas at work in the temples of the northern kingdom, where they had failed to save either shrines or people from destruction.

Deuteronomy's chief practical measure for this reform and purification was the centralization of worship upon the one sanctuary at Jerusalem (Deuteronomy 12:1-14). 'We are faced, therefore, with the strange ambivalence of Deuteronomy, that, while it divested the Jerusalem temple of its original meaning, it also demanded that it should be regarded as the only true shrine of Yahweh.'[1] The temple was thus demoted from the possession of any intrinsic significance or inevitable presence of Yahweh, and made dependent upon being first chosen and then granted the name-presence of the God who dwelt in the heavens. At the same time it was promoted to the position of sole and national sanctuary charged with the heavy responsibility of restoring the true covenant religion of Israel.

Something of the same ambivalence appears if we set the more positive attitudes of the prophets alongside those we have already outlined. Zion was the place chosen as Yahweh's dwelling and for revelation to Israel (Amos 1:2; Isaiah 6; 8:18; Jeremiah 3:17; 14:21; 17:12). For Ezekiel here was the glory of God (8:4) and here the destroyed temple would have to be rebuilt in even more glorious form. For the Isaiah of the sixth century the rebuilding of the temple was one of the objects of the return from exile (Isaiah 44:28; 54:11-14), and it was the prophets Haggai (1:13-14; 2:9) and Zechariah (1:16; 2:12-13) who spurred the builders into action. And as we have already seen it was around the temple that the prophets foresaw the future gathering of the nations in the pure worship of Yahweh, who, for Malachi, would first come in judgment to cleanse his temple (3:1-4).

5.2 EFFORTS TO RELIEVE THE TENSION

The different attitudes towards Israel's temple stand over against each other in various ways, but perhaps the most basic polarization occurs in the tension between an immanent presence and a transcendent deity that we have already set forth. Of the several attempts to mediate between these two emphases we have already referred to the Deuteronomic contribution whereby Yahweh whom no temple could possibly contain nevertheless graciously chose to 'place his Name there' as a means of establishing his presence without becoming localized and confined, bound to the physical sanctuary. Since the name expressed and represented the person this was a way of saying that Yahweh himself was really present without losing his transcendent existence and becoming merely a divinized part of the world at a sanctuary. Men could still come with their needs and prayers in confidence that Yahweh would be there to meet them, as the Deuteronomist continually promises. God is both in the heaven and on the earth below (Deuteronomy 4:39), and men are to meet him at the sanctuary he has chosen as 'the abiding place of his presence', the place of his Name (26:2).

Another and later attempt to provide a mediating concept in relief of the tension is found in the reinterpretations of Israel's history and temple that were demanded by the shattering experience of exile in heathen Babylon, and that assumed a collected form perhaps late in the sixth century B.C.. These writings of a priestly group show great concern for the restoration of the cult by laying down very precise regulations governing all aspects of worship, but at the same time they had to deal with the problem presented by Israel's lack of any temple for some two generations after 586 B.C.. If Yahweh and his people could still be together in these circumstances how was his presence to be envisaged in a rebuilt temple?

For answer the Priestly literature returns to one of the forms of theophany found in Israel's early experience, the revelation of Yahweh in the cloud that seems to have figured in the exodus and wilderness days. This was the Priestly alternative to the Deuteronomic Name-presence, a cloud which represents and contains the 'glory' of God, as the form in which his presence is sent forth to be with his people (Exodus 16:7, 10; 24:16; 40:34-38; Leviticus 9:6,23; Numbers 14:10; 16:19). This was a more vivid and concrete image than that of the Name, and more evidently not bound to one place, although at the same time the Priestly authors believed it had required a tabernacle in earlier history and now needed a temple. Since God's presence 'came down' or was 'sent forth' to men in this form, it could also be withdrawn, and so the long absence during the exile, coinciding with the lack of a temple, was accounted for in the Priestly theology.

The regularity of the appearance in Exodus 40:38 indicates that the cloud of glory 'is not merely a temporary manifestation of the divine glory, but is a permanent mode of his activity, and as such, is the way in which he comes to settle within Israel. This ... is neither unconditional not unchangeable, but is only a "tabernacling", and may be withdrawn in the face of national disobedience.'[2] This view of the presence amounts to Yahweh's 'settling impermanently' in a 'sustained theophany' or 'extended visit', thus being immanent in the temple while remaining his transcendent self.

The same view had been anticipated by Ezekiel who in all his visionary experience never reports having seen Yahweh, but only his glory as the mode of his presence on earth (1:28; 3:12); for him also the temple is essential for the future presence of God with his people, so dwelling among them in this particular way that Jerusalem itself will be called 'the Lord is there' (48:35).

In later rabbinic and intertestamental thought the mediating image took still other forms, such as the Word, Wisdom, or Spirit of Yahweh as the means of his presence among men. The chief of these further concepts was that of the Shekinah, something more than these personified divine attributes since the word itself means 'dwelling'. For the rabbis who used it, however, this was no mere revival of an identification between the deity and the sanctuary, but an effort to describe how intimate was the active presence of Yahweh in his special relation to the temple without detracting in the slightest from his transcendence. Under all these images — Name, Glory and Shekinah — which later co-existed and influenced each other, men sought to solve the problems that arose when they thought so highly of their temple and so profoundly about their God.

5.3 RADICAL OPPOSITION: NATHAN

In II Samuel 7 the story of the prophet Nathan's dream and his consequent dissuasion of David from the project to build a temple in Jerusalem provides one of the most important criticisms in the Old Testament of this type of sanctuary. The literary history of the material does not affect later discussion concerning interpretation; this has veered between non-theological explanations devoid of any criticism of the temple, and theological accounts implying a drastic opposition to such a sanctuary.

Most of the interpretations which avoid comment on the temple itself accept the story as an explanation of why Solomon rather than David was the builder, and so manage to remain favourable to both David and the temple. In one way or another it is shown that the time was not ripe in David's day. For instance, Nathan was really the spokesman for the great amount of conservative opposition still evident in the northern tribes of the new kingdom, so that David the southerner could not proceed with a temple in a capital that was not yet fully accepted; Solomon, however, was in such a secure and powerful position that he could ignore any lingering opposition. In the same vein Solomon's apology for David's failure to build is quoted (I Kings 5:3). Then again David is said to have recognized that he was unworthy for this sacred task after such a blood-stained career, and so given the credit of humility (I Chronicles 22:7-10). As an alternative it is suggested that the time was not yet ripe for Nathan, who is interpreted as a Jebusite priest opposed to any rival temple in a new cult in Jerusalem; later when he and his party came to support Solomon their attitude changed and one of them, Zadok, secured the chief position in the new temple.

These explanations all seem inadequate for such an impressive chapter. The decision of Yahweh revealed in a dream to Nathan would have
been sufficient to account for the delay on any of the above terms. The
subsequent lengthy criticism of temples as such, and the promise of a
dynastic 'house' for David instead of a sanctuary house for Yahweh,
tell against any building of a temple and especially against Solomon
proceeding so soon. It is impossible to avoid the force of Nathan's criticism. It is a serious theological statement, and those who accept it as
such must not therefore be dismissed as anti-liturgical protestants or
rationalists, as has been done. Nathan is not represented as criticizing
the cult, its external forms or sacrificial system, as some later prophets
did, nor is he merely contrasting an earthly man-made temple with the
heavenly temple which is God's true abode, as the Deuteronomist does
in Solomon's prayer at the opening. It is the temple as such that he
opposes, just as earlier the prophet Samuel had resisted the introduction of the monarchy. Indeed these were kindred developments, for
king and temple were twin foci in the religions of the neighbouring
nations and in the later religion of Israel, where temple and palace ad-
joined one another. Since both monarchy and Jerusalem temple were
copied from pagan peoples and represented a major departure from the
social and religious structure of Israel's previous formative centuries it
is in this direction that we must look to understand Nathan's attitude.

The essence of Nathan's opposition lies in his contrast between the
proposed temple and the tabernacle or tent sanctuary of the earlier
period. It is possible to see him as a genuine conservative theologically
convinced that the peculiar characteristics of Israel's religion and the
freedom of Yahweh himself were better served by the simplicity of
the tabernacle than by the Canaanite luxuries of the proposed temple
under royal patronage. The earlier Canaanite shrines adopted by Israel,
and even the main sanctuary at the Shiloh temple which is passed over
in silence, had managed to maintain the Mosaic tradition together with
the ark and perhaps the tabernacle also; but for the king deliberately
to plan a new official temple in the capital was following too closely in
the Canaanite path. In any event it must be admitted that the temple
in Jerusalem, like the monarchy, was a mixed blessing in Israel's religious history, and, as we have seen, a continual problem to her more

thoughtful minds. It might also be maintained that both Judaism and Christianity were the better for its final destruction, although this would be to anticipate our later enquiries. No one can say that Nathan's viewpoint was wrong.

Nor can it be said that this attitude was merely negative, for the greater part of the chapter is devoted to the positive theme presented as an alternative to the temple. We may summarize the chapter thus: David offers to build God a house, a temple (II Samuel 7:1-3); Nathan expresses the divine rejection of the proposal and reasserts the adequacy of the tabernacle tradition (vv. 4-10); God then promises to make a house for David, in the sense of a family or dynasty that shall be permanent (vv. 11-16); David wonderingly accepts, recalling the way God redeemed Israel from Egypt to be his own people for ever (vv. 18-29). A conversation that begins with the possibility of a temple ends with the assertion of a people, as the true concern of the God of Israel. Thus the initiative was transferred from David to Yahweh, and the subject changed from a sacred place to a holy people.

It is certain that David himself interpreted the situation in these terms and not as an injunction to allow the project to pass to his son. Marcel Simon, who has made extensive studies of both the Nathan incident and the figure of Stephen in the early Church, declares that Stephen also shares David's interpretation, for 'without doubt Stephen has seen a categorical repudiation of the Jerusalem sanctuary in the episode of Nathan's prophecy'.[3] In spite of all that we have been able to say about the spiritual values and insights supported by the temple type of sacred place, these two dissentient figures standing at the beginning and the end of the Jerusalem temple's history cannot be ignored.

5.4 RADICAL REPLACEMENT: THE HOLY COMMUNITY

The drastic replacement of a place by a people as the dwelling of God in this world, raised as a promise even before there was a Jerusalem temple, reappears in some of the great passages of the Old Testament. Jeremiah in one of his early oracles makes the astonishing pronouncement that the ark will not be so much as mentioned when the whole of Jerusalem has become in effect the throne of the Lord (3:16-17). That he has in mind the community rather than the physical city is indicated in his letter to the exiles after the temple was fallen; they will assuredly return and be in open and intimate relationship with Jahweh, but the only condition lies in the sincerity of their own hearts, and there is no mention of any need to rebuild the temple (29:1-23). The same emphasis appears in the restoration oracle of ch. 31, and especially in vv. 31-34 where Israel will be God's people by virtue of a new covenant written on their hearts.

Even Ezekiel, in spite of his great concern for a new and glorious temple in Jerusalem, sees the presence of Yahweh overflowing, as it were, the most glorious of sanctuaries. In fulfilment of the very promise made to David God's presence would be primarily in his purified people, to whom he had given a new spirit and a new heart (36:16-38). The emphasis is on the people rather than the place (37:24-28), and the city (community?) will be known as 'the Lord is there' (48:35). The import is that Yahweh himself will be his people's temple, while they in turn will be as a temple for his presence. The need for a physical sanctuary in these further reaches of Ezekiel's thought seems to have dropped out of sight.

A similar outlook appears in Psalm 22:3 when God is envisaged as enthroned upon the praises of Israel, and this image is developed twice in the fifth century Isaiah: Yahweh is enthroned both on high and also in the humble and contrite spirit rather than in any manner of house that men might build him (Isaiah 57:15; 66:1-2; see also Psalms 40, 50, 51).

This radical elimination of a physical temple is usually described as a spiritualization of worship, and in these terms it would be possible to trace similar revolutionary developments in many other religious traditions, especially among the moralists and philosophers of the Greek and Roman worlds. As witness listen to Seneca: 'We do not need to uplift our hands towards heaven, or beg the keeper of a temple to let us approach his idol's ear ... God is near you, he is with you, he is within you.' Or to the hellenized Jew, Philo, who spans both cultures: 'For what more worthy house could be found for God throughout the whole world ... than a soul that is perfectly purified.'[4] Here the human soul or spirit is the temple of God, but it is the individual man rather than man in community, and the spiritual element in man to the exclusion of the body.

A spiritualization of this kind is foreign to the religion of the Old Testament which sees man always as an embodied spirit, living as a man only in the community of God's people. Rather than speak of spiritualizing worship we prefer to call it a personalization, remembering that a person includes both body and soul and becomes truly personal only through community. It is this conception therefore that we have traced from David through Jeremiah and Ezekiel to the later chapters of Isaiah, the idea of a community of faithful persons becoming the true place of God's presence or dwelling, the true temple (see also Exodus 29:45-6; Leviticus 26:11-12). The discovery of the Dead Sea scrolls has shown that these ideas had passed beyond the visions of the prophets and in intertestamental times had been taken up in earnest by a community such as that at Qumran. We cannot do better than quote from Gärtner's admirable study:

> The leaders of the community were temple priests who had settled down by the shores of the Dead Sea in the hope of creating a new spiritual centre to replace the desecrated temple... to provide a new focus...; the community... called itself 'the Holy place' and 'the Holy of holies'...; they themselves were the 'new temple'...; they transferred the whole complex of ideas from the Jerusalem temple to the community. This... meant... the transference of the concrete entity, the temple building, to a more 'spiritual' realm in the living community, and of the sacrifices to deeds in the life according to the Law.[5]

It is true that one vein of thought at Qumran looked forward to a return to Jerusalem where God himself would build a new and perfect physical temple for the purified community, but there are other hopes also expressed where there is no mention of any Jerusalem temple and the community itself will continue indefinitely as the new form of the temple of God.

The radical transformation of the sanctuary into an entirely personalized new form of temple had therefore reached actual historical expression at Qumran and perhaps in other groups even while the

Jerusalem temple was being extended into a more glorious centre for the life and worship of the nation. Here we have the ultimate commentary on the sacred place from within the Old Testament tradition, and the first sign of a different form of temple that can be traced into the New Testament situation. This drastic transformation that began with the prophet Nathan is all the more striking in having emerged at Qumran. No longer can it be attributed to prophetic prejudice (or its modern equivalents) against cult and temple, for it was brought to this most complete and concrete expression here in a priestly group, who show themselves more sensitive than most to the limitations and impermanent nature of the temple type of sanctuary.

5.5 MODERN DISCUSSIONS: IN DEFENCE OF THE TEMPLE

The viewpoint of the Qumran documents certainly lends support to a statement such as the following, which represents one pole of the range of attitudes to the temple evident in modern studies: 'The temple was never an adequate expression of the religious life of Israel... never corresponded to the distinctive features of the religion of Israel... the Mosaic and prophetic streams.'[6] On the other hand we read elsewhere that 'it did in many ways serve to confirm in Israel ideas and practices that had been borrowed from Canaan, yet none the less it was and remained a thoroughly Israelite shrine... the God was Yahweh, God of Israel'.[7] The second passage represents current endeavours to avoid hasty dismissal of the temple and to seek out the ways in which Israel adapted the temple pattern to the peculiar nature of its own faith, and we must now examine some of these efforts in order to complete the picture of what was happening to this kind of sanctuary in the Israelite milieu.

It is commonly claimed that the distinctiveness of the religion of Israel is indicated by the imageless Holy of Holies as against the idol-filled shrines of other temples. There is no doubt about the forbidding of images of Yahweh, but we have already noted the empty throne as the symbol of the presence of a transcendent deity in other religious traditions; Israel was not unique in this respect. It is further claimed that Israel had replaced the usual divine images by its own peculiar cult-object, the ark, and that this was regarded as an object with an historical origin and reference and not as an inherently sacred object of mythological origin. In support we are referred to the Deuteronomic literature where the ark is regarded in a matter of fact manner as a mere receptacle for the records of the covenant law of Yahweh, and to the Priestly accounts of the ark having no intrinsic holiness but having first to be anointed with sacred oil. These facts alone do not make this cult object unique, for in other traditions there are many parallels wherein the most sacred objects have no holiness until they have been ritually installed, or are treated casually not only before but also on occasion after they have been consecrated. We have also observed the loss of the ark from the Jerusalem temple less than midway through the temple's history without any apparent difference in the functioning of the temple. These facts, taken together with our lack of certainty as to the exact nature and history of the ark, make it a very unsatisfactory support for the unique features of Israel's religion.

There remains the historical reference of the ark to the giving of the covenant in the Sinai period, and a recent study has stressed the importance of this constant reminder both of the covenant and of the classic formative experience in the wilderness where Yahweh proved to be an 'onward-going God', not anchored in any sanctuary but 'on the move' in history.[8] As visible sign of this there is frequent reference to the carrying poles fitted through rings on either side of the ark, and it was stressed that they must never be removed (Exodus 25:13-15); there they must have stayed for centuries, since the Deuteronomic historian records that the ends of the poles poked out into or through the curtain across the Holy of Holies in his day (I Kings 8:8). This is certainly a feature peculiar to Israel, but its easy disappearance from the scene indicates that it was not of vital importance in itself.

We have already referred to the differences of opinion concerning the degree of cosmic symbolism attached to the temple (p. 57); those who minimize this are thereby able to distinguish the Jerusalem temple from all others. Thus we are told that 'in reading the account of the building of the Jerusalem temple one does not get the impression that this cosmic symbolism had an intrinsic significance for the Israelites even remotely comparable to the place it generally occupied in the religions of antiquity'.[9] In specific support it is pointed out that the great rocky outcrop in the temple area probably had religious significance for the Jebusites in the previous era and most certainly figured in later Jewish legend and Muslim history, yet 'the Old Testament is strangely silent about this rock and its interpretation in Yahwism'.[10] These arguments from silence, when set against the other considerations we have adduced on this issue, provide somewhat uncertain testimony for the uniqueness of Israel's temple.

Another approach to the difference between Israel's temple and that of other peoples lies in the examination of the use she made of it, and of her peculiar rituals. It is probable that there were features of congregational worship within the temple precincts, and especially in its later history, that have more in common with Christian worship than with communal festivals in other temples. Above all, the main festivals themselves, although not confined to the temple, had been radically reinterpreted and shaped in a way that was completely new; they now subordinated the ancient mythological and fertility themes of the harvest festivals to the commemoration and re-presentation of the particular saving acts of Yahweh in the known history of Israel.

Such attempts to assimilate both temple and cult to a form of worship new in the history of religions are based upon a distinction between mythological and historical religions that is shared by both Christian and Jewish scholars. Among the latter Kaufmann has attempted to show that the Jerusalem temple was not a cult place of the kind familiar among the religions. He is impressed by Solomon's prayer at the opening of the temple: 'Alongside the Canaanite blueprint of the house in chapters 6-7, this remarkable prayer was placed as a sort of Israelite commentary on that document.'[11] There is not a word in this prayer concerning cultic functions, not even worship through hymn and psalm. It is not a house for the deity, guarded from attacks of evil powers, where man performs the cult necessary to protect and strengthen the deity. It is solely a house of prayer where man does nothing on behalf of the god but where Yahweh hears and answers, judges and pardons, shows compassion and delivers man. Kaufmann further suggests that the Priestly documents make no reference to the spoken word in the rites, and concludes that they were performed in silence. In this way the rituals inherited from the pre-Israelite worship were freed from the speech that articulated their magical-mythological sense, and so were able to become the vehicles of new Israelite meanings.

This seems to be an unnecessarily extreme view of the changes that did occur in the rituals, and to ignore the replacement of mythological by historical cultic recital that would be a much better antidote against the old pagan meanings than mere silence. And again, if the temple had become a house of priestly silence it was hardly yet a house of prayer, in the sense we must reserve for this term, the sense manifest in the synagogue, mosque or church. The very silence itself, as Kaufmann points out, 'served to heighten the awe of holiness', and this is one of the numinous effects characteristic of the *domus dei* sanctuary, rather than of a house of prayer. It is not disputed that the courts of the temple in Jerusalem were places of prayer as of many other activities both religious and secular, and that this continued even among members of the early Church; but again this was the regular practice in temples everywhere.

Kaufmann also stresses that the idea of a temple chosen by Yahweh originates with David and is emphasized in the Deuteronomic accounts. Over against this he sets the natural or inherent sanctity of non-Israelite holy places. The contrast is traced back to the portable sanctuary of Mosaic times, unconnected with any fixed sacred site; it lies behind the legends which linked the Canaanite sites with the patriarchs, 'explicitly providing a historical-revelational, rather than a natural basis for their sanctity'. In time, however, cultic sanctity was not to be found 'even in places that were consecrated by an ancient theophany, but only in the place that would be chosen by Yahweh...'.[12] There is no doubt as to this biblical emphasis: 'For the Lord hath chosen Zion, he has desired it for his dwelling place' (Psalm 132:13; also Psalm 78:68; Exodus 15:13). In the same way he chose Israel in the first place as a people, and later David and his house to lead it. But it is questionable whether 'historical choice' can provide a formal differentia for the Jerusalem temple. Neither Kaufmann's non-cultic temple nor the grounds on which he rests his case will withstand examination.

Another attempt to display the uniqueness of the temple in Jerusalem which overlaps with Kaufmann's at some points has been made by Childs, who starts with the same view of non-Israelite sanctuaries as possessing an inherent or natural sanctity which is traced back to the mythological beginnings of the world.[13] At the creation certain space received a holy content through the special part it played or the special way in which it shared in the primeval powers then active; this holy quality cannot be altered, although 'myth does allow a rhythmic fluctuation in the intensity with which a sacred place participates in the primeval power, and therefore it is the function of the cult to re-activate this latent power. The prophets, however, rejected this mystical understanding of sacred space. Holiness is not an impersonal force stemming from the primeval act, but that which belongs to the covenant God and shares his being. A place is never holy apart from its relation to Yahweh.'[14]

We must at once point out that neither are other sacred places holy apart from some relation to their deities, whether conceived mythically or in legendary or historical form. It is true that those which derive their sanctity from a primeval creation situation seem thereby to possess an unchangeable and permanent holiness that has become an inherent and necessary quality. But it is important to remember that there is also an element of contingency about them. As Childs has recognized, even their fluctuating participation in the primeval power requires a 'reactivation' that is contingent upon the due performance of the appropriate ritual and so is at the mercy of the carelessness, forgetfulness or unworthiness of the worshippers. A further element of contingency derives from the extent to which a sanctuary belongs to a transcendent deity who does not merely reside there in a localized and tied manner, but who visits it in theophanies which cannot be predicted or controlled, however much men may encourage or provoke them. This again is not peculiar to the Jerusalem temple. The functioning of all sacred places is dependent upon a certain element of choice, both human and divine, a fact which both Kaufmann and Childs seem to ignore when they endeavour to sharpen the antithesis between the so-called natural sanctuaries and the Israelite temple.

When, as Childs then points out, the prophets warned Israel against taking their sanctuary for granted as inviolably holy and as powerful to protect the nation it was not so much the reassertion of a historical and contingent view as the rejection of a mythical and necessary one; it is much better understood as a warning against the loss of the transcendent dimension and therefore of the contingency of the divine presence in the temple. When this happens and only a sense of the immanent presence remains religion is especially open to a danger that continually besets it, the subtle transformation of the authentic religious attitude into the magical outlook. This is the proper description when the sanctuary is regarded as identified with the deity whose power is now inherent in it, so that he who controls the temple controls also the powers it contains. This is what tends to happen when the tension between the transcendent and the immanent presence of the god is resolved in favour of the latter; only the human source of contingency then remains, only the human initiative matters, and men can proceed to use their temples and their gods like any other deposit of magic power employed entirely for human ends. This is a radical transformation of meaning and function to which all sanctuaries are liable, so that the basic antithesis here is not between history and myth, but between both myth and history as properly religious categories and the quite different world of magic that for ever hovers on their borders.

When it is said, with Childs, that the temple is never holy apart from its relation to Israel's God it is usual to assert that there was a moral quality in both the relationship and the god that marked out Israel's religion among the nations. Yahweh was a profoundly moral or 'righteous' god with a consistent moral character and will, and Israel stood in a covenanted relation with him that implied moral choice and acceptance as between the parties, and that entailed a life of moral obedience on the part of Israel. The functioning of the temple was therefore subject to this overriding moral obligation, and it was because Israel repeatedly failed at this point that the prophets were able to attack the temple and the cult as of no avail in themselves. This is clearly of the greatest importance in the Old Testament and in the religions that derive from it, and we have no desire to weaken the contrast with the immoralities that seem integral to the gods and to the practices of some other religious traditions. On the other hand other religions are not devoid of moral teachings and requirements that on occasion may be as impressive as any. We must also remember the extent to which codes of conduct, confessions of sin, atonements, expiations and penances for moral as well as for ritual shortcomings appear at the sanctuaries of many religious traditions. It may well be that there are superiorities in both the kind and the degree of morality identified with Yahweh and therefore required of those who would meet him at his temple, but the difficulty of establishing just what this uniqueness is prevents those who accept it from finding here the differentia of the Jerusalem temple.

We have already rejected the suggestion that these differentia lie in the simple contrast between myth and history, since other religions have historical as well as mythical references associated with their temples. Other worshippers knew who built their temples and when, or the religious experience that gave rise to a certain sanctuary, and other traditions had produced criticisms of temples as merely made by men's hands. Even when the historical temple becomes the depository and guardian of the corpus of myth, and the representative of the primeval and cosmic temples, this service of myth does not remove the historical features. But it does often overshadow them so that they make no contribution to a view of history as a continuous process in its own right, or as expressing the purposes of a creative god and leading to new developments in the future. Perhaps we may find a basis of differentiation in a reverse balance between myth and history occuring in Jerusalem.

Here we return to further elements in the discussions of Kaufmann and Childs. Both scholars have described the peculiar kind of historical setting of the Israelite temple, a history that dominated the continuing accents of myth and possessed a new eschatological dimension.

First let us note the central position historical concern holds in Israel's religion. Her religious literature contains extensive and accurate historical work in which places are recorded, known, accessible, and verifiable by later enquirers, and times specified in a related sequence of events. The people in these records are named and dated ancestors and almost certainly are historic figures. They live ordinary human lives in the context of the times. Whereas one might expect the remoter ancestors to have assumed more mythical forms surrounded by wonders and living in a primeval or paradisal age we find exactly the reverse;

the patriarchs exhibit a very ordinary pastoral existence where even the theophanies are regular types of the more vivid religious experiences rather than cataclysmic or mythical events. Such wonders and miracles as appear in the Old Testament are few in comparison with other religious traditions, and never overshadow the central historical events around which they chiefly gather — the slavery in Egypt, the escape, the wilderness survival and discipline, the settlement in Canaan; nor do they assume mythical proportions beyond the ordinary scale of events in nature and in history. The balance between history and myth has been reversed, and the latter assumes its place in the borderlands of history found in the early chapters of Genesis.

This concern with history is due to a new conception of particular events as not merely isolated incidental elements in human life or at best the occasional bearer of a theophany, but as parts of a whole which reveal to the eye of faith their share in the overall pattern. In their own context they reveal the continuing consistent will and purpose of Yahweh. This purpose is adequately expressed neither in some paradisal or primeval past era, nor in the present world order, but only in the achievement of a new world already planned in heaven and awaiting its earthly consummation. It is against this understanding of history that Kaufmann can say:

> The Deuteronomic temple of the future is diametrically opposed to the pagan temple whose sanctity is 'prehistoric', mythological. It is an eschatological temple to be established only after Israel arrives at 'the rest and the inheritance'. It will be entirely new, its sanctity a creation *ex nihilo*, unrelated to any ancient holiness. This historical-eschatological conception of the temple is the ultimate negation of pagan ideas of sanctity.[15]

The same view of history as leading to a new creation is found by Childs in the comparison between Eden and Zion in the Old Testament. There is first the identification between the two as places where complete harmony exists between God and his creation, in contrast to the present fallen world; Zion is Eden restored. But

> there is never a simple identification between the two as in the myth. At times the prophets relate Zion to Eden analogically: 'The Lord ... will make her (Zion's) wilderness *like* Eden, her deserts *like* the

garden of Yahweh' (Isaiah 51:3). Moreover... the content of Zion has been filled with new elements not present in the *Urzeit*. Zion is the site of the temple, the sanctuary of God's chosen people, the holy city of King David... these historically conditioned institutions are not assimilated by projecting them back into the beginning. The processes of history are viewed as producing something new over and above the sacred space of the primeval age.[16]
In place of concern with the periodic 'eternal returns' and the ultimate cyclic movements of life in other religious traditions we have an involvement in the new Jerusalem, the new hearts, the new community, the new world order among the nations to which the divine activity in history is leading. Instead of the 'rythmic fluctuations in the intensity with which the sacred place participates in the primeval power' we have the temple of Mt. Zion playing a historical role in the unfolding of this history, indeed acting as 'the pivot of human history' while still retaining the accents of a cosmic mythology. In this new balance between myth and history, rendered possible only through this new meaning in history itself, lies the differentia of the Jerusalem temple. But it is a balance and not an antithesis, for the temple retained many mythical interpretations and expressions of the relationship between God and man that it now sought to work out in the new historical world view. Indeed, 'the holy place became the means whereby the concrete historicity of the revelation could be most strongly emphasized'.[17] At the same time the functions we have earlier examined were not discarded, for the new context of history meant a more realistic and continuing effort to fulfill them.

Whether the physical temple remained essential to these religious functions was part of the controversies surrounding its later history. Kaufmann can say that 'the ultimate implication of the Deuteronomic reform was a new, popular cult without temple, sacrifice, and priest'.[18] Others looked for a purified temple. It is clear, however, that the distinctive features of the Israelite temple lie neither in its structures nor its functions but in its relation to a new and eschatological view of history. The future of temple depended on what happened in the further stages of that history; whether the actual temple on Mt. Zion had a permanent place in the ideal age to come or was but a temporary means towards its achievement was in the hands of factors outside itself. While it contributed to the historical process it no longer secured or controlled it; it was now a part of it. The denouement must be sought in later history itself.

5.6 CONCLUSIONS

The outcome of our study to this point is that both in physical form and in religious functions (as we have analyzed them) the Jerusalem temple furnishes an excellent example of the type of sacred place found also in archaic and non-Semitic religions; no peculiar features it may have possessed were sufficient to establish it as some further new type of sanctuary. The differentia lay not in the temple itself but in the part it was called upon to play in the context of a distinctive religion, the faith of Israel.

The fact that we have placed her temple so firmly in the category of temples in general should not be allowed to suggest a failure to appreciate the qualities of Israelite religion, or a desire to depreciate this temple. We hope we have said sufficient to demonstrate that the attitudes implicit or explicit in all temples and their functions reveal an impressive grasp of the spiritual complexities in the relation between men and the divine, and of the central importance of religion for human existence. So profound, in fact, are many of these views that they continually strain beyond the temple form for their adequate expression; in the end it becomes doubtful whether even the Jerusalem temple, which had brought many of these insights and demands to a sharper focus, could satisfy what it had helped to reveal. Its history was surrounded by tensions and ambiguities, by controversies and new interpretations. In one sense these represent the problems attaching to temples in all religious traditions;[19] in another regard they stemmed from the peculiar features of the religion of Israel. In neither sense was a solution to be found through the temple itself.

6

New Forms: Tabernacle and Synagogue

Before examining the solutions offered by further historical development in the New Testament and the Christian Church we must return
to a survey of two other places of worship that appeared at different
points in the life of Israel and the Jews, but which we have avoided
while concentrating on the temple. The tabernacle of the earliest period
before the temple, and the synagogue that survived and replaced the
temple are distinctive forms which lay foundations for the type of
'sanctuary' that was to arise as the main alternative to the temple.

6.1 THE TABERNACLE OR TENT

Unfortunately, little is known about the physical form of the tabernacle, in spite of the extensive accounts of its materials and construction. It is generally agreed that chapters 25-33 and 35-50 in Exodus
represent a double tradition of an elaborate tabernacle on the Jerusalem temple plan (in fact exactly half its size) set in the middle of the
encampment, and of a simple 'tent of witness' or 'of meeting' set outside the camp. The former was so large and elaborate that it would have
been beyond the material resources and skills of the few thousand Israelites to build, much less to transport throughout their wanderings in
the four wagons mentioned; it is also inexplicable why such a splendid
sanctuary should receive no mention between the settlement in Canaan
and the temple of Solomon.

For this reason it has been common since Wellhausen to dismiss the
more elaborate sanctuary as an ideal construction, based on the Solomonic temple, but projected back into the desert period by the later
priestly writers in order to find a Mosaic sanction for the second temple

and its rituals. This drastic solution is unnecessary, for the accounts of the more elaborate tabernacle may well be no more than a somewhat idealized version of a sanctuary that did exist towards the time of Solomon's building. One reconstruction of the history suggests that in the Mosaic period there was a tent as a portable shrine, at times inside and at times outside the camp; the later sanctuary at Shiloh represented a more permanent replacement of this, or perhaps even housed what remained of it or of its cult objects, especially the ark, and that after the destruction of Shiloh these had separate adventures until gathered into a new or second tabernacle set up by David in Jerusalem (II Samuel 6:17). This tabernacle was modelled on Moses' tabernacle but had developed further in the direction of the Canaanite and Jebusite temples, with an external altar for burnt offerings and an internal division to provide a special 'holy of holies' chamber. It was this which the priestly writers were referring to, and in its own way it was a link between the tent of Moses and the temple of Solomon.[1] The remaining difficulty is that we have no means of distinguishing in the Exodus accounts between the later idealizing and the actual historical facts from which the tabernacle began.

This does, however, help to clarify the earlier Mosaic tent by associating the more obviously temple-type features, such as the inner shrine, with later Canaanite sources; the ancestry of its own simpler tent form is then commonly found in the portable red leather tent-shrine found in Semitic peoples and surviving through various modifications and interpretations into modern Muslim usage.[2] The peculiar functions and interpretations of the Mosaic period are our main concern here, and especially their relation to the categories we are using for the analysis of sacred places and to the temple form. When so little is known about either the tent itself or about the other ancient sacred object, the ark, we are faced by considerable difficulties.

The relation, for instance, between tent and ark is the subject of much discussion; we have already seen the division of opinion as to whether the ark was of Canaanite or of Israelite origin. If the former is true then the ark has no integral connection with the Mosaic tent, but even if it was a cult object in Israel it may have belonged to another part of their religious practice that had nothing to do with the tent of meeting. Haran has argued strongly that 'the Tent and the Ark are two separate institutions derived from the different social and spiritual spheres of ancient Israelite life – prophecy... and priesthood – each of which evolved its own particular symbols and rites...'. 'Thus... two outstanding tents existed independently of each other in the Israelite camp: one of them... for the Ark... in the very centre of the camp... serves as the temporary abode of a priestly holy object... as it were an embryo of a House of God that is to be built in the Promised Land.'[3]

On this view the tent of meeting was always an empty shrine outside the camp with its own special functions apart from the regular cult in the centre of the community. This amounts to a radically non-cultic interpretation of the tent corresponding to Kaufmann's non-cultic view of the Jerusalem temple, and goes on to suggest that the two types of worship with their respective tents were combined into one at Shiloh, but with the cultic forms overshadowing those associated with the tent of meeting. This sharp dichotomy between a sacred place that is priestly and cultic and another that is entirely prophetic and non-cultic is reminiscent of the unsuccessful attempts to maintain the same clear division between priest and prophet during the period of the first temple, and would seem to be overdrawn. It also implies a view of the ark as a *domus dei* type of cult object, perhaps with a Semitic ancestry of this kind. All of this is quite speculative.

Although the ark is nowhere explicitly associated with the tent there is the later Deuteronomic interpretation that it was a receptacle for the records of the covenant, and this is in harmony with a number of references to the tent as the 'tent of the testimony', i.e. of the covenant (Numbers 9:15; 17:7-8; 18:2; Exodus 38:21); the same tradition appears in New Testament interpretations (Acts 7:44; Revelation 15:5). If in fact the ark was contained in the tent of meeting it does nothing to locate the tent in the temple category, for it was not necessarily an image of or dwelling for the deity. As the ark of the covenant, through its contents or even if empty, it would be a memorial of the eternal alliance between Yahweh and Israel rather than an instrument of the immanent divine presence.[4]

We do not need to adopt the extreme position of Haran in order to demonstrate the special features of the tent of meeting, or to appreciate the description that he offers (based on the Elohist and Deuteronomic materials):

Thus the tent was intended primarily for Moses, even if everyone who sought God's presence used also to go out to it.... The theophany does not occur inside the tent, but... at the entrance to it. It is true that Moses first goes into the tent, but he does not meet God while inside... the pillar of cloud descends and stands 'at the door of the tent'... the Lord... speaking from the cloud, actually *calls* Aaron and Miriam outside... at the entrance God speaks his word to them.... These unique descriptions of the theophany prove that the interior... serves merely as the place where the worshipper *presents himself*... set aside for the concentration and sharpening of all his faculties in *preparation*... for the revelation of the divine presence... revealed outside.... What we have here is not a cultic sanctuary housing the deity in its very centre, but a tent where the solitary worshipper might receive the divine inspiration in a voice coming from outside its empty interior. This is no permanent 'abode' of the godhead, after the usual pattern of sanctuaries and temples in the ancient orient, but a place appointed for the reception of an occasional prophetic vision.[5]

This is a coherent account, even if though we might disagree with the narrowing of the term cultic to exclude the prophetic function and the cloud theophany, which was a standard manifestation of sky or mountain gods and appropriate in any kind of sanctuary, either inside it or outside (cf. Exodus 40:34-5).[6]

If this was the nature of the chief sacred place of Israel in the Mosaic period, we can trace in it at least some of the usual features of sacred places. Whether at the time or in later tradition the tabernacle is regarded as fashioned in accordance with a revealed heavenly model, and this is endorsed by Stephen in the New Testament (Exodus 25:9,40; 26:30; Acts 7:44). In a real sense it served as the centre of reference in the life of Israel, even if it was not placed in the centre of the encampment. We cannot, however, see in it a microcosmic representation of the heavenly realms, unless one is to press an analogy between the tent and the firmament, together with the cloud of glory and the glory that fills the heavens, which is not impossible. On the other hand the tabernacle is a striking example of the sacred place as the meeting point between man and the divine. When it is called the 'tent of meeting' the latter word in Hebrew has the sense of meeting at a fixed time or by appointment (cf. Hosea 12:10), so that Moffatt can translate it as the 'trysting-tent'. This particular form of meeting in a cloud theophany declares that the tabernacle is the place of the presence, but in the form of intermittent visiting rather than continuous dwelling; the emphasis is therefore heavily upon the transcendence of the deity.

While it is clearly a sacred place it is also plain that it shows no signs of developing into the temple type, but rather stands in contrast to this form and so holds a rather unusual place in the history of the sacred use of space. We shall understand this better if we glance at the religion of the patriarchs that forms the most relevant part of its background. Here there is no emphasis on a god of the soil or on fixed holy places where the deity might dwell. Rather is he a 'most high God' (Genesis 14:18-20) who accompanies the patriarchal clans on their wanderings, perhaps represented by some Semitic tent-shrine, and having altars built to him at a succession of stopping points that have some significance: at Mamre (Genesis 13:18), Beersheba (26:23-25), Shechem (33: 18-20), Bethel (28:10-22). God reveals himself wherever he wishes and accordingly an altar of earth seems more in keeping with the situation than one of stone (Exodus 20:24). At the same time there are indications that men returned to particular altars or places of previous revelations (Genesis 13:4; 35:1-8; 46:1), thus pointing to the development of permanent sanctuaries as in any other religion, and to the two poles of immanence and transcendence between which the emphasis moves.

There is little suggestion, however, that these sanctuaries were regarded as the dwellings of a localized god, in static terms as a *domus dei*. All indications are of a dynamic relation with people rather than with places, with the God of Abraham, Isaac and Jacob rather than of Beersheba and Bethel. This of course is congruent with the life of semi-nomads for whom the community and its leaders were all important, although this sociological comment does not account for the religious fact itself. This highly personal religion sitting lightly by physical location would seem to be uncommon in the history of religions, but we do not need to press this point, much less to make it a unique religious development, in order to find here an ancestry that could contribute to the later tabernacle type of sanctuary. It is sufficient to note the similarity with Moses who goes to the tent of meeting to speak with Yahweh in an intimate and personal relationship, (e.g. Exodus 29:42-43) and the fact that the tent was entirely mobile and free from all suggestions of the house of God.

Similar features of the tabernacle are stressed in the later traditions about it. This is seen from a study of the usage of two Hebrew verbs, *yashab* meaning to inhabit or dwell, and *shakan* to sit down or 'tent' in a place. In the earlier writings when referring to God little distinction seems intended between the two, and the former is the commoner. With the Deuteronomic literature an important distinction emerges, *yashab* being used for God's dwelling in heaven and *shakan* for his tabernacling on earth. The priestly writers go one step further and never use *yashab* of God but always *shakan*, placing the whole emphasis upon Yahweh's tabernacling with men and calling the Mosaic sanctuary *mishkan*, indeed the *mishkan* or one tabernacle of the presence of God in this particular way. However much, therefore, the priestly writers were interested in the Davidic tabernacle as authenticating their later temple they were even more interested in the Mosaic tent of meeting as a solution to the problem of the divine immanence and transcendence. God was the high omnipotent Lord of the universe and yet had drawn near to Israel in the desert covenant and remained with her through subsequent history. How was such a God, who could not be regarded as dwelling in any shrine, yet be present with his people? The answer lay in the tabernacle, where Yahweh did not dwell (*yashab*), but where he 'settles impermanently' (*shakan*) in order to meet with Moses in the past, and in the same way, with his worshippers in the second temple. 'Priestly tradition has taken a concrete, archaic term, associated with Israel's desert tradition, and used it as an abstract term to express a theological concept.'[7]

It was in the light of this assimilation of the temple to the tent of meeting that the Jerusalem sanctuary could on occasion be called a tent (Psalms 15:1; 27:5; 61:5; 78:60). It was, however, still the temple to which this 'tabernacling' theory of the divine presence was applied, and it never managed to create an alternative sanctuary devoted to this view alone, or to suppress the whole complex of ideas belonging to the temple type. As Kaufmann admits, 'the Second Temple is but a pale reflection of the desert tent, because the tent's oracular, military, and prophetic aspects have disappeared'.[8] Even the priestly theology itself may have contributed to this for there are signs of the tabernacling presence being regarded as dwelling permanently rather than impermanently; this leads away from an 'appearance' theology towards the *domus dei* concept, albeit in the wilderness period, and so not yet anchored in any one location. (See Exodus 40:34-38.) It has also been suggested that Israel maintained a tent-cult and festival celebrated regularly by a kind of pilgrimage out into the desert to camp round a tabernacle or tent of meeting, as it appears Muslim Arabs have done in modern times;[9] even if this could be established the temple would still remain the great cultic sanctuary at the heart of Israel's life and worship.

The priestly writer's attempt at a 'corrective' to the natural bent of the temple form was scarcely a success, and by the time of the Chronicler the temple is the house of the ark and a characteristic example of the *domus dei*. The alternative tabernacle form which haunted the temple for so long and which reappears in New Testament thought never produced a continuing historical type of sacred place, but remained an influence of a symbolic and typological nature that we may now outline. In the first place it was a tent, presumably not dissimilar from the ordinary dwellings of Israel at the time; it was therefore domestic in character, suggestive of the more intimate and personal nature of the relations between God and men. It was also mobile; Moses himself could pack it up. In the striking phrase of II Samuel 7:7 Jahweh says 'I have not dwelt in any house.... I have walked in a tent... with all the children of Israel'. In contrast it is said of the Canaanite gods: 'Feet have they, but they walk not' (Psalm 115:7). No matter where Israel might be, God, through this portable tabernacle, would visit them. 'God becomes a nomad with his nomads.'[10] Indeed, the very temporary and inadequate nature of the tent dwelling indicates the pilgrim nature of the people of God, not only in the wilderness period, but throughout history, with no permanent city here on earth but looking forward to the city with sure foundations built by God – an image that is found in both the Old and New Testaments. The tabernacle therefore represents the dynamic and eschatological nature of existence as God's people, over against more static conceptions of a consummation indicated by the building of temples where the gods may dwell with men.

Further, the very simplicity and plainness of a tent of meeting stands in contrast to the luxury and grandeur of the temple type as it develops in history, including the history of the Jews; it therefore prefigures the later conceptions of God dwelling in the humble and contrite heart of the simplest of his worshippers, or, in New Testament thought, becoming incarnate in a manger and remaining incognito before men. There is no sign of any other people wanting to copy the tabernacle, and we can be sure there would have been many in the surrounding peoples to despise it, just as today it remains the somewhat contemptuous term for the buildings of Christian groups lacking in general esteem, for their 'horrible little tabernacles and conventicles'. Finally, this tent of the testimony with its possible relation to the records of the covenant and its certain relation to the period of the exodus and the Sinai revelation represents the radically new historicizing of religion that dates from these events.

It is therefore not surprising that some Christian groups have deliberately adopted the term tabernacle for their places of worship, even though some of these, like Spurgeon's famous Baptist Tabernacle in London, were essentially places of congregational assembly to hear a preacher. At least one architect has found in the wilderness tabernacle a pattern of permanent validity for Christian churches, and has suggested that

... the revolutionary basis of the design, resting on symbols, not the prevailing imagery... capable of a typological interpretation beyond the possibilities inherent in other houses of God of that age... [reveals the possibility that] in its general lines at least this God-prescribed arrangement... has an application to the worship of the new Israel when the time came for that to supersede the types of the law.[11]

The writer then tries to trace historical evidence of the influence of the tabernacle on early Church building, but the result is unimpressive. It is probably better to say that 'the tent as a prototype of church dwelling is of significance not in terms of form, but in terms of function'.[12]

Where the tent form has been adopted architecturally, as at the Church of the Holy Cross, Doncaster, in the Chapel of Unity at Coventry Cathedral, and for the Cathedral of Christ the King at Liverpool the suggestions are the reverse of anything mobile and transitory. Apart from such literal applications of the model, the tabernacle as a type of sacred place deserves fresh consideration on account of its symbolic features; to build plainly and simply for present uses instead of splendidly and monumentally for all time is a common injunction in current discussions of church architecture.

6.2 THE SYNAGOGUE

At the other end of Israel's history there stands the synagogue, which has remained the one place of worship for Judaism since the destruction of the Jerusalem temple, and which represents a completely new type in the history of religions. Its origins are obscure, but the commonly accepted view is that it derives from spontaneous meetings for community purposes, both secular and religious, among the sixth century exiles in Babylon, and that these meetings were continued and consolidated into institutional form in Palestine after the return. Another suggestion is that they began at the local shrines deprived of sacrificial rites in the Deuteronomic reform of 621 B.C., as an alternative form of worship that continued in the rural areas during the exile. Others seek to derive the synagogue from the temple itself, from alternative services developed both for the priests and for laymen, and there is evidence for at least one synagogue within the temple area; others again look to the Jewish dispersion in Egypt and elsewhere which was unable to reproduce the authentic Jerusalem cult.

These theories have one common factor — that the synagogue does not appear as an independent institution, but arises in some form of relationship to the Jerusalem temple, usually as a supplement, but possibly as an alternative to its worship. It is also apparent that if the synagogue did reach back to the sixth century its main development must have been outside Palestine or else so informal and unimportant as to escape attention in the later Old Testament literature; there is only one possible reference, in the late Psalm 74:8, where the phrase 'assemblies of God' has been translated as 'synagogues'. Since no Palestinian synagogues from biblical times have been discovered by archaeology and the main literary sources are post-biblical and rabbinic, we shall confine our account to what may reasonably be projected back into the earlier centuries from the abundance of later archaeological and textual evidence.

It seems certain that the term synagogue referred primarily to an assembly of people and not to a building or a place, although the Hebrew term *beth hakkeneseth* is literally 'house of assembly', or in more modern parlance, meeting house; Greek-speaking Jews in Rome and Egypt used *proseuche*, or 'prayer-house'. The formal requirement for the institution of a synagogue was the assembly of ten male Jews for this purpose. Moore points out that the term 'Great synagogue' was applied to a body of men in the period of Ezra, men who completed the collection of the books of the prophets, and introduced some of the regulations of later Judaism together with prayers for the synagogues.[13] This represents another form of the emphasis upon the people rather than the place of God which we have already observed.

This assembly was popular and democratic in nature, with a president and a caretaker, both laymen, and the business in the hands of elders. Presumably their responsibility extended to any aspect of the welfare of the community, but two main activities can be identified. The first of these was educational, both through a school for children and through the general instruction in the Law of God that formed the basis of the meeting for worship. While this emphasis upon instruction is not general in religions it was by no means peculiar to the Jews. Wherever religion is conceived as a way of life or emphasizes personal progress in spiritual development some means of receiving divine instruction appears, often in the form of regular disciples of a particular teacher or spiritual master, and sometimes through the association of these in guilds, schools, or monasteries. The new feature in the case of the synagogue may be expressed in the idea of totality: other deities were not so exclusive and intolerant as Jahweh, who was concerned with every aspect of the daily life of his worshippers and demanded a comprehensive and total obedience; Jahweh also required this obedience of his people as a whole. Other scriptures had been for the guidance of the priests; here was a revealed religion understood to apply to the whole life of a nation, so that the endeavour had to be made to educate the whole community in its faith, and through its scriptures. This was a new feature in the history of religions, a feature that continues also in Christianity and Islam; its uniqueness lay in the combination of lay activity, scriptural basis, and total moral claim upon the whole community. With this instrument which perfectly expressed their conception of religion the Pharisees were able to convert Galilee to Judaism in the last century B.C., and in one of these synagogues Jesus and his Galilean followers must have been taught the scriptures of Israel.[14]

On this basis the religious features of the synagogue worship were gradually extended. The Law was read in Hebrew and explained in Aramaic, being gradually arranged in sabbath portions for a three-year cycle. Anyone could rise to expound the Law through a discourse equivalent to a sermon. Prayers were added before the Law was read, and afterwards, together with the chanting of psalms and finally lessons from the prophetic writings. The result was a new cultic form, in spite of the elements it shared with temple worship in its psalms and prayers.

Judging by its later history synagogue worship was quite adequate to sustain and nourish the religious life of the individual and of the community, and it seems likely that for many the emphasis had shifted away from the temple long before it was destroyed. In fact Moore declares that 'in Palestine itself the synagogue had become... the real seat of religious worship... significant evidence... is the existence within the temple of a synagogue for the priests, and the interpolation... of features akin to the synagogue service in the ritual of the daily morning sacrifice, where, after preparation had been made for the offering, the priests left... and assembled in an adjacent hall to recite their Shema' and a series of Benedictions after which the sacrificial ritual was resumed'.[15] It appears that during their periodic temple duty, the laymen held services of their own, with prayers and scripture readings, when not actually required to stand by at the sacrificial rites of the priests.

This is striking evidence of the penetration of the new form into the old cult, and we can distinguish various factors at work to displace the temple from the exclusive position it had held, and never more than at the time of the Maccabean revolt in 169 B.C.. After the Maccabees the rise of the Pharisees as a popular party opposed to the priests separated the latter increasingly from the people. The Pharisees stood for a type of piety based on the full observance of the whole law, which extended beyond the cultic practices at the temple; these continued in their traditional splendour but came to be regarded as only one part of obedience to the Law, which was the ultimate end. All the other prescriptions of the Law were expounded by the Pharisees in the synagogue and applied in life outside the cult. When we remember that synagogues multiplied throughout the Dispersion we can realize how they provided everywhere a home for the 'portable fatherland', the book of the Law, and were the main support of Jews who could participate only very occasionally in the sacrificial system at the temple. This explains why the loss of the Temple in A.D. 70 was not the shattering blow it might have seemed to be; while other religions usually succumbed to the loss of their cult and their sanctuaries Judaism was equipped to survive as the religion of Law and synagogue.

So long as the two centres for worship existed together the synagogue building could remain primarily a utilitarian structure without any sacred character or temple features; the very little rabbinic legislation in the Mishnah concerning the synagogue ignores such matters as site, position, orientation and architecture. The articles of furniture peculiar to the synagogue and its special functions have Greek names rather than Hebrew – for the lectern, the reading platform, and the 'seat of Moses' (cathedra). Other articles were modelled to some extent on those of the temple – the scroll case was assimilated increasingly to the ark, the screen before it represented the temple veil, and the lamps the seven-branched candelabrum. After the temple came to an end its influence over the internal forms of the synagogue increased, as might be expected, and this influence can be detected in still further ways in the synagogues of reform or progressive Judaism in modern times. This study, however, belongs to the later history of the synagogue, and by the first century A.D. the effects of the temple are limited to the details we have noted together with certain other matters of a more general nature – the court for the proselytes perhaps corresponding to the Court of Gentiles, and the separation of men and women to their respective courts in Herod's temple.[16]

In spite of these echoes of the temple the synagogue, especially in its earlier forms, represents a radically new development in the history of places of worship. As against a building for a sacrificing priesthood, it served a non-sacrificing laity; in place of a cult that was largely individual, apart from the great seasonal festivals, it provided for worship that was entirely corporate; instead of being a *domus dei* with multi-cell plan and graded degrees of sanctity, it was a house for the assembly of the people of God, equivalent to a *domus ecclesiae*, and consisted essentially of a single cell or room; the one centralized supremely sacred place in Jerusalem had been set over against a multiplicity of places not sacred in themselves; and finally the typical themes expressed in sacred places and especially in temples seem absent in synagogues — there is no reference to their being divinely instituted as centres of the earth, the pattern of the heavenly, or the very entrance to heaven itself. The presence of God has been so completely detached from both places and buildings and so located in the faithful community gathered round the Law of God that one Midrash (upon Malachi 3:16) could say that when two men are sitting and studying the Law the presence is with them.[17]

What began as a subsidiary to the temple, or in default of ready access to its services became the sole place of worship in Judaism and has permanently replaced the temple, which not even a Jewry now restored to Palestine is likely to revive with its original functions. Indeed it has been suggested that 'the supreme calamity which Judaism could suffer today would be to have its temple restored and its prescribed system of animal sacrifices re-established', even though 'to great numbers the temple is still a mental rallying point and its ancient site a geographical expression of the unity of Judaism'.[18]

This shift of the divine presence from sacred place to holy people was no mere makeshift or substitute arrangement forced upon the Jews by the disaster of A.D. 70. We have observed the various ambiguities and tensions with which the temple was beset, the search for a more adequate instrument of the relationship bewteen God and man, and the belief that this would be found in a renewed or perfected community.

In the synagogue Judaism produced from its own resources its own answer to the limitations of the temple, but would seem to have been unaware that it had done so, and that a new centre for the religious life of the community was already in operation.

The nature and function of the synagogue were so new that we have been unable to speak of it as a sacred place but rather as a centre or place for worship. It represents the de-sacralization of places and buildings used for religious purposes and so stands as a new type in the phenomenology and history of religion that we may call the meeting-house, a house for the meeting of the people of God rather than a house for the god himself.[19] Its effectiveness and durability have been abundantly manifested in the troubled history of Jewry through all succeeding centuries, and it may be regarded as the precursor of similar forms in two other major religious traditions, the Christian church and the Muslim mosque. It is a major contribution of biblical religion to the religious life of mankind.

6.3 SYNAGOGUE AND TEMPLE

The uniqueness of the synagogue lay not only in its place in the wider history of religions but also in the way it gave expression to many of the central motifs and concerns in the religion of Israel. We have shown its relation to the problems that gathered round the temple, but it may also be said to have given new concrete expression to many of the values symbolized in the tabernacle. The synagogue also, in its beginnings, was more akin to the ordinary dwellings of the people and so suggestive of an intimate, personal or 'domestic' relation between God and men; it could be established with ease wherever the people of God were, in exile or in dispersion or in the smallest community, and so had a kind of mobility about it; the simplicity and plainness of the tent were reflected in the absence of monumental or luxurious features in the original synagogues and expressed the kind of life the Law required: and the place of this Law itself in the synagogue meeting and then physically in the way it was housed in the premises (reminiscent of the ark of the covenant) represents the historicizing and moralizing of Israel's religion that traces back to the tabernacle period.

The synagogue may also be regarded as especially appropriate to the prophetic tradition that found its sources of renewal in the Mosaic period and experienced repeated difficulty with the temple. It would be easy to imagine many of the prophets of the Old Testament period being quite at home in the synagogue and finding there a regular outlet for their contributions; if there is any truth in the pre-exilic theory for the origin of synagogues then this is in fact what did happen, with local prophets delivering their message to a synagogue-type gathering at the local shrines once these had been deprived of their sacrificial rituals. The connection cannot be pursued historically for the rise of the synagogues seems to have coincided with the decline of prophecy, but their affinity remains and the discourses of Jesus and of Paul in later synagogues were entirely appropriate.

When we give full weight to the fact that the synagogue was entirely a Jewish product and so in harmony with the basic biblical traditions that it could emerge inconspicuously and replace the temple with such ease, we are faced with the question why the latter remained the central and characteristic cult place and would have continued as such, so far as anyone can tell, but for the fatal clash with Rome. Even after 70 A.D., it was in the synagogue that loyalty to the temple was nurtured and the hope of its restoration maintained, and in some branches of Jewry this has continued into our own day. The fact that the Jerusalem sanctuary was such an excellent example of the temple-type of sacred place, set at the centre of a people whose religious history shows so many departures from the religions in the temple tradition, including the development of the alternative religious meeting house, forces us to attempt some comment upon this internal inconsistency, upon what many would regard as an arrested development, or a form of archaism.

If we set this situation alongside what happened to the archaic patterns of sacred time in the Old Testament period the problem is accentuated. It is widely recognized that in this sphere Israel was responsible for the most profound of transformations. Archaic conceptions of time or history as the vehicle only of decline or decay, or as repetitive and imprisoning, were replaced by a view of history as the agency of the divine purpose and as leading to a consummation from which life secured its ultimate meaning. Why then did Israel fail to accept wholeheartedly a corresponding transformation in the conception of space and place as they function in the religious life? It produced the synagogue yet remained wedded to the temple. When we remember that the great festivals of Israel, associated at least in part with the temple cultus, were themselves striking examples of sacred times as found in other religions that had been transformed into historical commemorations of the acts of God in Israel's history, then the failure to reinterpret sacred space is all the more evident. From this point of view it would seem that the Babylonian destruction of the first temple in the sixth century, and the subsequent rethinking that occurred during the exile, represent one of the mysterious lost opportunities in Israel's history.

The essentially conservative attitude to the place of the temple is even more puzzling if we consider the biblical view of the material world of matter that forms the content of the sacred place. Here again there had been a revolution in religious thought. Widespread views of the natural world as pregnant with divinity, or of the gods as being inherently immanent in the material realm as in other parts of the cosmos, were replaced by the sharper distinction between a transcendent God and his material creation. The latter was evacuated of notions of inherent or acquired sacredness, was neutralized as it were, and became a domain for man to control and enjoy but not to worship as the embodiment or even as the permanent dwelling of the gods. The same new attitude also disposed of all views of matter as illusory or unreal, or as hostile to the things of the spirit, as refractory or irredeemable; it was now established as the handiwork of the Creator, and therefore real and of positive value and function in the life of man.

The new outlook also implied rejection of the common notion of the earthly realm being patterned at all points on the heavenly sphere, with divine principles, order, or structure inherent and necessary because built into it from the beginning. Nature was now seen as contingent upon the divine, created by the divine fiat and sustained by the divine will and purpose. By an act of faith it is regarded as intelligible in principle, reflecting the order and the mind of the divine, but men cannot master the mind or will of God in advance. Therefore, they cannot merely deduce the pattern of nature from any reference to the heavenly, but must patiently explore what God has done and is doing in the universe around them, as in the inductive methods of the sciences which are themselves dependent on this attitude to matter.

We do not pretend that this view of the material realm was explicated to the extent that we have described or that the origin of the inductive sciences lies only in the thought of ancient Israel; intimations of a similar outlook may be found elsewhere in religious history, but Israel does seem to have been the first to have developed these ideas and incorporated them at the heart of her religious life.

It is not difficult to see that this more dynamic view of the relation between the divine and the historical and material realms is congruent with the tradition of the sacred place represented by the tent of meeting, or by the synagogue, rather than with the temple pattern. Since time and space and matter are such interwoven aspects of our experience it is difficult to explain their conspicuously differential development and interpretation. Israel had proved herself capable of such profound and creative transformations in the realms of time and of matter, possessed a potentially new form of sanctuary in her tabernacle tradition and produced a completely new place of worship in her synagogues, yet clung to the temple as her sacred place and indeed saw it brought to its full and splendid development in the Herodian sanctuary.[20]

We can only suggest that the still more radically personalized transformation of the place of meeting between God and men that the New Testament presents in the incarnation was of such a nature that it could not be anticipated in any preliminary or preparatory form, not even in any conceivable development of the tabernacle pattern, nor yet in that of the synagogue. The former was symbolic of what it could not itself achieve in historical form; the latter was appropriate for a community that had not yet appeared. The foundations for a new type of place of worship had been laid, but the day for building was not yet. In these circumstances the temple tradition was maintained against the time of its complete replacement. For most of the Jewish community this was forced on them by Rome, and the continuing nostalgia for the temple may be allowed to suggest that it would not have happened in any other way; for one part of this same community the replacement was more gradual and began before the temple was destroyed, but only because they believed they had seen the ultimate meeting of the divine and the human in a unique person.

The further history of the place of worship must take account of the later developments in synagogues, and the new and kindred forms that appeared in the mosques of Islam; it will however, be primarily concerned with the New Testament attitudes and the various forms the place of worship has taken in the Christian community, from its earliest house churches to its later Gothic cathedrals and Quaker meeting houses. Through all these Semitic traditions there will be found the same tension between the *domus dei*, and the *domus ecclesiae* that has emerged from our study of the history of Israel's places of worship.

7

The New Temple of the New Testament

The Jewish temple in Jerusalem serves as an example both of the achievements of the pre-Christian era in elaborating the sacred place where the divine and the human meet, and of the dissatisfactions that focussed on this most impressive achievement. This sense of the inadequacy of the best of temples appeared partly in the increasing influence of the synagogue as an alternative place of worship, and partly in the anticipations of some new development in the sacred meeting place that are evident in certain of the prophets, and among Jewish sectarian groups of the intertestamental period. It was nothing short of a radically 'new temple' that men sought, as has been well expressed by McKelvey:

> The new temple is a central idea of biblical eschatology.... It explains the priestly legislation and... interpretation of history...; it explains the great prophecies of the exile and post-exile periods... just as it provides an important key to the meaning of apocalyptic.... The essence... is the conviction that God will graciously condescend to dwell in the midst of his people in a new and unparalleled way and never again leave them.... The New Testament declares that God has fulfilled his word of promise made by the prophets and erected a new and more glorious temple.... The new temple is not indeed the kind of temple men expected but it is the long-expected temple none the less.[1]

Since the New Testament clearly centres upon the person of Jesus of Nazareth it is his practice and teaching we shall first examine, and, as in all our use of the New Testament, without reference to critical questions of historicity or authorship, which seldom affect our purposes.

7.1 THE PRACTICE OF JESUS

According to the infancy narratives in Luke's Gospel the personal relationship between Jesus and the temple begins even before his birth, with the vision Zechariah received when serving his turn as priest offering the incense in the holy place. His long-barren wife would have a son, to be called John, who would prepare the way for the Lord's coming (Luke 1:8 ff). Luke then proceeds with a series of incidents belonging to the infancy or childhood of Jesus himself, each set in the temple and implying a positive attitude to its services. His parents brought him after circumcision for the ritual dedication in the temple, together with the requisite sacrificial offering of doves and pigeons (2:22-24); there the saintly Simeon was led by the Spirit to discover the infant Jesus and make his prophecy over him (2:25-35); there too the aged prophetess Anna, who lived permanently in the temple precincts, sensed the significance of this child (2:36-38); and twelve years later Jesus is described as spending several days listening to the group of rabbis discussing the scriptures in the temple courts, and feeling that he belonged there, 'in his Father's house' (2:41-52). As a Gentile, writing to a Roman official, probably after 70 A.D., Luke might easily have ignored these stories: instead he has chosen to emphasize how the beginnings of Jesus' life and personal religious training were firmly and positively set in the context of the temple. For Luke there was no incongruity between the two.

For Jesus' practice in adult life we have only the evidence of the last few years of the ministry, but there is no reason to believe that he failed to share in the normal use of the temple for a Jew living as far away as Galilee. During the ministry itself it is clear that Jesus observed the main festivals along with his followers, and this normally meant some involvement in the sacrificial system of the cult. The records, however, are silent on the subject of participation in the temple sacrifices by Jesus, his followers, or the early Church, and the nearest specific reference is to the sacrifices his mother offered at his birth. It is dangerous to argue too much from this silence, but it might reasonably suggest a participation that required no comment, and avoided any open clash that would have found some place in the documents.

If Jesus had publicly dissociated himself from the cultic system he would surely have been charged with this during his frequenting of the temple precincts, for it was here that he came to pray and to teach; in the last part of his ministry he was daily in the temple that was still to him his Father's house (Luke 21:37-38; John 2:16). Whatever may have been his relation to the cult it is the temple as a non-cultic place of prayer and teaching or healing that figures in such picture as we have of his practice. For the rest, Jesus is shown attending the synagogue and taking part in its normal activities, and otherwise finding his own place for personal devotions. This ranged from the wilderness of Judaea, where he early went into retreat to meditate upon his work, to the quiet hillside for early morning prayer, and doubtless also the closet or storeroom in any private house, as he recommended to others. Once he chose the upstairs dining room of an ordinary house for the special religious meal that proved to be the last supper with his disciples. There is little to indicate that the temple held any exclusive position or indeed that any one place was more sacred than another.

7.2 THE TEACHING OF JESUS

We must first make clear that Jesus never attacked the cult or the temple as such, and that a number of recorded incidents show a respect for cultic practice or the temple. A leper who had been cleansed was told quite firmly to perform ritual thanksgiving as prescribed (Mark 1:44). Anyone who came with his offering to the altar while still in controversy with his brother was exhorted to go off and settle the matter before presenting his gift; this is not necessarily an exaltation of conduct over the cult, and may be read as taking the cult seriously and in the right spirit (Matthew 5:23-24). Some would see a respect for the temple in the rejection of the Devil's temptation that Jesus should use it as the most effective place for a public wonder or stunt (Matthew 4:5-7). Something of the same respect for the temple might also be detected in Jesus' attack on the casuistry of the Pharisees which made the gold in the sanctuary more important than the sanctuary and distinguished between swearing by the offering upon the altar and merely swearing by the altar itself; surely the altar was the more important sacred object, likewise the sanctuary where God himself dwelt (Matthew 23:16-22).

It is not surprising, therefore, that opposition between Jesus and the professional priests, the Sadducees, is shown only at the very end of his ministry. It is the Pharisees who were his constant opponents, and who received his sharpest criticisms. These were largely laymen, representatives and teachers of the Law as they had come to interpret it, men who had built up domestic piety in the homes, developed the synagogue service and taught there, and converted Galilee to the Jewish faith. Theirs was the most influential force in current Judaism, and upon their leadership its future was to depend when the temple was no more. It would seem that if Jesus could use, appreciate, even defend the temple this was because it had played a legitimate part in his people's history and was now about to give way to some other means of bringing God and men together; it could be superseded and was no challenge in itself to the mission of Jesus. This was not so with the new development in the religious tradition under the Pharisees whereby the emphasis upon the cult was being transferred to concern for the detailed regulation of conduct, and the religion of grace being replaced by faith in the Law. Jesus knew the limitations of the cult and the importance of conduct as much as any prophet in the past, but in the way of the Pharisees he could find only a complete challenge both to the true Mosaic tradition and to his own mission. Though both Jesus and the Pharisees were ultimately opposed to reliance on a continuing temple cultus the replacement he offered was so fundamentally different from their alternative that no accomodation could be effected between the two.

The absence of any attack upon the temple is quite consonant with Jesus' teaching that it would be superseded, and the conjunction of the two attitudes may be seen in the incident concerning his payment of the yearly tax on all Jews for the upkeep of the temple. Peter had been reassuring a tax collector that Jesus did pay it, and Jesus seized the opportunity to pursue the implications further with Peter: '"What do you think about this, Simon? From whom do earthly monarchs collect tax or toll? From their own citizens or from aliens?" "From aliens," said Peter. "Why then," said Jesus, "the citizens are exempt!

But as we do not want to cause difficulty... meet the tax for us both"'
(Matthew 17:24-27). 'Jesus is clearly saying at this point that he is a
stranger to the Temple and to its system of worship.... Hence at the
centre of a respect for the Temple that was in a sense provisional only,
the Master planted a seed of the latter's supersession, and this is, in its
way, a denial.'[2]

This more radical attitude of Jesus is revealed in a number of incidents and sayings whose import could not have been very clear at the
time. There was the discussion with the Pharisees about conduct appropriate to the Sabbath, when Jesus dealt with their strictness by re-
minding them of certain things that would seem to profane the temple
but which were not condemned; then the enigmatic conclusions: 'I tell
you, there is something greater than the temple here' and 'the Son of
Man is sovereign over the Sabbath' (Matthew 12:6-8). In the light of
the context and of the further teaching to be examined the mysterious
'something' can only be Jesus himself, destined to replace the whole
system that included reliance on sabbath-keeping and temple sanctity.

Somewhat plainer is his conclusion to the conversation with the
Samaritan woman he met at the well. It was a bold declaration that the
time had come when the worship of God tied to the holy mountain
and temple of Gerizim in Samaria, or to the temple of Jerusalem on
Mount Zion, would be replaced by a worship 'in spirit and in truth'
because not tied to particular holy places. It was even bolder to claim
to be the one who would vouch for this: 'I am he, I who am speaking
to you now' (John 4:19-26).

The day for such sanctuaries, or indeed for any special holy place,
was past. This worship in spirit and in truth could occur anywhere,
without benefit of shrine. The immemorial response of men, to en-
shrine all strongly-felt encounters with the divine, is manifest in Peter
when Jesus was transfigured before him and John high on a mountain,
and Moses and Elijah also appeared in the visionary experience. 'Lord',
said Peter, 'I will make three shelters here, one for you, one for Moses,
and one for Elijah.' But before he could say more there was a cloud
theophany directing them to Jesus himself. It was almost as if they were
told 'No more shrines, please! Attend to Jesus instead; he enshrines
the revelation now' (Matthew 17:1-8).

The most dramatic event in Jesus' dealings with the temple is in the story of its 'cleansing' (Mark 11:15-17; John 2:14-17). In one sense there were many who were distressed at the status of the temple, regarding the law of its holiness as broken ever since the profanation by Antiochus two centuries ago, or even since the Babylonian destruction four centuries further back. The Qumran community felt this so strongly that they dissociated themselves entirely from Jerusalem; less radical attitudes were found among the rabbis and various pious groups. The common desire was for some ritual purification and reform of the place, the premises, and the priesthood that would assure the presence of God in their midst, and the primary reference was to the sacrificial system.

Jesus' action was in no sense a purification of this kind or of the cult itself; it had no reference to the main work of the priesthood nor to the heart of the temple where they officiated. It occurred in the outer Court of the Gentiles, in sight of the famous notices preserving the sanctity of the inner courts by barring all who were not Jews from further entry. Its declared aim was not to support or purge the cultus of the temple but to throw this exclusive sacred place open to all nations as a house of prayer. As his two references to the Old Testament show (see Isaiah 56:7; Jeremiah 7:11) Jesus was reviving a long cherished hope for the temple as a centre of worship for all mankind, and was renewing the prophetic demand for moral conduct in the worshippers – hence the attack on the merchants 'robbing' their customers in the very precincts of the temple.

Some see the driving out of the oxen, sheep and pigeons which were to be bought for the sacrifices as an attack on the sacrificial cult itself; it was certainly not directed towards mere cultic reform. The chief significance, however, seems to lie in the location of the action which by-passed the cultic areas. 'It was through the portico there in the Court of the Jews and in the Court of the priests that prayer was said and worship was offered.... Why did He not enter into the conflict with the ecclesiastical laws and usages of the Temple authorities this time if He really wanted to restore the Temple as a place of prayer for all nations? Surely the answer is because the cultus, as the Temple had developed it, was at an end.'[3] The location in the Court of the Gentiles had therefore a double reference: positively towards the Gentile world for whose sake it had actually been built, and negatively towards the cultic fashions of the temple whose day was now passing.

More explicit and yet more enigmatic was Jesus' teaching about the destruction and restoration of the temple; John's Gospel gives a direct report of the occasion and places it immediately after the temple cleansing as a further development (John 2:18-22), while Matthew and Mark report it indirectly through the remarks of accusers at the Sanhedrin trial and of scoffers at the crucifixion (Matthew 26:61; 27:40; Mark 14:58; 15:30). The saying is given a high degree of authenticity on several grounds. It must have been a well-known statement of Jesus; his accusers did not wring it from him at the trial, nor did they invent it, for in either case it would hardly have been a ready taunt for a crowd of passers-by a few hours later. It was not the basis for his condemnation by the Sanhedrin, yet the early Church preserved it, even though it must have been uncongenial to Jewish Christians and must have provoked unwelcome controversies rather than solved any of their problems of conduct or of evangelism.[4]

There is still a question as to exactly what it was that Jesus said. His opponents at the trial and the crowd at the crucifixion clearly report the popular version that he himself threatened that he would, or could, destroy the temple and replace it in three days. This came very close to a direct attack upon the temple. John's Gospel simply says: 'Destroy this temple, and in three days I will raise it up again.' We can read this as a warning concerning the actions of his hearers, rather than a threat of his own action: 'You Jews are going the right way about destroying the temple by your nationalistic resistance to Rome.' The statement then follows the same line of thought as the warnings and predictions of the conflict to come, in Mark 13, or the lament over Jerusalem in Luke 13:35, when God would have clearly withdrawn his presence: 'Look! There is your temple, forsaken by God.' None of this was in criticism of the temple.

The exaggerated popular version is exactly what might be expected as a garbled misunderstanding of Jesus' more subtle statement. This would be more in character if it was not a direct attack upon the temple as such, which could have been made the basis of a successful charge at his trial. If then we adopt the less drastic interpretation of Jesus' own meaning we are still faced with the second part of the statement about rebuilding the temple in three days. The popular interpretation of course was to take it literally; a figurative reading could refer to an overthrow of the sacrificial cultus, but elsewhere Jesus seems to be indifferent to its reform or its fate. John's Gospel offers yet another understanding and implies that this was discovered by the disciples, although not till after the resurrection: 'But the temple he was speaking of was his body. After his resurrection his disciples recalled what he had said, and they believed... the words that Jesus had spoken' (John 2:21-22). It should also be noted that John used the word ναός (naos), thus referring to the temple proper with its inner shrine as the dwelling place of God, rather than ἱερόν (hieron) which would apply to the whole complex of buildings.

It seems, therefore, that Jesus was promising the replacement of that type of meeting place between God and men by another point of meeting, intimately connected with himself but not evident until after the resurrection. Whether he meant his own bodily resurrection, as John asserts, or his 'body' the Church which could be regarded as 'built' in the events of the three days from the cross to the resurrection, is immaterial for our present purpose; in any case the creation of the Church depended upon the resurrection of Jesus himself. It is clear that a personal form of meeting place between the divine and the human, intimately connected with Jesus, is to replace the physical sanctuary that had served for so long. 'At the same time Jesus did not turn his back so completely on the old order as to envisage a formless worship of God. What he did was to unite loyalty to the old traditional hope of Israel to the uniqueness of his own person. The new age would have its temple, and he himself would erect it.'[5]

This meant more than the spiritualization of worship that was a common enough quest in the Graeco-Roman world; it did more than replace the material temple by the temple of the soul or spirit of man, and so make the meeting place with the divine formless, subjective, and 'spiritual'. The physical place of meeting erected 'with hands' was to be replaced by something equally objective but 'not made with hands', by a personal meeting place to be found where both body and spirit united in the totality of his own person. He was the new temple, the positive replacement for all temples and cults on the Jerusalem pattern. His own body, whether interpreted individually or also corporately as the church, was the visible and historical reality that had become 'the medium for transcending the material and revealing spiritual qualities through the material'.[6]

The teaching on the replacement of the temple is all the more convincing when we remember the positive attitudes towards 'his Father's house' revealed in both word and action. Here was no extremist fanatical view unmindful of the contribution of the Jewish temple, and so of all temples, to religious history; indeed some such appreciation was the prerequisite for a genuine replacement. This might be hinted at, implied or presented enigmatically, rather than baldly stated in words too clear to be understood at the time, but that it was the import of Jesus' teaching is undeniable. For him, with his own sense of his person and mission, the day had come 'in which the concrete historical fact of the revelation itself decreed its own independence of any holy place – when it reached its fulfilment in a Man who could say of himself: "One greater than the Temple is here!"'[7] A more detailed study of this replacement and fulfilment of the physical by the personal will engage us shortly; the fact itself has now emerged and must be followed into the life and thinking of the early Church.

7.3 THE EARLY CHURCH: THE TEMPLE OLD AND NEW

There are no signs in the first generations of the Church that the tomb of Jesus became a holy place; it was only in later centuries that Constantine's Church of the Holy Sepulchre became a sanctuary like that of other religions to mark the tomb of the founder. The Christian belief in the empty tomb and the resurrection militated of course against a development that would have been incongruent both with Jesus' teaching and with the early Christian outlook. As for the temple, the practice of the first believers after the resurrection and ascension of Jesus is readily described, for it follows his own practice. There is at first no hint of opposition, for 'they kept up their daily attendance at the temple' (Acts 2:46). Whether this included full participation in the sacrificial cult cannot be determined unless we are to argue from the complete silence on the cult itself. Later even Paul acceded to the request of local Christains that he join in a purification ritual at the temple with some of their members (Acts 21:22-27), which suggests that various ritual uses continued for some twentyfive years after the beginnings of the Church. It was, however, mainly as a place of congregation and of prayer, where the leaders of the Church proclaimed the new gospel and worked miracles, that the temple appears in the records (see Acts 3:1; 5:25; Luke 24:53). Christians probably also maintained their customary attendance at the local synagogue, but otherwise their own distinctive activities of table fellowship occurred in private houses.

Some forty years elapsed between the birth of the Church and the final destruction of the Jerusalem temple, and when it did occur it seems to have been of no great moment since the Church made no clear reference in any of its subsequent literature to an event that must have been shattering for the continuing Jewish community. A number of factors account for this apparent indifference. Most obvious is the overwhelmingly Gentile composition of the Church by the end of this period, and for Gentile Christians the temple in Jerusalem had little historical meaning and no emotional significance. Within the whole Church, including Jewish Christians in Palestine, the implications of Jesus' teaching had been pursued, and through the thinking of Peter and especially of Paul Jesus' replacement of the temple had been interpreted in the teaching about the Church as itself the body of Christ and the new temple of God. Having this positive alternative view of the temple, together with the growth of their own liturgical life wherein the new view was expressed and consolidated, the Christians in Palestine must have been more responsive than most to criticisms of the temple that emanated from the various more thoughtful and pious groups among the Jews around them. When the disaster fell it was of no moment, for even those who perhaps still maintained some of the temple observances did so more from convention than conviction, or even for reasons of expediency like Paul in Acts 21:21-26.[8]

7.4 RADICAL OPPOSITION: STEPHEN

There is, however, one major incident in the first few years of the young Church that makes it appear surprising that the temple should have continued in use even for a generation. This was the attack upon both temple and cult made by Stephen in his trial before the Sanhedrin (Acts 7:44-50). Stephen was accused of 'for ever saying things against this holy place' and of claiming that Jesus would destroy it (6:13-14). The charge was therefore identical with one of the accusations against Jesus before the same tribunal only a few years previously. On this occasion it is possible that there was no exaggeration and that Stephen had said precisely this, for in his defence he reveals an open hostility to the temple that Jesus had never shown.

For Stephen the temple was merely a man-made house originating with Solomon; it had no connection with the tent of meeting that Moses had been commanded to set up on a divinely revealed pattern and that had continued until David's time. In Stephen the Nathan of II Samuel 7 and a whole series of Old Testament prophets spoke again, and if it was their voice rather than that of Jesus these were authorities the Sanhedrin might be expected to recognize; at the same time they represented the tradition that had culminated in Jesus himself, of whom Stephen proceeded to speak in the last sentence the Sanhedrin allowed him.

Whether Stephen wished for a revival of the tent of meeting, or regarded Jesus as both replacing the tabernacle and exposing the apostasy represented by the temple, is not clear from his defence alone. A study of the possible origins of his radical position confirms the second of these views as the more likely, even if not clearly worked out in Stephen's mind. It seems that he himself must have been a member of the Greek-speaking Jewish Christians to whom he was appointed as a deacon; his background would therefore be that of the Jewish dispersion where the desire for a more spiritual form of worship that they shared with certain Gentile groups led, in their case, to dissatisfaction with the Jewish temple system. At this point these Jews from the dispersion had much in common with the Qumran, the Ebionite and other reform movements of the time, and in view of Stephen's prominence in public proclamation of the new faith it is highly likely that he was well aware of these groups and of the attitudes to the temple found among them. There is no evidence of his having heard Jesus personally on this subject, but he had certainly found the teaching most congenial and had incorporated it, perhaps too literally, in his preaching, and paid for it with his life.

One of the unexpected consequences of Stephen's death was the persecution that followed and the scattering of Christians with their missionary witness into Samaria. When this led to the first Samaritan converts the question of the Jerusalem temple must have been raised acutely; did they now have to accept this temple and so reject their own rival temple on Mount Gerizim? And was the teaching of Jesus on this very issue, to the woman at the well in Samaria, so well known at this point that it helped to settle the matter? But settled it was, at least for the Samaritan converts, and against the temple in Jerusalem. Whether they continued for some time with their own temple rituals we cannot tell, although we may suppose they did.

More to our purpose is the effect of this development upon the members of the early Church in Jerusalem. What had happened, in the preaching of Stephen and in the acceptance of the Samaritans, was to prove a milestone in the expansion of the new faith to the Gentile world, yet in Jerusalem itself this radical attack on the temple seems to have had no influence on the thinking, nor as far as we can tell upon the practice, of the Church right up until the events of 70 A.D. made the issue irrelevant. The explanation seems to lie in the absence of any statement as to what it meant for Jesus to replace the temple, assuming that Stephen had gone even this far in his preaching, which is clear neither in the accusation against him nor in his defence. The most we can say is that he taught 'a supersession of the Temple "made with hands" in favour of some other form of worship, which is not directly particularized in his speech, but is analogous to the Tabernacle worship and is connected with Jesus of Nazareth'.[9]

This was not sufficient to take the Church much beyond the position of the various reform groups in Judaism; Stephen's only reference to Jesus was as 'the Righteous One'. Such slender doctrine offered no adequate replacement of the whole temple ideology; this had to await

Paul's approach to the question in new terms and his development of a Christology setting forth Jesus as the new presence of God among his people, and a view of the Church as both the body of Christ and the living temple of God. Nevertheless Stephen's radical attack and its indirect consequences played an important part in making the temple in this new sense the 'house of prayer for all nations' that Jesus desired.[10]

7.5 A THEOLOGY FOR THE NEW TEMPLE: PAUL

Although Paul had been present at the death of Stephen and must have known something of his teaching about the temple, he was an earnest Pharisee, more concerned with the Law than with the cult, and possibly less disturbed than some others by the attack on the temple. After his conversion he showed no signs of adopting Stephen's position, and seems to have both used and tolerated the temple. In his letters he is naturally more concerned with the new gospel's relation to the Law than to the cult, but nevertheless we also find a substantial contribution on the implications of this gospel for the temple.

The nearest Paul came to Stephen's statements was some two decades later when invited to explain his teaching to the Court of Areopagus; then he used the same argument about no temple 'made with hands' being adequate for the true God. This, however, was already a familiar idea in Stoic and other philosophic circles represented in this Athenian Court; it therefore gave no offence even though it applied to the Greek temples standing before them all, for it was coupled with a respectful attitude to other aspects of Greek religious practice (Acts 17:22-29). The burden of Paul's preaching was not an attack upon temples, but the subject which brought the meeting to an end, Jesus and the resurrection that had replaced all such forms of worship (vv. 18, 30-32).

Paul and the early Church were more concerned with exploring the nature of the new temple that existed somewhere in the interrelations of God, Jesus and the Christian community than in attacking the old that was being replaced. Paul's own thought appears distributed through a number of his letters and shows a certain development without ever having been gathered together and systematized in one place. The fullest statement occurs in II Corinthians 6:16–7:1, and it may also be the earliest, if it is correct (as some say) to regard this section as a displaced version of the 'previous letter' referred to in I Corinthians 5:9. Here Paul boldly transfers the temple concept from the physical building to the new community: 'For we are a temple of the living God, just as God said "I will live in them and move among them"'. The quotation draws upon the most intimate Old Testament pictures of how God will dwell with Israel (Leviticus 26:12; Ezekiel 37:27), and the identification of some four other Old Testament references in these verses 16-18 reveals Paul consciously presenting this new temple as the fulfilment of the ancient promise to his own people. To this extent Paul's doctrine was not itself new but was a continuation of the thought of the prophets and others, and of the interpretations of the synagogue and Qumran communities as to the place of the presence. There is little 'about the new temple beyond the fact that it is made of persons. We are not told what it is that makes the community of the faithful the temple, how God dwells in it, nor its relation to Christ.'[11] Paul has, however, placed the question in the proper context for a positive development.

The next stage appears in I Corinthians 3:16-17, with the implication that what he was saying was no new idea of his own but should be recognised as common knowledge. 'Surely you know that you are God's temple, where the Spirit of God dwells.... The temple of God is holy; and that temple you are.' Here the emphasis is on a dwelling of God that is more than a visit to or with his people, as in tabernacle or temple of old; it is nothing less than an indwelling, where the people themselves are the temple. The new development is in the mode of God's indwelling as the Holy Spirit, although this too had its earlier anticipations in the doctrines of God's presence through the Name, the Glory, the Word or Wisdom, and the Shekinah. This doctrine of the indwelling Holy Spirit, going beyond Qumran's idea of the divine presence in the community, was the point of departure for Paul's further thought on the place of Christ in the new temple.

Before pursuing this we must note the important contribution of I Corinthians 6:19-20 on the relation of the individual to the community: 'Do you know that your body is a shrine of the indwelling Spirit, and the Spirit is God's gift to you?... Then honour God in your body.' This is exactly the same doctrine, only now it is applied to the individual person as the temple of God, since 'body' for Paul has a wider reference than the merely physical meaning it has for us. There is no conflict between this application of the temple concept and the wider application to the whole community, for in Hebrew thought an individual exists as a person only when in community. 'Collectively speaking, the Church is ... God's temple, but the principle which makes her a temple exists in each individual believer and makes him also a temple.... All Christians as persons are God's temple. Where there is a believer, there also is a temple of God. Yet several believers are not several temples, for one Person dwells in and sanctifies them all.'[12]

In the doctrine of the indwelling through the Holy Spirit Paul has gone beyond both the Old Testament and the Qumran outlook. In his doctrines of the body and of the community he has surpassed the teaching of Philo, the Stoics and other thinkers who saw the mind or spirit of individual man as the temple of God. Paul starts from the community, not the individual, and only through continuing unity with the community in love can the individual retain the presence of the Spirit, who indwells his whole person, both body and mind. To include the material body in this way was abhorrent to the Greek thinkers; these also, like Qumran, regarded the presence of God in the human temple as due to natural endowment or spiritual effort and worthiness. Once again Paul has reached a new insight, that 'the Spirit is God's gift', the evidence of his grace and not of man's achievement.

Although for Paul the Holy Spirit is always the Spirit of Christ we have not yet had an explicit reference to the place of Christ in the new temple. We may see the beginnings of this in Paul's next letter, to the Romans, in a particular choice of words in ch. 3:25. He is dealing with God's grace in mercifully making Jesus Christ the means of dealing with human sin; Christ is described as the expiation or propitiation whereby guilt or defilement is removed. This is the sense of the Greek word used, ἱλαστήριον (hilasterion) although on the only other occasions where the same thought occurs the kindred word ἱλασμός (hilasmos) is employed (John 2:2; 4:10). Elsewhere in the New Testament ἱλαστήριον appears only once, in Hebrews 9:5, for the 'mercy seat' or cover of the ark of the covenant. In the Septuagint, however, it is used exclusively for the mercy seat, or whatever replaced this in Ezekiel's ideal temple where there was no ark.

The question then arises whether Paul might equally well have used ἱλασμός or whether he deliberately chose the alternative because of its association with ark and temple. Lest this seem to take a mere matter of words too seriously we may note the great importance found in this one verse by a wide range of Christian opinion; Luther spoke for many when he called it 'the chief point and the very central place of the Epistle, and of the whole Bible'.[13]

It is not too much to assume, therefore, that Paul was weighing his words, and was sensitive to the implications of ἱλαστήριον. If so, we are justified in recalling that the cover over the ark was the most sacred part of the Holy of Holies, where God dwelt as on his throne. In applying the word to Christ Paul was asserting

that the genuine mercy-seat, the true place of God's presence, is no longer over the Ark of the Covenant but in Christ crucified: 'God was in Christ reconciling the world to himself' (II Corinthians 5:19). Christ, therefore, has not only brought the temple system to a close; he himself is the spiritual temple, the new dwelling place of God with mankind. Further, the new ἱλαστήριον is said by Paul to have been exposed (πρόθετω – 'put forward before the public gaze') for all to see and have access to. The New Sanctuary is no longer hidden from the people by a veil as was the mercy-seat of the Holy of Holies. The veil of the Temple is now rent; the secrets of God ... manifested....[14]

If our argument is correct, at this point we are tapping a rich vein of Pauline thought about Jesus Christ replacing the Jewish temple by fulfilling its functions.

The climax of Paul's teaching on the relation of Christ to the new temple occurs in the explicit statements of one of his next letters, Ephesians 2:20-22. The preceding passage about the inclusion of the Ephesian Gentiles along with Jews in the one Church of God would inevitably recall the Old Testament longing for the day when all nations would come to worship together through the one temple at Jerusalem. Paul then describes the new Church through a combination of the images of building and temple: 'You are built upon the foundation laid by the apostles and prophets, and Christ Jesus himself is the foundation-stone. In him the whole building is bonded together and grows into a holy temple in the Lord. In him you too are being built with all the rest into a spiritual dwelling for God.'

In this rich and complex statement we recognize first the earlier thought that the whole community, now specifically reaching beyond the Jews, is the temple where God dwells. The Greek text and older translations make it plain that God dwells 'in or through the Spirit' in his people, exactly as in Paul's earlier accounts; the force and distinctiveness of this have been lost in the New English Bible translation above, as 'a spiritual dwelling', which also masks Paul's characteristic intimate relationship between the Holy Spirit and Jesus Christ contained in the last sentence. The new development in this statement is the centrality given to Christ who is firstly the foundation for all that the prophets and apostles have done in the creation of the Church, then the source of its unity, and finally the means of its growth into a holy dwelling place for God.

Paul therefore possessed a comprehensive and dynamic view of the new temple as community, including both its historical leadership, development and unity, and its transcendent origin and basis in the Christ whom God set forth as his own means of 'reconciling the world to himself'; it is Jesus Christ in unity with his body the Church, Jesus-in-community, who is the new temple where God graciously dwells in the Spirit, the new mercy-seat replacing the old ἰλαστήριον in the temple at Jerusalem. And all this without needing to attack the Jewish temple itself.

7.6 THE CONSENSUS OF THOUGHT: PETER, LUKE, HEBREWS, THE REVELATION
   OF JOHN

A briefer survey of other currents of thought in the early Church will show that Paul was not alone in the endeavour to interpret the relation of Jesus and the Church to the historic temple, and that whatever distinctive features other attempts possessed they still remained congruous with his formulation.

In I Peter 2:4-10 we have another major apostolic statement on Christ, the Church and the new temple. Christ is again the central figure, under the image of a 'living stone' who is also the 'cornerstone' (some would translate 'foundation stone') in a spiritual temple; this is made up of members of the Church who allow themselves, also as 'living stones', to be built up along with Christ. So far this is entirely Pauline, but instead of Paul's further development of the temple as God's dwelling Peter treats it as a place of worship, seeing it from the human rather than the divine side. The community-as-temple is 'a holy priesthood, to offer spiritual sacrifices acceptable to God through Jesus Christ'. Priesthood and sacrifice were central features of all temples, but now 'in contrast to Judaism, in which only a selected number from a single tribe functioned as priests, in this new Christian community all enter the *priesthood* and can, therefore, themselves constitute the sanctuary, in whose midst God's presence is manifested, and by whom worship is offered to God ... those now joined to Christ are sure of acceptance when they offer their sacrifices through Him.'[15] Here is the perfect complement to Paul's concentration on the temple building as a dwelling place; the old cult itself is replaced by a new priesthood offering a new form of sacrifice, but still 'through Jesus Christ'. And once again without any obvious attack upon the temple in Jerusalem.

The ability of both Peter and Paul to elaborate their new temple doctrine without open criticism of the old temple is all the more remarkable when we discover some of their own unpleasant experiences in the Jerusalem sanctuary; these are related in the two volumes of Luke, in his Gospel and the Acts. Twice Luke records expulsions from the temple. In Acts 4:1-3 Peter and John were arrested by the priestly authorities while preaching in Solomon's Cloister, imprisoned overnight, and next day examined by the Sanhedrin and formally forbidden to continue public preaching of the gospel of Jesus. Paul's experience was the more bitter because less to be expected. Acts 21:26-36 and the following chapters relate how he was actually participating in the traditional cult, along with fellow Jewish Christians with whom he had commenced a week-long purification ritual, when a mob dragged him out of the temple area to lynch him and he had to be rescued by Roman troops. After narrowly escaping a flogging he was released only to be rescued by troops a second time, from an excited Sanhedrin itself, and then whisked off by night under military escort to Caesarea to protect him from a plot to murder him. Thus began at least four years of imprisonment in Caesarea and Rome while under legal process of appeal and trial. And all this for one who had not only refrained from attack on the temple but who was still willing to share in its cultic activities.

Even if these experiences play no detectable part in the writings of Paul and Peter they do seem to contribute to Luke's theology.[16] After each account Luke relates a manifestation of the divine presence, a theophany that takes place outside the temple as if in compensation, or in comment upon the failure of both priests and worshippers in the temple to receive the revelation in Jesus (Acts 4:31; 23:11). This contrast, together with the particular selection and arrangement of his materials in the Gospel, suggests a reconstruction of his attitude to the temple on the following lines. As we have already noted, the infancy stories reveal a positive attitude: Luke regards the divine presence as having been in the temple. It is, however, no longer tied to the temple, and can leave it, as Jesus says it will (Luke 13:35). The presence is now linked to Jesus, as witness the further references to his divine glory in Luke's account of the transfiguration as compared with those of Matthew and Mark (Luke 9:28-36). The divine presence is now in the temple only when Jesus is there; then it resumes its functions, but only because Jesus has taken possession of it and 'cleansed' it. This was the object of his so-called entry into Jerusalem, which was really an entry into the temple for this purpose (Luke 19:28ff.). After the resurrection the presence is where Jesus is, not in the temple which fades out of the picture, but in his body the Church. Henceforth the temple and the Church stand in contrast with one another, and under divine guidance the Church appears to have actually invited conflict (Acts 5:20, 42). The leading apostles are expelled and the presence of God is manifested through theophanies in Christ's community, the Church. Thus does Luke trace the transition from loyalty to the temple and what it once could do, to loyalty to the Church of Christ as the new temple of God's presence. By this different route Luke reaches the same conclusions as Paul and Peter, and yet again, by his oblique criticisms, he avoids an open attack upon the Jewish temple which is clearly superseded. Peter's interest in the activities that occur in a temple as a place of worship is repeated in the very individual treatment of our theme in the Epistle to the Hebrews.[17] Priesthood and sacrifices are designed to secure access to God, and the author develops an elaborate contrast between the traditional Jewish cultic system as no more than an inadequate provisional attempt, and the new way opened up through Jesus Christ. He nowhere mentions the temple by name, nor does he use the temple language of ναός (naos) and ἱερόν (hieron), but gives a detailed account of what is clearly Jewish temple worship in terms of the tabernacle. Even this word is rarely used and instead we find a general term meaning holy place or sanctuary, τα ἅγια (ta hagia). The epistle is regarded as composed after the destruction of the Jerusalem temple, and while its account is based on the details of the Jewish cult these were sufficiently representative of the temple type of worship everywhere for the thrust of the argument to apply to sanctuaries in general.

We have here the most specific criticism of the Jewish and all other temples. Part of the attack coincides with the position of many contemporary proponents of a more spiritual worship; thrice temples are described, either directly or indirectly, as merely man-made (Hebrews 8:2; 9:11; 9:24) and once as being of this world, i.e. material (9:1). Throughout there is the implication that earthly temples are but shadows, copies, or mere symbols of the real thing (8:5; 9:24), and this is now clearly a defect rather than the virtue we have seen it to be in other interpretations of sacred places. The most sustained criticism appears in Hebrews 9:6-10, heightened by the contrasts in 9:11-28; the endless repetition of the sacrifices by the priests testify to their ineffectiveness; the restrictions surrounding sanctuaries and their holy inner shrines prevent full access by all to God; and external things like food and drink and ritual washing cannot bring the inner purity that will free men for the service of God.

The provisional and inadequate temple cults have now been replaced by a new, God-given, and entirely effective way of relating men to God. This has been pioneered by Jesus Christ, who has fulfilled all the aims of priesthood, sacrifice and sanctuary perfectly and once and for all by entering into the immediate presence of God, and indeed taking 'his seat at the right hand of the throne of God' (12:2). In terms of the old categories he is the true high priest, the perfect sacrifice in his death, and the real sanctuary where God is present – the separate features of the temple cult are now fused into the unity of his action and person.

This is a detailed and reasoned account of how Jesus replaced the temple, but it is not so specific on the nature of the new sanctuary itself. It is described as real, true, greater, more perfect, heavenly, even heaven itself, erected by the Lord and not man. Otherwise the emphasis is upon Christ as the one who establishes it, and upon what he does through it. This is expressed largely in terms of the worshippers now having full access to God. Through this 'way which he has opened' they are 'free to enter boldly into the sanctuary' (10:19), 'draw near to God' (7:19) and 'boldly approach the throne of our gracious God' (4:14; 7:25). Twice there are echoes of the veil in the Jerusalem temple that prevented access to the presence in the Holy of Holies: 'In through the veil, where Jesus has entered... as forerunner' (6:19) there now runs 'the new and living way... for us through the curtain' (10:19). Since this access to the presence of the divinity is the aim of all sanctuaries and the core of religion itself, these descriptions go to the heart of the matter and there is no need to dwell upon the sanctuary as a separate theme.

Here we notice the difference between the Epistle to the Hebrews and the positions of Peter and Paul, who identify the new temple with the community of the faithful and so present a vivid image of the Church as a temple-building erected from its members as 'living stones'. Hebrews never makes this identification and so its temple or sanctuary remains rather nebulous in itself, overshadowed by the person and work of Christ, into which it is absorbed. At the same time the Church is involved as the beneficiary of Christ's action at every point; he is its fore-runner opening up the access, 'its high priest making atonement for its sin and set over the household of God' (10:21), and 'we are that household of his' (3:6), invited to 'continually offer up the sacrifices of praise... through Jesus Christ' (13:15, 21). Indirectly, therefore, but nonetheless clearly, Hebrews shares with these other writers the same conception of the new temple as Jesus-in-his-community, and presents it in a form that was relevant not only to Jewish Christians among its readers, nostalgic for their shattered Jerusalem temple, but also to all men in a world of temples.

A further important contribution to the temple theme occurs in a still later book, the Revelation of John, where the image of the temple is employed in several different ways. The Church on earth is spoken of as a temple (Revelation 11:1-3), and in the letter to the Church at Philadelphia we glimpse a variation on the theme when the faithful individual is described as 'a pillar in the temple of my God' (Revelation 3:12), an obvious alternative to the 'living stone' structural image found elsewhere. The idea of church-as-temple is not pursued, even though the earthly community is regarded as in integral relation with the community of the saints whose worship in the heavenly temple is described at length in chs. 4-20. Here, as in the Epistle to the Hebrews, the emphasis is less on the sanctuary than on the worshippers themselves as a priesthood offering spiritual sacrifices in the immediate presence of God; again there is the same open access so central in Hebrews. The heavenly temple is mentioned only incidentally (Revelation 7:15; 14:17; 16:1) or intermingled with the tabernacle image — 15:5 speaks of the ναός of the tent of the testimony; only in 15:8 where the sanctuary is filled with 'smoke from the glory of God' does it appear to figure in the worship. The temple, then, is not an important feature in these successive scenes of the heavenly worship.

We discover why this is so when we examine what is said about the temple in the further visions of chs. 21-22. In a totally renewed universe John saw the new holy city of Jerusalem that was to be no man-made achievement but to come as gift of God, 'ready like a bride adorned for her husband' (21:1-2). This familiar image of the bride, together with subsequent references to Christ as the Lamb, show that John is thinking primarily of the city as the community, that is 'the people of God, in their ultimate state — the church redeemed and united in the eternal worship of God'.[18]

'Now at last God has his dwelling among men!' (21:3). We might expect this to be developed in terms of Jesus and his community the church being the dwelling-temple, as with earlier writers. Instead we find the blunt and radical statement: 'I saw no temple in the city; for its temple was the sovereign Lord God and the Lamb ... and his servants shall worship him; they shall see him face to face' (21:22; 22:4). Here we have the climax of biblical thought on the sacred place and its sanctuaries. These vanish from the scene when the functions they served are fulfilled without their physical mediation and in an entirely personal way, when Christ and his bride the Church stand in the immediate presence of God. This meeting between God, Christ and the Church was in such intimate unity that each might be said to 'dwell' or live in the other (but without fusion or loss of identity), and in this openness to one another, 'face to face', there was no need of any sanctuary or temple as the dwelling for the rendezvous between the divine and the human.

Although in this consummation God himself is the temple for his people, it is always 'God and the Lamb' in conjunction that figure in the image (21-22; 22:2, 3); since Christ the Lamb is indissolubly united with his bride, the Church also shares in the image as itself the temple of God with 'his name on their foreheads' (22:4). Although John starts at the divine end of what is really an all-embracing image his thought reaches out to the other pole where Paul had begun, the Church as God's temple. We can say that he sees 'God as a temple to the faithful and the faithful as a temple to God'.[19] While his thought has gone beyond that of the earlier New Testament writers to the ultimate limits where the temple loses its identity, he stills keeps company with them; the earthly Church can still call itself the temple, the Jesus-in-community where God dwells, and do so with all the more confidence when it turns to share John's vision of the Church triumphant serving as a temple to God even as God himself is a temple to them, with Christ as the bond of unity.

7.7 CONCLUSIONS

At the beginning of this survey of New Testament thought, when dealing with the teaching of Jesus, we were speaking of Jesus as himself the replacement of the temple. It is now clear that only part of the picture was then in view, for the early Church does not present Jesus Christ in himself and by himself as the new temple — Christ is never called the temple. It should also be noted that the Church is never called the temple of Christ, but always of God or the Holy Spirit. It is therefore Jesus Christ in union with his Church, or the Church as the body of Christ, that is the new temple where God dwells in or through the Spirit. If we recall the functions of temples as meeting points between God and men, as outlined in the first part of this study, we shall understand why the new temple cannot be confined to Jesus Christ in himself alone, nor, on the other hand, restricted to a dwelling for Christ but not for the fullness of the Godhead.

We have now followed the New Testament materials on the temple from the teaching and practice of Jesus through the thought and practice of the Church of the first century. There is no doubt of the result — that a major transformation in the interpretations and use of the temple form had occured, and that this consisted of the gradual abandonment of the Jewish temple as a material sanctuary defined in terms of physical place, and its replacement by a 'personal place', the place where Jesus was in his body the Church, as the new sanctuary. Although this was still as physical as the incarnation and as the Christ who was bodily resurrected, and also as the historical visible Church, it was no longer tied to any particular physical place or building. The Church in the New Testament is never the place or the building where it may be meeting, but always the community where Christ is with his people.

This revolution had emerged from the background of anticipations and experiments in the preceding centuries and in contemporary Judaism that we have referred to in the earlier chapters of this study; it had both fulfilled and exceeded these tentative ideas and developments, for in the action and person of Jesus Christ something new had appeared in the relations between God and men. Further, this revolutionary transformation, unlike most revolutions, managed to avoid attacking either its antecedents or the system it replaced, and in the practice of many Christians the transition from the one to the other must have been a gradual though inevitable process.

It should also be pointed out that the change begins in the teaching of Jesus, forty years before the destruction of the Jerusalem temple, and is developed in the writings of Paul and Peter well before this event; even the writings which are after 70 A.D. draw upon and are in harmony with traditions established in the early Church before this date. The new form of temple is therefore an authentic product springing from the heart of this new religious movement and in no sense an accomodation to the loss of the temple in Jerusalem, a hastily improvised and necessarily spiritual substitute. Neither Judaism itself with its new kind of worship in the synagogue, nor the early Church with its revolutionary new dwelling place for God, was in this desperate strait; each had already developed its own replacement, with an ensuing history we have yet to trace.

8

Phenomenological Analysis
of New Testament Contributions

In the previous chapter we studied the New Testament documents in
their own terms, employing in an elementary way the normal exege-
tical methods used by literary or biblical scholars and such theological
categories as emerged from the materials. Only occasionally did we
allow ourselves a reference to the general phenomenology of the sacred
place and of the temple that had been set forth at an earlier stage. Now
we propose to use the categories of this phenomenology for the analysis of the New Testament results we have reached. These have been
described as a revolution, and when we recall our earlier discussions
of temples this is not too strong a term. This new form of temple has,
however, sufficient concrete historical manifestations to be itself a
new phenomenon presenting data for study, and so the question now
arises whether it requires entirely new phenomenological categories
or can be contained and interpreted within those already used for the
study of the sacred place in general. The second position will obtain
if the new temple proves to be, at least in some important senses, an
unexpected extension of the forms already familiar. If this should be
so, then even these forms themselves will be better understood when
followed through into such new developments.

We shall therefore examine further some of the New Testament evidence and its resultant picture of the new temple to see if these repeat
in any way the five-featured pattern displayed in other temples.

8.1 DIVINE ORIGIN OF THE NEW SANCTUARY

We have already seen how the sacred place is selected and established
neither by the inherent suitabilities of natural phenomena nor by the

practical wisdom of men, but essentially by some divine revelation in dream, vision, miracle or other sign. So it is also with the institution of the new temple in Jesus. The advent was announced through angel visions and dreams to Zecharias, Joseph and Mary, and it was through similar vision, dream, heavenly sign, or Spirit guidance that first the shepherds, then the Eastern 'wise men' and finally the prophet Simeon in the temple were led to the new divinely-chosen 'sacred place' then being instituted in this person. Miracles, signs and theophanies attended the public ministry of Jesus, especially at his baptism, at his transfiguration on the mountain, and on the day of his death, and continued through the events of the resurrection and ascension into those of the day of Pentecost and the early Church. Whatever sceptical attitude might be adopted towards any individual event in this series, or towards the accounts we have of it, the total elimination of this dimension of revelation would undermine any Christian interpretation and by the same stroke remove these events from the place they so clearly hold in the general phenomenology of religion. This new sacred place was indicated from its inception and repeatedly confirmed by successive revelations of the divine presence in power or guidance.

The same phenomenological motif appears in the contrast between the old temple as man-made and the new as made by God. This appears most clearly in Mark's account of the accusation that Jesus had said he would destroy 'this temple, made with human hands, and in three days I will build another, not made with hands' (14:58). The Epistle to the Hebrews uses the same imagery: '... Christ has entered, not that sanctuary made by men's hands which is only a symbol of the reality', but, 'a greater and more perfect one, not made by men's hands...' (9:24, 11). This criticism of ordinary temples as merely man-made appears also in Stephen's attack (Acts 7:48), and in Paul's more moderate statements (Acts 17:24, 29); in the Old Testament the phrase was always pejorative and used of heathen idols or altars (e.g. Isaiah 17:8; 44:13) but it lies unexpressed behind the attitude to the Jerusalem temple we have examined in Nathan and in Solomon's prayer (II Samuel 7; I Kings 8:27).

This criticism might seem to contradict our interpretation above of the tremendous labours men have devoted to their temples in the conviction that they were obeying the will of the gods, and erecting a sanctuary on the divinely chosen site according to the plan revealed from heaven. No one then called this merely man-made. It must be remembered, however, that what men had fashioned remained solely a human construction until the gods had accepted it and been installed in the consecration rites. In the Egyptian consecration rites already quoted the gods had, as it were, gone one better still, and themselves built the temple, as men could never have done. No doubt something of the same interpretation attached to certain sanctuaries that seemed given ready-made by the gods in the form of fallen meteorite, grove or grotto, fountain or mountain. Far be it from man to attempt to alter or improve upon what the gods had shaped and given. And in what men themselves did construct with all divine counsel there remained the sense of an imperfection that was on occasion given the explicit architectural expression we have already noted.

In these various ways a feeling for the limitations of all things human ran through man's religious building, and as his insights deepened dissatisfaction with temples made with hands pressed upon him to the point where they were rejected on this account. It was this point that had been reached by the more thoughtful spirits in the world of antiquity; the Old Testament felt like this about the religious artefacts of other peoples and has the seeds of the same dissatisfaction with its own; intertestamental and contemporary Jewish thought reveals others who had turned away from temples; the New Testament takes up the same theme in its account of Stephen, but both Jesus and the New Testament writers are able to go beyond this and speak of the new temple, not made with human hands, that had now replaced the old. This was therefore the climax of a widespread search in the history of religions, rather than a novel phenomenon unrelated to the rest of religious experience.

The same emphasis upon the divine source of the new sanctuary finds other expression in the biblical theme of the grace of God. Even for the sanctuaries of the Old Testament 'the most decisive action was God's decision to bestow his Presence and this came entirely from him and not from any man. *The Temple was a gift of God.* Neither David nor Solomon, nor priestly rite or prophetic trance had "drawn down" his Presence or brought about his coming. He remained supreme and every communication made by him to his creature was a grace.'[1] As the Psalmist had seen, 'Except the Lord build the house, they labour in vain that build it' (127:1). The same note may be detected in the infancy narratives concerning Jesus, where the mercy and compassion of God in taking the initiative that is represented in Jesus form a recurring theme (e.g. Luke 1:48, 55, 78; 2:31) that reaches a mature and succinct statement later in John's Gospel: 'So the Word became flesh; he came to dwell among us, and we saw his glory... full of grace and truth' (1:14). Here indeed was no man-made dwelling-temple but one of such divine origin and nature as to satisfy this demand in all the forms it had taken in religious history.

8.2   THE NEW TEMPLE

8.2.1 *As centre*

We shall now test the radical fulfilment and transformation of the sacred place that is claimed in the New Testament by seeing how far Christ takes up into his person and work each of the four basic functions of the sanctuary that we have used in our earlier analyses, commencing with the function as centre.

The New Testament records leave no doubt that the centre of the new religious community was not an institution located in buildings or at a place — not even at Jerusalem, nor was it a hierarchy or ruling organization, nor yet a new ideal or way of life; it was simply and entirely the person, Jesus Christ. His centrality is evident at every point, and even though the terms used do not include literal reference to a centre the idea itself lies behind the various descriptions of the place of Christ. The New English Bible recognizes this when it renders Colossians 2:8 with an oblique use of 'centred... on Christ'. The same idea is embodied in Jesus' own statement: '... where two or three are gathered together in my name there I am in the midst of them' (Matthew 18:20).

A great variety of phrases express this centrality: 'It is no longer I who live, but Christ who lives in me' (Galatians 2:20); 'Christ is all and is in all'; 'live... in union with him. Be rooted in him; be built in him' (Colossians 3:11; 2:6-7). Christ is regularly called 'Lord', and this is kindred to the image of Christ as 'head' both of the Church (Ephesians 1:22; 5:23 ff.; Colossians 1:18; 2:19) and also of 'every power and authority in the universe' (Colossians 2:10). By another image he becomes the chief cornerstone or foundation in whom the whole structure is joined together (Ephesians 2:20-21).

There are many particular facets of this central reference point. For instance Christ is the source of strength, power or authority, being himself 'the power of God and the wisdom of God' (I Corinthians 1:24). Throughout the records the gospel is presented as the announcement of the power of God or of his kingdom manifested in Jesus Christ. Paul is especially fond of extolling 'how vast the resources of his power open to us' (Ephesians 1:19), of acknowledging that he is 'toiling with all the energy and power of Christ at work in me' (Colossians 1:29), and of recommending others 'to find your strength in the Lord, in his mighty power' (Ephesians 6:10). Jesus is described as giving others power to heal, to exorcise, to raise the dead, to forgive sins, and he himself is depicted as the power 'unto salvation' and the power over all created 'principalities and powers'. Likewise he claims 'full authority in heaven and on earth' (Matthew 28:18), and throughout his ministry claimed authority both by word and in deed.

A further aspect of the same centrality presents Christ as the inaugurator of a 'new creation' in his own person. He is understood as the centre of a new reality that is the only fully real existence and the source of true being for individual men, for the community, and indeed for the whole of a renewed creation or universe. In one image he is represented as the leader or first-born of a new humanity (I Corinthians 15: 20-23; Colossians 1:18; Ephesians 4:22-24); in another he is the 'bread of life' (John 6:30-58) or the 'living water' (John 4:8-15; 7:37-38) who had 'come that men may have life and may have it in all its fulness' (John 10:10).

The image of Jesus as the living water bringing real life contains an unmistakable reference to the same image in the Old Testament hope for the future. Ezekiel (47:1 ff.), Zechariah (14:8) and Joel (3:18) had all pictured the Jerusalem temple as the centre of a new age where blessing for mankind came from a spring of living water issuing from the temple. John's Gospel states that Jesus made his declaration on the last day of the Feast of Tabernacles when the climax was reached in a ritual of pouring water into the shaft opening at the side of the great altar, with prayers for rain in the year ahead. Jesus was therefore implying that he himself was now to replace the temple of Jerusalem as the centre of life and vitality for the world.

The same replacement of Jerusalem as the centre for the ingathering of the nations, is evident in John's further account of Jesus as the good shepherd, knowing his own sheep but concerned to gather in the 'other sheep of mine, not belonging to this fold. There will then be one flock, one shepherd' (John 10:14-16). This is clearly a reference to both Jews and Gentiles, and is followed up by John's story of some Greeks who came to seek Jesus out, and of Jesus' reaction to their coming as symbolic of his mission fulfilled; through his life and approaching death the nations would be drawn together around himself as centre of unity (John 12:20-33).[2]

A further wide-ranging image of the centrality of Jesus occurred when he was described as 'the real light which enlightens every man' (John 1:9), as 'a light that will be a revelation to the Gentiles' (Luke 2:32), and as the light of the cosmos when the sun and moon had been replaced in the new universe, for 'its lamp was the Lamb' (Revelation 21:23). This gathers up the functions of all temples dedicated to the heavenly luminaries, and of the Jerusalem temple sending forth light to the whole world, by placing Jesus at the centre as the source of all that light has represented in the history of religions.

A recent attempt has been made to distinguish a new sense in which Jerusalem remains a 'centre'.[3] In the previous era it was the centre to which all Jews looked and many came for worship, and where the nations would gather in the messianic age in a universal worship; here Jerusalem is a centripetal centre and the characteristic of this is pilgrimage. Then in the Christian era the city became the centre from which the gospel spread to the whole world; it had now become a centrifugal centre characterized by mission. In each era the world was to be seen as a 'polarized space' around a centre where events occur which are decisive for the whole surrounding space, even to its outer limits. This centre is fixed, both geographically and historically, and nothing can change it, so that the early Church which started in Jerusalem was led to witness 'in all Judaea and in Samaria, and unto the uttermost part of the earth' (Acts 1:8).

Historically and geographically this remains true, but in the second situation there has been a major change in the meaning of the term 'centre' that must also be emphasized. The mission that set forth from Jerusalem had a new source of direction and vitality, located in the person of Jesus Christ and not in the ancient city. When we remember the Jerusalem-Zion-Temple complex of ideas in the Old Testament we recognize the change in Jerusalem's status as but another facet of the transference from temple to Christ as person. And as in the case of the temple itself, the transference was a gradual rather than a sudden change. Jesus himself loved the city, wept over it, and finally went there to face death. In his own ministry, however, the emphasis was on Galilee, and Samaria also was included, while in the early Church we see Jerusalem treated with respect as the historical mother church, the object of loyalty and charity, but no more. In subsequent Christian history pilgrimages to Jerusalem would have educational and even devotional value but were no longer part of the religious structure, essential for the full meeting between man and God.[4]

If Jerusalem was the historical centre, Jesus Christ, or Jesus-in-his-community, was now the contemporary centre, which in a geographical sense had become pluriform. In the New Testament each congregation was the Church as much as any other. We have already observed the same plurality in both the images and the temples of a single god in other religious traditions, where an unlimited number of sacred places could each be considered the 'centre of the world'.[5] The early Church was therefore restoring a dimension of religion lost when Israel's worship was centralized on the Jerusalem temple (and unofficially regained in the synagogues); while the temple form itself was being revolutionized it was also regaining an important feature, albeit in this new personal mode.

The Christ who was the personal centre for the Church in each of its communities was also regarded as nothing less than the cosmic centre of a new unity and harmony in the whole universe. 'Through him God chose to reconcile the whole universe to himself... to reconcile all things, whether on earth or in heaven, through him alone' (Colossians 1:20); and in the new Jerusalem 'the city had no need of sun or moon ... for... its lamp was the Lamb' (Revelation 21:22-23). This cosmic reference found expression also in descriptions of the cross of Christ's death as a 'tree' (Acts 5:30;10:39;13:29;Galatians 3:13;I Peter 2:24). Behind this lies not only the literal pole in Deuteronomy 21:22-23 but the tree of life in the garden of Eden, with its affinity with the cosmic tree in a vast number of religious traditions. Christian legends were quick to develop around this theme, and also its cognate form where the place of the cross, Golgotha or Mount Calvary, appeared as the centre of the earth; here Adam was believed to have been created and buried, and here therefore Christ the Second Adam died for the re-creation of mankind. When Christ replaced the temple its functions as cosmic centre, expressed also in sacred tree and mountain, were subsumed in his action and person.[6]

It should be abundantly clear that all the functions of temples as 'centres' have been both taken over and clarified in the Christian interpretation of Jesus. He was the new centre of meaning, of power and authority; here was the 'heart of the real', the place of the truly human, the centre of the new creation for man and his entire world, the source of abundant life where man can quench his 'unquenchable ontological thirst for *being*'.[7] When the new religion claimed to supersede the old religions of the world it was not to dispense with the need for a centre, but to find it in a person rather than a place.

8.2.2 *As meeting point*

The meeting between the divine and the human with which sanctuaries have been concerned is also involved in the function of Jesus Christ as the new centre, where communication between men and God had been opened up in a new way. Jesus is regularly described as having been sent by God for this purpose – in John's Gospel the verbs for 'send' are used over forty times in this context. Throughout the New Testament he is interpreted as the point of communication where the divine revelation occurs for men, and where all nations may bring their prayers, praise and obedience in a religious response that is always 'through Christ'.

Jesus himself took up some of the ancient images of the meeting between the gods and men when he said 'I am the way... no one comes to the Father except by me' (John 14:6), and more pointedly still, 'I am the door' (John 10:7, 9). If the transference of temple functions to Jesus Christ be taken seriously then this was no mere happy illustration; rather was he gathering up into himself in an ontological fashion all that sacred places had endeavoured to do in religions through the doors, gates, thresholds and other 'entrance phenomena' we have already studied.

One of the standard 'communication forms' was also adopted by Jesus when he replied to Nathaniel: '... you shall see heaven wide open, and God's angels ascending and descending upon the Son of Man' (John 1:51). This is obviously a reference to the classic experience of Jacob in his dream at Bethel, with the ladder linking heaven and earth and the subsequent establishment of the sacred place (Genesis 28:10-17). There was also the possible reference to the Jerusalem temple, for Jewish traditions regarded the stone on which Jacob slept as the temple's foundation stone. 'Henceforth "the bridge between heaven and earth no longer leads as in the past to a particular place on earth... to a stone, but to a man in whom the glory of God is made visible".'[8]

At an earlier point we outlined the rabbinic views of the rock of Mt. Zion and the temple associated with it as the place of communication with both the lower and the heavenly worlds, the centre of the three cosmic realms. Jesus as the new temple is shown to be the link between the same three realms through his 'coming' from the Father, his life and ministry in this world, his descent into the underworld of the dead, and his return through the earthly realm to the heavenly by his resurrection and ascension. He thus forms a kind of axis at the 'centre' whereby communication is established throughout the cosmos just as the same axis was depicted by cosmic trees, pillars, and other images of communication in the various religions. An analogous action occurs in the experience of the believer who accepts the God revealed in Christ and by baptism descends into death and rises to life in the new creation (Romans 6:3-5).

Another way of expressing the new Testament interpretation of Jesus is to say that God had, as it were, projected himself in Jesus Christ, who was both Son of God and Son of Man and so the central meeting point between God and men. Human endeavour then could cease to be theocentric in its reference of all human activities and aspirations to the cultic centre of the gods at the sacred place; it could also abandon the anthropocentric search for ultimate truth and reality in the mind or soul of man; life was now to become Christocentric. Since Christ was regarded as both truly human and truly divine, those who made him their centre found themselves at one and the same time in encounter with the new humanity and the ultimate divinity. To be Christocentric was therefore to be both anthropocentric and theocentric. This real and permanent meeting of real man and real divinity in the one person of Jesus Christ, shared with his community the Church, was preserved in the Christological formulation of the later Christian Councils in their struggle against the heresies that would have weakened or dissolved the new personal meeting point.

Jesus' own statements of the unity he effected between God and men were exceedingly simple: 'as thou, Father, art in me, and I in thee, so also may they be in us'; 'I in them and thou in me' (John 17:21, 23). The New Testament accepted this person as an incarnation event where the heavenly and the earthly met in a unique union once and for all; this was where the divine had entered into the human in ontological fashion, and this in return was the 'break in the natural order' where the human could make the transition to the divine realm. Again the new religion fulfilled the widespread efforts to secure a meeting with the gods, and again did so through a person rather than a place.

8.2.3 *As microcosm*

Temples and sacred cities had often attempted to present an earthly microcosm of the cosmic dwellings of the gods, and their iconic images went further in seeking to supply a likeness of the gods themselves; in some cases even the temple building may have been intended as a theomorphic representation of the divinities, as seems possible in the neolithic temples of Malta, where the ground plan resembles the shapes of the gods as found in their images.[9]

The New Testament understanding of Jesus went beyond these categories. He was in no sense a representation of a heavenly realm or dwelling, nor was he a mere reflection, replica or copy of the godhead itself. Language is constantly strained in the attempt to declare that he shared in the very being of God, that he was theomorphic in the fullest or ontological sense, even though the doctrine of the Trinity had not yet been developed. So the Epistle to the Hebrews speaks of him as 'the Son who is the effulgence of God's splendour and the stamp of God's very being' (1:3); or Paul asserts that 'in him the complete being of God came to dwell' and that 'He is the image of the invisible God' (Colossians 1:19, 15; see also I Corinthians 11:7; II Corinthians 4:4). The word εἰκών (eikoon), translated as image, 'far from emphasizing... the unreality or the derivative nature of the image as compared with that of the original, signifies on the contrary that the image is an authentic and adequate expression of the original; in the image the thing itself is made present, manifest, visible. Thus, Christ is the image of God.'[10]

Other Greek words are used where the relationship is only that of a reflection or replica: thus in Hebrews 8:5 the term suggests 'the inadequate shadowy reflection of one thing by another' in a derivative way, and in James 3:9 where man is made 'in the image of God', the word ὁμοίωσις (homoioosis) 'expresses a likeness, a close relationship, which is not, however, an identity of substance'.[11]

The fuller meaning of image, including identity of substance, is most commonly expressed in the Christological title 'Son of God' which is used some hundred times. As John's Gospel puts it, 'No one has ever seen God; but God's only Son, He who is nearest to the Father's heart, He has made Him known' (1:18). Jesus himself is reported to have indicated this same unity: 'Anyone who has seen me has seen the Father' (John 14:9).

It might appear, therefore, that the function of the temple as microcosm is not fulfilled by Christ the new temple, and this is true as far as his divine nature is concerned. The distinction between microcosm and macrocosm did not apply. It was otherwise, however, with respect to his human nature, for the New Testament is equally emphatic as to his genuine humanity: 'God... sending His own Son in a form like that of our own sinful nature' (Romans 8:3); 'Christ Jesus... assuming the nature of a slave. Bearing the human likeness, revealed in human shape, He humbled himself, and... accepted even death' (Philippians 2:5-8); 'One who, because of His likeness to us, has been tested in every way, only without sin' (Hebrew 4:15). Again there is a title in the New Testament, 'Son of Man'; whatever else it may also mean, it at least indicates an actual human life terminated in the inevitable human way by death.

In many religious traditions to be human was to share in the analogy between man or his body, the temple or the house, and the cosmos or world, with the first two forms as microcosms of the last. This comprehensive analogy can be traced in oriental and primitive thought[12] and in Jewish legends;[13] we have also observed Paul's view of man as temple (e.g. I Corinthians 3:16; 6:19). The same idea is found in the biblical understanding of man as made in the image of God, and sufficiently akin to the divine for an incarnation to be possible. On the other hand, the word for image in Genesis 1:26-27 was also commonly used for heathen idols and so did not indicate anything of identity, as when Christ was called the image of God. There is the same limitation when James speaks of 'our fellowmen who are made in God's likeness' (3:9), for the word used is ὁμοίωσις, a mere likeness.

Jesus in his humanity was therefore also an image or likeness, in this different sense of being a microcosm of God. Further, he was the only member of the human race who could be thus described, for the biblical view is that the image of God in man has been defaced or distorted (some would say entirely lost) so that he is only partly human or subhuman. The whole divine exercise called 'salvation' was directed to the restoration of the full image of God in men, and this was done by establishing one pioneer instance in the person of Jesus Christ: 'For God knew his own... and ordained that they should be shaped to the likeness of his Son' (Romans 8:29). Men were therefor exhorted to 'put on the new nature, which is being constantly renewed in the image of its Creator and brought to know God' (Colossians 3:10).

A view of religious history now emerges in which men had been sufficiently aware of their own limitations and failures as over against the gods to seek the microcosm of the divine in their temples and images rather than in themselves. But even in their temples and idols there remained a sense of inadequacy or contingency that prevented any 'Luciferian confusion' between the human construction and the divine reality, and led the more sensitive and thoughtful to a critique of such sacred places. Now, in the event of this new person-as-temple, man's capacity to be an image or microcosm of the divine had been restored in the one perfect 'new temple'. The formulations of the later Christian Councils had therefore, of necessity, to preserve not only the indissoluble union between the human and divine natures of Christ (in order to maintain his function as meeting point), but also to insist on the distinction between them, without confusing the one with the other, so that he might also serve as microcosm or human image of the divine.

To put it yet another way: Christ was both theomorphic and anthropomorphic in the full ontological sense in each case. If we then speak of men becoming Christomorphic, we mean firstly that they become authentic men or truly anthropomorphic, as he was; but since a true anthropomorphism is itself a microcosm or reflection of the divine we also mean that they become theomorphic in the limited sense that is proper to created beings, although not in the absolute and ontological sense proper to the Son of God.

More simply, the Christian interpretation may say that in Christ we see the true pattern for earthly life, the exemplar, who at the same time also reveals the pattern of the heavenly since he is in the image of the Father. In Christ these two patterns are in the kind of full correspondence that enables the one to be the microcosm of the other, for he has restored the image of God in man. The attempt of physical images and sanctuaries to provide an earthly reflection of the divine has been fulfilled in the person who has replaced them.

8.2.4 *As immanent-transcendent presence*

As with our discussion of the immanent-transcendent presence of God in the Jerusalem temple, we find that this further function of the sacred place has been involved in our accounts of the other functions of the new temple. As centre and meeting point Jesus combined the human and divine natures in such indissoluble unity that the transcendent godhead was really present and immanent in his humanity, for this is what incarnation means. As microcosm Jesus' humanity again was in such perfect correpondence with the divine as to sustain the immanent presence of this transcendent God.

The earlier study of the Jerusalem temple included the various attempts, continuing into Jesus' day, to express the presence of Yahweh in a way that would both stress his immanence and yet preserve his transcendence: he was present in the cloud that both revealed and veiled, in his Name, in his Glory, or in later thought, through his Shekinah. The same expressions of the presence of God were taken up in the New Testament and applied to the person of Jesus.

When Jesus said 'I have come in my Father's name', 'I have made Thy name known' (John 5:43; 17:6, 26), or when he claimed to do his works 'in my Father's name' and that he had 'protected by the power of Thy name those whom Thou hast given me' (John 10:25; 17:12), he was identifying his own actions and person with the revealed presence of God in power, for this was what the name of God meant. At many points the New Testament writers apply to the name of Jesus actions or effects that anyone of Jewish background could attribute only to God. Thus men repent and are forgiven 'in the name of Jesus' (Luke 24:47; Acts 2:38; 10:43; I John 2:12); they are justified (I Corinthians 6:11) and saved (Romans 10:13), become children of God (John 1:12; I John 3:23; 5:13), and possess eternal life (Acts 20:13), all 'in the name of Jesus'. Whereas the proper name of God, Yahweh, had become sacred beyond utterance for a Jew, who replaced it by the term Lord, the New Testament knew no such inhibition; on the contrary it identified this personal name, Jesus, with the same Lord so that the earliest Christian confession was simply that 'Jesus is Lord'. For the Christian community this name, therefore, was 'the name above all names, that at the name of Jesus every knee should bow... and every tongue confess "Jesus is Lord"' (Philippians 2:9,10). The term Lord was used indiscriminately of both God and Jesus because he was the presence, the Name, of the Father, and in him the presence was immanent without ceasing to be transcendent.

The term glory for the active and radiant presence of God was likewise transferred to Jesus. In Paul's own experience the vision of Jesus had taken the same form as visions of God in the Old Testament, so that the glory of Christ was the same as the glory of God (Acts 22:6-8; cf. Stephen's vision in Acts 7:55). For him the message he thereafter preached was 'the gospel of the glory of Christ, who is the very image of God ... the revelation of the glory of God in the face of Jesus Christ' (II Corinthians 4:4, 6). In our account of Luke's views on Jesus and the temple we observed the gradual transference of emphasis from the temple to Jesus as the place where the glory of God was present; the temple was really the place of the glory or the presence only when Jesus was there. Luke's version of the transfiguration episode shows the same heightening of emphasis upon the glory belonging to the person of Jesus, and it has been suggested that he goes beyond the accounts of Matthew and Mark in the same way when he describes the ascension of Jesus.[14] It is John's Gospel, however, that emphasizes Jesus' manifestation of the glory of God on earth for those who can recognize Him (John 11:40). He possessed it before the world was created (17:5), and when 'the Word became flesh ... we saw His glory, such glory as befits the Father's only Son' (1:14). This glory shows Jesus to be sent by God (11:4), and is itself revealed when Jesus performs the miracles which John regards as 'signs' (2:11; 11:4,40); in fact, Jesus and God share in the glory that both reveals and yet hides the godhead (13:31-32). The glory that once was the presence in the temple is now present with its same immanence and transcendence in a person.

Very similar to glory is the rabbinic term *Shekinah* for the presence of God who dwelt among men without surrendering his trancendent nature, and we have seen that this was applied not only to presence in the temple but even more commonly to God's presence in any community of his people gathered for the study of the Law or for prayer. This maxim was so familiar that Jesus was inevitably identifying himself with the *Shekinah* when he said: 'For where two or three are gathered together in my name, there am I in the midst of them' (Matthew 18:20). In the light of this identification we can understand the claim to be 'greater than the Temple' (Matthew 12:6), which the author of this Gospel proceeds to explain as due to the Spirit or presence of God with Jesus (12:18). The point is reinforced by the incident Matthew places immediately afterwards, where the Pharisees said it was not God's Spirit, but that of Beelzebub, by which Jesus had healed the blind and dumb man; to which Jesus replied with a specific claim to the Spirit of God (12:24,28). This, too, was to assert that God was present in Jesus' action.

The transcendence of the God who was thus present is forcefully declared in many ways in the New Testament. Paul described Jesus as 'the image of the invisible God' (Colossians 1:15), and John asserted that 'God has never been seen by any man' (I John 4:12). Jesus frequently referred to having been 'sent' and to having to return whence he came, thus maintaining the Old Testament understanding of Yahweh 'visiting' his people rather than dwelling in their midst in his entirety. Yet John was equally emphatic that 'the eternal life which dwelt with the Father was made visible to us. What we have seen and heard we declare to you...' (I John 1:2-3). Likewise Paul, without contradicting his previous assertion, continued with the complementary statement that 'in him the complete being of God, by God's own choice, came to dwell... embodied' (Colossians 1:19; 2:9). The fully transcendent had become fully immanent in the one particular person where human nature was capable of this conjunction.

The further dimensions of Jesus Christ are strongly indicated in what the New Testament says about his pre-existence, incarnation, self-consciousness, death, resurrection and ascension, and his return to unite the whole cosmic order. The extent to which transcendent deity was immanent is seen in the incognito of the incarnation, in the complete historical particularity of the event, where 'the Divine is completely concealed in history. Nothing about the physiology, psychology, or the "culture" of Jesus gives one any glimpse of God the Father.... But, in reality, this "historical event" constituted by the existence of Jesus is a total theophany; what it presents is like an audacious effort to *save the historical event* in itself, by endowing it with the maximum of being.'[15] As with the other functions of Jesus Christ as new temple, this seemingly paradoxical dual function was also at stake in the subsequent creedal controversies. Finally Chalcedon affirmed that being ὁμόουσιος (homoousios) with respect to both God and man he was able to sustain both poles of God's presence.

The attempt to combine immanence and transcendence in their understanding of the presence of God has, as we have seen, preserved religions in general from crude literal idolatries and has helped to maintain a personal spiritual relation between the worshipper and the divinity. This attempt has, however, been under constant tension so that man's religious life has oscillated between high withdrawn gods devoid of local presence or concern, and a range of lesser divinities or spirits that were immanent enough but where the full dimension, power, and value of the divine had been attenuated. The New Testament and later interpretation of Jesus was that here in this person-as-new-temple the problem had been resolved, and the immanence and transcendence of deity combined in a way that not only consummated previous attempts but superseded them by the perfection and permanence with which it performed what they had sought to do.

8.3 THE TENT OF MEETING IN THE NEW TESTAMENT

In the first part of this study we examined the very different type of sacred place represented by the tabernacle or tent, and discovered that although it failed to achieve any historical development it nevertheless remained to haunt the temple tradition as the symbol of another form of divine presence. A brief reference must now be made to the reappearance of the tabernacle in New Testament thought, where it still performs a symbolic or typological function. We have seen the use Stephen made of the tabernacle as historically opposed to the temple, and as perhaps prefiguring the new kind of worship associated with Jesus that would replace the Jerusalem cult. Paul, even while using the temple metaphor for the Christian community, interprets it by a tabernacle reference from Leviticus 26:11-12: 'I will live in them and move among them' (as in II Corinthians 6:16). The tabernacle as ultimate prototype appears again in Revelation (15:5; 21:3,22), and indicates something of the form of the new worship where there is to be no temple. Although 'the Apocalypse sometimes mentions a "tent of meeting" at the same time and with the same meaning as "temple", it is... to recall the exodus on the one hand, and so to demonstrate the continuity of God's... dwelling among his people from the time of the exodus, in the earthly Jerusalem, in the Church, and finally in heaven; and on the other hand, it is because the oracles of God were revealed in the tent of meeting and now his judgments are pronounced from within his heavenly temple.'[16]

In discussing the Old Testament traditions focussed on the ark and the tent von Rad has drawn attention to the relative positions they occupy in the New Testament. The ark is seldom mentioned and then only in passing (Hebrews 9:4; Revelation 11:19), but the term for tent, and its derivatives, 'become once more expressions of the most profound theological insights.... The theology of the tent found... the fulfilment which was prophesied for it in the earliest times: here God speaks to men "as a man speaks to his friend".'[17]

This fulfilment is clearly what John has in mind when he opens his Gospel with the statement about the Word becoming flesh and dwelling among us (1:14). Literally translated, the verb for 'dwell' would be: 'set up or planted his tent, or camped' among us. John chose a word that recalled the way God was with his people in the tabernacle period under Moses. The implication is that now God is once more tabernacling with his people, but this time it is by his dwelling in Jesus among them, although Jesus is not actually called the new tabernacle.[18] The same identification is implied in the various accounts of the transfiguration of Jesus on the mountain, where the construction of the shelters Peter proposed is repudiated, and the shining cloud that covers Jesus shows where the new tabernacle is.

The New Testament, therefore, readily turns back to the ancient and undeveloped tradition of the tent of meeting which stood for an intimate and direct relationship between God and man, a relationship that was dynamic and personal rather than static and ritual. As such it was preparatory for the personalized transformation of the sacred place found in Jesus and the New Testament writers. Our earlier study showed how 'the idea of the presence dwelling in a place had begun to give way even in the Old Testament to the idea of the presence living in a person. But this personifying of the presence image of Old Testament faith took place fully in the person of Jesus Christ.... The tabernacle of the Old Testament as the place of the presence is the principal bridgehead in the Old Testament to the doctrine of the Incarnation.'[19] Thus the radical replacement of the temple by the person was mediated by the tabernacle tradition.

8.4 THE TRANSITION FROM PLACE TO PERSON AND ITS SYMBOL

The absolute and final nature of Jesus' replacement of the physical and spatial form of the sanctuary is dramatically expressed in the synoptic gospels' accounts of the rending of the temple veil on the day of Jesus' death. Whether the veil referred to was the inner veil protecting the Holy of Holies or the outer curtain between the vestibule and the Holy Place will affect only the detail of the symbolism: either the way to God's presence is now open for all, or else the whole temple, starting with its outer curtain, is to be destroyed. It seems to us that the overall symbolic meaning is much the same: the temple cult is ended. Mark's Gospel differs from the other accounts in concentrating attention upon the cross, and linking it closely with the rending of the veil and the conversion of the Roman centurion in charge of the crucifixion (Mark 15:37-39). Whatever the historicity of these last two events there could hardly be a causal connection between them, so that the conjunction is 'symbolic and interpretative ... the evangelist's way of telling his readers that the death of Jesus which he had already depicted as sacrificial means forgiveness and salvation for mankind. The destruction of the veil stands for the removal of what hides the face of God from mankind ... the barrier in the temple of Jerusalem but ... much more as well.'[20]

The rending of the temple veil is so intimately associated with the death of Christ because it is a vivid sign of the new order that was being inaugurated by this event at the heart of Christ's work. This new era was bringing to an end all that the temple stood for, which was more than the Jewish cult alone, for it represented the whole system of specially sacred places as found in man's religious history. Christ could do this because in his own person and function he now did for God and for men all that the temple type of holy place had sought to do in its own way. If we hold the view that the phenomenology of religion is concerned to discover the essence of all religious manifestations, then the New Testament events and their interpretation are of the utmost importance for phenomenological study. Here the essential functions of all sacred places were manifest in a new way, for it was believed that Jesus Christ fulfilled these functions more truly than any temple ever did; it was, then, no mere literary metaphor to speak of Jesus Christ-in-his-community as the temple of God, but an ontological statement in which the meaning of the word temple was at last laid bare. The rent veil was a sign that, as the Epistle to the Hebrews would put it, the earlier shadowy forms were of no further value now that the full reality was here.

This new and true temple was not tied to a single place, and operated not through holy objects but through personal relationships within a community, using only everyday things such as bread and wine, and an upstairs room in an ordinary house, any house. Since the resurrection and ascension this Jesus Christ had been freed from the spatial and temporal limitations of human life in this world, and continued his temple functions in his risen existence and through his community the Church, although this was still tied to times and places, and we shall have to reckon with this fact at a later stage. The sacred place was now where Christ was, and the conditions for finding and entering it were the conditions for apprehending Christ and being incorporated in his community.

We are now in a better position to understand the question raised earlier, why the biblical revolution in the religious use of space had to await the incarnation, and why, in spite of certain prefigurings in the tent of meeting, the temple had perforce to remain as the Jewish sanctuary and then suffer an abrogation. We also understand why Jesus bequeathed no sanctuaries, altars, sacred objects, nor any plans or instructions for these from which his followers might design a church building and its contents; nor does any legend giving dominical warrant for later Christian constructions of these objects appear to have developed.[21] There is only one instance in the gospels of Jesus deliberately choosing a place of assembly for a special religious purpose, and that was the upper room in a private house, where he also gave new shape and meaning to the traditional communal meal that was to become so important in Christian worship.

This setting of worship in the place of everyday life was matched by a similar transformation in the nature of the language employed about worship in the New Testament. A study of this question

> has shown that the New Testament uses neither *latreia* (Hebrews 9:16) nor *threskeia* (Acts 26:5) nor *sebasma* (Acts 17:23; 18:13) nor

even *leitourgia* (Hebrews 9:21, where it is used for service in the Old Testament sense...), forsakes cultic vocabulary altogether and uses terms from everyday life *sunagesthai* (Matthew 18:20; I Corinthians 5:4) or *en ekklesia sunerchesthai* (I Corinthians 11:18,20). These are the terms which cover most adequately what we mean today by worship or the 'Service'. It is significant that for a long period the Eucharist was actually called the Synaxis, until the word gradually gave way to the cultic term 'liturgy'. The only other phrase used by the New Testament for what we would call worship or the 'Service' is 'the breaking of bread'... again not a cultic word but a household word.[22]

Both place of worship and the language had been transposed from cultic to everyday domestic forms as the proper instruments for the new temple as person-in-community.

Let it be said at this point that the new way did not displace the old because the latter was evil, unspiritual and material but because, in spite of all its virtues, it was inadequate. One of these virtues was that it had on occasion inspired men to look beyond itself for a more satisfying expression of what it sought to do. This outreach had been conspicuous in the people of Israel, but not confined to them, and when the new form emerged from their particular religious history it claimed to satisfy the needs of all men. As Eliade has put it, in commenting on the universal 'accessibility' of Christianity: this development in Jesus Christ, 'although in the eyes of the alien observer it looks like a local history, is also en exemplary history, because it takes up and perfects these trans-temporal images'.[23] Christ in his community was now the exemplar of the temple across all times and all peoples.

8.5 NON-SACRED PLACES OF WORSHIP: THE MEETING ROOM

If the central revelation with which the New Testament is concerned had been a hierophany or theophany then we could have expected the addition of yet one more geographical sacred place to mark the spot where it occurred. Even if it had been simply an incarnation there might have been a burial place with ensuing tomb, shrine and pilgrimage in the manner usual in religions. Since it was an incarnation followed by a resurrection and an ascension there was no such development. Thus 'it is enormously significant that when the disciples come to Jesus' tomb to perform acts of traditional piety, they find it broken and empty. The doctrines of the Resurrection and the Ascension deal the final blow to any Christian ... deference to one place more than another.'[24] Any grave must surely have been known and become a sanctuary, and it is remarkable that even the site of the sepulchre where Jesus was entombed is uncertain. It is true that places allegedly associated with the birth, life and death of Jesus have become holy places for Christians, but the New Testament shows no such interest, and it is questionable whether these later developments as they have come to be understood and used are authentic Christian forms.

It is plain that for the New Testament holiness applies to persons and actions and not to things and places. When Jesus blessed bread or wine the real object of blessing was the people to whom these ministered through the whole action in which they played a part. Not a holy place, but a holy people sanctified through their union with the person who was the new sanctuary for both God and men, that is the New Testament position; in consequence the Church is always the community of Christ and never the place or building where it meets.

That there was a precedent for a non-sacred place of meeting for worship we have seen in our study of the synagogue as a new form in the history of religions; its pattern of worship definitely influenced early Christian practice, and it would be surprising if its nature as an ordinary unconsecrated meeting room did not encourage Christians to feel satisfied with their use of private houses for their assemblies. This was where they foregathered for their prayer and praise, 'breaking bread' and common meals. If there was any model that might consciously have been followed it would be the 'upper room' which Jesus had chosen, and where he had given the new meaning to this breaking of bread together. In Acts 20:7-8 we read of the Church meeting for these purposes in exactly such an upper room, but too much store must not be set by the 'upper' location nor indeed by the domestic setting itself; there was an inevitability about both features — where else could a larger assembly gather but in the only large room, the dining room on the top floor of the usual several-storied family house?

At the same time such a place for worship was completely congruent with the transformation Jesus had wrought.[25] The very nature of this room in an ordinary dwelling house, with no more sanctity about it than any other room in any other house in Jerusalem, threw the emphasis on to that nucleus of the holy people of God who themselves were only sanctified insofar as they were united with the Holy One of God in their midst. In spite of its inevitability, perhaps even because of it, we find here the beginnings of the authentically Christian place of worship that shared with the synagogue the significance of making a new departure in the history of religions. If certain modern Buddhist or Hindu movements have erected halls or chapels for congregational purposes, or if Sikh 'temples' may follow the same pattern, these are not characteristic of religion before the Judaeo-Christian development and will almost certainly be found to reflect the influence of the latter or of its kindred movement in Islam.

This new phenomenological form we propose to call the meeting room, or in its larger manifestations, the meeting house, and within the Christian tradition use the term *domus ecclesiae* in contrast to the *domus dei* represented by the temple. It is of the essence of this new form that the room itself has no special sanctity. It is quite different from those other forms of household religion focussed on a domestic shrine; in early Roman and ancient Vedic religion this was the only or most important sanctuary, and even where temples have multiplied the domestic altar or images have often retained their place. These, however, were sacred places in the same tradition as the temple and in no sense akin to the meeting room.

The position we have now reached is that the domestic house as the place of worship in the first Christian century embodied a new form in the history of religions, and provided a norm for this new tradition. This norm lay not in making a private house mandatory, but in setting the sanctuary free from bondage to particular holy places and buildings and locating it in the Christ-centred life of a community meeting wherever was most convenient. The house-church of early Christianity then becomes permanently significant, and can no longer be regarded as an unfortunate necessity, forced upon the early Church by the social or legal disabilities under which it laboured, and to be discarded for a 'proper church building' as soon as circumstances permitted. Some recovered recognition of this lasting significance is to be found in the house-church movement that has developed out of pastoral concern in recent times. It is our contention that there is also a liturgical, architectural, and theological significance that awaits a more thorough exploration, and this will engage us increasingly as we proceed to an examination of church building through the subsequent Christian centuries, together with a briefer study of further developments in the synagogue of Judaism and in the mosques of Islam.

PART TWO

Historical Application
Phenomenological Analysis of Places of Worship in the Semitic Religions

9

Churches in the Early Christian Centuries

'With the rise and spread of the Gospel, Christian architecture was born. This architecture was clearly something new, and it had its own unmistakeable characteristics. Yet it was not alien to its environment....'[1] With these words Cardinal Lercaro commenced his opening address to the Roman Catholic conference on sacred architecture at Bologna in 1955. Our enquiries so far suggest that if church architecture is governed by the effect of Jesus Christ upon sacred space then it ought to be something new and unmistakeable. Whether in fact it has been so is the question to which we now turn as we examine the history of the Christian place of worship.

As tools for historical analysis we now have the two phenomenological forms, the *domus dei* in its original physical sense rather than in its transformed personalized nature, and the *domus ecclesiae* or meeting room which serves the practical needs of the new temple that, in the Christian understanding, is Jesus-in-community. Since only the first of these forms is a sacred place we speak of them together as places of worship, or as religious buildings.

It will make for greater clarity if we state in advance the conclusions to which the following historical studies will lead. Our thesis is that when the authentic Christian conception, the *domus ecclesiae* that emerges from study of biblical religion, is applied to the study of church building we find that only limited use has been made of it in Christian history, and that the *domus dei* patterns have remained exceedingly influential. In particular, it appears that circumstances prevented the development of authentically Christian forms both in the early formative centuries, and again at the creative period of the sixteenth century, but that a new combination of circumstances in the later twentieth century may yet provide the first major opportunity in history for the development of a distinctively Christian place of worship. We are concerned, therefore, not so much with the technological, architectural or aesthetic aspects of churches as with their religious design and significance.*

9.1 WORSHIP IN A DOMESTIC SETTING

As we have already seen the Christian community began its own meetings in the private houses belonging to its members or friends, and continued to do so when it spread into other countries. The names of some of these have been recorded: Aquila and Prisca at Ephesus, Nymphas at Laodicea, and Philemon at Colossae.[2] For two centuries such house-churches were the home of the new religion, and on occasion part or even all of the house was adapted by internal alterations to make it more suitable for a growing congregation or for their peculiar activities. The reasons why no special buildings appeared are obvious enough: the Christians in any one place were usually not numerous and belonged on the whole to the poorer classes; local hostility was common and outbreaks of violence or of official persecution occurred from time to time until the early fourth century, so that there was every incentive to maintain an inconspicuous existence; and finally, the house-church was entirely congruent with the teaching of Jesus and with the community's own understanding of itself as a new spiritual temple that abrogated the Jerusalem temple and all such sacred places.

One of the most interesting and complete examples of a domestic dwelling adapted as a Christian meeting house has been discovered at Dura-Europos in Syria. This was built as a house early in the third century and adapted in 231 for communal use by the removal of an internal wall in order to provide a single room large enough for some fifty people. This was probably the main place of assembly, and a smaller room opening off it may have accommodated the catechumens or been used for the Lord's Supper and other meals; another room seems to

---

* Readers may find it helpful at this point to turn to the last three paragraphs of ch. 16.8, also 17.1 as further explanations of the method being pursued in Part II.

have been for baptisms and a fourth used as a sacristy. All these were located around the usual open court or atrium of a dwelling house; not far away a similar house had been used as a synagogue.

These domestic meeting places continued in use in Rome and elsewhere at least until late in the fourth century, and indeed have been found in all ages in Christian history, wherever the community was small and poor and on occasion when it was neither. At Lullingstone Park, near Enysford in Kent, excavations have revealed the remains of a Roman-type villa where the rooms on the north corner seem to have been sealed off from the rest of the house and provided with their own entrance so that they became an independent unit for use by others in the neighbourhood apart from the family. The rooms suggest a vestibule, an ante-chamber that may have been used by the catechumens, a chapel and a sacristy, and the walls were decorated with Christian symbols. About 380 the villa may have been abandoned as a residence, but the church portion may have continued in use for another twenty years. Even as late as this 'the only centres of Christianity in the country would be the semi-private chapels of Christian villa-owners'.[3]

With the growth and organization of the community many of these house-churches assumed a wide range of functions and acquired further rooms in the domestic complex, especially in the larger houses of wealthier members or the many-storied multi-roomed tenement buildings of a city like Rome. Rooms were required not only for worship, with perhaps special accommodation for the eucharist and for baptisms, but also for catechetical and charitable purposes, for the residence of ministers, for administration, meetings, social gatherings, as a library and as a reliquary, as a school, and as a hospice for the sick or the indigent, or for travelling Christians. Such a church had become what would in our times be called a Christian community centre, and had ceased to be a mere annexe within a private house.[4]

Where these many purposes could not be served by buying and altering existing domestic property, or where numbers were too large, the first Christian buildings were specially erected, but usually still in a domestic or very simple style. The first may even have been within a century of the death of Christ, by a bishop east of the Tigris between 123-136 A.D., and another was recorded as destroyed by a flood in the early Christian kingdom of Edessa in 201. In the third century there must have been many of these buildings for they are reported from widely different parts of the empire, with over forty in Rome itself by the turn of the century. These were still mainly in domestic architectural traditions, for public architecture in third century Rome carried pagan connotations derived from the gods of the State, the worship of the emperor, or the newer saviour cults; in one way or another palace or forum, assembly or army drill hall, temple or sanctuary of a religious sect, all these led back to the *domus dei* idea.

At the same time there are signs of the influence of the temple tradition, or at least of the human inclinations that lead in that direction, in the later third and early fourth centuries. In 265 the bishop of Antioch was demanding more impressive accommodation, furniture and ceremonies — he wanted an audience chamber, together with a throne on a dais in the worship hall, and acclamations upon his entry; a large church hall of St. Crisogono in Rome very early in the fourth century had a facade with three arched openings; internally and externally these developments identified the church with public buildings such as basilicas, and its leaders with the magistrates who officiated in them. Tending in the same direction were the spacious forecourt, the three doorways, the cedar ceilings, delicate carvings, and mosaic pavements of the new church opened at Tyre in 314, or the wealth of golden, silver and bronze utensils confiscated by imperial officials from the house-church at the small North African town of Cirta in 303. Such attention to the building and its appurtenances was out of harmony with the spirit of the *domus ecclesiae*, although this remained the style of the Church in general until it made its peace with the Roman Empire under Constantine in 313.

9.2 BACK TO THE *DOMUS DEI*

The situation of the Church was profoundly changed by this epochal event and all that ensued from it, and this change was nowhere more manifest than in the great wave of church building that then commenced. Buildings that had been confiscated or destroyed in the recent persecutions were now restored or rebuilt with state assistance, and the emperor himself is recorded as having built nine new churches in Rome, many more in Constantinople that became his new capital, and scores elsewhere in the empire, including many at biblical sites in Palestine. The standards and the general basilican design were already set by imperial palaces and state public buildings, and some of his great churches were magnificent, even sumptuous edifices with marble columns, gilded ceilings, mosaic pavements, carved rails and expensive screens; as he put it himself in his instructions for the church at Mamre in Palestine, they were to be 'worthy of my generosity and worthy of the catholic and apostolic church'.[5]

All this was outside the control of the Church itself, but had an inevitable effect upon it. The *domus ecclesiae* in the modest forms it still assumed was now too small for the swiftly growing membership, and for the increase in functions and in formalities associated with its new relation to the state. There was opportunity for something of more prestige, dignity and visibility, in keeping with the contributions of Constantine and with the new future emerging for the Christian religion, 'a new architecture of a higher order, public in character, resplendent in material, and spacious in layout'.[6] It is not surprising that the word *ecclesia*, which up till the third century had signified the Christian community at worship, was now applied to the church building; this had assumed an importance independent of the Christian community or its traditional needs, and had begun to make its own public testimony to the Christian God, in complete contrast to the previous desire for security through a quite obscure building.

The house-church in any of its developments provided little architectural guidance in this new situation. Synagogues supplied no model, for they too belonged to an unpopular minority group that had in addition been a rival of the Christians, and were also in the meeting house tradition that now seemed inadequate. It was inconceivable that pagan temples should have been copied, and these were in any case passing into obsolescence. In looking elsewhere for the ancestry of the new churches many possibilities have been canvassed. J. G. Davies has provided a critical survey of some eight types of building in the Graeco-Roman world that might have contributed the essential features; after considering the schola, cemetery chapels, private houses, imperial throne rooms, and various types of basilica he concludes that the Christian buildings derived from the civil basilican plan of a rectangular building arranged internally about its longitudinal axis.[7]

This was a flexible and comparatively simple form already put to a wide range of uses in Rome, in forums, palaces, baths, markets, law courts, reception rooms, etc.. It was basically a large meeting hall with a timber roof, usually terminating in a rectangular or apsidal tribunal. It was easily adapted for Christian worship, and indeed its functions in Roman civic use were often not so different from those of the larger Christian meeting houses. From the public point of view the Christian basilica was but one more species of the 'monumental public meeting halls with religious overtones' that had already been borrowed by some of the other new religions. This form of church, with the Christian variants to which it lent itself, became the usual place of worship built from the third century onwards, and was distributed throughout the Roman Empire; in fact, this 'Constantinian Christian architecture turned out to be the last phase of the architecture of Late Antiquity'.[8]

This civil basilica has its own architectural ancestry, which Davies finds in the Greek temple:

> The ... civil basilica preserves the central axis and main features of narrow oblong Greek ναός or temple. At Rome ... there was one single building that exercised a predominant influence on architectural style and that was the *curia oblongata*, the meeting hall of the senate, which was little else than a Greek ναός with a narrow facade ... and so the Christian basilica can be classified as a direct descendant of the civil basilica, itself deriving from the Greek temple.[9]

The basilican church remained the characteristic design in Western Christianity for a thousand years, but in the East it was replaced by the rise in the sixth century of a different type marked by a central vertical axis concluding in a vaulted and domed stone roof, instead of the pitched and gabled wooden roof of the west. This gave rise to the characteristic churches of Eastern or Orthodox Christendom where the basic structural unit is a square surmounted by a dome; with many variations this spread through the Balkans and Russia, ousted the basilica and became the dominant form in the East for over a thousand years, and even influenced the mosque builders of Western Asia. The largest and most famous, though not quite typical, example of these churches still stands as the Church of Sancta Sophia, or Hagia Sophia, in Istanbul, dedicated in 537.

The central axis plan had long been familiar in the Christian martyria, the small buildings erected over a site made sacred by some event connected with the life and death of Christ or by the burial of one of the martyrs. These became shrines at sacred places, and therefore very much in the older tradition that culminated in the *domus dei*, and remote from anything like a meeting house as found in Christian practice. As for the structural form of dome and square, Davies asserts that at least one of its main forms, 'the cross-in-square is closely connected with certain types of temple which are to be found in the region to the south east of the Mediterranean...'.[10] In northern Mesopotamia and Anatolia there are also smaller groups of churches showing different forms again, with transverse naves, side doors, and the beginnings of western towers; and of one of these groups Davies is able to say that the 'plan derives directly from Assyrian and Babylonian temples', and others show Hittite influence.[11]

It is somewhat surprising to discover that the temple plan which was so decisively rejected in the first Christian century has reappeared as the dominant architectural inheritance and influence in the first great age of church building, from the fourth to the sixth centuries, both in the basilicas of the West and the centralized structures of the East. This was not necessarily disastrous, for the basilican form itself was already widely used for purposes primarily secular, and the Christian faith has baptized many a pagan feature into its own life; indeed this might be said to have occurred already wherever the new churches developed a complex of ancillary rooms around the main worship space to accommodate the varied activities of the house-church — the whole might still be called a *domus ecclesiae*, even though there was something more like a *domus dei* in its midst![12]

It was probably the uses to which the new churches were put, the forms of worship and church life, and especially the influence of funerary practices that determined which of these two models was to mark the subsequent development of church buildings; on the other hand, while the architectural inheritance might have been adapted to the *domus ecclesiae*, it also lent itself easily to the building of churches that were temple-like rather than meeting houses. If the new Christian movement had been free to express its needs architecturally from the beginning it might have developed the new domestic form in a distinctive way that would have made visible its radical departure from the temple tradition. Historical circumstances did not allow this, so that the first Christian architecture, when ultimately it did become possible, has been described as 'a final expression of the architectural concepts which were dominant in the Eastern Mediterranean centres and coastal areas of the Late Roman world'.[13]

9.3 FUNERARY INFLUENCES

Burial places have been intimately associated with religion since prehistoric times and form one of the characteristic sacred places of most religious traditions. Death as a kind of rebirth has naturally been associated with the sanctuary, the place which is the creative centre, the source of reality and of life. Although 'the grave is... the symbol of separation between the dead and the living'... 'turning it into a shrine for the living-dead [i.e. the ancestors] converts it into the point of meeting between the two worlds'.[14] This was written of the Abaluyia people of East Africa and applies to a very simple shrine, but evidence for the derivation of the most elaborate temples from tombs can be adduced for the Hittite and Egyptian[15] religions, for Buddhism, and for many other religious areas. The tomb of the ancestor, the chief or king, the culture hero, or the holy man becomes a place of commemoration and of communion on the part of the living, and then of pilgrimage; in the course of time it assumes the form of a simple shrine and may finally become a temple.

It is not surprising to find this same mode of thought continued in the early Christian Church, with its strong belief in the resurrection and in the 'communion of saints'. While this developed especially around the burial places of their own heroes, the martyrs and the especially holy members they regarded as saints, it began even earlier for their ordinary members. This was merely in continuation of the general practice of the community at large, whereby visits for memorial meals were paid to the tomb at various intervals after the burial, as on the third, ninth, and thirtieth days, and then annually on the date of the deceased person's burial or birthday. Christians had their own variations on the pattern, and similar customs are to be found among Christians in parts of West Africa today. Practical provision for the memorial meal ranged from a simple table at the tomb to provision for preparing the meal and even something like a dining room.

The larger number attracted to the grave of a martyr than to a family tomb, together with the increasing desire of Christians to be buried near the martyr, increased the need for some kind of shrine structure. 'This would be the origin of the martyrium. Such places had no priesthood, for there was no congregation. There was no altar, only a table (*mensa*) placed near the martyr's grave as well as other tables for the remaining dead. Architecturally, the martyrium had a central plan rather than a rectilinear plan....'[16] Although not erected for worship, as the funerary banquets became memorial eucharists and the annual feast days for the martyrs of the whole Church were regularised and increased in number these martyria became in effect places of worship; but they were still within the pagan funerary traditions rather than expressions of the new religion.

The pagan association was heightened by the way in which the tomb shrines of saints and martyrs replaced the minor sanctuaries of local divinities, especially in country districts. It was comparatively easy to transfer the search for spiritual help from the old gods and spirits of the locality to the new 'holy ones', who would be equally concerned about their own home areas and were now influential in heaven. In parts of Asia Minor the many traditional hill-top sanctuaries of the pagan gods were replaced by the martyria of the Christian saints. The frequency of these martyria in the East was one factor in the development of the later churches with a similar central axis plan, and the ousting of the Western basilican form. It is interesting to learn of the same influence from central-plan tomb to church detected in modern times in India: the Padres Santos cemetery chapel at Lashkarpur, Agra has been described as 'an octagonal domed building, just like a fairsized Mughal tomb'.[17]

In the West, from the end of the second century, there was some de-velopment of underground chambers or catacombs for burials. These obviously provided a certain measure of security, assisted by the legal protection Roman law gave to tombs, and some funeral banquets and services were held within them. They were, however, so small, damp and dark that most memorial services were held in buildings on the surface, and especially in the open-air cemeteries that Christians acquired from the beginning of the third century. Here there were simple graves, with a funeral banquet table above, or free-standing tombs, and in between small mausolea, or open-air precincts, courtyards, loggia or roofed din-ing chambers. Where there was also a martyr's grave or a site associated with some saint, confessor or other manifestation of God's power, then the buildings assumed more monumental proportions and became a centre of pilgrimage.

The construction of funerary buildings of various forms was there-fore the first architectural activity of the early Church, apart from modification of dwellings for the house-church. When the peace of the Church arrived under Constantine a firm relationship was already es-tablished between some forms of Christian worship and funerary prac-tices closely connected with pagan thought and custom.

In the Constantinian period the same practices continued, with an in-crease in scale and monumentality due to the new freedom and wealth available. These factors, together with the great increase in numbers, the still growing cult of the martyrs and the popular desire to be buried near a martyr's grave or shrine made existing provisions inadequate. In consequence there developed a new building, the covered cemetery in simple basilican form; examples of these, dating from early in Con-stantine's rule, have been identified in recent years.[18] They lay outside the walls of Rome as it then was, in the cemetery areas, and were each associated with a martyrium, although this was a separate structure. The funeral hall itself was very large — known examples were from 80 to 104 metres long — and its floor was covered with graves. Originally it had no priesthood, no proper altar, and no congregation; it housed memorial services and funeral banquets, served from tables including a special one for the martyr; when the ceremonies concluded with the eucharist this too was served form one of these tables. In the course of the next two centuries they became arranged more like the basilican churches built in the period, and housed the ordinary worship of the suburban population around them.

It may be surprising to learn that the original St. Peter's in Rome began in this way as a covered cemetery. There was an existing shrine of St. Peter, which is the oldest known martyrium, dating from the second century and located in a cemetery outside the city. Here Constantine decided to erect a much larger building for the vast crowds of pilgrims attracted to the shrine, and to combine it with a vast funeral hall for the usual purposes of burial and of memorial services. The latter was the common basilican shape, and the former consisted of a transverse building across the end of the basilica, and projecting beyond its sides to form an overall T-plan. Had it not been for the separation from the funeral hall by an arch and rows of pillars, and the quite distinct use as a shrine-room housing the memoria of the great apostle, the whole building might have been seen as a nave with transepts at one end, although as a church form this did not appear generally in the West till some centuries later. There was no permanent altar; when the whole building was required for great occasions of worship which included the eucharist a temporary altar was set up in the martyrium section, now used as a chancel, and the congregation filled the covered cemetery portion. This was a clumsy adaption that was partly improved upon by later alterations to make it suitable as the chief church of Western Christendom until it was destroyed early in the sixteenth century.

In Palestine Constantine built a number of elaborate edifices that combined the functions of congregational worship for the local community and veneration of some sacred site associated with Christ or with Old Testament theophanies by pilgrims. Thus the basilican meeting hall was joined in various ways with a martyrium usually modelled on the traditional central-plan mausolea; the whole structure had nothing to do with burials, but shared in funerary influences through the architectural nature of the martyrium. This combination was not continued after Constantine, when martyria became separate circular shrines detached from basilican provision for a congregation.

In other parts of the Empire yet other associations of burial and congregational structures occurred. For example in the Rhineland area of Trier, where Constantine and later emperors maintained an imperial residence, ancient pagan underground burial vaults have been found with the structure extended into a chamber above ground for funeral and memorial feasts. This pattern was possibly adopted by the Christians, for the earliest churches at Trier seem to have been small and simple meeting-places above the burial vaults where the bishops were interred.[19]

Throughout the first centuries of church building there was therefore a constant association with the burial practices and funeral architecture of the pagan world that were retained in the Christian community.[20] Pagan understandings of sacred places and the buildings erected upon them, a world of thought that issued in the *domus dei* kind of sanctuary, hovered over the first Christian buildings before congregational architecture had opportunity to produce and to consolidate forms distinctive of the new faith. The basilica might well have been converted to this purpose as a *domus ecclesiae*, but there were other influences that frustrated such a simple solution, and we must examine these in some detail if we are to comprehend the peculiar situation in which the church buildings first took shape.

9.4 THE CULT OF THE SAINTS

Within this general funerary influence the special cultic practices associated with saints, confessors, and martyrs require separate attention, although their effect was on the internal arrangements and furnishings, and on the interpretation of what churches were for, rather than on the architecture of the building itself. Our previous section has indicated that any martyrium, and especially the splendid ones erected in Palestine, readily gave the site on which it stood the special status of a sacred place, where one was nearer to the divine and had more access to spiritual power than elsewhere; hence the desire to be buried there oneself, or to make pilgrimage in pursuit of special blessing. All this was in explicit denial of the New Testament revolution, and depreciated what occurred in the ordinary congregational meeting houses.

The inadequate holiness of the latter was soon remedied, and by various means. One of these was the development already noted whereby a basilican type of funeral hall associated with a nearby martyrium, or even incorporating such a shrine in its own overall structure, came to be used as the regular congregational church; it could then claim to be a specially sacred church and to attract people from a distance.

Where the church did not have this initial advantage the desired effect was secured in another way. There had been an association between tombs and the altar table through the celebrations of the eucharist that concluded some of the memorial services; on occasion the stone slab covering the sarcophagus had been used as a table, as in the cramped conditions of the catacombs, although more often a separate table would be set up. In the open-air cemeteries this was of stone rather than of wood as in the house-churches. There existed therefore an association between tomb, stone table, and the eucharist.

In the fifth century buildings designed as churches and not as funeral halls came to be erected over the grave or relics of a martyr, and it was natural that the grave should remain associated with the table for the eucharist which was stationed above it, and like the tomb itself was also of stone. Where a church had not been built over an existing martyrium strenuous efforts were made to secure relics of a saint or martyr and to deposit them in a reliquary under the altar, and so to secure the the same result. Popular demand was such that fictive instead of real relics were sometimes employed, and Church Councils decreed that every altar must have its relics.[21] Originally these were deposited in a separate chamber under the altar, but in later practice they were placed in the body of the altar or in a cavity called a sepulchre in the table slab; thus the altar had become also a tomb, where the death and beneficial presence of the martyr physically represented by the relics was associated with the death of Christ and his presence. This presence came to be identified with the consecrated elements, so that when the elements were reserved or kept in the 'tabernacle' after the service was over they combined with the relics to assure the faithful that the presence of God dwelt permanently in this sacred place.

This development obscured the primitive form of the eucharist at a table, for this had become much more like a temple altar. The nadir of the whole process was reached in the popular magical practice of bringing cloths, oil etc., to be impregnated with spiritual power for healing or other blessings by contact with the sacred relics themselves, through specially provided holes or channels cut in the altar-tomb. Further, the multiplication of relics in the one church building was an important factor in the multiplication of altars, at first in side chapels, but later in the main area. To glorify and emphasize the altar as the sacred place an ancient pagan custom was transferred to churches by building a baldachin or canopy over it, and when this framework was used to support veils around the altar we have a Western counterpart of the Eastern iconostasis that totally screened the altar from the sight of the laity. We are back to the inner sacred cell, the holy of holies, of the temple plan. In all these developments the *domus dei* was effectively replacing the *domus ecclesiae.*

At the same time 'as the main worship of the Church absorbed the martyr cult... the eucharist with the dead was... suppressed. In Ambrose and Augustine we read of the struggle to halt the cult of the dead. It succeeded with the following resulting compromise. Meals for the dead were still allowed, but no table could be involved in any way which would allow a eucharistic interpretation. The funeral meal was simply a social event.'[22] The change was accelerated by the excesses that had come to mark the memorial meals, with gluttony, drunkenness and riots, and it was made possible by restricting the cult of the dead to that of the martyrs elaborated in the ways we have outlined.

The cult of the martyrs was therefore, in some respects, a reform. It is also possible to find in it a version of the New Testament doctrine of the people of God, in fellowship with Jesus Christ, as the new temple. A modern apologist argues that 'Every Christian is entitled to the name of "saint" and the title of "temple". But pure souls... are his temple in a more special way.' He then quotes an earlier writer to the same effect:

Among all visible creatures, human nature alone can truly be an altar, while all that is made by man's hands is only a copy of this image and type.... In fact, nothing is more closely related to the Eucharistic Christ than the martyrs.... Moreover, the true temple, the real altar are these relics. The building is merely an imitation. Hence it was fitting that these bones should be incorporated in the building, that they should perfect the building....[23]

This appears to present a quantitative notion of the new temple, correlated with degrees of human sanctity that comports ill with the 'quantitative' acknowledgments of one of the most notable of saints, Paul, that he was 'the least of the apostles' and 'the chief of sinners' (I Corinthians 15:9; I Timothy 1:15). It must be recognised, however, that these defences begin from the soundly New Testament position of a personalized temple, and the question for the moment is whether or not this is contradicted by identifying it with the physical remains of even the saintliest of saints, thus giving these physical objects a different theological status from that of the physical building in which they are housed. Such relics may be granted historical, pedagogical and even devotional value, but this apologia gives them theological significance. By the same token, any Christian cemetery filled with the remains of saints of 'lesser degree' should be, to a certain extent, 'the true temple', a sacred place with unique access to God. Once the distinction between the *domus dei* and the *domus ecclesiae* is obscured the triumph of the former is sooner or later inevitable, and it is impossible to separate the cult of the martyrs from the cult of the dead in general in the hope that this victory will not occur.

As a final example of the way in which funerary influences instinct with the old traditions of sacred place overshadowed the development of church building we take the history of the consecration rite for churches. At first these were dedicated as anything else might be offered for the service of God, and the significant action was the celebration of the first eucharist in the new building, perhaps with a special prayer of preface, as in the Gregorian Sacramentary. This was not a consecration establishing a holy place or building, although it might be a very special occasion in other ways. On the other hand special rites for the deposition of relics of the martyrs in churches existed from an early stage of this practice. These amounted to a consecration of the tomb or reliquary, and the associated altar, as sacred objects in a sacred place, and the church building acquired importance and sanctity indirectly through these. When special church dedication or consecration rites developed, perhaps in the second half of the sixth century, it was still concentrated on the deposition of relics and the consecration of the altar, with less attention to the building itself.[24] In fact, one Council declared that 'if in future a bishop consecrates a church not having relics he shall be deposed'. The balance, however, between the two components of the rite reflects a distinction between the temple tradition of sacred place and the newer form of the *domus ecclesiae*, which had not yet been entirely assimilated at this point.

This assimilation was furthered by elements added to the consecration rite for churches from another practice, the rite for the transference of a former pagan temple to use as a Christian church. This included exorcisms of the former divine occupants, now demoted to the status of evil spirits or demons, together with lustrations and anointings that completed the purification. 'It suggested ... a kind of baptism of the stone structure.... But, it must be admitted, there was some degradation of the idea of baptism in such a literal extension of the concept of man's regeneration to his external dwelling.... The most serious error ... was the eventual reduction to the status of an appendage of that which had been fundamental in the Christian ritual: the celebration of the first Mass in the place prepared for it.'[25] This last component, properly understood, would have preserved the idea of the new temple as the presence of Christ amidst his people, but these exorcisms and lustrations, together with the cult of the martyrs, served to identify the church building as a rehabilitated form of the old temple or sacred place.

9.5 FURTHER INFLUENCES OF THE TEMPLE TRADITION

The conversion of pagan temples to Christian worship has been mentioned; this occurred when the Pantheon in Rome became the church of St. Mary of the Martyrs, or the temple of Athena was adopted for the cathedral at Syracuse, and the Parthenon became a church in Athens; Pope Gregory actually recommended this as a missionary method to Augustine of Canterbury. The wisdom of such a policy may be doubted, in view of the practices and ideas that tended to remain associated with the building; thus Christians continued to sleep in churches in order to obtain revelations through dreams with a view to guidance or healing, just as they do once again in some of the independent churches of modern Africa. The same idea of the church, and especially the altar, as a place of refuge or sanctuary where one was safe from forcible arrest was a continuation of the traditional inviolability of temples. Not surprisingly there was a transference of the term *templum* itself to church buildings, together with other words such as ναός, and even those which referred to the inner holy of holies — *penetralia* and *adytum*.[26] As we shall see, this inappropriate use of the word temple continues in the most unexpected Christian quarters even today.

This continuity between the old faith and the new was unavoidable in view of the great geographical and numerical expansion of the Church after the peace with Rome that brought into her membership large numbers of half-converted pagans who naturally thought in terms of temples. They would have little difficulty in feeling at home in buildings that were so similar in many of their uses and interpretations to the temples from which they had come. It has been pointed out that the new emphasis upon monumentality, and upon creating an effect of awe and dread through the architecture of the building coincides with the influx of masses of recent pagans and the 'decline of both offering and communion among the laity'.[27] The size and splendour of many of the new churches enabled them to create a feeling of the numinous through physical media, although this was quite foreign to the worship of the earlier house-churches and radically opposed to the New Testament transformation of sacred space; at the same time it was completely appropriate to the temple type, and made the church a worthy *domus dei*. The movement towards the monumental was assisted not only by the Constantinian models and the new public status of the Church but also by the earlier influence of pagan funerary architecture, which was marked by this same feature.

In the plan of the church the apse became a regular element in both East and West. This was the direct descendent of the very heart of the pagan temple, the *cella* or shrine of the god, the holy of holies, and wherever it has appeared in church architecture it has tended to carry with it this association of a special place more holy than the rest of the building, and so has reintroduced the characteristics temple idea of graded degrees of sanctity in man's approach to the deity. Davies suggests that when the rectangular sanctuary was introduced as an alternative form to the semicircular apse this too was of pagan origin.[28] In either case it was completely congruous with the same idea of degrees of holiness found in the cult of the martyrs whose relics lay in the sanctuary.

As a further development in the same direction the ancestor of the chancel, the *cancelli*, became a normal part of the church layout. These balustrades or low walls served to define the more sacred area where the clergy officiated, which culminated in the apse and the altar, and so separated the laity from the sanctuary and the later chancel. This again has no point of origin in the earliest Christian tradition of the *domus ecclesiae* but represents one of the most basic and elementary features of ancient religions, the circles of stones or other enclosures that defined and protected the sacred place. A kindred development, which seems to have originated in Syria in the fourth century, was the erection of a curtain or veil to hide the sanctuary from the laity; in the West this became associated with the baldachin, and in the East it was the beginnings of the iconostasis, the screen entirely separating the action at the altar from the lower clergy and the laity. 'As often as I worship in a Greek Cathedral', wrote Professor William Malcolm Macgregor in a facetious vein, 'and watch the service being carried through afar off, and but dimly heard, always what occurs to me is this, "So the veil of the temple has been stitched together again".'[29]

In the address to which we referred at the opening of this chapter Cardinal Lercaro proceeded to illustrate the Christian adaptation of pagan basilicas, as he saw it. In

the new Christian basilica... the sides were now walled up to create an environment hushed in austere silence. A domestic atrium was added on the side of the entrance to effect a degree of separation from the profane world. The cantharus [or fountain] reminded the faithful of the need of internal purification.... The wall opposite the entrance was bent to form a semi-circular apse: the congregation could now arrange itself in an order which revealed its hierarchical structure. Finally, under the triumphal arch, at the point of contact between the clergy and the *plebs sancta*, there rose the altar, the centre of liturgical activity.[30]

If our analysis of the distinctively Christian idea is correct then the interpretation of most of these developments as forms of Christian impress upon fourth century civil basilicas will not stand. In particular, an 'environment hushed in austere silence', the idea of 'separation from the profane world', a building designed to confine certain sections of the worshippers to a limited area, and the altar as the single centre of activity, are all integral features of the temple plan, not represented in the earlier house churches. Such buildings in the fourth century were moving away from a Christian form, not towards it.

Further illustrations of the reversion to the temple type are to be found in the symbolism that began to attach to church buildings, especially in the Byzantine churches of the East. The basic principle behind this symbolism was the familiar conviction that the earthly is patterned on the heavenly, and that the sacred place in particular reveals this correspondence. Thus the Byzantine church became an image of man, and of the entire cosmos. The nave represented man's body, the chancel his soul, and the altar his spirit; the altar at the east end might also stand for Paradise, which lay in that direction; the door to Paradise was later seen in the door through the iconostasis across the sanctuary; the west end was the realm of darkness and death; in between, the middle of the church represented the earth, and above it the dome was the vault of heaven, with the whole church signifying the universe, and its four sides the four cardinal directions. Thus the church building as a true copy of the cosmos 'incarnates and at the same time sanctifies the world'.[31] It revealed once again the richness of the temple symbolism, and as a building deserved a reverence that the house-church could never sustain. Although much of this symbolism might be confined to the sophisticated intellectual, the effects of this new sanctity in the building itself were felt by all. For example, whereas a mid-fourth century Council had encouraged the continuance of the love-feasts as acts of fellowship and charity in the Asia Minor churches, later Councils both in East and West forbade the 'so-called Agapè' in the church building, or, as it had come to be called in a way that matched the attitude to it, 'the house of God'.[32]

9.6 CONCLUSIONS

In surveying the fourth to the sixth centuries we have been examining the first great age of church building, and some who have sought to penetrate behind later historical developments to a primitive form that might be regarded as normative have found this in the fourth century. It is true that there is no earlier century where churches were freely built or on a sufficient scale to supply us with such a norm; neither can it be provided by the first century of the peace with Rome, for too many contrary factors were at work to permit an authentically Christian model to emerge.

At the same time it would be a mistake to make this period the villain of Christian architectural history, and it is not our purpose to apportion blame, but to clarify what happened in this sphere. At the beginning of the new development the Church had little share in Constantine's own contributions and could not prevent them; nor could it escape many of the other factors that affected its buildings, and if we should criticize the outcome at many points, it was a misfortune rather than a fault. Indeed, it has been asserted of the Christians in Rome that on the whole they held at bay the heritage of classical buildings with their pagan associations through the greater part of the fourth century, and that in this they differed from the Church in the East and in the northern parts of the Empire; it was not till paganism had finally collapsed in Rome in 395 and the whole classical inheritance been threatened by the barbarian invasions that the Church in Rome became fully identified with the monumental classic style, so that the greatest age of church building began in the third decade of the fifth century.[33]

After allowing for all such qualifications our application of the two main types of place of worship to the history of church building in the first six centuries enables us to summarize the overall development in three statements:

1. Christian architecture began in association with tombs and memorial shrines, which had pagan associations and interpretations; these shrines both ante-dated the general construction of church buildings, and then invaded them with the same connotations.

2. Both main types of church building, characteristic of the two main

areas of Christendom, were developed from an ancestry in the temple tradition, with its built-in interpretations of sacred space and of the relationship between the earthly and the heavenly.

3. All adaptations and developments of inherited forms were restricted by this architectural heritage and overshadowed by the cult of the dead, and especially of the martyrs.

In short, church building and design had neither a clear start nor a fair chance. The first great creative period of the Church, marked by doctrinal definition, liturgical development and a vast expansion into a universal community, had seen the new and authentically Christian form, the *domus ecclesiae*, become submerged in revived and extended forms of the *domus dei*. It is this legacy, we believe, that has influenced much subsequent understanding and building of churches as places for Christian worship.

10

A Thousand Years of the *Domus Dei*

In the long middle period of Christian history the developments we have surveyed in the earlier centuries were expanded into new forms and consolidated into the very conception of a church building, a conception that still remains as a kind of archetype in Christian thinking. The few developments that might have led men back to explore the *domus ecclesiae* tradition again were either marginal to the main forms, somewhat short lived, or too late in the period to counter the dominant *domus dei* tradition before the upheavals of the sixteenth century.

The two main types of building, the basilican and the central plan, continued throughout these thousand years and on into our own times. The basilican was simple and economical to build, and could hold a large number of people; except for a period in the seventh and eighth centuries when Eastern forms invaded the West and even Italy itself, the basilicas that provided the first churches in Rome remained the predominant plan for a church in Western Christendom — even the novel Gothic building retained the basilican plan in a different style and structure. In the same way the East retained the centralized plan, whether round, polygonal, or in variations of the Greek cross, surmounted by a domed roof in stone. This plan was also a minority form in the West throughout the period, and was represented by buildings such as St. Stephen-the-Round in fifth century Rome, St. Mark's in Venice of the ninth century, and the two original Greek cross plans for the present St. Peter's in Rome, those of Bramante and Michel Angelo in the sixteenth century. There was also a constant copying of certain famous ancient churches of this form, especially the round church of the Holy Sepulchre in Jerusalem. In both East and West combinations of the two types occurred wherever Eastern churches developed a more distinct nave with a longitudinal axis, and Western basilicas were roofed with domes.

There was nothing inherent in either of these forms, regarded simply as buildings, that anchored them in the traditions of the temple; each was quite capable of being applied to the purposes of Christian worship and of supporting the meeting house tradition, as has been shown in modern churches consciously seeking this kind of use. Even the pagan religious associations carried by buildings of these two types were not inherent to their general structure, and in the course of time both might have been baptized into an authentically Christian form and significance.

It seems that this did in fact occur in one subsidiary part of Christian building activity, the baptisteries which were independent or semi-independent structures for this one Christian sacrament. The earliest of these were small square buildings found in Rome into the fifth century and outside Rome up till the seventh. They were replaced by round or octagonal baptisteries, with eight columns or supports, and these provided the standard pattern thereafter, albeit elaborated with niches and ambulatories. How did this change come about, and was there a model in existing Roman architecture for this very distinctive baptistery form?[1]

Since baptism was seen, among other things, as a kind of cleansing it would not be surprising if the Roman baths had provided the pattern of the building for the Christian purification rite. These, however, do not appear to be the ancestor, but rather the Roman mausolea of the third and fourth centuries, which show all the variations later found in Christian baptisteries. Christian mausolea or martyria had already copied the same model, and produced a domed central room surrounded by eight or twelve columns and inner and outer ambulatories, as at the Holy Sepulchre in Jerusalem and Sta. Constanza in Rome, both fourth century. The association of baptism with burial was exemplified not only in this funerary architectural ancestry but also in the occasional location of baptisteries in catacombs or cemetery basilicas; likewise burial of notable Christians sometimes took place in baptisteries, and even had to be prohibited by the Council of Auxerre in 578 — but without much effect, for as late as 1419 John XXIII, the Pisan Council's 'Pope', was buried in the baptistery of S. Giovanni at Florence.

In view of the pagan nature of other funerary influences upon Christian practice in the early period we might expect to find a similar effect from the manifold funerary associations of the baptistery. In this case, however, there was a natural link between the ideas of burial and of baptism, for Christian interpretation followed the New Testament in regarding the latter as a kind of death and burial, in a mystical imitation of the death and burial of Christ. The 'old Adam' had to die and be buried, symbolized by total immersion, in order that the 'new man' might arise as a regenerate creature ready to share in the resurrection of Christ. This was a thoroughly Christian understanding, enriched by the very funerary associations that this type of building may still have carried, and extended to include the octagonal symbolism, for the number eight represented regeneration, salvation and resurrection in the symbolism of St. Ambrose and other authors. Here pagan forms had been laid under contribution to an authentically Christian development. Baptisteries, however, were not the commonest or the main buildings, and the churches themselves were not so fortunate in their own history.

10.1 THE RETURN OF THE SACRED PLACE

The first generations of Christians reveal no special interest in the sanctity of sites associated with Old Testament events or the life of Christ, and this was in keeping with the revolution in the form of the sacred place in which they had shared. In the third century the desire for pilgrimage to the Holy Land begins to appear, and this was encouraged by Constantine's building of shrines and churches at many of the important sites. We have also examined the similar erection of shrines for the saints and martyrs and the deposition of their relics in martyria and churches. Both developments implied that sanctity belonged to physical objects and places because of their association with unusual manifestations of divine presence and power, and were therefore places where special access to deity could be secured and consequent blessings obtained. This outlook, which belongs entirely to the older tradition of the sacred place, became deeply embedded in the widespread medieval practice of making pilgrimage to the holy places of Christian history.

Palestine, of course, was the chief attraction, but by reasons of distance or of control by its later Muslim conquerors this pilgrimage was not always possible, and Rome became an early alternative. Here there were the shrines of the great apostles Peter and Paul, together with hosts of other relics of saints and martyrs. In the succeeding centuries similar famous shrines appeared all over Europe, and not least in the British Isles; there was Glastonbury, associated with Joseph of Arimathea and St. Patrick and possessing a wonderful collection of relics, and the shrines of Our Lady of Walsingham in Norfolk, of St. Patrick's Purgatory in Ireland, St. Winifred at Holywell in Wales, and Saints Martin and Ninian at Whithorn in Scotland; later the shrine of St. Thomas à Becket at Canterbury became so popular that Henry VIII had it destroyed.

Some of these shrines were located at places with a long sacred history in pre-Christian times, especially where wells had been associated with healing and other miracles, and so were continuing a mode of thought that had remained immune to the New Testament development; this was true at Holywell, at Glastonbury, and at the famous French church at Chartres; when the predecessor of the present cathedral was burnt down in 1194, the lament recorded was not for the destruction of the house of the congregation but for 'the loss of the home of the Virgin, the peculiar glory of the city... the incomparable place of prayer'.[2]

The cult of the saints and the medieval pilgrimage habit which it sustained had noticeable effects on the church buildings of the period. The multiplication of saints, and the depositing of their bodies or their relics in churches led to an increase in altars, shrines, and apses to contain them; likewise the vast crowds of pilgrims these attracted required larger churches, with more aisles, longer naves, and space for their ritual devotions as well as for the processions on the saints' days. The church was no longer primarily a place for monks to say their offices or a congregation to engage in Christian worship; it had often become 'an immense reliquary' for the general public, and thus a far cry from the *domus ecclesiae*. The latter pattern might still be seen in many an ordinary local church, but the churches of pilgrimage were so numerous and of such prestige that they dominated the conception of what a church building was for and what it ought to be like.

A Christian critique of the habit of pilgrimage to holy places is well expressed in a dissentient statement from the earlier part of this period, albeit a somewhat marginal and heretical voice from a Syrian Nestorian synod in 858:

> Canon xv proclaims that the faithful ought to give their offerings and perform their vows for the remission of their sins in the places where they live.... Why should they go to distant places... with the idea that God will there favour them more... if they wander about as people who have lost their God, not knowing where they will find Him or where He will hear them, they are sick souls....[3]

This expresses the heart of the matter, that 'God will there favour them more', as well as the associated idea that the cost and difficulty of a pilgrimage were a work of merit and made the journey suitable as a vow. Together these notions supported the temple tradition of sanctity and divinity being located in a particular place or building.

Another version of the same idea occurred in the practice of building a church as a replica of one erected at an original Christian holy place. Just as there were fictive relics when originals were not available, or to duplicate the more famous of the originals, so also 'fictive' holy places were created through imitative buildings, and thus the local worshipper could share in the benefits of pilgrimage to the Holy Land, but vicariously and at a distance. The most common, but not the only, subject for such imitation was the Church of the Holy Sepulchre built by Constantine at Jerusalem, with its alleged tomb of Christ. Replicas of this appeared all over Europe from the fifth to the seventeenth centuries, and it was even imitated for an imperial mausoleum at Potsdam in the late nineteenth century; sometimes the relationship was indicated by the name being borrowed also, as in the churches of the Holy Sepulchre at Cambridge and Northampton. As might be expected, the chapels of the military orders formed to assist pilgrims to the Holy Land, the Knights Templars and the Hospitallers, also copied the Jerusalem church.

A study of churches inspired by the Holy Sepulchre has revealed that the interest was religious rather than architectural, so that it is often impossible on first inspection to see any connection between the copy and the original.[4] Modern copying of an ancient building would be revealed in the style, shapes, and even decorative detail, but a medieval

replica was not concerned with such architectural reproduction. A selection might be made from the various component features of the original, or they might be rearranged and combined with new elements to
produce a church that was no mere architectural copy. The main concern was to reproduce the essential religious content, and this was represented by certain selected elements in the prototype. In the case of
the Holy Sepulchre these consisted of the name itself and of the tomb,
together with the round building (interpreted in any polygonal fashion), a selected group of important measurements such as those of the
tomb or the spacing of the piers, and the number of supporting pillars
in the rotunda. There were in fact eight piers in diagonal pairs, with
twelve columns filling the intervening spaces in four groups of three.
Replicas were usually satisfied to possess either the eight or the twelve,
although Templar churches such as the one known still as the Temple in
London might have six. The numbers had important symbolic meaning;
we have already noted this for the number eight, and it would be obvious for twelve as the twelve apostles; indeed, in the Jerusalem Holy
Sepulchre the grouping of the columns into four sets of three 'linked
the number of the four regions of the world with that of the Trinity
whose gospel was spread by the Apostles throughout the world'.[5]

Sometimes the replica was consecrated with the name 'Jerusalem',
or a whole complex of buildings sought to repeat several of the Jerusalem holy places; thus at Bologna there was a group of structures at
Sto. Stefano representing the Holy Sepulchre, the chapel of Golgotha,
and the church of the Invention of the Holy Cross, all together known
as Jerusalem. Here the pilgrim was enabled 'to visit the Holy places in
effigy and in the very sequence which they have in the prototype. He
could come and venerate here the Tomb of Christ, there His Cross or
the site where the Cross was found', and so 'share at least in the reflection of the blessings which he would have enjoyed if he had been able
to visit the Holy Site in reality'.[6] It would be insensitive to depreciate
the religious devotion inspired in these ways but it clearly belongs to
the tradition of specially privileged status for particular sacred places
and not to the manner of the New Testament.

The same tradition of the sacred place was exhibited much more
widely in the almost universal orientation of church buildings so that

the altar was towards the east and the entrances at the west end. This ancient feature of sanctuaries was examined in the earlier part of our study. The house-churches were indifferent to the practice, although prayers towards the east were mentioned by both the *Apostolic Constitutions* and Tertullian; earlier church buildings reveal considerable variety and many Constantinian and later Roman churches had their doors at the east end, while some churches were north and south. Uniformity of practice began first in the Eastern and Coptic churches and spread into Western Europe so that on occasion churches had their internal arrangements reversed in order to comply. The analogy between the rising sun and the resurrection of Christ is perfectly appropriate, but when such orientation becomes mandatory if the building is to be properly a church, or when the altar and sanctuary are regarded as nearer to God and holier because at the east end, then legitimate Christian symbolism has given way to the old ontology of sacred places, and churches have rejoined the temple tradition.

As a final example of the continuance of the same outlook we may mention the universal desire to be buried in or near a sacred place that we have already traced back to the early centuries. To be buried in the church itself, or in its porches, vestibule or cloisters was best of all, but otherwise one would hope to lie in consecrated ground, in the graveyard beside the church. The idea itself, and many of the funeral rites that developed, were of pagan origin, and as late as the sixth century a number of councils tried to stop the practice, but in vain. In a sense it was capable of Christian interpretation, with 'God's acre' as a constant symbol of the fellowship between the congregation and its 'living-dead'. When, however, men feared to be buried on the north or 'evil' side of the church, or in unconsecrated ground, lest their eternal salvation be imperilled, then the ancient outlook had returned and the cemetery around the church had become a kind of temenos or precinct with a temple or shrine in its midst.

10.2 CHURCHES AS SACRED BUILDINGS

As the medieval period advanced there was further development of
the notion of degrees of holiness expressed in the structure of ancient
places, and found in elementary forms fairly early in the history of
churches. The church itself, as a sacred building, could not be entered
without some ritual of purification, and for this purpose fountains were
erected in a courtyard or atrium before the church as early as the fourth
century. In the vestibules the worshippers prepared themselves by peni-
tence or by sprinkling or crossing themselves from the stoups of holy
water that still exist in some churches today. Likewise one of the reasons for the placing of the baptismal font near the entrance door lies in
the same idea of preparing to enter the holy place by a ritual cleansing.

10.2.1 *The gradation of sanctity*

Inside the building there was the lengthening of naves already referred
to, and an enlargement of apses or chancels. The combined effect was to
produce a splendid view from the more profane end of the church towards the distant altar in the holy sanctuary — a royal path, as Eusebius
called it even in its less developed days, along which the worshippers
approach the altar of Christ, enthroned as King; or, as B. L. Manning
used to put it, speaking from within the tradition of the *domus eccle-*
siae in modern times, a 'superstituous vista'!
    This lengthening was the easiest way to enlarge a basilican or cruci-
form church and in England the lengthened chancels together with the
naves produced many of the longest churches in the world. Anselm's
rebuilding of Canterbury Cathedral in the twelfth century has been
offered as the point of departure for the longer chancels, for he had
transferred the choir of monks from the east end of the nave into the
chancel, which now required two spaces, a sanctuary for the clergy and
a choir for the monks, and this innovation was widely copied.[7] At the
same time it reflected a similar development in many countries and led
to the familiar pattern of a church with three main chambers or spaces,
nave, choir and sanctuary, corresponding to a progressive increase in
holiness from the laity to the priests.

The same differentiation was assisted by other features, such as the raising of each area above the previous one by steps, the separation of the chancel by a screen across its nave end, and the demarcation of the altar or sanctuary proper by a railing. In a larger building the whole chancel area might be screened off on all sides and become a specially sacred chapel for the holy ministers set within the body of the church. Inside the sanctuary in this new and narrower sense the bishop's seat was removed from behind the altar-table where he had led the earlier Christian community in their common worship, and the altar against the east wall took its place, the clergy officiating at it with their backs to the congregation.

The altar itself became more ornate, often honoured with the canopy or ciborium on four enclosing posts; this undoubtedly made it 'a token of the old $\nu\bar{\alpha}\acute{o}\varsigma$ of antiquity; that it to say, it was the most intimate part, the most sacred place of all in the temple, in which the image of God was kept'.[8] With the addition of the doctrine of the transubstantiation of the eucharistic elements the return to the view of a God dwelling in the inner cell of the temple was complete.

We have been describing the situation as it developed in the West, but equivalent changes occurred in the Eastern Church where the iconostasis created an even more impressive inner sanctuary of the divine presence. 'This screen indicates the limit separating the world of sense from the spiritual world, and it is for this reason that the icons appear at this point, as uniting the two worlds, as the world of imagination in man stands between his spiritual nature and his sensory faculties. Beyond the screen is the... holy of holies or the divine dwelling place.'[9] In the other direction the entrance doors of the church lead out to the world of death and the devil.

These gradations of holiness might be described in terms of a horizontal hierarchy running along the main axis of the building; in the eastern churches there developed an even more elaborate vertical hierarchy of holiness which is best understood by examining its stages from the highest to the lowest. The whole scheme is represented in the mosaics and paintings with which the interior of the church is covered, and embraces three main levels: the heavenly uncreated world of the divine, the paradisal created world before the entry of evil, and the present human world of the Christian community in process of being re-stored through union with the new creation in Jesus Christ.

The divine world is set forth in the main dome and the high vaults, where Christus Pantocrator, Christ in majesty, is shown as the ruler of all, and the centre of the universe which the whole church building represents. Below and around him there are the angels acting like inter-mediaries between the divine realm and the created world beneath. This is shown first in its restored or paradisal form as seen in the incarnate life of Christ on earth, the chief scenes being represented in terms of the twelve main feasts of the Christian year; these are distributed over the secondary vaults, the squinches and pendentives and upper parts of the walls. Below this again comes the present life of the Christian in process of sanctification. First there stand the figures of the saints and martyrs on the lower parts of the walls as testimonies to the re-creating power of Christ in those already sanctified; then on the floor of the church is the living congregation who have commenced on their way towards the higher levels of life represented on the walls and roof above them.[10] No pagan temple ever had a more coherent and explicit manifestation of its function as a microcosm of the universe than is to be found in the combined horizontal and vertical hierarchies of a Byzantine church.

10.2.2 *Symbolism in churches*

From the two previous sections it will be apparent that the rich cosmic symbolism characteristic of the temple type of sanctuary was devel-oped in most impressive manner in the middle ages, and it remains to add a few further examples that draw attention to this feature. The cosmic directions, for instance, are also known as the points of the compass or cardinal directions, and these were represented not only in the eastward direction of the sanctuary but also in other ways: the south became the sign of the Holy Spirit and conversely the north stood for darkness and estrangement from God; the world of the flesh and the devil lay in the west to which the baptismal candidate turned when renouncing him and all his works, after which he faced to the east and paradise in order to profess his faith in Christ; similarly the four cardinal directions were identified with the four ends of the cross.

The dome, which as one modern writer says 'automatically inspires' an emotional experience,[11] was inevitably the symbol of heaven or the universe, and has actually been used as a name for great cathedral churches — in German, as the Dom at Mainz, and in Italian, Il Duomo at Florence and elsewhere. The same symbolism appeared in the stars on a blue surface found on the underside of the four-posted ciborium in imitation of the heavens. Then 'in ascending the steps of the sanctuary the sacred ministers go as it were into the heavenly sphere to "join with angels and archangels and the whole company of heaven" in offering the Holy Sacrifice in union with the eternal High Priest, who, having passed through the veil, is exalted at the right hand of the Majesty on high'.[12] The use of New Testament language must not be allowed to obscure the essentially archaic and pagan nature of this symbolism, as is revealed when the author of our quotations points out the very close analogy between this kind of sanctuary with its ritual and a Pawnee fire ceremony performed with a similar set of four posts supporting the domed roof of the sky.

The medieval symbolism of numbers that has also been before us was capable of endless application to every conceivable feature of the church building and its contents: any single central feature was apt to stand for God, every pair of objects for the two natures of Christ, every set of three for the Trinity, and of seven for the seven gifts of the Spirit. This riot of symbolism and allegory was gathered up in the thirteenth century work of the French bishop William Durandus, the *Rationale Divinorum Officiorum*, which became a standard handbook for the later middle ages and again in the nineteenth century for the Ecclesiologists. We shall be referring to this again in more detail and content ourselves here with one extract to show how far the interpretation of any particular item could go: 'Bells do signify preachers.... Also the cavity of the bell denoteth the mouth of the preacher ... the hardness of the metal signifieth fortitude in the mind of the preacher. The clapper or iron, which by striking on either side maketh the sound, doth denote the tongue of the preacher... the wood of the frame upon which the bell hangeth doth signify the wood of our Lord's Cross. The rope hanging from this, by which the bell is struck, is humility or the life of the

Preacher.'[13] And more still, in the same vein, on bells alone.

Much of this is harmless enough and could serve a didactic purpose, but in general the elaboration of symbolism distracts attention from the essentials of Christian worship and from the personalized temple-in-community; to place the emphasis on the building and its furnishings restores these once more to the status of a specially holy place. It should be remembered, however, that the very compexity of such symbolism removed it from the capacity of less sophisticated minds than that of Durandus, and that much of this interpretation was a later symbolic reading of existing features rather than the point from which churches were conciously designed.

10.3 GOTHIC: A NEW AND CHRISTIAN FORM?

The twelfth century saw a quite new development in church architecture, the Gothic form that emerged first at the Abbey of St. Denis (1132-44) in the Isle de France, and spread rapidly through western Europe and down into Spain and northern Italy. We are accustomed to the analysis of Gothic into components such as pointed arches, ribbed vaults, and flying buttresses, or we are trained to identify the various styles in the course of Gothic development, especially in Britain; but those who raised the first great Gothic buildings do not seem to have been concerned with architectural questions of structures, styles and decoration. As Krautheimer has pointed out,

no mediaeval source ever stresses the design of an edifice or its construction, apart from the material which has been used. On the other hand the practical or liturgical functions are always taken into consideration; they lead on to questions of the religious significance of an edifice.... Not once ... does Suger refer to the revolutionary problems of vaulting and design in his new building at St. Denis.... Time and again Suger discusses the dedications of altars to certain Saints. Questions of the symbolical significance of the layout or of the parts of a structure are prominent... and of the relation of its shape... to a specific religious... purpose.[14]

Among these religious purposes we find a need for space to say twenty masses simultaneously, and of a building worthy to house the relics of St. Denis, the 'Apostle of Gaul', and fit to be the religious centre for the kings of France.

Since this close connection between architectural form and religious concern occurred during the climax to the 'great ages of faith' Gothic has often been presented as the long-delayed appearance of a new and distinctively Christian form of church building; as we shall see below, it was deliberately revived in the nineteenth century as the only Christian type for all time. Our concern here is whether the analysis we are employing will sustain such judgments, and not with the technological, economic or aesthetic aspects of Gothic architecture; in this way we share the predominantly religious interests of the founders of this new form.

It is clear both from the expressed intentions of Abbot Suger and from a cursory inspection of a typical Gothic building that it is a *domus dei* rather than a congregational meeting place. Its very distinctiveness, until copied in secular buildings, coupled with its soaring style, place it visibly at the centre of the communities it dominates. Likewise the richness of its carved stonework, its figure sculpture and stained glass set it in the midst of later medieval artistic imagination and effort, and enlisted these to beautify the house of God, and to make it a worthy centre for a culture focussed upon the Christian faith.

Gothic glass and sculpture were the western alternative to the rich mosaics and paintings of the Eastern Church, and conveyed the same sense of worshipping amid a great community of the sanctified with its hierarchical orders: Christ and the angels, apostles, saints and martyrs, Christian bishops, scholars and rulers. The building itself, however, possessed a rather different symbolism; instead of enclosing the whole universe from the earth beneath to the domed heaven above, as in the Eastern buildings, it pointed to the heavens rather than contained them. As a modern writer put it, 'the whole building seems chained to earth in fixed flight.... It rises like an exhalation from the soil.... No architecture like the Gothic so spiritualizes, refines and casts heavenward the substance which it handles.'[15] Indeed, its very walls rise up to 'meet like hands joined in tense perpetual prayer'.[16]

To this most obvious symbolism of the Gothic building other symbolic functions have been added by modern interpreters. The dynamic life-giving quality of the Christian faith is matched by this fabric that 'seems almost organic and tremulous with life',[17] where 'stone vaulting gives the roof the appearance of springing from the pillars rather than of being supported by them, less of a load than a product', in contrast to the 'angular lines and geometrical forms' of other churches.[18]

The analogy with the Christian life is pursued further when the subordination of the parts to the whole is likened to the interrelations of individuals in the Christian community: 'The equilibrium of the genuine Gothic church is the result, not of mere accumulated weight, but of balanced thrusts, pointing to the organic structure of nature — and further still to St. Paul's analogy of "the whole building fitly framed and perfected"...'.[19] The symbolism is carried even further into the life and work of Christ, who as 'the Greek Christ... lived a life of perfect rhythm and harmony and perfection', and as 'the Gothic Christ... lived a life of suffering and agony, which nevertheless resolved these contradictory elements into a unity of poise and victorious upward thrust'.[20] Finally a note of absolute sincerity is claimed for Gothic, 'in that its interior corresponds to its exterior; there is no disappointment of unfulfilled promise. We may say that while Greek religion illuminated the stone from *without*, Christian religion shone through it and transfigured it from within. That is surely one of the profoundest symbols of the Christian faith....'[21]

There are two kinds of symbolism within these statements, the one cosmic and akin to that of the *domus dei* in history, and the other apparently anchored in the New Testament and its view of Christ and his community. How far the latter is the product of the ecstatic and imaginative writing on Gothic architecture that marks the century after Pugin, and how far it is integral to the Gothic church but recognized only in modern times, is a matter of considerable doubt. It seems to us to be a later sophisticated interpretation of didactic value, but far from the minds of those who erected and worshipped in this new church type. The symbolism recognized by the medieval builders was similar to that of the earlier western churches, for the Gothic church was still a basilica with sanctuary or apse. To this symbolism was added the one inescapable new effect of Gothic, its soaring flight from earth to heaven, and this effect was deliberately sought when towers and spires were pushed higher and higher until the cathedral at Ulm rose up a hundred and sixtythree metres, when finally completed in 1890.

We have here one of the two most striking religious features of this type of church. It is a new version of the temple as meeting place between God and man, with the emphasis on the human aspiration after the divine. Rudolf Otto found Gothic analogous to the search of the mystic: 'Just as the slender colums and responds of the Gothic rise and climb and do not finish in the repose of a semicircle, but by an urge after the infinite thrust up in the incompleteness of the pointed arch, so Eckhart demands "the climbing spirit"... of a Gothic soul, striving after... a goal most limitless'.[22] P.T. Forsyth, speaking from within a very different ecclesiastical tradition, finds the same effect when he calls the Gothic church 'the lovely symbol of a man's thirst for the infinite', and proceeds in a lyrical and much-quoted passage:

> It is 'thrust like a fine question heavenward',.... The pointed arch, reproduced in great and small throughout the fabric, the upright line instead of the classic horizontal, the vast height of the pillars prolonged into the roof, the effect produced by bundles of small pillars rolled into one column, and carrying the eye upward along their small light shafts, the judicious use of external carving, so as to add to the effect of height instead of reducing it, the pinnacles and finials which run up everywhere on the outside, the tower, and still more the spire, placed above all these – the total effect was to make the spirit travel upwards with the eye and lose itself in the infinity of space... the Gothic... volatilises the stone. It gives the garment of praise for the spirit of heaviness.[23]

This aspiration towards a meeting with the divine is a most powerful recognition of the transcendence of the heavenly being. The other notable religious feature is the complementary sense of the mysterious numinous divine presence created by Gothic within its lofty and richly worked interior space. One modern study regards the Gothic cathedral as a conscious attempt to provide an awe-inspiring setting for the mysteries of the mass in medieval worship, a more ethereal structure 'less earth-bound than the heavy buildings of the Roman Empire', whose 'soaring arches and great expanses of shimmering glass created that luminous atmosphere... fitting for the re-enactment of a mysterious and dramatic spectacle'.[24]

It is this aspect of Gothic that has appealed to those among its modern revivers who find here the most effective means of creating the right 'mood' for worship. The great apostle of the Gothic revival in the United States earlier this century was R. A. Cram, who could speak of the exalting solemnity of divine worship... surrounded by the dim shadows of mysterious aisles, where lofty piers of stones softened high overhead into sweeping arches and shadowy vaults, where golden light struck down through storied windows, painted with the benignant faces of saints and angels; where the eye rested at every turn upon a painted and carven Bible... where every wall, every foot of floor, bore its silent memorial to the dead, its thankoffering to God; where was always... the still atmosphere of prayer and praise.[25]

There can be no doubt of the numinous qualities of medieval Gothic and of its capacity to produce religious experiences of these kinds; even in the present secularized and irreverent age it is still able to produce a minor religious response from the hordes of tourists who gaze upon its wonders and are impelled to lower the voice a little and quieten the step in deference to this house of God. In this respect it resembles the great domes of the Eastern churches which we were told automatically produce an emotional experience, and it does so in spite of the complete contrast between the two architectural forms and the ways in which they secure these effects. Whereas Gothic forms, both inside and outside, rise from earth to heaven, 'a Byzantine building... is essentially "hanging" architecture; its vaults drip from above without any weight of their own; the columns are not supports but descending tentacles; the whole develops downwards in accordance with the hierarchical spirit manifest throughout Byzantine life'.[26] Each form of church, Western and Eastern, provides an excellent example of a numinous sacred place, instinct with a presence that is at once immanent and transcendent.

When this quality is considered, together with the symbolism that continues as in previous churches, and the special ways in which Gothic is equipped to serve as centre and meeting point between man and the divine, it is clear that we are dealing with a very distinctive development within the temple tradition, in fact with a form that is further from the *domus ecclesiae* than any other. It must be remembered that we speak only of the religious nature of the Gothic church, and not of its architectural or aesthetic qualities. It might be regarded as the supreme form of the pagan temple, a religious building *par excellence*, capable of its own autonomous witness in ways that surpass the churches of Eastern Christendom. These in their earlier and characteristic form spoke eloquently from within, but like the earlier churches of the West, were extremely plain on the outside, and sought no particular effect from this viewpoint. With Gothic we have a rich interior matched to an exterior as statue-covered and decorated as many an Indian temple, and proclaiming the glories and majesty of its God to the whole world around.

The comparison with the churches of the East can be pressed still further. From the standpoint of an orthodox Christian theology the 'hanging architecture' described above may be regarded as an appropriate expression of the 'joy of heaven to earth come down', the movement of God to man in the incarnation. By this symbolism Gothic must be seen as a powerful statement of the reverse movement from man to God; when viewed only from the outside world and without its own internal statement of God's presence with man, then the vertical movement of the Gothic church speaks solely of human search and aspiration, and not of man's response to a God who has first sought him. As a religious testimony in the public manner this is the reverse of any Christian gospel.

Instead of a new and possibly definitive Christian form we have in the Gothic church a major contribution in the archaic temple manner, and one that has survived to bedevil the development of authentic Christian forms of the *domus ecclesiae* in modern times. Nevertheless we can appreciate it as a superb religious building, giving moving expression to the human thirst for the divine, and with a rich sense of the numinous in our midst. As an attempt to say with a building what religions are all about it has never been surpassed; but if we are correct in our analysis of what had already happened to such sacred places in the Semitic traditions then it came some twelve centuries too late.

10.4 THE RENAISSANCE : A NEW THEORY OF CHURCH ARCHITECTURE

The first explicit attempt to develop a theory of church architecture and to build accordingly is found within the Renaissance movement in the Italy of the fifteenth and sixteenth centuries, in the heart of western Christendom where Gothic had never penetrated. Indeed, it was here that the latter received its name, as the 'monstrous and barbaric' architecture of a semi-civilized northern Europe, in contrast to the churches of the south which showed a continuous succession within the classical tradition of Roman culture.

The common interpretation of the Renaissance as a humanistic movement, glorifying man and the beauty and resources of this world is misleading when applied to an understanding of the new churches it produced, as if they were mere temples to the human spirit devoid of all concern for the transcendent reality of the divine. If this were so then they would have represented a completely new departure in the history of religions, whereas in point of fact they provide a full scale development of religious principles derived from the world of classical antiquity. The Renaissance designers were inspired and controlled by the fifteenth century discovery of a treatise on architecture by Vitruvius Pollio, a Roman architect in the time of the emperor Augustus. Vitruvius Pollio's theory of temple building led the Renaissance theorists, especially Alberti (d. 1472) and Palladio (d. 1580), to make a close study of the temples of ancient Rome and to expand their own theories on the basis Vitruvius had provided. They used the word 'temple' for the Christian church, and for symbolic reasons which we shall shortly examine they were drawn to the circular form found among the temples of antiquity, though less frequently than they imagined. Thus it was that churches closely resembling Roman temples and, in particular, buildings with a central axis began to appear in the first half of the fifteenth century, and became the typical Renaissance form by the time the movement was at its height in the first quarter of the following century.

There was nothing especially new in deriving churches from the temples of the past for the temple in Jerusalem had been invoked as a model by many, including Abbot Suger and William Durandus, in the previous centuries. This model had legitimated the three-cell elongated basilican churches of the middle ages; such divisions were impossible in the centralized building which was not designed to serve a congregation of hierarchical structure, or to create a numinous interior focussed on a distant sanctuary in the Gothic manner. The first round church in the new mode was Brunelleschi's S. Maria degli Angeli begun in Florence in 1434; this was octagonal and reminiscent of the temple of Minerva Medica in Rome. The same architect began the basilica of Santo Spirito two years later in the same city; while this was not centralized it represented another basic feature of Renaissance churches, the carefully determined mathematical relations between its parts; for instance, the nave was twice as high as it was wide, and the ground floor height was the same as that of the clerestory. The combination of concern for harmony and proportion with a central plan distinguishes the churches of the Renaissance in the next century, and reveals the extent to which they were no mere copies from past forms but an important new creation.

At the same time they remained firmly within the temple tradition and, like Gothic, gave this type of holy place a new fulness of expression through their own peculiar developments. In terms of our analysis of the sacred place, Renaissance church theory sought to define a sanctuary that would stand at the centre of the community, but marked off from the profane world as a meeting point between the human and the divine. Thus for Alberti and for Palladio the church building

> should not only stand on elevated ground, free on all sides, in a beautiful square, but it should be isolated by a substructure, a high base, from the everyday life that surrounds it... windows should be so high that no contact with the fleeting everyday life outside is possible and that one can see nothing but the sky.[27]

To ascend the broad flights of steps to such a temple can inspire only awe and devotion.

Given such a setting the church must then be planned so as to serve as the instrument for the meeting of God and man. These plans were determined not by architectural imagination or practical needs but by the very nature of God himself. The perfect beauty, order and harmony in God were reflected in the presence of the same qualities in the universe he had made, and also in the human body and soul when these achieved their true nature. As Vitruvius had said, the form of the temple should be 'analogous to the character of the divinity';[28] since both man and the universe exhibited this same analogy there was one pattern running throughout reality, and both man and temple appeared as microcosmic exemplars of the macrocosmic order and of the gods themselves. In proof of this relationship and in demonstration of the basic features of the orderly pattern Vitruvius 'described how a well-built man fits with extended hands and feet exactly into the most perfect geometrical figures, circle and square. This simple picture seemed to reveal a deep and fundamental truth about man and the world, and its importance for Renaissance architects can hardly be overestimated. The image haunted their imagination' and 'became a symbol of the mathematical sympathy between microcosm and macrocosm. How could the relation of man to God be better expressed... than by building the house of God in accordance with the fundamental geometry of square and circle?'[29]

The Renaissance church architects went further than Vitruvius in establishing a certain priority for the circle, which Alberti found distributed through natural phenomena such as the heavenly bodies, the trees, the nests of birds and many other things. Palladio gave this impirical justification a theoretical basis in his account of the circle:

> It is enclosed by one circumference only, in which is to be found neither beginning nor end, and the one is indistinguishable from the other; its parts correspond to each other and all of them participate in the shape of the whole; and moreover every part being equidistant from the centre such a building demonstrates extremely well the unity, the infinite essence, the uniformity and the justice of God.[30]

A centralized church, even if polygonal or on the Greek cross plan, is therefore in harmony with the most perfect form in the universe and thus with the nature of God himself; since man also is made to conform to the image of God there is a spiritual kinship between a church of this kind and man's own nature. In such a church 'we react instinctively; an inner sense tells us, even without rational analysis, when the building we are in partakes of the vital force which lies behind all matter and binds the universe together.Without such sympathy between the microcosm of man and the macrocosm of God, prayer cannot be effective.'[31]

In a beautiful church, instinct with this rich symbolism, and in keeping with the harmonies of the physical universe and with God's own nature, man is purged of his disordered existence and encouraged through prayer and piety to a like harmony in his own soul. But it is not only man who depends on this place of worship; it would appear that God himself also depends upon it for a full revelation of his nature. The church has become the essential meeting point between God and man, revealing the one and recreating the other in the perfect divine image.

The Renaissance church was therefore a house of God in a very special way and must reflect its divine owner at every point. Its beauty depended on the rational and mathematical harmony of its parts whereby each possessed a size and shape that contributed to the whole and could not be altered, any more than the nature of God could be altered. The materials used should be the richest and best that can be found; the colour should be predominantly white for the purity of God, and the whole building dignified and strong, able to survive for all ages.

This type of church, and the theory that controlled it, plainly exhibit the *domus dei* as centre, as meeting point, and as microcosm; the extent to which it also provides for the immanent-transcendent presence is less clear. It can scarcely be called a numinous building in the sense made familiar by Rudolf Otto and found unmistakeably in Gothic. It is too rational, too controlled, too clear in its light and whiteness for this. It sets forth plainly what it has to say about the divine, instead of suggesting the hidden mysteries. Even when of great size it does not overawe as it might, for the discipline and simplicity of its parts make it look smaller than it really is; St. Peter's in Rome does not really look like the largest church in the world, whereas a much smaller Gothic church may appear immense both inside and out. As one comment has put it: 'The Southerner did not thirst for the mysterious and the indefinite, taking life as he found it beneath a glowing sky.'[32]

An attempt to make the interior more numinous appeared in the controversy as to whether the altar should represent the presence of God by standing at the centre of the circular space, or be set on the periphery. The second position was supported by some on the grounds that to place it as far as possible from the entrance door was to declare the infinite distance between man and God; this suggests a search for the remoter and more numinous sanctuary familiar in the basilican and Gothic churches, and not easily secured in the centralized types. Central or vertical and longitudinal axes are not easily combined, and the continuing effort to do so may be detected in many churches over the next two centuries and indicates one of the major problems emphasized by Renaissance churches.

Although the sense of a numinous presence was not carried by these buildings, their designers intended their perfections to declare the immanence of God in a more rational and sophisticated way, as well as to point to the transcendent glories that lie beyond this earthly realm. The Renaissance church, therefore, gives its own particular expression to this aspect of the temple tradition, albeit one less likely to reach the mass of the worshippers.

It stands as a new type of the *domus dei* which, like its Gothic rival, sought to declare the religious message in an architectural statement, and differed from the Gothic in being entirely planned to this end on the basis of a highly articulated theory. There is genuine religious feeling behind it, although controlled more by a religious philosophy with Platonic roots than by the practical needs of a Christian congregation or by New Testament teaching. The emphasis might be said to have passed from the Christ of the Cross represented in the cruciform basilicas and Gothic churches to 'the Greek Christ' of perfection and harmony who was more akin to the ruler of the universe seen in the domes of Eastern Christendom. As we have seen the risen and cosmic Christ is inescapable in the New Testament, and the biblical view is fully aware of the majesty and grandeur of God and of the beauty and perfections of the universe he has created. To concentrate on these, however, leads to the idea of a universe sufficiently perfect in itself to reveal its creator, and then of a church building that can do likewise. Revelation and holiness are found once again in sacred places and material edifices.

The Christian view, on the other hand, is that these are inadequate to the task. The ultimate revelation has occurred, not through the harmonies of the natural order or their repetitions in human constructions, but through the tensions and conflicts between good and evil in history, with all its disorders, imperfections and contingencies, culminating in the supreme conflict, the ultimate disorder and ugliness of the cross. In

the person in whom this conflict reached a triumphant conclusion the
new 'sacred place' was now given to men. The Renaissance church, like
the Gothic before it, may be accepted for its aesthetic and architectural achievements and as a magnificent expression of a sophisticated
religious spirit, but from a Christian standpoint it was a useless repetition of an outmoded type in the temple manner. It manifested a grand
theory, but not a Christian one.

10.5 OTHER FORMS IN THE MIDDLE AGES

It must not be forgotten that not all medieval churches were large
buildings on the temple pattern, whether basilican, Latin cross, Gothic
or Renaissance. There were many small and simple churches more akin
to the ancient basilican and domestic models, both in rural areas and in
the larger towns, where in addition to the magnificent central churches
there were many smaller ones that still surprise us with their proximity
to one another. These were not distinguished by the possession of relics, by internal subdivisions or numinous effects, and they provided
for the assembly of a congregation and for its participation in the worship in a reasonably satisfactory way. Their very smallness, as in some
of the Saxon churches in England, held them closer to the *domus ecclesiae* form and use.

In Italy there were always buildings that were more congregational
in character, with wide spaces and an open view of the altar, so that
the effect of an assembly of Christians under its president or bishop
was never lost; with the advent of a choir of monks and canons the
placing of this group on the other side of the altar from the lay congregation avoided the divisive and hierarchical effects we have noted
in Northern Europe.

Similar forms appeared in fourteenth century Spain where churches
were built for congregational participation with wide naves or even
square in shape, a small sanctuary or apse, and the choir at the west
end or in a central enclosure in the nave. This left a large space between
the altar and the choir for pulpit and worshippers, who were really in
the centre of the action; in this respect there was a return to the *domus*

ecclesiae, even if the temple tradition still produced a magnificent building possessed of its own religious eloquence.[33]

The dominance of this latter tradition was partly due to the growth of the monasteries whose size and wealth were reflected in their abbey churches, and whose worship, where they shared the same building, was separated from that of the laity. Such developments were in denial of the humility, simplicity and austerity that marked the beginnings of the monastic movements, and the history of the orders presents a series of reforms seeking to return to the ideals of the founders, and so to a simpler form of church building.

This is well illustrated in the reform of the Benedictine tradition when Bernard of Clairvaux dominated the newly-founded Cistercian order early in the twelfth century, and declared the principles their churches were to follow in his *Apologia* (ca. 1124). He criticized churches of 'immense height... immoderate length... superfluous breadth' which 'somehow remind me of the old Jewish ritual'. His immediate point of departure was the Benedictine Abbey of Cluny which had grown into an immensely influential cultural and political centre, and whose third church (1086-1121) had seven towers, seventeen apses and the longest overall length in the world. The Cistercians therefore repudiated large and costly churches, with stone towers, figured sculpture on their facades, triforiums, and sumptuous stained glass. Their first stone church at Pontigny was probably a simple rectangle without aisles or ornamentation.

A recent study of Cistercian architectural principles has pointed out that they were of a negative nature. The Cistercian theories

consisted first of the Augustinian principle demanding a structure without *affectus*, that is without emotional expression. Secondly, corresponding to Benedict's stipulation that the monastic church should be nothing but an *officina*, the oratories were to be ideal workshops for 'the art of holiness'. To this St. Bernard added that an architecture whose aim is to create a vivid emotional response would be unworthy of the independent spirit of... monks, who must transcend 'a meaningless hull of stone'.[34]

On this basis, and governed by the Cistercian demand for uniformity within the order, a typical plan developed as the abbeys of the new order built their churches all over Europe and as far afield as Cyprus and Syria. It was basilican in form, with shallow rectangular sanctuary; this form with its continuous lean-to roofs, was simpler and cheaper to build, albeit with a somewhat barn-like overall effect, both inside and out. The extreme simplicity, however, could sustain a beauty of its own as seen in the Cistercian abbey churches of Fountains and Rievaulx in England.

St. Bernard had made it clear that this concentration upon the community and its worship rather than upon the building as the ideal expression of the Christian faith was for monks alone, and that the general populace needed the stimulation of a lavish church. It is not so surprising, therefore, that later churches of the order saw a departure from the austere standards of St. Bernard, the introduction of paintings and tomb sculpture, and the adoption of Gothic and finally even of Baroque styles. The weakness of the Cistercian reforms lay in embodying a reaction against the *domus dei* tradition rather than a new statement of an authentically Christian building.

Another and very different monastic influence arose with the mendicant orders of the Franciscans and Dominicans of the thirteenth century. Their concern with conveying the gospel to the masses of the population led to the erection of simple preaching halls of a rectangular shape, with a wide nave but no chancel for a choir or sanctuary, merely an altar at the east end, and often free of pillars or aisles. They were not designed for full liturgical activity, but rather as a supplement to the parish church; yet they were influential models when older churches came to be rebuilt, and were not unsuitable for the kind of worship that was to appear in the sixteenth century reformation.

Little seems to be known of the places of worship of the large number of heretical and reforming 'sects' that appeared in the later middle ages. These commonly adopted voluntary poverty and an exceedingly simple style of living, together with a reassertion of various New Testament principles. Many of these dissenters, such as Henry of Le Mans, Peter of Bruys, and others among Cathars and Waldensians entirely rejected the need for special church buildings or consecrated cemeteries, and asserted that God could be worshipped as well, if not better, in groves, taverns or market-places; some even advocated the destruction of existing buildings. Such ideals, together with the persecutions they endured, inevitably meant a return to the house church, and prevented a new architectural expression of their understanding of Christian worship. In consequence they left no concrete legacy for the future, although we may detect a revival of their attitudes and practices in many of the groups that made up the later 'radical Reformation'.[35]

10.6 THE ORTHODOX CHURCH OF ETHIOPIA

It must not be forgotten that during the thousand years we have been surveying there arose another form of Christianity, outside the orbit of either East or West, the Orthodox Church of Ethiopia. This Church and its buildings have escaped the dialectic found elsewhere in Christian history, enjoy a continuity of development and of form, and possess a strong Jewish inheritance without parallel in other parts of the Christian world. Although scholars are still exploring the complex of possible channels of this Jewish influence, Ethiopian traditions trace it back as far as the fabled Queen of Sheba whose son by Solomon became Menelik I. This Menelik stole the Ark of the Covenant from the Jerusalem Temple and installed it in Aksum, his capital. On this legendary basis the Ark has become central in Ethiopian Christian worship, with supposed replicas of the original in every church, but now reduced to the essentials, the contents of the Ark or the Decalogue Tables in the form of the *Tabot* or tablet resting on the altar. This is the most sacred object in the church, which after consecration by the bishop lends its sanctity to the whole building. This explicit continuity with the Jerusalem Temple is matched by the threefold form of the church building, which is usually round and in three concentric parts — the inner Sanctuary for the priests, the surrounding 'Holy Place' for the people at the eucharist, and the outer choir area, where hymns are sung and the cantors stand. Even in octagonal or rectagonal buildings this same threefold form remains, and in all forms there are four doors facing the cardinal points.

The accents of the *domus dei* are unmistakeable, and these are emphasized by the extensive indebtedness of the Ethiopian Church to the

Jewish tradition — in its attachment to the Psalter in the liturgy, in the observance of the Sabbath as well as Sunday, in the festivals and their sacrifices, in the system of fasts and in other customs too numerous to mention. It would seem that the *domus ecclesiae* conception has never taken root, that there is no parallel with the forms of the earliest Christian centuries, and that Ethiopian Christianity which dates from the fourth century began with churches in the same tradition as those then developing elsewhere — albeit for different reasons.[36]

It appears, therefore, that for nigh on a thousand years in the East and the West, and into our own day in Ethiopia, the dominant church forms exemplified the *domus dei.*

11

Reformations and their Aftermaths

The Protestant Reformation in the sixteenth century may be said to
have produced the first great 'liturgical movement' in the modern
sense, and to have anticipated forms of liturgical renewal which have
featured in the twentieth century liturgical movement. These have been
belatedly discovered by other Christian traditions and re-discovered by
the heirs of the Reformation who had lost much of their inheritance in
the intervening centuries. The sixteenth century Reformers recovered
the primitive communal nature of worship with the result that the distinction between the clergy and laity was removed from the place it
had assumed in the life of the church, the sacrament was restored to
the laity, and the Lord's Supper was celebrated from behind a table set
near the people instead of from before a remote altar. The unity of the
word and the sacraments was re-established so that pulpit and table
were placed closer together where all could both hear and see, and the
subdivision of the interior space was abandoned. The cult of the saints
and the funerary motifs were suppressed, likewise all that bespoke luxury and splendour. With this new emphasis upon the Church as the
community of Christ's people sharing in a common worship the church
building was conceived once again as a *domus ecclesiae* rather than a
domus dei.

A Roman Catholic writer recognises that there was more concern
with convenient and practical ways of expressing this new outlook than
with the building itself and its symbolism: 'The first concern in the
Reformed churches was to form, so to speak, a ring of prayer around
the pulpit, the altar and the organ, which were to be as near to each
other as possible. Catholic symbolism, on the contrary, required space
between them, and established a spacial and spiritual progression from
the doorway to the pulpit, and from the pulpit to the altar.'[1] It is not

surprising, therefore, that while there was a great deal of discussion of the nature of the Christian community and of its worship there were no major treatments of the church building and nothing at all comparable to the great treatises that provided a theory for the Catholic symbolism of the Renaissance churches. Reformation activity was focussed more on the development of liturgies, and explicit statements about the buildings tend to be rather incidental or limited to their internal arrangements.

11.1 PROTESTANT STATEMENTS

Such evidence as there is of Luther's attitude has recently been marshalled for us[2] and shows that for him churches were a secondary concern, to be viewed in a practical and sensible manner but not treated as specially holy places, and therefore not to be consecrated as in the past. On the other hand it is asserted that he consecrated the first new chapel built for Lutheran worship, at the castle at Torgau in 1544;[3] it may well be a reminder of the essential conservatism of Luther in so many matters, and the chapel itself which has been called '"The first Protestant church"... already shows all the characteristic features of Protestant church building which prevailed until the 19th century'.[4] There was no chancel, and the altar had become a 'simple monumental table'. It was over a century before a Lutheran architectural treatise appeared: after the end of the Thirty Years' War, in 1649, the city architect of Ulm, Joseph Furttembach, produced his book on *Kirchengebau* as a guide to the building of rural churches in the areas devastated by the war. He recommended plain domestic rectangular buildings, with pulpit, table and font together where all could see and hear.

Calvin's treatment of the subject is also somewhat incidental, but the elements of a theory of the place of worship may be constructed from his various brief references. He recognized that pagan temples could serve the purposes of divine revelation, for he declares that 'Xerxes... rashly destroyed all the temples of Greece' thinking it 'absurd for gods ... to be shut up within walls and roofs. As if it were not in God's power to come down to us, in order to be near us, yet without changing place or confining us to earthly means; but rather by these to bear us up as if in chariots to his heavenly glory...'. 'It was especially to this end that ... in ancient times under the law all believers were commanded to assemble at the sanctuary' though Moses plainly taught 'that there can be no use of the place apart from ... godliness.... Accordingly the Temple is called ... (to remove all cause for superstition) his "footstool".... Whatever temples the Gentiles built for God on any other principle were a mere profanation of his worship. To a degree the Jews fell into this, though not with equal grossness'.[5] The Jerusalem temple is here placed in the same category as pagan temples, with the same possibilities of use in the right or the wrong ways.

As for churches, which Calvin sometimes called temples, there ought 'to be public temples wherein'...'common prayers for believers' are held, and this is 'the lawful use of church buildings'.[6] But 'the Lord nowhere recognizes any temple as his save where his Word is heard and scrupulously observed'. Otherwise 'he moves elsewhere and strips the place of holiness'.[7] The buildings, it seems, have a relative or derived holiness only, depending on the kind of worship offered in them; we must therefore

> guard against either taking them to be God's proper dwelling places, whence he may more easily incline his ear to us – as they began to be regarded some centuries ago – or feigning for them some secret holiness or other, which would render prayer more sacred before God. For since we ourselves are God's true temples, if we would call upon God in his holy temple, we must pray within ourselves.[8]

Hence

> It is wrong that a love of walls has seized you; wrong that you venerate the church of God in roofs and buildings.[9]

On the contrary,

> Our God does us the honour of appointing us to be sanctuaries and temples... each Christian is a temple of the Holy Spirit.[10]

These statements could well serve as a theological framework for the Christian interpretation of the sacred place in any religious tradition; in practice they provided realistic and biblical guidance on the attitude Reformed Christians were to adopt towards the churches they had inherited, rather than a charter for an exploration in Protestant church building. Something of the same practical emphasis appears in the first *Book of Discipline* drawn up in 1560 at the inauguration of the reform movement in the Church of Scotland:

Lest the Word of God, and ministration of the Sacraments, come into contempt by unseemliness of the place, churches and places where the people publicly convene should ... be repaired ... and provided within with such preparations as appertain to the majesty of the Word of God as well as unto the ease and commodity of the people.... Every church must have ... a bell ... a pulpit, a basin for baptism, and tables for the administration of the Lord's Supper.[11]

The same practical concern with the functional aspects of the building is seen in Martin Bucer's efforts to rearrange the interior for the better participation of the congregation – at Strassburg as early as 1533, and in England when advising on the Prayer Book of 1549. After recognizing the need for churches, which was not true of all sections of the Reformation, he declared 'that the choir should be so distantly separated from the rest of the temple, and the service (which pertains to the whole people and the clergy) be set forth in it alone, is anti-Christian'. This arrangement suggests that the ministers are 'nearer to God than lay people', and also 'confirms the pernicious superstition by which reading ... the Scriptures and prayers, without intelligence and without understanding of faith, is thought a worship pleasing to God'.[12] For these reasons, and from a misapprehension as to the frequency of round churches in antiquity, Bucer favoured a building of this shape as the ideal form.

Among the most widely read statements on our theme in the sixteenth century was the Second Helvetic Confession, drawn up by Heinrich Bullinger in 1561 and adopted by the Swiss churches in 1566. This runs parallel to the Scottish statement of the same period when it exhorts that 'places where the faithful meet together be decent, and in all respects fit for God's Church. Therefore, let houses be chosen for that purpose, or churches, that are large and fair, so that they be purged from all such things as do not beseem the Church. And let all things be ordered as is most meet ... that nothing be wanting which is requisite for rites and orders, and the necessary uses of the Church.' At the same time, 'the true ornament of churches does not consist in ivory, gold, and precious stones, but in the sobriety, godliness, and virtues of those who are in the church'.[13] While recognizing in biblical fashion that 'God does not inhabit temples made with men's hands', nevertheless 'places dedicated to God and to his service are no longer profane but consecrated by reason of the Word of God and the use of holy things for which they are employed'. When the congregation is there at worship 'they are in a holy place, in the presence of God and his holy angels'.[14]

Similar sentiments were expressed in contemporary statements in England to be found in the second *Book of Homilies* or sermons appointed to be read in the time of Elizabeth. The titles alone indicate their concerns, speaking 'Of the Right Use of the Church or Temple of God, and of the Reverence Due to the Same', 'Against... the superfluous Decking of Churches', or 'Of the Place... of Prayer'. The emphasis is typically reformed: God's true temple is found in his people and not in man-made buildings. 'The church or temple is counted... holy, yet not of itself but because God's people resorting thereto are holy and exercise themselves in holy... things.' At the same time, 'God doth allow the material temple made with lime and stone (so oft as his people come together into it, to praise his holy name) to be his house, where he will hear the prayers of them that call upon him', although it is recognized that 'prayers were heard in whatsoever place... in caves, in woods, and in deserts...'. The holiness of the building is clearly derivative, and contingent upon its being 'thus godly used' by Christian people. It is unfortunate that this position is somewhat undermined by constant use of the Jerusalem temple as a model, and by unbiblical terminology: 'The church is called by the word of God (as it is indeed) the temple of the Lord and the house of God.'[15]

These statements from the first sixty years of the Reformation reflect a common outlook and concern. There is first a recognition that churches are usually necessary, though there are signs that 'other places' or houses might also serve the purposes of worship. The main emphasis is on function, on their being arranged and equipped for the reformed conception of corporate worship, and if possible as a single chamber. While they should not be elaborate, they should be well maintained and worthy of the relative or derived sanctity they acquire when God is present among his worshipping people through Word and Sacrament;

this, however, does not make them holy places in themselves. There can be no doubt that we are back in the atmosphere of the *domus ecclesiae* with an attempt to express the implications of the New Testament revolution in the place of worship; it is also evident that all sections of the reform movement, whether on the Continent or in England or Scotland, shared in this attempt.

There were, however, two points in these statements where the contrast between the two kinds of place of worship was liable to be obscured and therefore the desired reforms weakened. One lay in the continued use of the term 'temple' for the church building; this implied a continuity with the Jerusalem temple, which was sometimes explicitly acknowledged. The other occurred in the ascription of a relative or derived holiness to the building, which encouraged the continuation of consecration rites and the return to the idea of the *domus dei.* Both these tendencies may be seen in the work of Richard Hooker, writing at the end of the century in England, with a more extensive and systematic statement than anything that had gone before.

Hooker recognizes, if somewhat obliquely, that church buildings were not essential in all situations, and that for Christians who were derided in the early centuries for their lack of worthy temples 'their most convenient answer was that "The best temples which we can dedicate to God, are our sanctified souls and bodies"'.[16] On the buildings themselves some of his statements have a functional emphasis akin to that in earlier Reformed documents: 'It behoveth that the place where God shall be served by the whole Church, be a public place, for the avoiding of privy conventicles, which ... may serve unto dangerous practices.'[17] Hence 'our churches are places provided that the people might there assemble themselves in due and decent manner'.[18] He also asserts that their 'end being the public worship of God, they are in this consideration houses of greater dignity than any provided for meaner purposes'.[19]

These statements might have come from any section of the Reformation, but Hooker was led by his own temperament and the extremer Puritans, as he saw them, to an extensive discussion that led back to the temple tradition. He felt he had to answer 'a special refined sect of Christian believers ... exceedingly grieved at our solemnities in erecting churches, at the names which we suffer them to hold, at their form and fashion, at the stateliness of them and costliness, at the opinion which we have of them, and at the manifold superstitious abuses whereunto they have been put'.[20] On the question of 'sumptuousness of churches' Hooker replies that 'as touching these two contrary ways of providing in meaner or costlier sort for the honour of Almighty God... they are in their season both allowable: the one when the state of the Church is poor, the other when God hath enriched it with plenty'.[21] This sounds eminently sensible, but Hooker clearly preferred the latter and supported his position with exaggerated views of the 'spacious and ample churches... erected throughout every city' in the third century.

It is entirely congruent with this preference that he should call the first Christian churches 'temples', and refer to the church in his own day as a house fit for the dwelling place of the God of heaven. Similarly he appears to regard churches and the Jewish temple as belonging to the same genus, with the difference that the former has only two divisions, for the clergy and the laity, although these are observed 'not with any great strictness or curiosity'.[22] The effect of the Reformation is evident in the qualification, even if destroyed by the use of this analogy with the temple. It is also in keeping with the analogy that Hooker should defend the consecration of churches, although his statement is not so dissimilar from the earlier Reformed language about the building: 'When... we sanctify or hallow churches, that which we do is only to testify that we make them places of public resort, that we invest God himself with them, that we sever them from common uses.'[23]

The extent of the divergence of Hooker's position from that of the Reformation is seen when he describes the religious influence of the building itself: '... the very majesty and holiness of the place, where God is worshipped, hath *in regard of us* great virtue, force, and efficacy, for that it serveth as a sensible help to stir up devotion, and *in that respect* no doubt *bettereth* even our holiest and best actions in this kind... we think not any place *so good* as the church...'.[24] This would appear to go beyond the other Reformed statements on the suitability of the building, and to invest the latter with an independent religious eloquence and influence akin to that of a *domus dei*. Hooker's judgment on the religious effects of the building will receive further attention when we examine this most difficult of questions towards the end of our study, but taken together with his other statements it suggests that he cannot be recognized as an explicit exponent of the meeting house tradition implied in Reformation theology and worship. However much he may have been 'the judicious Hooker' in other matters, his attempt at balance and comprehensiveness in this field might be regarded as theologically and liturgically rather injudicious; and in the event, the ensuing religious history of England exacerbated the divisions he sought to remove.

11.2 FRUSTRATED INSIGHTS

Before thinking too harshly of Hooker's compromises or of the failure of the Reformers to produce a substantial exposition of church architecture from the new viewpoint, we must understand the peculiar combination of circumstances that rendered their situation almost exactly the reverse of that of the fourth and fifth centuries, and prevented any extensive architectural expression of the reformed outlook. In lands where the Reformation was not successful or did not develop there was no opportunity for small Protestant minorities to design their own churches with any freedom. Where the reformed outlook did obtain, in other areas of Europe, it was common for the monastic orders to be suppressed, and for their churches, chapels and cathedrals to be taken over for congregational worship; many of these are still used in this way today. This resulted in an excess of church buildings so that there was little scope for new architectural embodiment of the reformed liturgical understanding and pastoral concern. It has been claimed that 'during Elizabeth's reign there was less church building than at any time in English history for 800 years',[25] and the few college chapels erected in this period gravitated towards the traditional monastic rather than the congregational pattern. If Reformed Churches had come into being by succession from a continuing Catholicism, and had been granted freedom to develop alongside the older faith, as at the later Disruption in the Church of Scotland, then they would perforce have built their own churches to express their own outlook. The comparatively complete success of the Reformation in the areas where it ultimately prevailed brought with it a rich architectural legacy from the middle ages that virtually denied this manifestation of the new insights.

The appearance of a new Protestant architecture was also inhibited by the incessant warfare, compounded of both civil and religious factors, that marred the first century and a half of the new faith. In France, where the population might have divided into Roman or Reformed sections, there was continued strife with intermittent 'wars of religion' from 1562 till 1594, and the few new churches in a distinctive Protestant style were usually destroyed by rioting after a brief existence. The Netherlands were struggling for freedom from Catholic Spain from 1566 till 1609; Germany experienced armed struggles between the Emperor and the Protestant princes until the Peace of Augsburg in 1555, but troubles continued until the end of the Thirty Years' War brought a viable compromise in 1649; Scotland was more fortunate, with less actual warfare but plenty of political troubles from the Stuart rulers as well as involvement in the civil war of the English in the succeeding century; Switzerland also had been divided by two civil wars early in the Reformation period. The times were certainly most unpropitious for an exercise such as church building that required economic resources, civil order, and religious freedom.

As a further influence upon a situation already unfavourable to new developments we must mention the fact that for many Protestants the church was not as important as it had been in the past, for their emphasis was upon the community and not the building. Many learnt to worship in the open bereft of any shelter, others gathered in hiding in obscure buildings, in barns or private houses, and those who were fortunate enough to inherit the existing churches were content to adapt them as best they might to the requirements of the new ways. Since these latter were in the majority and many of their alterations have survived into our own times or can be documented, we must look to the rearrangements of the medieval churches for the chief concrete manifestation of reformed attempts to revive the *domus ecclesiae*.

11.3 ADAPTING AND TRANSFORMING THE OLD CHURCHES

It could be said that the main architectural problem was how to adapt for reformed worship as the people of God a building that had been designed in the medieval tradition as the house of God. By the nature of the case the problem was not acute in many of the smaller churches, which therefore remained substantially as they were. Likewise there was less change in Germany, where Luther's conservatism made him content to leave the altar against the east wall, and where his reform of the liturgy retained the intoning of the Scriptures as being acousti-cally more effective than speech in the high-roofed medieval churches. Later Lutheran practice was to bring table, pulpit, font and organ to-gether as a common focus for worship.

A common solution involving the minimal adaptation was to accept the double-chambered nature of the building, using the nave for the preaching of the Word, and the chancel or choir as the place where the congregation proceeded for the Lord's Supper at the table that had replaced the high altar. There was then no question of a sanctuary to which the laity could not be admitted, and the people might even gath-er kneeling round the wooden table, as seems to have been the common practice in Elizabethan England. Here the service was read from the nave, but the chancel screens were retained, albeit cut down to a lower level, to preserve the two-roomed building, notwithstanding that the communicants might be so numerous as to overflow into the eastern end of the nave. As the 1549 *Book of Common Prayer* put it, the wor-shippers were required to 'tarry still in the quire, or in some convenient place nigh the quire'.[26] An adaptation of the same principles has re-mained to this day in the Grote Kerk at Haarlem in the Netherlands. The copper screen across the chancel, completed only in 1517, was re-tained; the nave is used for preaching with seating facing it from three directions; in the apse where the high altar once stood a large tablet was erected, bearing in Dutch the words of the institution of the Lord's Supper, which is celebrated in the choir with the communicants around long tables set up for the sacrament on each occasion.[27]

This dual use of the building was not entirely satisfactory and failed to set forth the unity of the Word and Sacraments that was important in Reformation theology. A more radical adaptation, therefore, was to transfer the table to the nave, and this seems to have been implied in the regulations for the reform of worship in the German principality of Hesse as early as 1526:

> But all the faithful are admonished to be present at public prayer and the reading of the Gospel, as also at the Last Supper of our Lord. Moreover, these rites shall from now on be no longer celebrated in the choir, but shall be performed with due decorum in the midst of the church so that all people ... may learn to sing in harmony and with one heart may glorify God's name, for all have become priests in Christ.[28]

In England in 1550 the Bishop of Gloucester and Worcester, John Hooper, was advocating the closing of the chancels and placing the whole service in the nave, so that all could see and hear better and the the minister be inspired to greater care by the proximity of the congregation! While he failed to have the chancels closed he was able to order the removal of chancel screens and all other such partitions from churches in his dioceses, as being reminiscent of the veil of the Jewish temple that kept the people from the Holy of Holies. A little later, in 1567, the diocese of Durham ordered that the Communion should always be celebrated in the nave.[29] At Leeds parish church the table was brought out into the nave for the Lord's Supper as late as the nineteenth century, and the bread and wine were being carried to the people where they sat when Newman became vicar of St. Mary's in Oxford.

With this unification of the service and the shifting of the centre of action to the nave the chancel was available for other puposes. Sometimes it was used to seat a portion of the worshippers, facing towards the nave, as when the cathedral of S. Pierre at Geneva was rearranged. An English example occurs in the parish church at Slaidburn in Yorkshire, where the pulpit is placed half way down the south side, with pews facing it from east, west, and north, and those in the chancel looking down the church through the Tudor screen.[30] In Scotland, after the Act of Annexation of 1587, the chancel was taken over by a layman representing the religious house that had been despoiled; the place where the high altar had stood became the family burial place, and a gallery erected across the chancel contained their pews for worship.[31]

Sometimes the chancel when cleared of the altar was given to burials, as at Bradwell-near-Coggleshall in Essex where there was a fine Jacobean tomb belonging to the local squire's family.[32] In the spacious chancel of the Nieuwe Kerk in Amsterdam the tomb of Admiral de Ruyter stands where the high altar had been, and the rest of the chancel is used for weddings or other semi-secular purposes; the pulpit and seating are arranged much as in the Grote Kerk in Haarlem, and for Communion large tables seating a hundred worshippers are placed down the centre of the nave.[33]

There are Dutch churches today where the medieval chancel serves as a bicycle park, and in some Scottish churches it was simply walled off and left to fall into ruin, as at Kirkliston and Dalkeith. Even old St. Paul's in London had the choir bricked off in the seventeenth century during the Long Parliament. Elsewhere it might simply be left empty and ignored, as in the cathedral and other churches in Basel.[34] At St. Martin's Church, now the cathedral, in Leicester, the chancel was shut off and turned into a library in the sixteenth century; all side chapels and altars were suppressed, and a wooden table on trestles was set up in the nave as required for Holy Communion. Even after Laud ordered the restoration of the chancel and this was done, the Bishop of Lincoln directed that the sacrament should still be administered from a table nearer the people. Now this cathedral church is arranged much as it must have been originally except that the chancel was actually extended to include the crossing in the nineteen-twenties; it might therefore be said to have been both reformed and doubly de-reformed; might it yet be re-reformed in the twentieth century manner?[35]

Yet another solution was to wall off a still smaller part of a very large church or cathedral for use as a parish church, as at Haddington in Scotland, or even to divide these very large buildings between several congregations; thus St. Giles in Edinburgh was divided up for no less than five distinct congregations until its restoration in the nineteenth century, and the large Church of St. John the Baptist in Perth, which before the Reformation had forty altars, was later divided by stone walls and housed three separate churches known in the early nineteenth century as the East, Middle and West Churches of St. John's.

All these shifts and improvisations were controlled by the central

Reformation emphasis upon the unity of Word and Sacrament, the unity of ministry and laity in one worshipping community, the effective participation of all in the liturgical action, and upon the building as the servant of the holy people of God rather than as a holy place in itself. This absence of a false sentiment about the church was an essential factor in the sixteenth century efforts at making their more unsuitable buildings serve the new liturgy. Some of their methods may seem curious to us, but they were surprisingly successful and many are still in operation.

It is interesting to observe the belated application of some of the same methods in the twentieth century to buildings that were unaltered or remained in Roman Catholic hands four centuries ago. This time it is the modern liturgical movement that has given rise to the same insights about the unity of the people of God, the importance of the Word and its relation to the Sacraments, and corporate participation in the action of the liturgy. Hammond has given an interesting survey of churches in Germany where the apse or chancel has been put to new use as a baptistery, as a week-day chapel, as a choir space with seats facing west, or even walled off permanently from the rest of the church. He also refers to churches in England where similar rearrangements have been effected once the east end altar has been brought forward to the people and become more suggestive of a table.[36] More recently Salisbury and Hereford Cathedrals have removed their chancel screens against the opposition of local bodies and the Royal Fine Arts Commission, in a determination to adapt their medieval buildings for more effective corporate worship by uniting the nave and the choir. Many of the nineteenth century churches built in a deliberately revived medieval manner must be calling for similar treatment. The sixteenth century situation is indeed still very much with us.

11.4 TOKENS OF WHAT MIGHT HAVE BEEN

Although speaking of the general effect of the Reformation century in these ways we do not suggest that it has no more to offer us than lessons in adaptation; a small number of most significant new churches did appear, and we may regard these as tokens of a development that was stifled for other reasons.

The 'first Protestant church', the Lutheran castle chapel at Torgau, has recently been mentioned, and its new features have been analysed for us by an architect as follows:

We can recognize in it the central orientation of the congregation, the open space in the centre and the pulpit against the central column. Typical elements in the centralized church plan can also be seen in such arrangements as the setting of the communion table and organ to face each other and the two rows of continuous galleries. The communion table which in accordance with Luther's doctrine originally stood free, was not replaced by the retable altar till the beginning of the 17th century, a reminiscence of the medieval church which was then generally adopted by the Lutherans.[37]

The first new church on a basilican plan but with a single liturgical centre seems to have been in the village of Nidda in Upper Hesse in 1618; here the pulpit, font and table were grouped together at one end, although the table was in an arched recess in continuing deference to medieval notions. There were, however, more adventurous designs in the same period, including some novel shapes such as the twelve-sided church at Hanau (1622-54), and the L-shaped Freudenstadt Church (1601-8) with free-standing table, pulpit and font all at the junction of the arms.

The most interesting new church forms appeared in France where the Huguenots managed to erect several 'temples', as they called them, even amid the desultory fighting of the second half of the century. In 1564 three were built in identical form at Lyons, round buildings with the seating forming an ellipse and the pulpit at one of its foci; these were all destroyed three years later. At La Rochelle an octagonal 'Grand Temple' was erected in 1577 to seat three thousand five hundred worshippers, and a similar church at Sedan in 1593. The Edict of Nantes brought relative peace for the Protestants in 1598, and allowed them to build churches at certain designated places and of certain limited size. Accordingly we find new churches on the same centralized principle: a dodecahedron near Rouen in 1601, and others at Dieppe (1600), Saint-Martin-en-Montbeliard (1604), Caen (1611), and Charenton on the outskirts of Paris (1601). The latter was a small rectangular church and was burnt by rioting Catholics in 1621; Louis XIII specially authorized its replacement with a new church in 1623 that became famous in its day, and served as a model for Protestant buildings in Germany and Holland, and even, it is said, as late as 1843 at Algiers and 1926 at Marseilles.[38] Its architect, Salomon de Brosse, also designed the Luxembourg; similarly the La Rochelle temple had been the work of another prominent architect, Philibert de l'Orme, who was responsible for the Tuileries; indeed, the profession seems to have been intrigued by the possibilities of Protestant churches, for the architect Jacques Perret included plans for hypothetical churches in books published in 1592 and 1602, just as Leonardo da Vinci had enjoyed sketching centralized Renaissance churches earlier in the century. This interest, however, had little scope for expression as the Protestants remained restricted and their free and imaginative excursions into a new form came to an end with the revocation of the Edict of Nantes in 1685; their churches were destroyed (Charenton with some difficulty), many members dispersed to other lands as refugees, and their faith was proscribed until its gradual return to public existence in the nineteenth century.

Whatever their shape, rectangular, oval or polygonal, a centralized arrangement was followed, but for functional and not for symbolic reasons. The restrictions imposed by the Edict of Nantes compelled the Protestants to accomodate as many as possible in the one building, so that Dieppe was reported to hold six thousand and the second church at Charenton between four and five thousand; this could be achieved only through the use of galleries — Charenton had two tiers running round all four sides. The pulpit therefore stood out from the wall on a platform that had space in front of the pulpit for the celebration of the sacraments; all in the vast assembly could see and hear the whole liturgical action, even if those in the gallery were at a distinct disadvantage as regards the Lord's Supper. They were thus more effective as preaching halls than as buildings for the fullest participation in all parts of the liturgy.

At the same time they served well as meeting houses that encouraged a strong sense of community.

Unambiguously, everything was orientated towards the centre, with the different groups of the congregation ... facing inwards. Everyone was in immediate relation with the rest of the meeting and with what went on in the divine service ... the gathering of the community was the visible sign of the Church. It was made up of distinct groups drawn towards the centre, where took place baptism (at the beginning) and the Lord's Supper (at the end). The encounter of these different groups, achieved through everyone's concentration on the centre, corresponded with the structure of the liturgy.[39]
In accord with this emphasis upon the people rather than upon the building the external appearance was plain and functional, looking like the large meeting house that it was. 'The exterior of Charenton did not suggest the theatre, nor was it intended to awe and overwhelm. The tenuous political privilege which made the church possible was too uncertain to permit much ostentation ... the building had no true facade.'[40] In this description we should see more than a reflection of the political situation, for it is entirely in keeping with the whole rationale of Protestant worship to which the French churches gave such emphatic expression.

In Holland there was similar experimentation with new plans and one of the earliest of the new buildings is still used – the brick octagon built at Willemstad (1596-1607) with the pulpit in the centre of one wall and pews in two rows of varying length across the body of the church. Another common central plan took the shape of a regular cross with short arms or transepts, the old Greek cross form, as in the Noorderkerk in Amsterdam (1623), with the pulpit near the centre of the crossing. As a variation on this there might be two sets of short transepts intersecting a rectangular nave, as in the Westerkerk in Amsterdam (1630), where the pulpit stands in the short cross arm on one side of the nave. Others again favoured the simple rectangle, and in one case at least copied the Charenton church almost exactly – the Arminian church in Amsterdam of 1630. By this date 'Dutch architects had tried almost every major experiment to which English and American builders of the late seventeenth and eighteenth century finally turned'.[41] Fortunately, unlike those in France, sufficient of the Dutch churches of the period have survived to testify to this further endeavour to build places of worship suitable as a *domus ecclesiae.* The first post-Reformation church of any consequence to be built in Scotland was St. Columba's at Burntisland, in 1592. In this 'solitary example of a consistently planned reformed church',[42] which is said to resemble Dutch churches of the period, there is a square plan with four central pillars supporting the roof, and a gallery running round all walls. The pulpit is at one of the massive pillars and the communion table and font within the square defined by the pillars, with the congregation seated on all four sides. Most new building awaited the more settled conditions after the re-establishment of episcopacy in 1610. In 1612 there was the new church of Old Greyfriars in Edinburgh, and although this had a medieval Gothic nave there was no chancel or altar at an east end. Others early in the seventeenth century were simple rectangles with the pulpit in the middle of one long wall, and perhaps galleries across the short sides. With the addition of a transept in the long wall opposite the pulpit there emerged the T-plan that was characteristic into the next century; examples are to be seen in Anstruther East (1636) and the Tron Church in Edinburgh (1637). In all these forms there was the same effort to make the building serve the liturgy as in the other countries of the Reformation.[43]

Only one building remains in England from the period 1600-1640 to exhibit the nature of a new Protestant church as it was conceived in the Anglican tradition. Inigo Jones' chapel of ease for the Covent Garden residential square, St. Paul's Church of 1640, has survived in its original form as a simple rectangle with high windows of clear glass, a flat ceiling, and a gallery along the two sides. It is a functional preaching church of the type that was to be further developed later in the century in the churches of Christopher Wren. As for the Puritans, their own special contributions did not appear until after the period we have taken as the first Reformation century, so that St. Paul's remains the one surviving building 'to fully interpret the Plain Style in England before the Great Fire of London'.[44]

The term 'Protestant Plain Style' is eminently suitable as a summary of the developments we have been examining in the various areas of the Reformation. Garvan claims that a European tradition of this kind is manifest through all the experiments with manifold forms that mark

the era, and that when the great Puritan migration began to New England in 1630 it took with it a well-formed notion of how churches
ought to be designed. In consequence the meeting houses of New England 'were not haphazard or accidental responses to the demands of
the American forest', and whatever changes took place in materials
and whatever variations appeared in the different American colonies
the basic principles of the new style were still followed. 'In each, space
was closely defined, linear and well lighted; ornamentation was con-
strained and abstract; and construction direct, simple, and apparent.
Here was a lucid shelter within which the rational literate Protestant
might reach his god.'[45] If this is so then there is a continuity between
the Protestant architecture of the New World and that of the old, and
both present a clear answer to the question of how to break from all
aspects of the temple tradition and present the Reformed churches
with a genuine *domus ecclesiae*. The only pity is that the great majority
of Protestants were confined to medieval buildings and their adaptations, so that the new style remained no more than a token of what
could have been the great revolution in the churches of this section of
Christendom.

11.5 OTHER REFORMATIONS: LEFT WING AND RIGHT

We have dealt at length with the main or Protestant section of the sixteenth century movement, but we must not overlook the Counter or
Catholic Reformation and that third section recently called the Radical
Reformation and known at the time as the Anabaptists.[46] These were
smaller groups who sought to by-pass all the Christian centuries if only
they might recover the pattern of the early Christian church and follow
nothing but the express authority of Scripture. Their communities
were gathered churches, based on mature religious experience of rebirth, and professing an austere life of high moral standards separated
from the community at large. Many were pacifist, most rejected infant
baptism (hence the name of Anabaptists), some practised community
of goods and a few became polygamous. Inevitably they were often in
conflict with the state, as also with the Catholic authorities and the

Protestant Reformers. To all of these they seemed like lawless revolutionaries who would lead to chaos in church and society, in morals and in religion. The main groups included the Mennonites, and later the Amish section of these, the Hutterites and the Bohemian Brethren; the equivalents at a slightly later stage in England were the Baptists, the Independents, and then the Quakers.

Many of these, like the Waldensians before them and the first Methodists in the eighteenth century, continued to worship in the parish churches, even if only to avoid suspicion; otherwise they usually met as inconspicuously as possible in their own houses, or when under more extreme persecution secretly in woods and barns. The city of Zurich was an early centre of anabaptism in the sixteen twenties, and one of the first of these congregations met in a peasant house at Zollikon nearby for re-baptism and the celebration of the Lord's Supper. In 1536 those in the Cassel district are reported to have used an abandoned church, and in 1530 a demand was made at Strassburg that a church be assigned to the Anabaptist community; both the circumstances and the inclinations of the majority, however, preserved them from inheriting and then having to adapt medieval buildings.

The extremer Anabaptists were opposed on principle to any special buildings, even in the simple meeting-house style, and this tradition survives in the Old Amish in the United States, who insist on the church community meeting in homes. Others were content to buy or rent houses or warehouses for the larger congregations, and to adapt them as meeting houses, much as the early Church had done; when persecutions receded they followed the early Christians again in building their own simple meeting places, looking much like dwelling houses; indeed in some places such as Holland they were forbidden to resemble a church building, with towers or bells. One domestic example may be seen on an Austrian charity postage stamp in 1953, and, appropriately, for the Vienna Evangelical School rebuilding fund. This shows a surviving meeting house at Steyr, which was the centre for John Hut, 'the apostle of Austria'; the building has three floors and an attic under a high roof like any ordinary house in the area.

The meeting house was usually a plain square or later a rectangular space, sometimes with galleries, and a high pulpit with table on either the short or the long side; they were therefore akin to some of the new Protestant buildings we have already examined. This meeting house style was much the same wherever Anabaptist groups appeared, from Russia to the New World, and it is only gradually and in more recent times that their places of worship have been assimilated in name and in form to the churches of other Christians.

One of the interesting might-have-beens of the Reformation occurred in Poland where there was considerable movement towards Protestantism among both aristocratic families and the peasants, in the fifteen fifties. In 1555 the Diet of Warsaw allowed the nobility to introduce any form of worship they desired into their houses or on their estates. In the same year the Bohemian Brethren who had been expelled from Bohemia in 1548 entered a permanent union with the Calvinist section of the Polish Protestants, in striking contrast to the hostility that existed elsewhere between these two forms of the Protestant faith. We are told that worship was held in the large houses of the nobles, and 'in spireless, whitewashed stone meeting-houses constructed on their estates or in the towns they governed...'.[47] The combination of these two parties in a favourable situation might have established a valuable new architectural tradition in the *domus ecclesiae* manner; but once again we have no more than a token of the possibilities, for in the following decade a great Catholic revival led by the Jesuits and then supported by royal enforcement of the decrees of the Council of Trent won Poland back to the older faith.

In general we may say that the section of the Reformation that might have given the most drastic re-orientation to church building was unable to secure any abiding place where it could express its own interpretation of the church and of Christian worship in architectural form; the influence of these Anabaptist groups was not apparent in the first century of the Reformation in Europe, and must be sought at a later period in the Dissenters and Independents of England and in the Puritan migrants to the New England in America.

The sixteenth century reform movements were not confined to Protestantism and the buildings of the Catholic or Counter Reformation also repay attention. Among the pioneers of the Catholic reform were the Jesuits, who were at first in favour of circular or octagonal churches, just as this form was sponsored by some of the earlier Roman Catholic liturgical reformers of the present century. We have already examined the Renaissance centralized churches of the immediately preceding period which provided an abundance of models, and we have placed them in the *domus dei* type; at the same time their centralized nature made them more suitable than their medieval predecessors for congregational worship with full participation. It was this aspect that appealed to the Jesuits, who, whether through this form or through a rectangular plan, were concerned that preaching and instruction should reach all the worshippers. Chancels and apses were also suppressed, and the altar placed against the main rear wall of the church, where the sacrament was within sight and hearing of everyone. The reasons for this, in Jesuit churches of the sixteenth and seventeenth centuries, are given by Cardinal Lercaro: '... this was done for a functional purpose.... For the spirituality of St. Ignatius emphasized the active life, and counterbalanced this emphasis by the practice of mental prayer, which is eminently individualistic. Thus the choir was suppressed because it was the expression of the monastic spirituality, which is eminently communal.'[48] This explanation is difficult to follow unless we regard the Jesuits as substituting a wider congregational fellowship for the narrower monastic community; if that is so then they had a good deal in common, in what they were trying to do through the building, with the Protestant reformers.

The most influential building of the Jesuits was their mother church in Rome, the Gesù (1568-84), which has been widely imitated in the Latin world of both Europe and South America. It has been described as an 'edifice without mystery', a preaching church with a single broad nave, no aisles, and only narrow transepts, so that all were close to every aspect of the liturgical action. In its original form it had little internal decoration coupled with a plain but impressive exterior. It was, however, no mere auditorium for everyone could see the action at the altar and follow the mass, and it was this part of worship that was given ever greater effect and more dramatic setting in the later highly ornate theatrical Baroque churches of the Jesuits.

The chief expression and instrument of the Catholic Reformation was the Council of Trent (1545 intermittently to 1563), but no express statements were made about church architecture. It was after the Council that Charles Borromeo, who had become archbishop of Milan in 1559, applied the spirit of the Council to church building. In his directives on the subject he rejected centralized buildings as pagan and supported the revival of the medieval Latin cross plan, but although this lead was widely followed centralized churches have been built in every subsequent century, and so have served something of the original Jesuit ideals.

It appears, therefore, that in all parts of the ecclesiastical spectrum from the Anabaptists, through the Lutheran and the Reformed, to the Jesuits, ideas were present which might have led to a widespread reform in the understanding and practice of liturgical architecture. When we examine the overall history of the first century of the Reformation we realise that the scales were heavily weighted against this particular development. A great creative period in the life of the Christian Church, which has influenced subsequent history in so many other ways, seems to have bequeathed the Protestant plain style to a minority section but little firm architectural legacy to the rest of Western Christendom. Once again, as in the fourth and fifth centuries, but this time for different reasons, church architecture had neither a clear start nor a fair chance.

12

Advances and Retreats

12.1 DEVELOPING THE PROTESTANT PLAIN STYLE

In the seventeenth and eighteenth centuries church building in Britain, in North America and much of Protestant Europe revealed an extensive experimentation with the Protestant plain style that we regard as the main legacy from the Reformation era. The most influential and widely diffused statements expressing this view of the place of worship were those which emerged from 'the Assembly of Divines at Westminster with the assistance of Commissioners from the Church of Scotland as a part of the Covenanted Uniformity in Religion betwixt the Churches ... of Scotland, England and Ireland'. Strangely enough the documents drawn up between 1643 and 1646 by this assembly of almost a hundred episcopally ordained ministers of the Church of England, together with a mere eleven commissioners from Scotland, were rejected by the Church of England in 1661, but have continued as the official standards of the Church of Scotland ever since 1649. In addition they were subsequently accepted by Presbyterian settlers and the various later Presbyterian churches in North America, and in other parts of the English speaking world. No theological documents composed in the English language can have had a wider effect, so that their references to the place of worship may be taken as thoroughly representative of the Protestant position.

The Westminster *Confession of Faith* took its stand upon Scripture for all matters of faith and conduct, but recognized that 'there are some circumstances concerning the worship of God... common to human actions and societies, which are to be ordered by the light of nature and Christian prudence, according to the general rules of the word, which are always to be observed'.[1] In this spirit, and recognizing that churches were not specifically dealt with in the Bible, the Confession proceeded to declare that 'neither prayer, nor any part of religious worship is now, under the gospel, either tied unto, or made more acceptable by any place in which it is performed, or toward which it is directed; but God is to be worshipped everywhere in spirit and in truth, as in private families daily, and in secret... [and] more solemnly in the public assemblies....'[2]

In *The Directory for the Public Worship of God*, issued two years earlier in 1644, it is perhaps a sign of this same 'Christian prudence' that a subject which had been the occasion of so much recent controversy between the Puritans and Caroline divines should be relegated to a single short appendix, 'Touching Days and Places for Worship'. Here it was stated that 'as no place is capable of any holiness under pretence of whatsoever dedication or consecration; so neither is it subject to such pollution by any superstition formerly used, and now laid aside, as may render it unlawful or inconvenient for Christians to meet together therein for the public worship of God. And therefore we hold it requisite, that the places of public assembling for worship among us should be continued and employed for that use.' This, of course, is what Christians in the Reformed Churches had been doing for a century.

The polemics of the period in England had produced many individual statements,[3] and we content ourselves here with quoting from George Gillespie, a noted Presbyterian in Scotland writing in 1637: '... Unto us Christians no land is strange, no ground unholy; ... every faithful company, yea every faithful body [is] a Temple to serve God... whereas the presence of Christ among two or three gathered together in his Name... maketh any place a Church, even as the presence of a King with his attendants maketh any place a court'.[4] This goes to the heart of the New Testament position, and is not inconsistent with the Westminster divines' concern for church buildings. There were some, however, who saw an opposition between the two viewpoints due to the persistent association of churches with temples in the arguments of the anti-Puritan writers.

The most forthright opponent of church buildings in the seventeenth century was George Fox, who never tired of attacking the use of the term church for the building, and of criticizing those who regarded what he persisted in calling 'steeple-houses' as sacred places. 'The steeple-houses and pulpits,' he declared in 1651, 'were offensive to my mind because both priests and people called them "the houses of God", and idolized them, reckoning that God dwelt there in the outward house. Whereas they should have looked for... their bodies to be made temples of God....' He explicitly rejected the analogy with the temple; for Fox, 'their houses called churches were more like Jeroboam's calf-houses (even the old mass-houses) which they had set up in the dark times of popery... which God never commanded; for that temple which God had commanded at Jerusalem Christ came to end'.[5] Thus it was that the Quakers became the most radical exponents of the Protestant position, with their meeting houses expressing the most literal sense of the words, benches the only furniture needed, and both pulpit and table abandoned along with the distinction between clergyman and layman. This produced what is really a highly liturgical form of corporate worship in which the whole meeting room has become an undifferentiated worship space. Insofar as the Quakers seem to be the only section of Christendom that has remained true to its original insights and unaffected by the confusions of the nineteenth century their radical position seems to have been largely justified.

This, however, is to anticipate, for the building of meeting houses was a somewhat later development. Those who held a less radical form of the Protestant position were in somewhat the same position as their predecessors in the Reformation century: they had plenty of churches at their disposal during the Puritan ascendancy and the Commonwealth period, and when they lost control of these the disabilities they suffered after the Restoration of 1660 prevented their building many alternative places of worship in their own manner. For the most part they worshipped in warehouses or barns, private houses, guild or other rented halls, although a few plain-style 'chapels' as they were called, akin to meeting houses, were built before 1689, and the Congregational Chapel at remote Horningsham in Wiltshire may go back as far as 1566.[6] The main opportunity for the dissenters in the England of the seventeenth century came with the passing of the Act of Toleration in 1689, when the meeting house tradition of Continental Anabaptism and of English dissent was suddenly freed for architectural expression. In the next ten years over two thousand four hundred nonconformist places of worship were registered, although by no means all were new buildings, and many were adaptations from disused churches or other structures. Externally they were domestic in style, on a square plan and with none of the usual distinguishing marks of the older churches; internally they followed a central-plan arrangement, the seating being placed around a large communion table with a pulpit behind it, and if the building assumed a rectangular shape this was on the long wall. It was essentially a functional building for the meeting of a community gathered round the ministry of word and sacrament, a true *domus ecclesiae*, as may still be seen in the Unitarian and Independent chapels surviving from this period.

It is true that the inconspicuous situation in a side lane and the plain domestic interior without pointed windows, spires or bells, were dictated partly by economic necessity and partly by the continuing uncertainties of the dissenters' position, for Tory mobs were still liable to attack their chapels. It is also true that even under freer conditions the same style would have emerged, for this was essentially the manner of building that became the standard pattern in New England in the seventeenth century and well into the eighteenth. Here there is the continuing testimony of Old Ship Meeting House at Hingham, Massachusetts (1680), which may be compared with one of the larger extant examples in England, the Congregational 'Old Meeting' at Norwich (1693). In both the old world and the new, the Protestant Plain Style had a common rationale that was opposed to everything in the *domus dei* tradition.

12.2 THE NEW ANGLICAN TRADITION

We have seen that one of the ways in which the Church of England adapted its medieval buildings for reformed worship was to bring the table forward into the middle of the chancel or even into the nave for the sacrament; it then became common to leave it there even between times. This led to unseemly practices such as sitting on it, or using it as a depository for coats and hats. We can therefore sympathize with the campaign conducted by the future archbishop Laud, from 1616 when he became dean of Gloucester, to protect the table by restoring it to the east wall in the altar position, and to enclose it with rails. Behind this care for decency and order there lay a view of the church building as possessing that 'derivative and relative holiness in places... dedicated to the honour and service of God [that was] common in the Old Testament; and... in the New...'; coupled with this went a view of the altar 'as the greatest place of God's residence upon earth'.[7]

Whatever the reasons for Laud's attitude,[8] it certainly led back beyond the not dissimilar language of Hooker to the *domus dei* tradition, and it was supported by similar views in other prominent Caroline divines, who, like Lancelot Andrewes, were ready to revive the analogy between church and Jewish temple. The remarkable feature of the century is that despite the provocation of the extremer Puritan statements and the failure of the more explicitly Protestant bid for control of the Church of England, it was not the Laudian view of the church building that prevailed. While supporters of Laud were reviving the pre-Reformation tradition Inigo Jones was building St. Paul's, Covent Garden, which we have already described as a clear example of the Protestant plain style in England. This proved to be the true index of the future, for although Gothic would have better served the emphases of the Laudian view, in fact this form was not used in any Anglican church built in the two centuries after St. John's, Leeds, of 1634.

When the troubles of the civil war and the Commonwealth were over the great fire of London in 1666 presented the established church with an unexpected opportunity for a large-scale expression of its attitude to the church building. In the next forty-five years Christopher Wren designed over fifty churches, including a new St. Paul's Cathedral in London. Behind this lay a century of experience of the *Book of Common Prayer* as a pattern for reformed worship, and perhaps also the recent and revealing experience of having to use former Puritan preaching halls while the new churches were being built. An architect has summed up Wren's work as follows:

The varied forms of the city churches were always a consistent statement of the doctrine of the priesthood of all believers. Spatial unity permitted participation of all worshippers in the service both visu-

ally and physically. This form ... symbolized the new emphasis on the
enlightenend exposition of the word of God. Inside all was bright
and light; there were no shadows and mysticism. The high ornately
carved pulpits also drew attention to this aspect of doctrine.... In
these ways Wren's city churches were the first good architectural
representation of Protestant doctrine.[9]
Wren thus abandoned the 'superstitious vista' focussed on a distant and
elaborate altar, and designed simpler one-chamber buildings without
chancels that have been called the 'auditory type'. It must not, however, be suggested that Wren designed mere preaching halls. As a high
Churchman in the reformed manner he provided the architectural setting for a closer unity between word and sacrament, and for the people
to share in the ministry of both. This was achieved in a building that
was most often rectangular, though occasionally square, oval, or polygonal where the site demanded a different form; the chancel, if present,
was never more than a shallow recess for a central communion table,
still with the Laudian rails; a pulpit stood on the left, reading desk
sometimes in balance on the right, choir and organ in the west end of
the gallery, and font near the main door. A fine architectural treatment
inside and out was completed by a handsome spired tower. Here was
both a satisfying meeting house for the full range of Christian worship
and a notable addition to the townscape.

Both the quantity and the quality of Wren's buildings served to establish the pattern for most Anglican church building over nearly a century and a half, and this is still the model that has been suggested for
current Anglican practice by Addleshaw and Etchells.[10] So thoroughly
had the chancel and all that it usually signified vanished from the scene
that a late eighteenth century writer had to explain what the word
meant. From the same fundamental premises, but with such different
histories, both Nonconformity and the Establishment had arrived at
their own versions of the *domus ecclesiae*, and these had more in common with each other than either had with most of the churches built
between the fourth and the sixteenth centuries.

When Methodism emerged as a movement from within the Church
of England in the eighteenth century it created no new forms. Its
members were expected to continue in their parish churches for the

sacraments, and their own meetings were supplementary services for mutual pastoral care and the preaching of the Gospel. At first they met where they could, like the dissenters in the previous century, and when they did erect their own buildings these were regarded as 'preaching houses' even if furnished with an altar and rails, as a few were in the course of time, for the rare occasions when an ordained minister was present. The earliest of these was the 'New Room' so well preserved at Bristol, a plain rectangular building with galleries on each side and a two-decker pulpit at the end (1739). In 1757 Wesley was very taken with the octagonal meeting house erected by the Presbyterians at Norwich the previous year for the unusually large sum of £5,000; for a time this became a popular Methodist plan for its chapels, even as far afield as Aberdeen, where the first Methodist building was called 'The Octagon'. This plan was officially commended by the Conference of 1770 on account of its functional properties. It was, however, the City Road Chapel in London (1778) which became the official norm in 1790—a rectangular building with shallow apse containing communion table and rails, with a high pulpit in front of this, and galleries on three sides. This plan aimed at a meeting house for preaching and the sacrament, and was not uncommon in Anglican churches of the period. Methodism was now largely assimilated to the building model of its Anglican parent and has since made no distinctive contribution to the form of a church, unless it be the Akron plan to be mentioned below.

12.3 THE PROTESTANT PLAIN STYLE IN OTHER AREAS

We have already noted the central-plan buildings that appeared in Scotland by the end of the Reformation century, and the development of the common T-plan from the rectangular church arranged transversely, as may be seen at Ayr (1654). In the eighteenth century more explicitly central plans took various forms: the oval of St. Andrew's as part of the 'New Town' plan in Edinburgh of 1765, the large plain octagon to seat three thousand at Kelso in 1773 and other octagons at Dreghorn (1788) and Eaglesham (1790), and the square with extensions on each side at Lasswade (1794). All of these tended to be designed as meeting and preaching houses, but to make no fixed provision for a communion table, which was commonly set up only when required for the quarterly or even less frequent celebration — in one parish no sacrament was observed for fifty years.

The same sacramental practice appeared in the Protestant churches of Holland, where the many experiments already mentioned were continued through a great variety of central-type ground plans, octagonal, square, Greek cross, T-shaped, etc., and all with internal arrangements of a convergent nature focussing on the pulpit as the dominant liturgical feature. Again in Switzerland the churches of the Reformation were designed on the same principles, except that here the communion table was more likely to be a permanent feature in the very middle of the seating, with the pulpit on the long wall, as at Wadenswil (1764) and Horgen (1780).

The somewhat different development of Lutheranism in Germany maintained the unity of word and sacrament, which was expressed by a close grouping of pulpit, table, font, and even organ, and sometimes by designing the pulpit and the table as one massive piece of liturgical furniture providing for the two main foci of the service. Otherwise there was the same experimenting with novel ground plans, although rectangles arranged longitudinally, and sometimes with chancels, prevailed. Simple rectangular churches appeared in rural areas in the second half of the seventeenth century to replace those destroyed in the Thirty Years War, and while there were still lighted candles and a crucifix on the altar-table the building was domestic in appearance and encouraged all to engage in the action.

These buildings followed principles enunciated by the first Lutheran writer on church architecture, Joseph Furttembach whom we mentioned above. In the next generation another influential architect, Leonhard Christoph Sturm (1669-1729), developed the central plan more specifically and in ways suited to the larger numbers and greater resources of town congregations. He attacked the cruciform plan and emphasis on chancels, and advocated a squarish form or a rectangular church arranged with pulpit and altar on a longer side so that all could see and hear, and with the liturgical centres placed close together. In the first half of the eighteenth century many churches on a great variety of ground plans sought to follow these principles.[11]

Sturm had drawn the rather dubious analogy between a Greek theatre and a Christian church, meaning by this to support the principle
of the central plan. This form was also found in most Roman Catholic
churches built in southern Europe during this period. It was not difficult, therefore, for both Lutheran and Catholic churches to share in
the Baroque style with its central opera-style plan and its markedly
theatrical effects, as it developed in southern Germany and Austria.
Baroque was very much a product of the culture and society of the day
with its numerous princes and courts, and their patronage of the arts
as well as of the Church. The buildings of the latter were assimilated
to Baroque culture in two ways that have been well expressed by Professor Davies: 'Since God is the King of Kings... his residence has to
display even more splendour than that which is lavished on princes.' It
was further 'inspired by the desire to offer to God all the riches of the
world, to gather together in edifices consecrated to him and in which
he resides all forms of beauty, sanctified by the sacred character of
their function'.[12] These are not in themselves ignoble attitudes, and
they have produced some of the most magnificent temple edifices and
church buildings in human history. This was akin to the spirit in which
Constantine had endowed the church of the fourth century with its
most splendid buildings. But we have seen how this attitude inevitably
issues in buildings of the temple type and loses contact with the New
Testament revolution. Early in the development of Baroque this was
shown in Anne of Austria's instructions to the architect of the Parisian
church of Val-de-Grâce, in 1645: 'The church must be a sumptuous
and magnificent sanctuary in order to compensate as much as possible
for the extreme vulgarity and poverty of the place where the Eternal
Word chose to be born.'[13] In other words, the church building must
correct the unfortunate impression created by the Incarnation rather
than find its form therein.

The most famous example of Protestant Baroque was the Lutheran
Frauenkirche at Dresden (1726-38) which expressed the principles of
Sturm in the new style, until destroyed in World War II. Externally it
could be mistaken for an opera house, and internally it could well have
served this purpose for the seven thousand it accomodated. The plan

was basically circular with no less than five tiers of galleries facing a stage-like apse framed in a large arch. The pulpit was fixed to the left pillar of the arch; curved stairways ascended to the platform that projected forward from the apse and carried a central lectern with a font behind it; then on a still higher platform towards the rear of the apse stood the altar with a splendid reredos, and above this in the upper reaches the organ crowned the whole effect. As a setting for the dramatic spectacle of a high mass in which few participated the building was excellent, both as to sight and sound; as a meeting place for a community gathered round to share in word and sacrament it was quite unserviceable. Fortunately Baroque remained a minority development that was short lived in the Protestant world, although it had considerable influence in the Catholic churches built during the Spanish and Portuguese periods in Latin America.

Another centre of Christian activity in the seventeenth and eighteenth centuries lay in North America where the Protestant plain form was continued by the settlers and developed into the New England or colonial forms of the Georgian style, in which the influence of Wren may be clearly detected. The whole evolution of this form has been traced from the earliest square meeting houses through several stages. First, the square became a rectangle, but still with the entrance on one long side facing the pulpit on the other side, and perhaps with a tower at the end. Then a second door was provided under the tower, and finally this became the only entrance, with the original doorway closed up and the pulpit shifted to the shorter wall at the far end from the tower, and the seating arranged as in a hall down the length of the 'church'.[14] The very name had changed in company with the loss of the original meeting house effect, but it was still a pleasing example of the Protestant plain style, and it became the model for the churches of many later denominations, including even the Roman Catholic Cathedral of St. Joseph at Bardstown in Kentucky. Only in later times when chancels were added was there any substantial interference with a building that remained fundamentally a *domus ecclesiae*. This principle also governed many eighteenth century Anglican buildings, as in the plain squarish-plan churches of South Carolina.

There was therefore less experiment with all kinds of ground plans among the American Protestants than there was in Europe during these two centuries. But behind these differences there lay a consensus about the place of worship that extended also into some sections of Catholicism: in one way or another it had become more of a central plan building in a simpler style, concentrated on a single chamber which needed no chancel, and functioning as a house where the people of God met with their ministers to share together in the liturgical action. Nothing like this had happened on such a scale since the fourth century, and it might seem that at last Christendom was producing a place of worship rooted in its own origins and true to its distinctive nature. But once again the course of church building was deflected into other channels, for the nineteenth century proved to be a period of reactions and of extremes from which we are painfully recovering today.

12.4 THE LOSS OF THE *DOMUS ECCLESIAE*: THE AUDITORIUM

One of the basic requirements in churches of most denominations in the centuries after the Reformation was that it should be an 'auditory' building, a place where whatever was said in connection with word and sacrament was clearly heard by all. Most places of worship, from the theatrical Baroque to the non-sacramental Quaker meeting house, could satisfy this demand. The movement we are now to trace, that reached its height in the later nineteenth century, concentrated upon this admirable feature and upon the preaching that it facilitated, but in the end transformed the auditory meeting house into a preaching auditorium and concert hall that ceased to be a suitable home for the Christian community.

Signs of this development have already been indicated—in the subordinate place occupied by the sacrament and by the table that provided for it, together with its infrequent celebration or even total neglect. In Holland and in Scotland it was the preaching that mattered and the arrangement of many churches made this only too plain. Even in the Baroque churches something of the same effect was created, for while those in the tiers of galleries were effectively related to the high pulpit they were isolated from any active participation in the sacrament, which was extremely difficult from the galleries. Among Presbyterians and independents in England the development was in this same direction. A Unitarian writer has traced the evolution of Unitarian church building from its earlier Presbyterian meeting houses, and shown how the large table round which or near which the participants sat for the sacrament shrank in size, and became a railed-in token table and rather inconspicuous beneath a pulpit that dominated the building. This change was part of the same development as the one we have traced in the New England meeting house, the elongation of the building and the placing of the pulpit at the far end from the entrance. As a result, whereas 'formerly the preacher stood like the father of a family, with the rest gathered round him, because the old building reflected Calvin's belief that the Communion was a supper round a table. Now the preacher is like a schoolmaster facing a class, and minister and people are separated in a way against which the Puritans protested.'[15]

The emphasis upon the word at the expense of the sacrament, and all that this implied in the nature of the building, was therefore well advanced in some sections of the Protestant world when the great evangelical movements on both sides of the Atlantic in the nineteenth century led still further in this same direction. The conversion of the individual was now the major concern and the gifted evangelical preacher the chief instrument. The result was a new conception of the church building as a place where large numbers of people could feel as much at home as in any secular meeting hall and could be brought into the closest possible encounter with the message and the personality of the preacher. Instead of a splendid pulpit giving authority and prestige to the sermon, no matter how ordinary the preacher, there now appeared the attenuated preacher's desk set on a large open platform that gave greater scope and visibility to the idiosyncrasies of the preacher himself. Here he could leave the shelter of a pulpit in order to come face to face with his hearers, pleading with them as man to man, kneeling in prayer for them, or walking to and fro as he used all the dramatic arts to convey his appeal.

To meet this situation large preaching churches were built on a squarish or central axis ground plan with one or more tiers of galleries surrounding the projecting platform on three sides, so that every one of the thousands of hearers was as close as possible to the preacher. On the fourth side and behind the pulpit area the space was filled with the ranks of the choir that reinforced the appeal of the preacher with its devotional singing, and behind the choir rose the large pipe-organ. If there was a communion table it was probably small and rather inconspicuous at or near the ground floor level below the pulpit platform. As a building it was highly efficient for its purposes in the days when large crowds regularly hung upon the words of the famous preachers for which the nineteenth century was notable.

Several outstanding churches of this nature were built in London within the short space of fifteen years. In 1860 there was the building in South London known simply as Spurgeon's Tabernacle, built on a circular plan so that five thousand people in three tiers of galleries could hear the great Baptist preacher. Five years later the Congregationalists had completed Westminster Chapel with two tiers of galleries, and here for a century visitors from all over the world have come to hear its famous preachers – Campbell Morgan, J. H. Jowett, John Hutton, and Martin Lloyd-Jones. In 1874 the City Temple was built at the cost of £70,000 and its minister, the Congregationalist Joseph Parker, could command as his telegraphic address simply 'Preacher, London'; the 'pulpit' could hold forty people.

Many other famous churches that were fundamentally auditoria appeared in other areas in the same period: for instance, St. George's West in Edinburgh and Queen's Park St. George's in Glasgow,[16] and across the Atlantic the Congregational Church in Brooklyn built for the two thousand five hundred who listened to Henry Ward Beecher. Nor was the Anglican tradition exempt. In 1877 Trinity Episcopal Church was built in Boston, Massachusetts, for the greatest American preacher of the century, Phillips Brooks. This was basically an auditorium with a large central preaching space formed by a Greek cross plan with short wide arms; in this case the communion table was better treated, being placed in a shallow apse that still kept it in close relation to the people. In the next twenty years it was imitated in many parts of the United States, although it was later 'made more liturgical' with altar and baldachino. To the same period belongs the widely used Akron plan which originated in the Methodist Episcopal Church at Akron, Ohio. Here a square auditorium was arranged on a diagonal axis: a gallery around two adjacent sides faced the opposite corner where there was a combination of pulpit platform with choir behind and table in front at a lower level; one of the free side walls between gallery and platform could be opened up so that the adjacent large Sunday School room could become part of the church space when needed. This again was a highly functional building within its limited conception of the activities appropriate in Christian worship.

The auditorium plan has survived into the present century and in various traditions. For example the Methodists built Newland Church, Hull, in 1928 on this principle, and as recently as 1969 the Rev. Ian Paisley's Martyrs Memorial Free Presbyterian Church, costing over £160,000, was opened in Belfast. With the help of a large gallery there is seating for some two and a half thousand people facing a pulpit that will hold eight ministers, but not much sign of a communion table; as Mr. Paisley said at the opening, there was 'nothing on ministers as priests in the New Testament but plenty on preaching', a statement that has its own measure of truth.

The lamentable decay of preaching in the twentieth century, coupled with a new sense of the full dimensions of the Christian community and of its worship, have combined to brand the auditorium church as a period piece, a remarkable testimony to the individual personalities who sustained it, and to the performances they and their choirs provided. It was certainly efficient for its purpose, and it made its own contribution at that stage in Christian history. But as a preaching church carried to an extreme form upon the outstanding gifts of individual men it no longer offered a normal pattern for churches where most of those who ministered would never be great preachers; nor was it a meeting house providing for worship that was truly corporate and comprehensive. The gathering of a huge audience chattering with suppressed excitement over what was to be expected today from the central figure is hardly a picture of the assembly of Christ's people for its common worship. To call the building an 'upholstered auditorium, with its secular platform, fetish-like organ pipes, and balcony suggestive of the running track of a gymnasium'[17] may be going too far, but it has the truth of a caricature. Such a church might be the antithesis of medievalism, but it was also a far cry from the upper room and from a true *domus ecclesiae.*

12.5 THE RETURN OF THE *DOMUS DEI*: THE GOTHIC REVIVAL

The auditorium development, with its emphasis upon the dramatic performance of minister and choir, has been explained as a low-Protestant substitute for the lost drama of the mass celebrated amid the mysteries of the sanctuary. This criticism would consort well with the contrary and equally extreme reaction associated with the Gothic Revival movement of the nineteenth century to which we now turn.

The astonishingly sudden and unheralded nature of this movement is seen only if we first observe the nature of church building in the first few decades of the century. The eighteenth century consensus was carried over into the nineteenth, so that as John Betjeman has put it,

there was little to choose between an early nineteenth century Methodist, New Jerusalem, Roman, Independent or Unitarian chapel in a large town ... and a Proprietary chapel or new chapel of ease erected for the Established Church. They did not have bells or towers, but their internal arrangements were similar.... The pulpit dominated the altar... those which retained the rectangular plan... had exceedingly shallow chancels and the pulpit was... often in front of the table.[18]

This general form was continued in the churches built from the one and a half million pounds voted by Parliament in 1818 and 1824 to provide for the unchurched masses in the growing towns. In all, by 1858 three million pounds had been spent on over six hundred churches erected by the Church Building Commission. The new churches reflected in their exteriors and styles the rediscovery of both Classical and Gothic architecture that marked the first two or three decades of the century; these, however, were no more than styles apparent in windows and facades, and in towers or spires where these were added, but not affecting the ground plan or the interior arrangements in any important way. The Commissioners were undoctrinaire in attitude and followed the proved eighteenth century patterns in a well-balanced if rather undistinguished manner; they insisted, for instance, on good auditory qualities as well as on a free-standing table that was appropriately emphasized, usually in a shallow recess some ten feet deep at the shorter end of the rectangular space.

There was, therefore, little suggestion of the explosion that occurred in the eighteen thirties, and produced the second and even more influential of the two major influences of the century — the Gothic Revival; this had nothing to do with the Gothic churches of the Commissioners, which were repudiated as degenerate and 'protestant'. It is beyond our scope and purposes here to trace in detail the many factors that were compounded in this new Gothic enthusiasm. In the background lay the romantic movement in general, and especially Sir Walter Scott's romanticized version of the Middle Ages. In Oxford there was the Tractarian movement that broke surface in 1833, with its deep concern for the reform of worship by taking the ministry and the sacraments more seriously. In Leeds in 1841 there was the rebuilding of the parish church in a new manner, and the novelty of a surpliced lay choir placed in the chancel to provide a daily choral service; this was the work of a great reforming vicar, W. F. Hook, and a colleague John Jebb, both of whom owed their inspiration to Jebb's uncle, an evangelical High Church bishop of Limerick. In Cambridge, the years 1836-1839 saw the appearance of a speedily influential student society, the Camden Society founded by John Mason Neale, E. J. Boyce and Benjamin Webb, consolidated in 1839 with the aid of one of their tutors, Thomas Thorp — all, of course, Anglicans. Two years later their journal, *The Ecclesiologist*, was dispensing a new theory of church architecture that was rapidly put into practice in many areas. The same decade saw the emergence of the most striking individual protagonist of the Gothic gospel, a young architect of French Protestant extraction named Augustus Welby Northmore Pugin, who was converted to Roman Catholicism in 1834 at the age of twenty-two, and who published his first broadside, *Contrasts*, in 1836. This was a series of beautifully drawn satirical sketches contrasting the 'Christian' architecture of the Gothic Middle Ages with the 'pagan' forms of his own day, and was followed in 1841 by *The True Principles of Pointed or Christian Architecture*.

From the interaction of all these initiatives the Gothic Revival took shape, and we can do no more than outline some of the main emphases in the theories and practice associated with the movement, and the influence that it has exerted to this day through most Christian denominations and in many parts of the world.

12.5.1 *Theories in the Gothic Revival*

The basic position was composed of a certain theory of the relation between architecture and culture, intermingled with a particular interpretation of Christian history. A culture and its architecture were regarded as integral to each other, so that each culture produced its own appropriate and distinctive architectural forms; these reflected its own climate, materials, customs and religion and could not be successfully borrowed for use in another milieu. Thus the pyramid, the obelisk, the temple and the pagoda belonged to their respective pagan societies, and those churches since the Renaissance which had been modelled on Greek or Roman temples, especially those reflecting the influence of the recent Classical revival, were quite unfit for use in a Christian culture. By the same token, a Christian culture would produce its own truly Christian form of architecture for its churches, and this was believed to have happened when the Christian religion had been most pervasive and powerful in the so-called 'ages of faith', and especially at their climax in the fourteenth century. Earlier, 'the Church in her suffering state' had not been free for this expression; but then her extended triumph 'in beauty and luxuriant foliage over the earth'[19] had been manifested in the perfect architectural form of decorated Gothic. A church must therefore be on a cruciform plan and in the 'pointed' style, as Pugin called it.

There is a measure of truth in this cultural theory of architecture if not pressed to these doctrinaire extremes. There was much less truth in the idealized picture of the fourteenth century as a 'Merrie England' of profound and orthodox piety that had been destroyed by the increasing power of state over church, the corrosions of the pagan Renaissance and the heretical Reformation, and the blight of the industrial revolution; to have lived in the period and seen what the faith of the age really was and how the churches were actually used would have been a shattering experience for any of the Gothic revivalists. Such, however, was the innocence and the conviction of the more extreme among them that they seriously proposed the rebuilding of the Norman Cathedral at Peterborough in decorated Gothic, although (true to the cultural theory of architecture) they advised Bishop Selwyn in New Zealand that Norman would be better suited to the natives there in their present stage of development! Even St. Peter's in Rome joined the demolition list.

Implicit in this theory of architecture lies the 'ethical fallacy' developed in a theological direction, the assertion of a direct correlation between the morality or orthodoxy of the architect and the nature of the building he produces. As Neale and Webb put it, 'in ancient times, the finest buildings were designed by the holiest bishops, and such must always be the case'. This was supported by the Old Testament view of the Spirit of God as the source of all skill and wisdom. Hence 'there cannot be a more painful idea than that a separatist should be allowed to build a House of God... or again to think that any churchman should allow himself to build a conventicle...'. In other words, only an honest, noble, Catholic Christian architect can build an honest, noble, Catholic Christian church, and he should build nothing else, not even a secular building, although 'as things are we cannot expect so much as this now'.[20]

This architectural doctrine was associated with revived medieval views of the Christian community as a hierarchical society in which the basic distinction lay between the laity and the clergy, for the latter were 'endowed with high privileges as being those consecrated to the immediate service of the sanctuary'. Therefore 'the material edifice displayed a like division: the nave and chancel preach to posterity the sacredness of Holy Orders, and the... relation in which the flock stand to their shepherds'.[21] The office of the minister was now to provide a sacerdotal and sacramental service in all the mystery of holiness, offered on behalf of the people rather than along with them in any corporate fashion, yet designed to elicit their response in adoration.

The church building in this view was no longer the house of the people of God for their common worship, but the House of God which they were allowed to enter with due reverence; they must remain in the nave and refrain from entering the chancel which was for the choir, or the sanctuary reserved for the priesthood. The post-Reformation

Anglican view of the building having only a relative and derived holiness was replaced by a revived theory of the church as a holy place, on the specific analogy of the Jerusalem temple. For this Neale and Webb could find only a tenuous basis: 'The probability that in the earliest Christian churches there was at least this resemblance to the Temple: that there should be in both a Holy of Holies and an outer-court. Supposing this distinction to have been only made by a curtain, our point is nevertheless gained.' Further, 'any one designed parallel being granted, the inference for others is easy'.[22]

This tendentious account of the most ancient places of Christian worship was supported by quotations from the Fathers employing the analogy with the Jewish temple, and amounted to a deliberate revival of the *domus dei* tradition. The chief manifestation of this was the insistence on chancels to distinguish true churches from mere conventicles; the chancel, according to the first issue of *The Ecclesiologist*, ought to be at least a third of the length of the nave, and divided into the choir and the raised altar-sanctuary; it should also be separated from the nave by several steps, and a screen which might be said to stand 'between two worlds, the one immovable, the other changeful; the one of gods (or heaven) the other of mortals (or earth); that is to say between the choir and the nave, between the clergy and the laity'.[23] For Pugin, screens represented 'the very vitals of Catholic architecture', for 'faith in the Holy Eucharist could not survive their destruction'.[24]

A further consequence of the re-establishment of a sanctuary was that fonts, which had sometimes stood near the altar-table, must now be moved to the other end of the church, near the entrance, lest any infant be allowed into the holiest part of the church before its baptism. In the sanctuary the Camden Society campaigned for lighted and vested stone altars, for a credence table, for flowers, incense and crosses, and for the use of vestments and the sacerdotal eastward posture; most of this was quite foreign to the early members of the Oxford Movement and adopted only by the later Anglo-Catholics. It is doubtful, however, whether much of this would have been taken up if Hook and Jebb at Leeds had not provided a more acceptable rationale for chancels by dignified daily services of matins and evensong sung by the clergy and a small choir.

12.5.2 *Gothic Revival symbolism*

In keeping with the temple tradition the building itself must not only
create a sense of awe and mystery but also represent the richest and
most splendid offering that man can make to God. Churches, said Pugin, should exhibit 'the truly Catholic principle of dedicating the best
(men) possessed to God', and 'be more vast and beautiful than those
(buildings) in which they dwell'. In fact, 'a man who builds a church
draws down a blessing on himself both for this life and that of the world
to come'.[25] Gothic, by its very nature, was peculiarly fitted for such
an offering to the glory of God. It also gave full scope for the idea of
the church building as symbolic not only of the numinous presence
of God and of the devoted response of men, but also of almost every
conceivable aspect of Christian belief and practice.

For the Gothic revivalists the roots of this symbolism were also to
be found in the medieval period, in the great love of allegory applied
not only to the interpretation of Scripture but also to the details of
the liturgy and of the church building. This reached its classic and most
influential expression in the *Rationale Divinorum Officiorum* of Durandus, whose inventiveness in this field we have already sampled.[26] His
translators, Neale and Webb, however, did equally well on their own
account, as we may see by letting them speak for themselves in their
'general view of the symbolism of a Catholic church'.

> Far away, and long ere we catch our first view of the city itself, the
> three spires of its cathedral, rising high amid its din and turmoil,
> preach to us of the Most Holy and Undivided Trinity. As we ap-
> proach, the transepts, striking out cross-wide, tell of the Atonement:
> the Communion of Saints is set forth by the chapels clustering round
> choir and nave: the mystical weathercock bids us to watch and pray
> and endure hardness: the hideous forms that seem hurrying from
> the eaves speak the misery of those who are cast out of the Church:
> spire, pinnacle, and finial, the upward curl of the sculptured foliage,
> the upward spring of the flying buttress, the sharp rise of the window
> arch, the high-thrown pitch of the roof, all these, overpowering the
> horizontal tendency of string course and parapet, teach us, that van-
> quishing earthly desires, we should also ascend in heart and mind....

We enter. The triple breadth of nave and aisles, the triple height of pier arch, triforium, and clerestory, the triple length of choir, transepts, and nave, again set forth the Holy Trinity. ... Close by us is the font ... it is deep and capacious, for we are buried in baptism with Christ: it is of stone; for He is the Rock: and its spiry cover teaches us ... to seek those things that are above. Before us, in long drawn vista, are the massy piers, which are the Apostles and Prophets: they are each of many members, for many are the graces of each saint: there is delicate foliage round the head of all; for all were plentiful of good works. Beneath our feet are the badges of pomp and glory, the charges of kings and nobles and knights: all in the presence of God as dross and worthlessness. Over us swells the vast 'valley' of the high-pitched roof ... in its centre stands the Lamb ... around Him the Celestial Host ... look down peacefully on the worshippers below ... one is the song of the Church in earth and in heaven.[27]

The theme of the hierarchy joining the Church militant and the Church triumphant, the prophets and apostles, the saints and martyrs, is then developed in relation to the structure of the building for a further page, and inevitably recalls exactly the same cosmic symbolism we have already described in the churches of Eastern Orthodoxy.

This might be accepted as a rather imaginative devotional or pedagogical exercise, but there was more precision in much of the other symbolism attributed to the building. Trinitarianism resided in the altar steps, which must be in threes, and of course in every three-light window. If it was of two lights, then these were the two natures of Christ; or the double leaves of the entrance doors under one arch were the two natures in one person. If there were six trefoils in a circular window they were assigned to the six attributes of the Deity, although Neale and Webb admitted that the symbolism of complicated Decorated windows was so difficult that 'who will now pretend to expound it?'

Gothic architecture, by its inherent nature, was therefore regarded as containing an inexhaustible potentiality for Christian symbolism, and so provided the single and final style for a church; no other form revealed its essential inner connection with the Christian faith, or could ever hope to serve it truly. The difference was akin to that between the revelation contained in the Bible and whatever qualities the rest of the world's literature might contain. Neale and Webb asserted that it was 'of no consequence whatever, whether the early builders of (Gothic) churches intended this particular arrangement to be symbolical'.[28] A form which had emerged from an intensely Christian culture was inevitably eloquent of its origins, but only after men had learned to listen to its message could they deliberately accept and perpetuate it as the one Christian style, the one true house of God.

12.6 THE NEW-OLD IMAGE OF A CHURCH

It is difficult to find adequate explanation for the immediate, widespread and continuing influence of the Gothic revivalists, for it is to this source that we must trace the dominant image of a 'proper' church building in the English-speaking world. How was it that this form of building was so soon adopted (to the dismay of the Camdenians) by those who bitterly opposed the type of worship with which it was associated and for which it was intended – by the evangelical and low church Anglicans and many nonconformists? And, on the other hand, why was its influence so limited in the one quarter where there would seem to be a natural affinity – in the rapidly reviving Roman Catholic Church in Britain? Although Pugin designed four new Catholic cathedrals Cardinal Wiseman disliked Gothic, and Newman regarded Pugin as an intolerant bigot, even 'heretical and a little more'. How did the Camden Society continue its influence when the first flush of enthusiasm that drew in seven hundred members began to collapse within four years, so that by 1864 it was forced to change its name to the Ecclesiological Society and remove to London in order to survive? What was it that countered the strong criticisms of many architects in one of the professional journals?

We may find answers to some of these questions, such as Ruskin's influence on the Evangelicals, but we remain astonished at the result: 'For fifty years almost every new Anglican Church was built and furnished according to their [the Ecclesiologists'] instructions; that is to say, in a manner opposed to utility, economy, or good sense – a very wonderful achievement in the mid-nineteenth century.'[29] When we look back upon the combination of utility, economy and good sense with a genuine *domus ecclesiae* in the seventeenth and eighteenth centuries, the problem of explanation is enlarged still further.

The consequence, however, is quite clear: the standard Anglican parish church as we have known it over the past century, especially in the towns, with its cruciform shape, deep chancel for surpliced choir, railed sanctuary at the far end, covered altar with candlesticks and a cross, rather inconspicuous side pulpit, litany desks, and prominent brass eagle-lectern. It is difficult to realize what a novelty much of this was until a mere hundred and forty years ago. In keeping with the parish church the renewal of Anglican cathedral building exhibits the same Gothic style — Truro (1879-1910), and in the present century first Liverpool and then Guildford, with the later Coventry Cathedral maintaining much the same internal arrangements albeit with a different form of building.

The Nonconformist response to the new fashion is equally striking, and not least because it seems to have begun among the rationally minded and non-ritualistic Unitarians. Their Upper Brook Street Church in Manchester is described as 'the first Nonconformist church to be built in full Gothic', although it still had a central pulpit. The next step, with side pulpit and chancel complete with table, occurred in 1848 in Hyde Chapel, Cheshire, and Mill Hill Chapel, Leeds, and 'about 1850 a Unitarian magazine announced with pride that the newest Unitarian church was "a perfect replica of an English parish church of the 15th Century"'.[30] Even sadder was the intrusion of Gothic revival elements into existing meeting houses, as in the Unitarian Chapel at Leicester. Great Meeting in Bond Street was built by the Presbyterians in 1708 and is one of the loveliest examples of the meeting house type. By the eighteen sixties it was the home of a prosperous Unitarian congregation whose members were prominent in public affairs, and who apparently desired to improve upon the domestic simplicity of their meeting place by following the current fashion and acquiring a chancel, with divided choir stalls, table and all. The result of their efforts protrudes like an architectural sore thumb and has ruined a classic building of its kind.

The Congregationalists in the middle of the century were also enjoying an economic and social status akin to that of the Unitarians, and were therefore prone to abandon their simpler meeting house ancestry for a more opulent style. The first large Gothic church in London was Christ Church (1872) in Westminster Bridge Road, which could hold two thousand five hundred people; only the spired tower survived World War II. Older buildings were remodelled and given chancels, as the King's Weigh House Chapel in 1901, and many new churches followed the Gothic fashion; their Mansfield College buildings (1889-90), were described by Heiler as 'the most Catholic place in Oxford'!

It is not altogether surprising, therefore, that we have already quoted their greatest modern theologian, P. T. Forsyth, in appreciation of the Gothic church. Forsyth showed a profound sensitivity to its religious qualities. He observed the 'inwardness' of Gothic, 'as if to enclose the worshipper with Deity'; the 'broken and tempered' daylight produced a 'dim, bowed, mysterious sadness'; there was an aspiration after infinity about it, a rich beauty inside and out and a unity that bound the exterior to the interior and led to a feeling of 'dynamic peace'. In consequence Gothic provided the perfect shrine for the spectacular ritual of the Mass, and was 'the purest, most adequate, and most congenial expression of the Christian spirit in architecture'. In spite of this last statement Forsyth had no doubts whatsoever that Gothic was quite unsuitable for an evangelical Christianity where the emphasis was on the preached word and communal worship; this view of Christianity 'seals the fate of the Gothic style', if only because good aesthetics cannot replace bad acoustics.[31] Unfortunately for Congregationalism, Forsyth spoke nearly half a century too late.

Even earlier, the Unitarians had been followed by the Methodists, who had their own more sober Pugin in Dr. Frederick Jobson. Before entering the Wesleyan Methodist ministry in 1834 he had been articled to a Roman Catholic architect who was one of the early exponents of the Gothic Revival, and he retained a professional interest in the theory and practice of church architecture throughout his ministry. His tastes made him sensitive to much of the drabness in Methodist buildings, and when he held appointment at the influential City Road Chapel in London in the eighteen forties he wrote a series of articles setting forth a theory of Gothic as the ideal Christian form that was very similar to the views of Pugin and of the Camden Society. These were published on Conference authority in 1850 as *Chapel and School Architecture, as Appropriate to the Buildings of Nonconformists*.... Model designs for a village chapel and a suburban church were drawn up in the Gothic style, although at first there were no chancels but a railed-in table in front of a central pulpit. This was no different from earlier arrangements, but the adoption of Gothic as a style led in the end to the developments that usually went with it, and gave Methodism its own tradition of churches in the *domus dei* manner. Some branches of Methodism continued the early meeting house pattern well into the twentieth century, but these have been overshadowed by those anxious for Methodism to have a 'proper church', and it is the latter who were still supporting buildings derived from the Gothic Revival a century after Jobson. Thus an architect was able to comment on the *Methodist Buildings Report of 1958*:

Although the buildings illustrated in this document would be generally considered as 'contemporary' in style, they are practically all long and narrow, with the communion table set against a curtain at the end of a vista. This position gives the table a symbolic significance analogous to that of an altar, a significance which is further emphasized in some examples by the table having a cubic form.... Also the long, narrow, high building is far from ideal for preaching or for the development of Christian community.[32]

Some would explain this as an example of the constant tendency to put the emphasis on the building when the virtue of the community declines.

Other communions which might be thought to have their roots more directly planted in the Reformation tradition came under the spell of the same Gothic Revival. The more prosperous Baptist congregations showed that they too could build as well as the rest, as witness the appropriately named Victoria Road Church (1865) in Leicester, complete with chancel. The nearest the Baptists have approached to a Gothic cathedral is in the great Coats Memorial Church in Paisley (1893), with its massive portal, central tower, and deep chancel containing a communion table in front and baptistery behind.

Nor were the Scottish Presbyterians immune, not even the Free Church which since the Disruption had known many a plain and improvised building. Yet when it began to build more permanently later in the century it was usually in the Gothic manner, albeit sometimes impossibly based on square or circular plans, or combined with an auditorium as at the Barclay Church, Edinburgh (1862). The Church of Scotland saw a revival of interest in public worship and its setting, and had its own Church Service Society from 1865 and an Ecclesiological Society from 1886. There was, however, sufficient confusion for the seventeenth century Old Greyfriars, Edinburgh, to be rebuilt in a thirteenth century Gothic manner (1857), and for another rebuilding at St. Cuthbert's in Edinburgh (1894) which avoided the Gothic only to perpetrate a meeting house church with a chancel and altar-like marble table. Even the more scholarly reformers often seemed ignorant of the possibilities of their own inheritance, and therefore 'fell back on the tradition of the one communion they knew which had never completely surrendered the unity of Word and Sacrament, notably the Anglican. It was unfortunate, however, that this... should have taken place at a time when Anglicanism itself was experiencing a considerable architectural sea-change as a result of the Oxford movement.... It thus becomes one of the ironies of history' that much of the architectural expression of the liturgical reformation in Scotland 'should have been precisely that which the first Reformers had given up'.[33] Some of the churches might be very good Gothic, or impressive examples of Gothic in a free modern idiom, such as the splendid Reid Memorial Church in Edinburgh as late as 1929-32, but all inclined to the *domus dei* rather than the *domus ecclesiae*, or represented an unsatisfactory compromise between the two.

It is surprising, at first sight, that the major denomination least influenced by the Gothic Revival should have been the Roman Catholic Church. The Revival, however, was very much an English religious and cultural movement, while in general the Catholic Church, despite Pugin's cathedrals, remained loyal to Italianate architecture and Roman liturgical use. Its major cathedral at Westminster is a wide Byzantine basilica with galleries and apse not unsuitable as a large preaching church. For similar reasons Catholicism on the Continent was also less influenced by the Gothic movement, although in a sense the climax of the whole revival might be found in the highly original and quite fantastic Sagrada Familia church in Barcelona, begun in 1884 but still unfinished.

Continental Protestantism, however, especially in Germany, had its own Gothic revival reinforced by subsequent influence from England. Here again there was the same combination of romanticism and revived medievalism, with the added support of two successive kings of Prussia, Frederick William III and Frederick William IV. In 1861 the Eisenach Conference on Church Architecture set the seal on Gothic as the best form for new churches; orientation was recommended once more, and side pulpits so that the altar might be sufficiently prominent. English influence is attested in the choice of Sir Giles Gilbert Scott as architect for the great church of St. Nicholas (1845-1863) in Hamburg, and it was the particular form of the Gothic Revival in England that determined the international style it was to become.[34]

12.7 AN INTERNATIONAL PATTERN

12.7.1 *Gothic Revivals in the United States*

In the United States of America there was a remarkable parallel with developments in England. Gothic was first promoted as an architectural style without liturgical effects, especially by John Henry Hopkins (1792-1868) who graduated from practical secular activities to the Protestant Episcopal ministry and finally became senior bishop in this communion. In 1823 he designed his first church, Trinity at Pittsburgh, to hold a thousand people in a plain Gothic rectangle with galleries on three sides and on the other a pulpit, reading desk, table and font, one in front of the other and centrally placed. Once, however, he had discovered an analogy between Gothic and the Jerusalem Temple and asserted therefore that Gothic was the most ancient form of religious architecture the way was prepared for subsequent development towards the *domus dei*. By 1840 Hopkins had come to share the Camdenian views of the altar as the principal feature within the church; when he remodelled St. Paul's Episcopal Church, Burlington, in 1851 he gave it the now 'correct' chancel divided into choir and sanctuary with communion rails; at a further rebuilding in 1866 transepts were added.[35] The same influences were at work in another immigrant from Britain, this time a professional architect, Richard Upjohn, whose Trinity Protestant Episcopal Church (1839-1846) in New York was in Gothic, with a deep chancel, choir stalls, altar and reredos.

The Protestant Episcopal Church also produced its own conscious imitation of the Cambridge Camdenians in the formation of the New York Ecclesiological Society in 1848, based on its General Theological Seminary in that city. As a recent study has put it, this also engaged in 'the quest for the Temple', produced its own *New York Ecclesiologist*, and did battle therein against churches with square box pews and three decker pulpits in favour of long chancels separated from the nave.[36] As in Britain, the Gothic Revival affected other denominations also, and the Congregationalists began to forsake the colonial meeting house style for the new fashion in their churches at Asylum Hill, Hartford, Connecticut (1865) and in Boston the Central Congregational Church (1867, designed by Upjohn's son), both in Gothic and with chancels. By this time the new image of a church building was firmly planted in the American Protestant mind.

The major difference from the modern history of Gothic in Britain is that the great days of Gothic were reserved for what has been called the 'second revival', in the twentieth century, although there is a certain reminiscence of the English scene in two of the chief exponents – an Anglo-Catholic architect, Ralph Adams Cram (1863-1942), and a Unitarian minister, Van Ogden Vogt (b. 1879). Cram was a colourful figure who developed a theory of Christian history running in five hundred year periods; crises marked the end of each era, and culture flourished in the intervals; the greatest flowering had been in the later Middle Ages, and the most destructive crisis had been that of the Reformation; a new cultural development to reclaim the medieval inheritance had begun in the nineteenth century, and must repudiate Protestantism and all its works. 'There is one style, and one truly, that we have a right to; and that is Gothic as it was when all art was destroyed at the time of the Reformation.'[37] For Cram this meant perpendicular Gothic rather than the decorated period canonized in England.

This attitude produced the same difficulties as those experienced by the English Ecclesiologists when they found Nonconformists or a non-Catholic culture prepared to adopt their medieval Gothic. Instead of the Camdenian's Norman for New Zealand, Cram reported that 'we did our best to induce our "Nonconformist" (sic, and in the U.S.A.!) clients to let us do Colonial structures for them' since 'there was something incongruous in using Catholic Gothic to express the ethos of that Protestantism which had ... done its best to destroy (Catholic) architectural and other artistic manifestations'.[38]

These qualms were silenced by Cram's faith in the missionary eloquence of Gothic on the full medieval plan, so that when he accepted commissions from 'nonconformist' churches he felt he was serving them better than they knew. He recognized that 'it would have ... horrified Doctors Calvin and Knox in their day, but we are permitted to believe they are better informed now'.[39]

A further difference in the American attitude to Gothic lies in the emphasis upon its numinous qualities rather than upon its symbolic significance in the Durandus manner, or its alliance with a hierarchical conception of the church and its ministry. Hopkins was concerned with the creation of a devotional attitude in the individual worshipper, and relied on Gothic for 'an impression of sublimity more exalted than any other sort of architecture can produce'. Likewise for Cram, 'the first desideratum of a church' is the creation of a 'sense of awe and mystery and devotion' in those who enter it.[40] But the major exponent was the liberal non-ritualist Unitarian, Van Ogden Vogt, who compensated for the limitations of his theology with a sentimental emphasis upon 'the intimations of Gothic buildings' which were 'not chiefly intellectual ... but emotional and mystical' and where 'the high vaulted aisles ... lead the imagination to find some communion with the infinite unknown'.[41] In twentieth century American Christianity this desire for an 'inspirational or devotional experience' promoted by the deliberate creation of a 'worshipful atmosphere' is deeply ingrained; for satisfaction it has usually turned to some form of Gothic, or at least to the internal arrangements of divided chancel and sanctuary associated with this style more than with any other.

Only the briefest reference is possible here to some of the landmarks in the present century's Gothic revival in the United States. The Protestant Episcopal Church has its three greatest cathedrals — Grace Church in San Francisco (albeit in 'naked reinforced concrete'), the national cathedral in Washington, and the mammoth cathedral of St. John the Divine in New York, which was begun in a Romanesque style in 1891 and later given to Cram to finish in Decorated Gothic (it may now never be finished, for work was stopped in the sixties in view of the clamant needs of America's own submerged peoples and of the Third World). The nineteen twenties saw Gothic chapels arise on many university campuses, notably at Chicago in a modern style and at Princeton in more traditional manner. At the same time even the Baptists produced a magnificent 'cathedral', the Riverside Church (1926-1931) built for Dr. Fosdick and a congregation of two thousand five hundred in thirteenth century French Gothic, with divided choir and a solid stone altar-table in a sanctuary; and above all, a tower one hundred and twentythree metres high. Once again the Methodists offered a norm for church building, with a scale reproduction of a model chancel in the correct manner, with antiphonal choir seating, altar set against a carved reredos and raised on four steps, pulpit and lectern balancing each other outside the chancel arch, but with the communicant's rail extending across the nave in front of these so that everything professional is separated from the worshippers.[42] This was promoted by the Methodist Episcopal Church (North) Bureau of Church Architecture before World War II, under a director who appropriately published a work entitled *Building the House of God.*[43]

12.7.2 *Across all lands and denominations*

One could follow the course of the Gothic church wherever English-speaking denominations were established in the nineteenth and twentieth centuries. It could be found in attempts at a Gothic style in mud and thatch or timber churches in many a mission field, or in the early wooden churches of pioneer settlers in New Zealand and other colonies, who ignored the Camdenian recommendation of Norman and pressed on to greater things in stone — as the English settlers did with their Gothic cathedral in the centre of Christchurch, or the Free Church Scots with their beautifully proportioned First Church (1873) in Dunedin. Often enough in these situations it was only a style, for the internal arrangements were far from 'correct' — the chancel, if there was one, might be filled with pulpit and organ and lack any sign of a communion table. And yet the building was there, calling for its appropriate use, and the present century has seen a wave of remodellings of these interiors to clear or extend chancels, equip them with raised central tables, and create a sanctuary atmosphere.

The ramifications of the idea of a church that we owe to the Gothic revival extend to the plainest of hall-churches where there is no suggestion of Gothic in the building but clear signs of the sanctuary pattern it encouraged. One would not expect this among the Pentecostal churches, yet when the Assemblies of God in Leicester erected a hall as a temporary meeting place until the New Trinity Church proper is built, they equipped it with the appurtenances of a sanctuary. A raised platform railed-in across the full width of the hall contains a central pulpit-desk in front of a shallow apse that leads into a rectangular recess; the devotional focus is a wall-vase of flowers in the middle of the recess, spot-lighted for 'effect'; only a table for the Breaking of Bread outside the 'sanctuary' and on the main floor level testifies to the meeting-house tradition that is more congenial to this community.

It is also interesting to observe how commonly Pentecostal communities use the terms sanctuary and temple for their places of worship or meeting. The British Apostolic Church reports the opening of 'A New Sanctuary' at Blaenavon in 1970, and a 'temporary temple' was erected for the convention of its Lagos, Nigeria, branch in 1969. We learn also that the 'Evangelical Pentecostal Church Brazil for Christ', admitted to the World Council of Churches in 1969, has 'recently dedicated a sanctuary that will ultimately seat 24,000'. And in East Providence, Rhode Island, there is a Zion Gospel Temple, just as English Methodism produced the facade noted by Betjeman at Great Yarmouth: '1829 – The Methodist Temple – 1875'. One recalls, of course, that churches have often born the name of 'temple' in the past, as with the Knights Templars' Temple Church in London, or the Temple (Anglican) Church in Bristol, and the French Protestant 'temples' of the Reformation period. It is nonetheless surprising to find completely inappropriate terms such as temple and sanctuary so freely adopted by the spiritual heirs of the sixteenth and seventeenth century communities where such language would have been anathema. It may be due in part to a misguided biblicism, but we suspect that even here the Gothic Revival's image of the church as the house or temple of God has not been without its influence.[44]

12.8 CONCLUSION

The retreat towards the *domus dei* and the dissolution of the *domus ecclesiae* into an auditorium 'meant the obliteration of a liturgical understanding and of an architectural tradition which had survived all the vicissitudes of church history from the Reformation, through the ages of orthodoxy, enlightenment and pietism ... an abandonment of the tradition of Protestant church building which was no less radical than the original revolution'.[45] To explain this would require a profound exploration of the inner life of modern Christianity and of the surrounding influences. It is sufficient for us to record the nineteenth and early twentieth centuries as the great age of confusion in the understanding of the Christian place of worship, and to survey its chief manifestations.

Although there were other architectural forms revived or developed in this period — Byzantine, Renaissance, Classical and twentieth century 'modern'— these added nothing new to the basic types we have identified as auditorium or sanctuary churches. Church building oscillated between these two conceptions, or even attempted to combine them, but it was the second which has enjoyed the more pervasive influence. This has been most evident in the Anglican communion, but has so affected all denominations that it is often impossible to identify to whom a church belongs merely by inspection; likewise sanctuary forms have penetrated the practice of evangelical and pentecostal groups which would strongly repudiate all sacerdotal and hierarchical ideas.

It might be said that the repeated revivals of the *domus dei* in Christian history testify to its inherent value in ministering to the hunger of the human spirit for a sacred place instinct with the Divine Presence. This we do not dispute, for we have set forth the virtues of the temple type at some length in the first part of this work. What is to be questioned once again is whether, in spite of all the glories of its Gothic renascence, it is the authentic Christian form, and what place, if any, it may be allowed in the new image of the church being sought in the later twentieth century — a subject to which we shall return in Ch. 16. In the meantime, we may appreciate the sober achievements of the seventeenth and eighteenth centuries in their attempts at a worthy *domus ecclesiae*. The meeting house may be the more difficult and exacting form to develop and to commend to men, but the varied attempts made since the mediaeval period are not to be despised.

13

The Experience of Other Traditions: Islam

Our survey of the history of churches will now be supported by a similar analysis of their counterparts in Judaism and in Islam. Synagogues, churches and mosques are all non-sacral places of worship, belonging to the meeting house type pioneered in the history of religions by the synagogue, which together with the mosque now possesses a long history under divers historical and cultural influences. We shall enquire first into how Islam, as the larger and more independent tradition, has developed its places of worship since it emerged early in the seventh century.

13.1 ISLAM'S ANCIENT TEMPLE

There is a quite remarkable parallel in the Christian and Muslim traditions between their original places of worship and their subsequent development. Islam also was born in a sacred city of long standing, Mecca, and with an ancient temple complex, the Ka'bah and its temenos, as a chief sanctuary in the *domus dei* pattern, and known as 'bayt Allah', the house of God. The Ka'bah (the common Arabic term for temple) may have been a rather different and unimpressive roofless building until it was rebuilt and enlarged about the year 608, just before Muhammad began to experience his visionary revelations; since then it has remained substantially the same as a roughly cubic single-chamber building of approximately the same size and shape as the inner Holy of Holies of the Jerusalem Temple. According to the traditions attached to the Ka'bah both before and after Muhammad it was rich with cosmic symbolisms similar to those found at Jerusalem. Here also was the centre of the world and the navel of the earth, a reflection of the heavenly prototype and orientated in the cosmic directions – in this case the four corners faced the four cardinal points. To this famous place of pilgrimage men came from afar to make their offerings, vows and sacrifices to the many deities whose cultic stones and images stood both within and outside the Ka'bah; at this point it resembled the Jerusalem Temple only in those decadent periods when its image-less purity had been destroyed by the invading cults of the surrounding peoples. Such was the sanctuary which dominated the city in which Muhammad was born.

Although specific evidence is absent there is every reason to presume that the founder of Islam, like Jesus in that other holy city, shared from boyhood in all the temple rituals, making the circuits of the Ka'bah and kissing the Black Stone, and also sharing in the sacrifices at associated sacred places such as the *musalla* of the Banu Salima or open sanctuary just south-west of the city with its two annual festivals. There is some basis for believing that Muhammad in the early stages of his teaching in Mecca, again like Jesus in Jerusalem, used the temple precincts for non-cultic purposes, for his own private prayers, and for discussion and dispute on religious matters. As we shall see, the followers of the Prophet use the sanctuary in Mecca in somewhat the same way to this day, just as we may suppose Jews would have maintained their cultic practices at their Temple had it not been destroyed.

We have already examined in some detail the ambivalent attitude to this Jerusalem temple in both the practice and teaching of Jesus, and a similar ambivalence may be observed in the relation between Muhammad and the Meccan sanctuary. Although this holy place provided the setting for his own religious experience there is no mention of it in Qur'anic revelations during the Meccan period from about 610 to 622; in this same period he was concentrating upon the small but growing band of those who accepted his divine call and teaching, and coming into increasing conflict with the Meccan authorities over this independent development and over his strict monotheism in declaring three of the chief goddesses of the sanctuary to be unreal. His own call had been associated with his practice of going out to the hills around Mecca for prayer and meditation, and as soon as he arrived in Medina from Mecca after the hegira of 622 his worship and that of his followers was associated with no local sanctuary but with the courtyard of his own house

Yet Muhammad's policy for the remaining decade of his life featured the Ka'bah as an essential place of pilgrimage. During the very first year or so at Medina, after one of the early raids of his Medina supporters upon a Meccan caravan, Muhammad was able to answer the criticism that he had encouraged war during the sacred month when it was banned in Arabia by asserting that 'to turn [men] from the way of God and to disbelieve in the sacred temple and to drive his people from it is more serious with God... than killing' (Sūrah 2.214).[1] In the next few years Muhammad declared that the traditional pilgrimage to the Meccan temple would remain central in his new religion, and by 628 he had established the treaty right for his followers to make a three-day pilgrimage the following year, which they did in an entirely peacable and traditional manner.

Further conflicts led to his advance on Mecca in 630 and its swift capitulation. After resting for a while he visited the Ka'bah to pay his ceremonial respects by riding round the building and touching the Black Stone, and by praying within, after which he performed a 'cleansing of the temple' reminiscent of that of Jesus in Jerusalem. He destroyed the cultic images and other objects (tradition mentions three hundred and sixty idols) and so converted it into a sanctuary suitable for a strictly monotheistic faith, and a house of prayer for all nations, as it was to become. His own reported comment is illuminating: 'No man before me was permitted to injure this sacred place, and no man after me shall do it. I myself have only been permitted to do it for a part of one day.' The pilgrimages thereafter continued at the proper time, that of 631 being led by Abu Bakr his closest companion and that of 632 by Muhammad himself, in the year of his death. This 'farewell pilgrimage' set the seal on all the traditional ceremonies connected with the Meccan sanctuary — the circumambulation of the Ka'bah, the kissing of the Black Stone, the running between the small hills Safa and Marwa, the visits to 'Arafāt and Muzdalifa some miles east, the offering of sacrificial animals at Mina' (where Abraham, according to current Arab tradition, prepared to offer Ishmael), the casting stones at Satan at al-'Aqaba, and the observation of the various tabus.

This thoroughgoing incorporation of the ancient sanctuary and its rites into the Islamic faith was legitimized for Muhammad by revelations which associated the Ka'bah with Abraham himself as the true pioneer of monotheistic religion. The foundations of the Ka'bah had been laid by Abraham and its sanctity derived from God's covenant with him: 'Behold the first sanctuary ever founded for man was that of Mecca – a blessed one and a guidance to all the world' (see Sūrah 2:119-23; 3:90, 91). As J. Obermann has put it, 'the Abrahamization of Islam had led Mohammed so far as to include the age-old national center of Arab worship in his institutionalized monotheism; now this stark residue of pre-Islamic paganism is in turn Islamicized by being anchored in God's primeval design for the salvation of man....'[2] It is on this basis that later Islamic mythology has traced the building of the first Ka'bah still further back to Seth, the son of Adam, or even to an angel, with Abraham merely rebuilding after the deluge had destroyed it.

Thus it is that Muslims throughout the world possess a single sacred centre that retains so much of the temple form and of the rites and mythology that belong to this type of place of worship. It is interesting to speculate upon the place that might have been found for the Jerusalem Temple in Christian practice, as a corresponding inheritance from the past, had it survived within a Christianized community. In spite of its destruction, at times it has provided a model, as we have seen, for Christian churches. The Ka'bah, on the other hand, like Allah, was unique and has never become the pattern for Muslim places of worship.

13.2 MUHAMMAD'S NEW FORM

The mosque has a quite different ancestry, akin to that of the synagogue, and of the house church of the early Christians. Its origins lie in the attitude of Muhammad to the requirements for daily worship and in his own personal practice, especially in the formative years at Medina. For Muhammad a sanctuary was not necessary, since every place was the same to God and God was everywhere: 'To God belongs the East and the West; whichever way you turn, God's presence is there....

There is no piety in turning your faces towards the East or... the West'
(Sūrah 2:115, 177). As one tradition has it, 'all the world is a *masjid*',
i.e. a place of prostration, or mosque, and this word has so general a
meaning that it could cover not only the later Islamic places of worship
but also pre-Islamic sanctuaries in Arabia, the churches and temples
of other religions, and places where worship occurred without benefit
of buildings at all. There are, however, exceptions, for prayer is prohibited in lavatories, slaughterhouses and Christian cemeteries.

Consistent with this teaching was Muhammad's practice both in
Mecca and after he had left for Medina. In Mecca he and his followers
had prayed together in private houses or quiet open places, and when
a simple house was built for him in Medina he continued in this manner, using the roofed shelter at one side of the domestic courtyard.
There was no sanctity about it, nor ritual objects, and in the courtyard
itself the household chores proceeded, the community's affairs were
regulated, visitors camped, and at one side individuals said their prayers
or the community worshipped. Other places of worship in Medina were
equally simple and domestic, or consisted of no more than an open
prayer square. The only specific feature to develop was the *qibla*, the
direction to face during prayer, at first towards Jerusalem but later towards Mecca, and indicated by a wall or niche. Thus were the simple
liturgical essentials of Islam established – a community praying towards the historic place where its founding experience had been given,
and for its regular worship entirely abandoning the tradition of the
domus dei and all its manifestations: cosmic symbolism had been replaced by historic revelation as the link between man and the divine. Of
the older tradition only the cleansed and reformed Ka'bah remained,
but with no more than occasional functions in the religious life.

Nearly six centuries earlier the first Christians had been in a remarkably similar position with their house churches. The founder of their
faith, however, had left no more than an 'upper room' model for the
place of worship, on a single occasion and on the last night of his life.
The founder of this new faith had taught and demonstrated this way of
worship for some two decades and for his last ten years had presented
the model of his Medina home. It is not surprising, therefore, that we
find here the permanent pattern for the Muslim mosque, with basic

features that have persisted in spite of later and somewhat contradictory influences shortly to be examined.

The earliest mosques, as at Basra (635), were usually no more than
square or rectangular open areas marked off by a ditch or a light pali-
sade with a simple roofed but wall-less shelter at the *qibla* side. These
were even simpler than the Medina model which itself became a public
mosque in the more formal sense over two decades after the Prophet's
death in 632. By the early years of the following century the mosque
had developed a more detailed form with various functional components, but still observing the original principles. It now consisted of a
rectangular or square enclosure containing an open court (*sahn*) with
arcades (*riwaqs*) around two or three of its sides for shelter and for
ablutions, a *qibla* wall with a niche (*mihrāb*) in its centre like a very
small apse for the prayer leader (*imām*), a larger covered area (*haram*,
with arches or *līwāns*) along the *qibla* side of the enclosure, and under
this (mainly in larger or central mosques) a pulpit or throne (*minbar*)
for the Friday preacher, and a screened-off more private area (*maqsū-
rah*) for use by a caliph or imam; the minaret or slender tower from
which the call to prayer is made was borrowed later from Syrian models and has never been a universal or essential feature. Apart from minor
variations such as Sunni, Ismaili or other mosques without a *mihrāb*,
this general form has remained definitive ever since, for 'no matter
how complex the architectural structure, whether we are dealing with
the frozen forest of marble that is the Mosque of Cordova, or the mudbrick mosque of a Nilotic village, the articulation of its parts is invari-
ably the same'.[3]

This new mosque form has no connection with worship that is priestly, sacrificial or ritualistic; it houses a congregational assembly of laymen for their simple forms of prayer, preaching and scripture reading.
It is respected, but not set apart as a holy place through consecration;
neither is it confined to the more explicitly religious use of worship,
for, like the domestic courtyard of its origin, it remains in principle
a multi-purpose building even when ancillary accomodation is later
developed to cater for specific functions such as school or hospice. In
no sense is it ever a shrine for the divinity. The orientation of the worshippers towards the *qibla* unites the world-wide Islamic community in

remembrance of the place of the historic revelation; it does not lead them to any special dwelling place of Allah. This is not denied by the suggestion that 'in Islam it is more the direction which is holy than any particular liturgical object'— or place, and by a practice such as turning away from the *qibla* if the worshipper feels the need to spit, for to do so towards the *qibla* would amount to 'expectorating in the face of God';[4] but this no more enshrines the deity in a sanctuary than does kneeling, bowing, or other appropriate behaviour in the Judaeo-Christian tradition.

Similarly the respect paid to the *mihrāb* through decoration as the focal point of the building, and through a sanctuary lamp hanging in front to illuminate it, does not turn it into a miniature shrine or holy place. In origin it may owe something to the synagogue Ark or cupboard for the Scriptures, or more certainly to the apse of basilican churches and especially a similar niche in Coptic churches in Egypt; it was, however, completely empty, with neither Sacred Book nor altar and so less likely to attract the notion of special sanctity that did appear in churches and synagogues. Although we have spoken of the 'sanctuary' lamp in the *haram* or 'sanctuary' the use of this term for the area in front of the niche must be understood in an architectural sense only, freed from the usual sacral meanings attached to its liturgical use. The mosque is clearly a non-sacral place of worship, albeit of a distinctive nature derived from the geographical and cultural location of its origin.

13.3 RETURN OF THE TEMPLE TRADITION

In the early and rapid expansion of the new Islamic faith into Western Asia and northern Africa the simplicity of the Medina tradition was at first preserved. In Iraq the Arab conquerors of the 630s founded new towns and provided mosques that were no more than demarcated open spaces with a small roofed shelter. In 641/2 'Amr ibn al-'Ās, the conqueror of Egypt, built the mosque named after him with mudbrick walls and a low palm-leaf roof on palm-trunk pillars. In newly captured towns it was usual to avoid using the sanctuaries of other faiths and to be satisfied with the erection of a very simple mosque somewhere in the centre; thus in Jerusalem there was only a very primitive square with a temporary roofed structure. It was perhaps inevitable that these early simplicities could not long prevail when Islam spread into the wider world and gained imperial power, as had happened to the Christians and their churches a few centuries before. Once again we may trace the re-emergence of the *domus dei* tradition to the influence of such factors as imperial wealth and patronage, the influx of people of other faiths with their own temple forms, and the development of what we have called funerary practices – the cult of the saints and of relics and the associated pilgrimages to tomb sanctuaries.

Within a century of the founder's death the Islamic faith commanded an imperial structure that held sway from the shores of the Atlantic almost to the borders of China. Since there was no institutional separation of religion and politics within a community totally committed to the service of Allah, and since mosques were the places for the installation of rulers, for public announcements and trials, and for civic assemblies of all kinds with the caliph as both civil and religious leader, this change of status, of scale and of resources could not but affect the form of the mosque. Buildings are a major expression of the power and wealth of any society, and so it is with the 'Great mosques' of Islam. Only some thirty years after the establishment of some of the earliest mosques we have mentioned they were being rebuilt in a larger and grander manner – Basra in 665, Kufa in 670, and 'Amr in 673: these now featured many-pillared roofed aisles with high ceilings, and arcades that were more decorative than functional. For the first time Islam now possessed architecturally significant buildings.

Just as Constantine had extended his imperial patronage to the erection of splendid shrines at the sacred places of Palestine so also we find a caliph, 'Abd al-Malik, erecting the splendid Dome of the Rock on the sacred place where the Jerusalem Temple's open-air altar had once stood, and where Muhammad was said to have ascended to heaven – and this within sixty years of the death of the Prophet, and in spite of his reported strictures on such activities: 'The most unnecessary activity that eats up the wealth of a believer is building.' This remains as the oldest surviving Muslim monument, not a mosque but a shrine of wonderfully harmonious proportions built with expensive marbles and glass mosaics, and intended to outshine the Christian churches in Jerusalem.

The next caliph turned his attention to Medina, the place of the prototype itself, where Muhammad's original house had already been rebuilt as a mosque. In 707/9 al-Walīd replaced this with a great mosque complete with a semi-circular *mihrāb*, four corner minarets, and marble and mosaic decorations, and all this on the very site where the founder lay buried. At the same time al-Walīd began the Great Mosque at Damascus, 'the oldest mosque still in use in its original shape..., the first monumental expression of the Muslim ritual'.[5] This again was built to surpass the Syrian Christian churches from which at the same time it borrowed the new architectural feature of a nave with gabled roof in front of the *mihrāb*; the latter was cut from a single block of rock crystal, and the expensive upper walls of sanctuary and courtyard were covered with mosaics of landscapes and cities.

In one sense the climax of the early period must have been the great mosque of 852 at Samarra, north of Bagdad, somewhat uncertainly claimed to be the largest ever built although now in ruins. The *haram* alone contained two hundred and sixteen pillars forming twentyfive aisles and the whole mosque area embraced some thirtyeight thousand square metres; beyond this rose the single and still-standing minaret, a massive conical tower with outside helicoidal stairway fifty metres high. With decorations rivalling those of Damascus this colossal structure must have aroused a sense of awe bordering on the numinous associated with the great temples of other traditions.

The sense of the numinous is more explicit in one of the splendid mosques of later Islamic history, the Mosque of Sultan Ahmed in Istanbul built in the early seventeenth century to outshine the nearby Hagia Sophia, the sixth century Christian church that is one of the most monumental of *domus dei* forms. The external symmetry of cumulated dome upon dome framed within the six slender three-galleried minarets, and the vast internal prayer space under its richly decorated and cosmically-domed canopy combine to induce in the worshipper the feeling of creaturehood and of spell-bound awe that Otto associates with the numinous. Undoubtedly 'the emotion in such a mosque is religious, but scarcely Islamic; we do not experience it in the buildings of an earlier date'.[6]

It is possible to trace accents of the same grandeur with cosmic overtones in certain Sikh gurdwaras (also called temples) and in other religions associated with the Islamic tradition; thus Baha'i calls its places of worship 'temples', and to the general mosque form adds the requireof nine sides, since as the largest single number this symbolizes unity and comprehensiveness.

There were, however, other factors also at work to revive the temple tradition within Islam. The pre-Islamic sanctuary of the Ka'bah had been reformed and as it were isolated from the new mosque development, but the temples of other peoples were to become influential. In some cases the sanctuaries of conquered peoples were turned to use as mosques. A pagan temple of Shamash became a Masjid al-Shams; firetemples of Persia accomodated the new worship, and at a later stage temple halls in China were readily adapted by the addition of a *mihrāb*. As was noted in the earlier Christian history the mass influx of semiconverted pagans brought a continuing allegiance to sacred places into a religion that denoted a break from this mode of thought.

The chief influence from non-islamic forms seems to have been that of Christian churches, and it is somewhat ironic that by now the revival of the *domus dei* tradition should have been so far advanced that the Christian influence often served to distort rather than to support the Islamic development. We have already observed monumental churches serving as both rival and model in the emergence of the great mosques of Islam, and where there were mass conversions from the older faith to the new the churches themselves especially in the villages were converted into mosques. In Syria, where the churches faced east and where Mecca was almost due south the turning of the worshippers through ninety degrees towards a *mihrāb* installed in the southern wall was all that was necessary. Later, in Istanbul, a token *mihrāb* could be set up in the south-eastern section of the apse and the congregation aligned much as before. This adoption of church buildings has remained a possibility for Islam: for instance, in 1970 the Catholic Cathedral of the Sacred Heart of Jesus in Tripoli was converted by the government into the Gamel Abdel Nassar Mosque, and there are more examples in

Algeria; in 1972 a Catholic church only eighteen years old in Lille, France, underwent the same transformation; in Britain the conversion of redundant churches into mosques, as also into Sikh gurdwaras and Hindu temples, is now a live issue that raises awkward theological questions for those who view the church as a consecrated holy place, but not for Muslims where such ideas are irrelevant.

There will be further occasion to examine the relation of church and mosque, but it is clear that the ambivalent position of so many church buildings has resulted in an equally ambivalent influence over the course of Islamic mosque development. A further influence in the revival of the tradition of the sacred place, at once more clear-cut and more internal to Islam itself, has been the complex of practices we have designated as funerary. Islam must have become increasingly acquainted with the Christian funerary practices we have examined, but these in turn derived from widespread and ancient forms to be met in many cultures. Any Christian influence, therefore, could only reinforce factors already at work.

The first Muslims, however, like the first Christians, showed no special interest in sacred places, not even in the burial place of Muhammad himself, which did not become a sanctuary or shrine for pilgrimage until later. Collections of tradition made in the third Muslim century exhibit discussion as to whether tombs could become places of prayer with mosques erected over them, but the practice was strongly rejected. Ancient habits, however, supported by the Christian cult of saints, were too strong and a visit to the grave of Muhammad soon became an optional part of the pilgrimage to Mecca; earth from the grave was taken away and any relics of the Prophet such as fragments of his mantle or specimens of his hair were preserved in chests and visited by the faithful. Increasingly the mosque at Medina became a pilgrimage shrine and was parallelled by the erection of further mosques at places especially associated with Muhammad in and around Mecca and Medina; by the reverse process other mosques on occasion developed stories connecting them with the Prophet in order to assume this special status. Shrine-mosques were also built over the tombs of members of the Prophet's family or of his early companions and of other holy men and martyrs as far afield as Mesopotamia and Persia; even pre-islamic shrines or sanctuaries were incorporated into the Muslim faith by a re-interpretation of their local traditions to associate them with the saints of Islam.

The pilgrims to these holy places sought to touch the tomb for access of power, or for healing of a barren woman, or came simply to pray, and in due course there appeared the desire to be buried close to the holy person.[7] In modern times this practice has been exemplified by the efforts of the Shī'ite Muslims of Iran to be buried near one of the shrines devoted to al-Husayn, a grandson of the Prophet, whom they regard as in the only true succession from Muhammad, and whose death at Karbalā' in 680 is interpreted as a martyrdom. Shī'ite dead were therefore conveyed from Iran to Karbalā' in Iraq, or to other similar shrines at Najaf and Samarra, mostly by caravan but even by an airline specializing in this traffic, which in 1932 was estimated to involve some two hundred thousand corpses. Finally, for political reasons, the Iran government banned the export and directed the relatives with their dead towards the Persian holy cities of Qum and Meshed. On the other hand the burial even of saintly Muslims within a mosque is now generally strictly forbidden in Wahhabi countries.

Certain other practices which suggest the identification of mosque with sacred place may be briefly mentioned in order to dismiss them. The fact that business and marriage contracts and oaths made in a mosque are more binding need signify no more than being made in a court of law, which the mosque often was, or may serve as a reminder of the presence of God without implying that He dwelt in this sacred place. Similarly the removal of footwear is both a sign of respect and a necessary form of cleanliness that applied equally in private houses, as anyone familiar with the muck in bazaar alleys would appreciate; the lustrations before entry are a preparation of the person for prayer, not the place, and apply also at any casual place of prayer while travelling. Exclusion of non-Muslims is confined to some sects only and in most mosques all are welcome; the restrictions on women are not original, for they stood behind the men in Muhammad's time, and in any case are more socio-cultural than derivative from views on spatial sanctity.

It is certain regular architectural features that may be more significant in sustaining the sense of a sacred place through their cosmic symbolism. We have already identified this effect in the great monumental mosques, and it is still possible that even in the smaller plainer mosques there remains a symbolism of the transcendent inherent in the structure of dome, the light it often provides through its supporting drum, and the *mihrāb* it illuminates.[8] The almost unavoidable heavenly suggestion of domes has been sufficiently remarked. The metaphor of light is used of God in Sūrah 24:35-36 where 'Allah is the Light of the heavens and the earth. The similitude of His Light is as a niche wherein is a lamp.... [This lamp is found] in houses which Allah hath allowed to be exalted, and that His name shall be remembered therein....' Light is therefore a chief mode through which 'the Islamic notion of divinity expresses itself, and illumination has always been of paramount importance in mosques, and especially in the vicinity of the *mihrāb*'.[9] As for the *mihrāb* itself, this 'is but an Islamicized version of one of man's oldest symbols, a gate or symbolic door opening on the beyond'.[10]

It would seem therefore that in going beyond the simplicities of the primitive Medina model at each of these points mosques have inevitably incorporated something of the built-in symbolism of the temple type of sacred place, albeit in a minor key. To this we may add the symbolic declaration of the Divine presence that some have found in the overall effect of the characteristic mosque form. Here

Nothing expresses effort... there is no tension, not any antithesis between heaven and earth. 'There is none of that sensation of heaven descending from above as in the Hagia Sophia, nor the ascending tendency of a Gothic cathedral.... It is by its immobolity that the atmosphere of a mosque is distinguished from all things ephemeral. Here infinity is not attained by a transformation from one side of a dialectical antithesis to the other; in this architecture the beyond is not merely a goal, it is lived here and now, in a freedom exempt from all tendencies; there is a repose free from all aspiration; its omnipotence is incorporated in the edifice....'[11]

On the other hand, even if we grant recognition to this aspect of the mosque it is still doubtful how far it provides evidence of a *domus dei* place of worship, for would not many a Quaker, in simpler language, say something of the same for his own plain meeting house? Perhaps at this point there is some convergence of the two types we have been presenting as antithetical.

13.4 SURVIVAL OF THE ORIGINAL FORMS

In spite of such manifestations of the temple form of sacred place as remain indisputable it is remarkable that the essential principles of the primitive mosque form are still discernible; however overlaid with other themes even the grandest of mosques incorporates the same traditional basic elements, and functions as the prayer house of a lay community. Even if the mosque should have to be closed for repairs or cannot accomodate all on a great occasion the adjacent courtyard remains adequate as an authentic *masjid*, the place of prostration, for the building is not essential.

This survival of the original principles is all the more remarkable when we observe that they are unprotected by reference to divine revelation. As we have seen, temple forms claiming an origin in dream or vision, or some act of divinity, were usually most faithfully conserved through their subsequent history. While there are records of individuals being directed in a dream to build a mosque as an act of piety or service, the divine warrant seldom extends to the detailed form or structure, which continues to follow the one tradition.

The history of the three most revered Muslim structures – the Ka'-bah, the surrounding Mosque at Mecca, and the Mosque of the Prophet at Medina – is instructive in this regard. The Ka'bah, as we have observed already, retains roughly the same shape and size that it possessed in Muhammad's time, but there is nothing in the Qur'an or in the Sunna, the tradition, to prohibit changes, and in fact there have been considerable variations in detail and in decoration and some minor innovations in the course of a history marked by the vicissitudes of siege, fire and flood, or the penury or prosperity of the rulers of Mecca; perhaps its chief protection has lain in the natural conservatism of the inhabitants of the city.

The Great Mosque of Mecca, the Masjid al-Haram, which embraces the Ka'bah, also reflects the changes consequent upon extensions and improvements effected at many different periods and in various styles, and continuing in recent times under the patronage of King Saud and King Faisal; in particular there have been many and various pulpits differing in size, form and material, and 'the changes of these pulpits... show that there is no rigid rule that such and such pulpit set up by such and such a person only is sacred'.[12]

The Mosque of the Prophet at Medina, which one might have expected to be anchored to early canonical forms, has undergone the greatest changes of all. The freedom seen in its early development has already been noted; in 1256 it was completely destroyed by fire and in 1328 the new structure accepted a complete innovation, the addition of two galleries to accomodate the increasing volume of pilgrims. After being again destroyed in 1471 by lightning (which might have been a disastrous omen for a traditional sacred place), and again rebuilt, it became grander still with new minaret and dome built by caliphs in the next few centuries. By 1849 it was in such poor state that in the next twelve years it was almost totally reconstructed in a much altered form. 'Since the traditional composite parts of the mosques... are not sacred... there was no harm in removing or changing these parts whenever it was necessary. The reverence that was attached to these places was only because of the historical association of the Prophet....'[13]

Within the community of Islam there have always been voices raised against any sacralization of the objects or buildings at its holy places. The second caliph Omar, is said to have addressed the Black Stone set in the corner of the Ka'bah in accents authentically Islamic: 'I know that thou art a stone, that neither helps nor hurts, and if the messenger of Allah had not kissed thee, I would not kiss thee.' And then he kissed the stone.[14] Something of the same attitude marks the Sufi and mystical tradition, where visits to the tombs of the saints and the pilgrimage to the Ka'bah remain important. At the same time the famous Persian Sufi poet and theologian, Maulana Jalal ud-Din Rumi of the thirteenth century, could write that 'the heart of a human being is better than a thousand Ka'bahs'; and when the Sufi Rabiah wanted to visit the Ka'bah to prostrate before God in the holy sanctuary she received the vision of the Ka'bah itself coming to prostrate before her. Even more radical was Ibn Taimiya a generation later, a traditionalist and jurist, fanatically anti-Sufi, who issued what has been called the 'most famous *fatwā* (i.e. pronouncement) in Islamic history',[15] condemning invocation of saints and prophets, and the pilgrimage to their tombs, even including the tomb of Muhammad at Medina, as a form of idolatry. The Wahhabi sect which dominates Saudi Arabia arose under his influence and continues this strict opposition to what it regards as polytheism, although it has not extended this attitude to the Ka'bah which lies in its own area.[16]

Other Islamic sects have preserved primitive mosque forms and resisted any moves towards more temple-like developments. Thus the Ibadhis, who represent the first sect within Islam, the puritan and egalitarian Kharijites, think it wrong for one Muslim to stand higher than another and shout commands at him, and have no minarets in their mosques in north and east Africa; the mosque itself is called Jama'at Khaneh (house of assembly). The Ismailis possess extremely domestic forms of mosque, with no orientation towards Mecca, and may have a divan and perhaps a garlanded picture of their well-known leader the Aga Khan in place of even so early a feature as the *mihrāb*.

It must also be remembered that the vast majority of mosques have been small and humble buildings or even no more than designated open spaces in rural areas; when we read reports of seven hundred mosques once counted in Palermo, or of seven thousand in Basra and even twelve thousand in Alexandria, we must remember that most of these may have been no more than single rooms in bazaars and residences, rather than free-standing buildings. These urban and rural simplicities remind us that prayers in a community remain the essential requirement, and that the portable prayer mat serves the travelling Muslim as his place of worship with as much acceptance as the grandest of mosques.

The tradition of the simple shelter for prayer is maintained in some of the contemporary mosque buildings, even in such sophisticated surroundings as the campus of the University of Ibadan where the mosque erected in the 1950s is essentially an open air place with a central portion roofed over by a semi-spherical concrete shell. The new mosque built at the Hague at the end of the 1960s has the domestic appearance of a two-storied house, except for the token minaret shaft at the rear. On the other hand the grand mosque, representing political and other

aspirations, is to be found once more in the magnificent so-called National Mosque of Malaysia opened in Kuala Lumpur in 1965 by the
King; it cost a million and a quarter pounds, holds eight thousand in
the main prayer hall, and is constructed in an entirely modern manner
of reinforced concrete faced with Italian marble and decorated with
calligraphy in gold overlay. Although built in a country of small and
modest mosques, there is no necessary contradiction here for the classic simplicities of the basic Islamic form survive within its splendours.[17]
The same might be said of the notable series of much more richly decorated but less modernistic mosques erected in Alexandria between
1920 and 1960.[18]

13.5 HOMOGENEITY OF MOSQUE HISTORY

Our survey of the history of Islam's places of worship indicates a very
close similarity with the history of Christian churches. Both traditions
spring from a founder who combined a certain respect for the ancient
temple forms with a radical shift of emphasis from the place to the
person. Both exhibit the revival of temple influences from the same
sources and with similar results, although the major expansion and
identification with a world political power that took three centuries
for the Christians was telescoped into less than three generations for
the Muslims. In each case their foundation norms have survived to
control the subsequent developments.

But there the overall similarity ends, for within the two great faiths
there are also striking contrasts in this field. Islam has never so surrendered to the temple tradition as to present the antithesis represented
by an elongated Gothic cathedral such as Salisbury and the Quaker
meeting house. In its larger and more splendid mosques it has admitted
certain numinous and cosmic suggestions, but it has not introduced
other notions of distance, differentiation and gradation associated
with the lengthening of the single axis in churches; as the mosque en-
larges it spread outwards but not lengthwise, whether as pillared hall
or under clustered domes. The *mihrāb* may be enriched and reverenced
but it has never become a sanctuary of greater holiness as the domicile

of the divinity. The liturgical history of Islam has therefore been more peaceful than that of the Christians; it has been free of such strongly contrasting forms as cathedral and meeting house, or Eastern central axis and Western horizontal axis churches, free of new theories of church architecture such as Gothic and Renaissance, and of iconoclastic controversies until the Wahhabis discovered the forgotten writings of Ibn Taimīya.

This continuing identity within the mosque history has not been achieved by uniformity for Islam displays in its place of worship the full range of the cultural styles, from Moorish to Chinese, that it has imitated and absorbed in the course of its wide expansion. The full explanation of this identity must doubtless be sought in the inner dynamics of Islam and we must rest content with this study of its historical and phenomenological forms. But perhaps the following description also points to deeper explanations:

'... the mosque sets itself against a profound tendency of human nature – the tendency to think one place holier than another.... It does not fulfill what is to most of us the function of a religious building: the outward expression of an inward ecstasy. It embodies no crisis, leads up through no gradation of nave and choir, and employs no hierarchy of priests. Equality before God – so doubtfully proclaimed by Christianity – lies at the very root of Islam; and the mosque is essentially a courtyard for the faithful to worship in, either in solitude or under due supervision.'[19]

14

The Experience of Other Traditions: Judaism

The emergence of the synagogue as a radically new non-sacral form in the history of religions, and its reciprocal relation to the Jerusalem Temple which it finally replaced, have been examined in an earlier chapter. It now remains to explore the further history of this pioneer form, which has been overshadowed by its younger semitic cousins, the church and the mosque, and to discover its own experience of the persistence or revival of temple traditions.

14.1 SYNAGOGUES IN ANTIQUITY

The earliest synagogues have left us no evidence, either literary or archaeological, of their form. There are no biblical instructions about synagogues, as there were for the tabernacle and the Temple, and it is only in later Talmudic literature that a very few general rules occur.[1] The synagogue is to be built on the highest site in a town, without other buildings above it; it must have windows, and the doors are to be in the east wall; concerning the bimah or reading platform and the ark or provision for the scrolls of the Torah there are only a few disputed statements. In practice even these few directions never became general or normative. 'This amazing silence of a vast tradition which in other areas is ... bewildering articulate, ... is a constant reminder that the central vehicle in Judaism is the Jew as an individual and as a member of a congregation.'[2] The building is instrumental, rather than a *domus dei* in its own right, and the emphasis is on the people, not the place, of God, much in the same way as in early Christianity.

This comparative indifference to the building is congruent with the classic understanding of Israel as the chosen people that ante-dated the whole temple development, and with the lay, democratic and spiritual tendencies associated with the various movements — Hasidim, Pharisees, Essenes, Qumran community, etc. — of the last few centuries before the destruction of the Temple. This widespread emphasis upon holy people rather than holy place meant that the synagogue replaced the Temple not merely through the unfortunate accidents of history but also because it satisfied spiritual needs unmet before.

This function was fulfilled by a basilican form of meeting hall that characterizes the later synagogues of antiquity known to us through archaeological remains; these for the most part represent the larger and more substantial buildings, but most synagogues must have been quite small and simple, for there were large numbers in some cities, such as the precise figure of 394 given for those in Jerusalem when the Temple was destroyed. On the other hand the second century synagogue of the wealthy community at Sardis in Asia Minor was large and sumptuous, but preserved the basilican form with an apse at the western end and entrances at the east. Other buildings, such as the synagogues of 244/5 at Dura Europos, and of Eshtemoa (*c.* 4th century) were broad rooms rather than basilican in form, but still clearly within the meeting hall type. The fifteen or more synagogues identified in Galilee and dating from the third and fourth centuries are well represented in Capernaum — a rectangular hall with facade and doors facing Jerusalem, a small annexe for scroll storage, and interior stone benches along two or three walls with a gallery on all sides except that of the facade. In later synagogues the main addition is the apse for the scrolls in their ark, which we shall discuss below. The exterior was usually inconspicuous, and decoration was confined to interior murals, pavement mosaics and the movable objects; even though they had received Roman citizenship under Caracella in 212 the Jews had no desire to call attention to themselves. In this and other aspects their places of worship closely resembled those of the Christians of the same period, and both were indebted primarily to the civil assembly hall of the Graeco-Roman world, the basilica.[3]

In later antiquity, however, and throughout the Middle Ages the synagogue and church follow very different developments for the Jewish community escaped most of the forces that combined to revive the tradition of the *domus dei* among the Christians. Judaism after the fall of the second commonwealth was not to enjoy independent political power again until recent times, much less to attain the imperial wealth and status that befell both Islam and Christianity, and distorted their own original traditions. It is true that synagogues were sometimes donated by the socially important and wealthy, and although the emperor Alexander Severus is reported to have founded synagogues, as in Arca of Liban, within a decade or so of Caracella's edict of citizenship, this exceptional procedure is in no way comparable to the patronage of Constantine and his successors.

Likewise the Jewish faith never witnessed the vast expansion in numbers and the influx of peoples of many races and faiths with their own traditions of temple worship that mark the history of Christianity and of Islam. In this way it was spared another of the factors leading the church and the mosque away from their own norms. It is possible that temple influences can be detected at a later point in some of the remoter communities of Jews, as in China where the synagogue (1163 and many reconstructions) at Kaifeng, once the Chinese capital, showed a remarkable external resemblance to the traditional Chinese temple compound with its series of entrance porticos and courts, its table for offerings and incense, and its raised shrine at the far end.[4] Even if this could be accepted as a substantial movement towards the temple form rather than a merely exterior style, it was too far removed to influence the mainstream of Jewish development.

We have observed the extensive effects of the complex of funerary practices upon the first Christian churches and the similar process in Islam; there is almost nothing comparable in the Judaism of antiquity. Here was a faith orientated to this life rather than the next, where burial and mourning held only a peripheral place, and where the few relevant prescriptions are negative, as in the Holiness Code's concern for the purity of worshippers endangered by contact with the dead (Deut. 26:14). A curious example of the contrast between Christian and Jewish developments occurs with the seven Maccabean brothers martyred under Antiochus Epiphanes and honoured for their faithfulness by both religions. The early Christians knew them as the 'holy Maccabees' and there is a strong tradition of their tomb being in an Antioch church that had itself been converted from a synagogue where they had been buried, or — as is much more likely — that had been named in their memory. On the other hand the Rabbinic literature does not call them holy and makes no mention of their tombs, much less of a synagogue built over these as a kind of shrine. It is possible that this reflects a more 'official' suppression of such funerary practices, for in the later Hasmonean period Graeco-Roman influence had encouraged the erection of ornate and monumental memorials for important figures, and popular religion had probably always been more involved with the graves of the saintly — so much so that canonical literature includes what seems like a prophetic protest against a tomb-cult (Isaiah 65:4). In the case of the seven Maccabees synagogues dedicated to their memory existed later in Constantinople, Rome and Cologne, and it is not improbable that a synagogue had actually been built over the tomb of the martyrs in Jerusalem and that it had been one of the first erected after A.D. 70.[5]

Further funerary influences have been identified in the pagan symbolic elements borrowed for the internal decorations, especially mosaics, in synagogues in Graeco-Roman areas of the West in a manner that does not occur in the more conservative eastern buildings of Babylonia.[6] However this may be, it seems plain that such effects are superficial and that neither the funerary customs of classical antiquity nor the undercurrents of popular paganism within Judaism itself were of any consequence in the development of the synagogue.

Our first account of the synagogue (Ch. 6) made brief mention of various features which may be described as echoes of the Jerusalem Temple, and it was from this direction if any that a *domus dei* influence may be detected. As long as the Temple existed there was no need to interpret or to develop the synagogue in this sacral manner, but after A.D. 70 there are signs of the holiness and certain of the functions of the Temple being transfered to the synagogue. One sage interpreted Psalm 90:1, 'Lord, thou hast been our dwelling place', as meaning the synagogue, and others declared that God was to be found there rather than elsewhere, or that prayer was heard only in the synagogue; likewise the statement in Ezekiel 11:16, 'for a while I became their sanctuary (or little sanctuary) in the countries to which they had gone', was understood as a reference to the synagogues of Babylonia.

The building itself was sometimes referred to as the 'holy synagogue', or 'this holy place',[7] and assigned a holiness similar to that of the Temple. One authority, therefore, detailed at great length the kinds of behaviour forbidden in the synagogue: idle talk, sleeping, eating or drinking (for which annexes came to be provided), doing business, entering with an unsheathed knife or to escape bad weather. A minority went even further and banned menstruant women and lepers. In general women became confined to galleries or annexes although this had not been an issue earlier when few women attended and they joined the men in the main hall; the separation reflected the pattern of the Temple. Other prescriptions forbade dirt and rubbish or dirt on one's shoes, and any use of the upper stories for purposes incongruent with the spirit of a sanctuary. The various objects used in the synagogue possessed a derivative sanctity, graded according to their closeness of association with the Torah scroll itself; thus a chair rated less than the curtains of the ark, and these less than the ark itself, and when no longer serviceable they must not be destroyed but simply stored away. The bimah and the ark will be examined fully in a later section, but we may note here the development of the latter from a moveable utilitarian chest to a fixed and most holy object specially provided with its own niche, apse or cabinet, and elaborated into one of the two main foci of worship. Most of the attitudes implied in these rules and developments are those appropriate to the House of God, and it is no surprise therefore to learn that the very term *avodah* used of the sacrificial ritual in the Mt. Zion Temple was transferred to the worship of the synagogue — 'the *avodah* or ritual of the heart'.

With these influences at work it is important to observe that the synagogue did not in fact become a *domus dei* as did so many churches. Judaism was aware that the Jerusalem Temple was unique and that many of its functions could not be transferred elsewhere; one could only live and pray for the day when it might be restored. In the meantime the synagogue contained these reminders or echoes of the Temple, and was loved and respected for what it meant in the life of the Jewish people. Otherwise it was a non-sacral building, open to the Gentiles and even on occasion sold to them, or bought from them, and dedicated by the installation of the Torah and the lighting of the perpetual lamp hung before it, but not consecrated as a dwelling for Jahweh. In particular it remained largely free from cosmic symbolism, and the extensive symbolic reference that did develop was historical rather than cosmic in intent. Orientation had once been prescribed but this was to be towards Jerusalem the historic centre, and when many synagogues later were built on an east-west axis there was no emphasis on the cosmic implications of this. The historical reference has remained predominant in the elaboration of symbols that has continued into modern times — twelve windows for the twelve tribes of Israel (as still in Yemenite synagogues), or thirty-nine small windows for the number of Old Testament books, five steps up to the bimah for the five books of Moses, two high walls flanking the ark for the two tables of the Decalogue, together with the seven-branched candlestick, the eternal lamp before the ark, and the ark curtian — not as cosmic symbols in themselves repeating their functions in another temple but as reminders of their originals in the one historic Temple. Despite the close analogy at some of these points with the symbolism of the Gothic revival churches they have not served to sanctify the synagogue but rather to preserve the historic identity of an Israel deprived of its sacred temple. Unlike Christian churches the synagogue itself emerged from antiquity still basilican in form and in principle a *domus ecclesiae* that had remained true to its origins and purpose as a meeting house.

14.2 THE INCONSPICUOUS THOUSAND YEARS

Little is heard of synagogues in the succeeding centuries of the Dark Ages. The Jewish communities were small and poor and their meeting places must often have been no more than rooms set aside for prayer. The general insecurity, especially under the Byzantine Christian empire, and the existence in ghettos magnified the functions of the synagogue as a community centre that embraced many aspects of Jewish life. When mourners were comforted within its walls or prospective bridegrooms congratulated, when lost and found notices and stolen goods announcements were made, legal judgments proclaimed and properties for sale advertised, we can only conclude that any earlier attitudes towards it as a place to be kept apart and revered had been seriously eroded. This of course planted it still more firmly in the meeting house tradition.

There was, however, a considerable development of the funerary influences that have affected Christian and to a lesser degree Islamic places of worship. Some pilgrimage to Jerusalem and the site of the Temple had continued as circumstances allowed ever since the first century, but from the earlier Middle Ages and especially after Saladin conquered Palestine and allowed free access from 1187 Jewish pilgrimages became more numerous. Jewish doctrine could tolerate and even encourage pilgrimage to the historic sites as an act of piety and for edification, but as usual in this sphere popular religion was ill content with such bounds and sought more specific benefits of healing and access of spiritual power. And again, as with the Christians and the Muslims, these boons were to be had by pilgrimage to the tombs of the saints — to the graves of biblical figures such as Samuel the prophet at Nabi Samwil, of Rachel near Bethlehem and her son Joseph in Shechem, of the rabbis of the Talmud in Galilee, and of later saints, scholars and heroes. Traditions had grown up around these holy places, sanctuaries or shrines had been erected over their graves, and the cult of the dead with the offering of prayers, the burning of incense and candles, and the pledging of vows flourished in the Jewish context. Early in the tenth century a Karaite scholar, Sahl b.Mazli'ah, was driven to complain: 'How can I remain silent when some of the Jews are behaving like idolaters? They sit at the graves, sometimes sleeping there at night, and appeal to the dead: "Oh! Rabbi Yose ha-Gelili! Heal me! Grant me children!" They kindle lights there and offer incense....'[8]

A later Jewish traveller, Benjamin of Tudela, recorded his extensive pilgrimages about the 1160s to a long list of synagogues that had been built as shrines at the graves of prophets, saints and heroes, much as we have suggested earlier had occurred at the tomb of the seven Maccabean martyrs. Although further detail is lacking this must have been an influential force towards the transformation of synagogues into sacred buildings with temple overtones; that it did not succeed may owe something to the vicissitudes of Jewish history but perhaps more to the staying power of the basilican and similar meeting house forms as they continued to serve the spiritual and social life of the Diaspora.

Other influences that might have led back to the *domus dei* in the Middle Ages were to be found in the splendid Byzantine and Gothic churches of the Christians. The repressive attitude of the Byzantine Empire towards the Jews and the lack of opportunity to build new synagogues, coupled with the conservatism of mediaeval Jewry may explain the absence of Byzantine influence till more recent times. In the freer conditions of northern Europe some use was made of Gothic, as in the Bamberg synagogue in thirteenth century Germany, with a Gothic ribbed vault and emphasis on the longitudinal axis, and in other examples in the same century in Prague and later in Cracow and especially in Bohemia and Galicia. In all cases, however, the synagogue remained a rectangular basilica in form and avoided the full development of Gothic with chancel and cruciform plan that would have led it away from its own tradition. This has remained true even in modern times when synagogue builders (if we may anticipate later history) succumbed to the prestige of the Gothic revival in the mid-nineteenth century and occasionally followed this style both in Europe (the Meisel Synagogue in Prague and others in Vienna) and in North America; only very exceptionally has the full Gothic cruciform plan been followed, as by the church architect who presented the Congregation Mikve Israel in Savannah with pure fourteenth century Gothic in 1877, or in the Temple B'rith Sholom in Louisville, Kentucky. In general this is the one Christian style that Jewish scholars have explicitly rejected, for 'the pointed arches... and the soaring spires which point upwards are the theological symbols of Christianity's primary concern with... the after-life...; Judaism, per contra, is preoccupied with life on earth, not in heaven... and relegates to lesser concern the after-life'.[9] This may not be a satisfactory understanding of the Christian position but it coincides in spirit with our own critique of Gothic as a religious but non-Christian form; it is also significant that this rejection should have arisen within the one Semitic tradition that has followed the *domus ecclesiae* principle most faithfully.

Although Jews had been under Christian influence for a longer period and over more extensive areas, it was Islam that exercised the greater influence on the mediaeval synagogue. The Arab invasions from the eighth century released many Jewish communities from Byzantine oppression and Jews discovered a new confidence under rulers who were Semites like themselves. It is the *Itinerary* of Benjamin of Tudela which again supplies information on eastern synagogues for he described the great synagogue of Bagdad as a columned hall opening onto a courtyard and decorated with calligraphy in typical mosque manner. The synagogue at Aleppo was quite specifically Islamic in the early internal courtyard style: the congregation sat in the porticos around the courtyard, a separately roofed bimah took the place of the usual fountain in the middle of the courtyard, and the ark was placed in the position corresponding to that of the mihrab.

In north Africa and especially in Spain from the eighth century under the Moors Jewish and Islamic cultures enjoyed a mutually stimulating relationship that flowered into a golden age for each community. The synagogues built in Spain belonged to this distinctive Muslim civilization and although none has survived from the Moorish period the same influence governed those built later under the Christians in the twelfth to fourteenth centuries. Two of these survive at Toledo: one from the thirteenth century exists today as the Church of Santa Maria la Blanca, and the other built about 1357 became the El Transito Church; both exhibit a typical Moorish mosque rectangular plan and structure, with plain exterior and richly wrought interior decorated with biblical calligraphy, and with horseshoe-shaped arches to their arcades. In their magnificence they might be said to look in the direction of the temple tradition, as did other splendid mosques in Islam, but basically they remained within the general basilican form of meeting hall.

It is convenient here to anticipate history once again and glance at the later revival of Moorish influence in the synagogues of Europe and North America. In their groping amid the many revivals and new forms of the nineteenth century and perhaps with a desire to emphasize Judaism's oriental origin as against Christian Gothic and other western styles, synagogue builders turned again to the golden period of Spanish Jewry and adopted their Islamic forms, with bulbous domes, horseshoe arches, Moorish-style arks and minaret-like towers. This revival can be traced from the Oranienburgerstrasse Synagogue in Berlin of 1855-66, and others at Cologne (1861), and Nuremburg (1874) in Germany, the Central Synagogue of 1870 in London, the great synagogue at Florence with heavy Moorish decoration in 1880, and one at St. Petersburg in 1893. At the same time the Moorish form appeared in the United States, with the Plum Street Temple in Cincinnati (1866) displaying its thirteen domes and two minarets, and others in New York (Temple Emmanuel, 1868), and in Philadelphia (Rodef Shalom, 1870), and dozens elsewhere, all looking like Turkish mosques. While this exotic fashion faded it does represent perhaps some sense of the inherent kinship between mosque and synagogue as places of worship.

14.3 PERSISTENCE OF THE MEETING HOUSE: 16TH TO 18TH CENTURIES

With the expulsions of Jews from so many western European countries towards the end of the Middle Ages the story of synagogue building moves eastwards, and especially to Bohemia, Moravia, Galicia and Poland where large numbers of Jews lived in relative prosperity within Roman Catholic cultures. They were therefore influenced in the early modern period by the advent of Renaissance and later Baroque churches, which as we have seen, were better able than Gothic to preserve the meeting house form of single chambered building. Up to the eighteenth century European Jewry existed for the most part as an oppressed or restricted minority, excluded from the mediaeval trades guilds and unable to acquire a tradition of building and architectural skills of their own. When, therefore, in the intermittent periods of relative freedom they were able to erect larger purpose-built synagogues they had perforce to resort to Christian builders and designers, and to accept the prevailing forms of church building. This resulted in notable synagogues such as the Klauz in Prague, built in the sixteenth and altered in the seventeenth century in a local barrel-vaulted Renaissance idiom with a definite longitudinal axis; others were the R. Isaac Nachmanovich synagogue in Lvov of 1582, and, among many others in Cracow, the R. Isaac Jacobowiczy Synagogue of 1644 with a rectangular meeting space of twelve by nineteen metres and the bimah almost in the centre. In Bohemia and Moravia it was the Baroque of south Germany and Austria that issued in eighteenth century synagogues with a square plan and even with an ark resembling a Baroque Catholic high altar, as at Neuzedlisch in 1786.

It was in Poland that we find in this period the most distinctive architectural contribution ever made by Judaism. Troubled times had descended upon Polish Jews in the seventeenth century as seen in the great massacres of 1648-49, and these were reflected in the desire to build in less conspicuous non-church forms and in the necessity to use local craftsmen and materials. The result was the Polish wooden synagogue often built by Jewish builders and employing much of the local vernacular wooden style as seen in smaller wooden churches. The oldest known example was at Chodorov near Lvov in 1651, and large numbers were built in the next two generations not only in Poland but westwards as far as Germany where they adapted to the local half-timbered style. The exterior was plain and almost shed-like, the walls were usually timber lined on both sides, and the roof mounted high sometimes in successive almost pagoda-like stages over an internal ceiling of a highly imaginative and complex design combining ogival and barrel-shaped vaulting. The plan was a fairly compact rectangle with a central axis emphasis derived from the group of four timber pillars that supported the roof and enclosed the bimah. As a structure it was a triumph of folk-carpentry which maintained the prayer-house tradition in an original manner.

In the seventeenth century Jews moved north-westward into the Protestant countries to escape from the Polish troubles and from the Inquisition in southern Catholic Europe. Spanish and Portuguese Jews in particular were welcome in Holland, which had made its own escape from Spanish rule, and there they once again made use of the local forms we have already described as examples of the Protestant Plain Style. Thus the Sephardic (i.e. Spanish and Portuguese) Synagogue of 1675 in Amsterdam was built by a Gentile architect in classical basilican manner with barrel-vaulted ceiling in the same way as many Protestant churches in Holland and some in France. In like manner the Bevis Marks Synagogue of 1701 in London resembled the Nonconformist meeting houses of the period, and other eighteenth century synagogues were akin to the new churches of Christopher Wren. These Sephardic Synagogues in Holland and England were copied by the Ashkenazic (i.e. Polish and Russian) Jews and spread to North America and other parts of the world. In the United States, for instance, there is the surviving Touro Synagogue completed in 1763 at Newport, Rhode Island, and exhibiting a Georgian colonial wooden style on a square plan, with a women's gallery on three sides, twelve columns for the Twelve Tribes of Israel, and a central bimah.

As the neo-classical revival overtook church building in western Europe and North America in the late eighteenth and early nineteenth centuries so also it affected the stylistic design of synagogues as seen in the Great Synagogue in London in 1790 with rows of Ionic pillars and a small round-arched apse for the ark. Other classical examples appeared in the Rue Notre Dame in Paris (1820), in Vienna (1824), Budapest (1821), Munich (1826), and in the New Synagogue of 1838 in London. In all these synagogues the neo-classical was but a style imposed on a basically rectangular meeting hall which had managed to persist through all the vicissitudes and diverse imitations of the early modern period.

14.4 THE SPATIAL PROBLEM OF THE SYNAGOGUE INTERIOR

The basic structure of the Jewish liturgy has remained remarkably constant since it became the sole form for Jewish worship after the fall of the Temple. Liturgical variety has been more concerned with the arrangements within the synagogue for the performance of the liturgy, and in particular on the inter-relationship of the people, the bimah or reading platform, and the ark or container for the scrolls of the scriptures, the Torah. In the earliest synagogues there is no sign of a fixed place for the chest or ark of the scrolls, and these were probably kept in a storeroom outside the prayer hall and later in a chest that came to be carried or wheeled in; It was the bimah which was the sole and essential fixture upon which the service focussed as the prayers were led and the scriptures read from this raised platform. The congregation was distributed around the bimah along the walls and the whole clearly displayed a central axis form of meeting house.

There was therefore no problem until the increasing emphasis upon the holiness of the ark led to its permanent installation on the end wall and to elaboration of the ark itself and of its surroundings in a manner that presented another and competing focus for the worshippers: what had begun as a humble chest became a monumental built-in feature exhibiting the best artistic skills of the day. Either it overshadowed the bimah, which amounted to a major dislocation of the liturgy, or if the latter was also elaborated with pillars and canopies and rich carving then the tension between the two was equally serious. If the service had been primarily a matter of prayer then the fully developed ark form would have provided a focus comparable to that of the altar-table in a Christian church, and the single-axis suggestion would have been entirely appropriate. If the liturgy had been confined to the reading of the Torah and its exposition then the bimah would have served with similar satisfaction. And in either case it had to be remembered that the synagogue was basically a place of assembly, a meeting house for the congregation. 'The relative proximity between the two foci in one interior... and the search for a balance between them... constitutes an aggravating architectural problem... the principal conceptual and ideological factor in synagogue design.'[10] When in modern times exposition turned into preaching as such and so required a still different relation to the congregation, then the problem became compounded. It is obviously very similar to the Christian problem of the relationship between the provision for the celebration of the sacraments, the reading of the Word, the preaching of the Gospel, and leadership in the prayers. If the development of the ark had never occurred in the synagogue, but the scriptures had been carried in straight to the bimah as they are in some Christian churches, then much of the problem would not have arisen.

That it did arise is due in large measure to the human desire for a special holy place, aggravated in this case by the loss of the Temple and not satisfied by the offer of a radically new form of temple as in the New Testament. The original term used for the container of the Torah was *tebah*, the ordinary word used for the arks associated with the infant Moses and with Noah, and this usage continued into the Middle Ages among rabbinic circles. Alongside this and among Hellenized Jews the word *'aron* which referred to the ark of the covenant in the Jewish Temple replaced the merely secular word; when qualified as *'aron kodesh* (holy ark) as by Ashkenazic Jews, or given the term *heikhal* (sanctuary) by the Sephardim, the sacralization of the Torah chest was completed. This change, however, was long resisted by the Palestine conservatives, for whom there could be no substitute for the Holy Temple and its sacred objects.

The progressive elaboration and sacralization of the *Aron* is a study in itself which we can barely sketch. It includes the appearance in the ark ensemble of various symbols and architectural features associated with the Temple: the twin pillars, the gables and doors of the Temple, the lion symbols and the seven-branched candelabrum, the curtains or marble screen that separated the new Holy of Holies from the congregation, and the *Ner Tamid* (perpetual light) sanctuary lamp hung in front of the *Aron* to indicate the light of the Law and thus the presence of God, in a way that the lamp before the *mihrab* of the mosque never managed to suggest. Accompanying these developments there was the installation of the ark as a fixed cabinet on the wall and then as a built-in feature sometimes provided with a niche or larger apse, or as in the case of a Cairo synagogue with a shallow chancel raised five steps and enclosed by a stone balustrade with a central entrance. On occasion raised and projecting platforms enclosed by pillars and balustrades and surmounted by gables or canopies created the impression of the splendid entrance porch to a temple. The parallel elaboration of the Christian altar and its reredos and approaches was not without influence in the history of the ark, and in the Baroque period there is record of richly worked Baroque altars being bought from churches and monasteries closed under the Emperor Joseph II of Austria and installed in synagogues; in the Sephardic synagogue of Amsterdam the Baroque ark extends across the whole width of the nave, and in the eighteenth century the style had spread to Eastern Europe with much zoological carving and open scroll work. In another altar-like version the ark might resemble a marble sarcophagus with reredos, recessed on a platform, as in the Shaarey Zedek Synagogue in Winnipeg, Canada.

It is not surprising, therefore, that much Jewish law and custom is concerned with the ark as the holiest part of the synagogue after the scrolls of the Torah. Other appurtenances within the synagogue might be sold to buy an ark, because they possess less holiness, but an ark must not be sold even to assist the building of a synagogue itself; if it becomes unusable it must be respectfully placed in storage. One must not sleep in its vicinity nor sit facing away from it, and while it is open it is customary to stand. On certain occasions it is not left empty but has a lighted candle inside while the scrolls are removed. On the occasions of special fasts or rituals it is opened for prayers, and sometimes for the special prayers of individuals for healing and for other troubles.[11]

The attitude to the ark as holy is still very much alive in some contemporary Jewish circles. Thus a sophisticated American rabbi can assert that 'it is the presence of an *Aron Ha Kodesh* containing the scrolls of the Torah that transforms any room into a synagogue'.[12] This implies a rather drastic judgment on the earliest synagogue forms. The same rabbi continued with the demand that the ark 'occupy the most commanding position structurally... as the modern counterpart of the ancient Holy of Holies in the Temple.... Our Modern Ark must be proportionately large and lofty and imposing.' Indeed some modern arks are quite overwhelming in their height and splendour, and perhaps covered in gold leaf or arranged for the rays of the sun to play upon them.

On the other hand it is fair to indicate the criticisms of these developments also to be found in American Jewry. At the same conference at which the rabbi we have quoted spoke other voices warned that 'the scroll and the Ark van easily become an idol', and that 'the frequent analogy between the Ark and the Holy of Holies in... Jerusalem is but an *ex post facto* justification for an over-emphasis on the Ark which comes into Judaism from alien sources'.[13] Another speaker proclaimed the danger of 'allowing the Ark to dominate the end wall... but we worship neither the Ark nor the Torah. Since the Ark is not an end in itself, is it right that it should form a visual and hence psychological termination to the house of worship?... Should we not bring the Ark out of its niche and express it for the worldly and transient thing it is ...?'[14] These two contrasting viewpoints will engage us later when we examine the different sections of modern Judaism.

The bimah, on the other hand, acquired its importance not from any suggestions of holiness but from the central place it occupied in the synagogue liturgy from earliest times. We have already commented on this new form of worship, which has been well described in a modern statement: 'Here for the first time in human history, the religious books were opened to all the people, not only to be read aloud to them, but also to be translated into the spoken Aramaic and expounded and interpreted so that all would understand... universal enlightenment was looked upon as an ideal and deemed indispensible to the true worship of God....'[15] The main element in the liturgy was therefore the reading of the Torah, and the most important item in the synagogue was the bimah, the platform with reading desk whose free-standing or central position was ideal both symbolically and functionally. It was to the bimah that the Torah scrolls were carried ceremonially and then read for as much as an hour; men walked to the bimah to recite the blessings, to read the prayers, and to hold the Torah; from the bimah the Torah was carried back with due dignity to its ark; and here the Torah was expounded, the shofar blown in the New Year ritual, and various ceremonies such as circumcision performed. Other faiths had nothing like it their liturgies or assemblies; this is indeed 'the one genuinely Jewish structural form brought into being as a requirement of Jewish ritual'.[16]

The entirely appropriate emphasis upon the bimah as the spiritual and architectural centre of the synagogue encouraged an elaboration of its arrangements, with dual flights of steps to a platform as much as three metres from the floor, with carved bannisters, balustrades, desks and seats, with ornamental grills in ironwork, and canopies and roofs supported on impressive columns that had become part of the new form of building structure. No matter how dignified and splendid the bimah and its associated ritual became it is impossible to find even in these developments a transposition from the principle of the meeting house to that of the temple.

At this point we should note the diverse ways in which the two chief foci have been related in the course of synagogue history. The earliest pattern consisted of a central bimah with the ark on the eastern or end wall; this became firmly established in antiquity and in the mediaeval period and has remained the plan found among oriental Jews ever since.

In the twelfth century there began a series of architectural developments which presented different ways of providing a central bimah,
especially in larger buildings. One of these was the double-naved synagogue formed by two columns on the main axis, which divided the
space into six bays and located the bimah in the centre between the
columns. This plan first appeared at the synagogue in Worms late in
the twelfth century and became common in mediaeval central Europe,
sometimes in a simpler version employing only one column. The final
development in this direction occurred when the bimah was established
centrally within the sub-space created by four pillars which together
carried the roof; here the whole building structure and the bimah were
integrally connected and the emphasis had reached its climax. Alongside these variations the ark was receiving its own enhancement and
the tension between the two was never solved.

Another approach was to place the bimah on the west or end wall
opposite to that accomodating the ark and so to attempt a balance
between the two foci along the same axis. This began in Spain at least
by the thirteenth century and came to full development in Italy in the
sixteenth and seventeenth centuries. In this bi-polar hall the congregation sat in two parts facing each other across the central aisle along
which the Torah was carried; the bimah was sometimes elevated sufficiently to allow for the main entrance beneath it, flanked by symmetrical flights of steps, and treated in an ornate Baroque manner. In
this arrangement every worshipper is equally related to both ark and
bimah and the conflict might be thought solved. It has, however, not
been more widely adopted, and partly on account of the factors that
led to the third form.

In this particular and modern plan both ark and bimah are located at
the same end. This usually results in a central ark that holds the single
dominant position, and in front of it a platform with seats, lectern,
prayer desk and pulpit, these three being commonly reduced to twin
ambos in symmetrical support of the ark. One of the main factors en-
couraging this radical change, besides the increasing sacralization of the
ark, was the revival in the nineteenth century of the sermon that had
fallen into disuse in the Middle Ages. Preaching in the full sense as distinct from exposition of the Torah required a more direct confronta-

tion with the whole congregation which was most readily secured from a position in front of or near the ark. This revealed the problem of a large empty space between preacher and bimah, and the solution was to combine all the activities of the bimah together with the preaching on a platform across the ark wall and to rearrange the congregation in rows facing this wall.

The immediate result was to decrease the sense of being a participating community of praying Jews with their lay leaders in their midst and to heighten the suggestion of an audience led by professionals who performed for their benefit on a platform. This arrangement is very common in modern American synagogues; that of Sinai Congregation built in Chicago in the 1950s holds two thousand people within a semicircular plan focussed on the 'stage' and is inevitably spoken of as the auditorium. Only the central splendour of the Holy Ark prevents complete identification with the concert or lecture hall.

Such a drastic change was not effected without considerable opposition especially from the Orthodox section of Judaism, although even their synagogues have not proved immune. Nor has this development avoided the same reaction we noted in connection with the sacralization of the ark, a desire to restore the emphasis on the Torah, and on the procession of the scrolls to the bimah which has been telescoped to no more than a few inconspicuous steps. A compromise solution has been to advance the bimah platform into the congregation, much as with an apron stage in a theatre, or more radically to place it in a novel position half way along the side wall much as a Christian pulpit might be placed against a pillar several bays distant from the chancel. It is to be doubted whether either of these changes could lead to the restoration of the distinctive features of the Jewish community and its worship, which some are once again seeking in terms of the ancient central plan.

14.5 FROM MEETING HOUSE TO TEMPLE:
THE VARIANT INFLUENCE OF MODERN JEWISH DENOMINATIONS

We have conducted our discussion so far with little reference to the older divisions within Jewry which were not of great moment in relation to our theme. The modern parties, however, which have arisen since the eighteenth century show considerable divergence in their attitude to the synagogue, with a spectrum ranging from meeting house to temple emphases.

The first of these is found in the modern Hasidim, a pietist movement within Orthodoxy which appeared in the second half of the eighteenth century in Poland and Lithuania and spread southwards and finally to the United States. The Hasidim laid stress on spiritual experience and on people, rather than on the synagogue building, its furnishings and rituals. The result was a more informal service, without paid officials, in a smaller plainer synagogue called the *shtibl* (small room) often not purpose-built, and also used for any kind of meeting, for study, and for common meals. This amounted to a revival of the earliest forms of synagogue interpreted and used very much as a meeting house. The Hasidim therefore represented the same *domus ecclesiae* emphasis that had been recaptured by the radical groups of the Protestant Reformation, the English dissenters and Quakers, and the German pietists.

The Hasidim have, however, become increasingly archaic and the main groups in modern Jewry have been the Orthodox, the Conservative, and the Reform Jews (called Liberal in Britain); we shall confine our attention to Orthodox and Reform, for the Conservatives lie between these two distinctive and opposing groups.

Orthodoxy as an identifiable section of Judaism appeared first in Germany and Hungary among Jews who were prepared to accept the political emancipation that began in the late eighteenth century, but who set themselves against any form of assimilation to modern Western ideas, which for them were associated with Christianity. Under the new freedom of the past two centuries, and as the Orthodox position has spread westwards to North America, its synagogues have often been splendid, elaborate buildings with services of great decorum and dignity, but they have remained close to traditional forms in several respects that concern our thesis. The bimah is retained as a distinct structure and usually remains in a more central position; the congregation is either placed on the two sides of the bimah or grouped around it in a circular manner; women have their own gallery. A modern form of Orthodoxy is represented in the Shaarci Shomayim Synagogue (1968) in Toronto where the free-standing central bimah has the congregation round it in a large semi-circle which also faces the ark, and where the women's section is now on the same floor at the rear and to one side, enclosed by a low wall. Some few Orthodox in North America have gone further and adopted the ark-with-platform arrangement, with the women allotted one side of the auditorium separated only by a centre aisle. In modern Israel, on the other hand, where the great majority of synagogues are Orthodox, we find the bimah still central and a screened or curtained women's gallery.

It is highly significant that the Orthodox do not sacralize the synagogue or treat it as a temple, in spite of sharing in the sacralization of the ark. Although in the United States Orthodox have succumbed to the Reform practice of calling the building a 'temple' this has been resisted in Europe and above all in Israel. Many Orthodox hope for the rebuilding of the Temple when the Messiah comes, and occasionally one hears of plans to proceed at once with its restoration; on the other hand the term 'Jerusalem Great Synagogue' has been employed for one current attempt to provide a central large place of worship in Israel for world Jewry. The distinction between Temple and synagogue is vital for Orthodoxy and is manifest in practice by the kind of behaviour that is acceptable in the latter, where men may dance at services celebrating the giving of the Decalogue and women throw sweets down from the gallery, where children may sound rattles and shout when Haman is mentioned during the reading of the book of Esther, and where women use the place as a meeting house and enjoy conversation. However much the synagogue acquired certain temple overtones, especially in connection with the ark, in principle the distinction has remained firm throughout most of the Orthodox Jewish world and not least within the modern return to Palestine.

In contrast to Orthodoxy stands Reform Judaism, originating in Germany and Western Europe and now influential in North America and other parts of the world except eastern Europe, Israel and the Orient. The reaction against the formal rigidities of Orthodoxy that issued in the Hasidim in eastern Europe took a different turn in the west where the influence of the Enlightenment and the progressive emancipation of the Jews initiated in the American and French Revolutions led to movements specifically called 'Reform', and focussed especially on the worship of the synagogue. It was felt that a religion that had survived by the conservation of the traditions and the unity of an oppressed people might vanish with the abandonment of the ghetto and the response to the new freedoms; its future depended upon a modernizing development of new forms suited to the new situation. These convictions first took shape in Germany at the turn of the nineteenth century and were expresserd in a school chapel at Seesen in 1810 where there were choir, instrumental music, and a sermon preached in German; it was known as 'Jacob's Temple' in dedication to the father of the teacher, Israel Jacobson; the latter had lived under French occupation in Westphalia and regarded the French Calvinist Reformation (with its use of the term 'temple') as similar to his own movement.

Orthodox pressure secured government closure of this venture but better success attended the new temple of the Hamburg Reform Association in 1818 with its organ, its new prayer book, its use of German in the service (Jewish translations of the scriptures into German had begun in the 1780s), its abolition of the screen separating the women, and its moving of the bimah from the centre to just in front of the ark. The use of the term 'temple' arose from the conviction that Israel was no longer in exile, and that a temple was not necessarily associated with a sacrificial cult but was to be found in every house of worship. The new designation became universal in Reform Judaism and has spread beyond it in the West; in more recent times it has been applied to the whole complex, including ancillary buildings for all the purposes of a community centre, so that the room reserved for worship is known as the 'sanctuary'— or even more colloquially as the 'prayerie'!

Reform spread in Holland and Britain, where the West London Synagogue was erected in 1840, and to the United States as early as 1825 — the first notable building was the Temple Emanu-El in New York in the mid-century. Other changes included drastic reduction of the length of Torah readings and new emphasis on the sermon, not only as an exposition of scripture but for the general discussion of religion. Traditional prayers were purged of elements that now appeared superstitious or outmoded, such as prayer for the restoration of the sacrificial cult or the coming of the personal Messiah – the latter notion was transformed into belief in a messianic age which some felt was now dawning; references offensive to non-Jews were also reduced to innocuous forms. In these changes the intention of much of the Reform section was to remain true to Jewish tradition, and appeal was made to rabbinic authorities wherever possible; only the more extreme humanist and secularizing wing of the movement departed from this allegiance.

One of the departures from traditional forms effected by Reform Judaism has been the adoption of paid professional leaders who have added the functions of the Christian minister to those of the traditional rabbi – preaching, pastoral care, and the conduct of a greater range of modern religious services suitable for all occasions, as a priest responsible for the rituals. It has also been suggested that many of the priestly functions exercised in the Jerusalem Temple are now found in the services of the Reform Synagogue, where

the daily prayers are a symbol of the sacrifices in the Temple. The priestly blessing in the daily worship of the synagogue is a symbol of the priest's blessing in the Temple after the daily offering... the various Hosannah prayers, with the lulav procession are a recollection of the procession round the Altar in the Temple. The whole synagogue service is to a large extent a symbolic recollection of the Temple.[17]

Despite the meeting-house suggestions of the auditorium it is the *domus dei* outlook which has overtaken the Reform synagogue as it has progressively abandoned the distinctives of the Jewish prayer hall; this appears in the loss of lay leaders at a central bimah and of the surrounding congregation, in the separation of the latter from a professionalized ministry with priestly functions, in the conversion of synagogues into 'temples' with 'sanctuaries' reserved for the single purpose of the sacred liturgy and dominated by the Holy Ark, and in the increased interest in liturgy as such since the late 1930s in the United States – these entirely congruous developments all lead back to the temple form of place of worship.

The same conception appears in modern Reform discussions of the building itself and of its interior effects. The ark, as we have pointed out, has become the focal emphasis, often secured through giving great height for the sanctuary wall (in Congregation Shaarey Zedek, Detroit), or through richness of materials; for example, one specification offered 'a simple rule ... that the nearer an object is to the Holy of Holies (the chamber containing the Ark) the rarer and costlier the materials'.[18] This suggestion of graded sanctities is also found in the use of light 'to capture the drama of the service' (i.e. to make the platform more like a theatre stage) and to suggest the glory of the heavens descending upon the Holy Ark in the sanctuary – usually by strong overhead natural or artificial lighting. This light may even be allowed to spill over into the seating area so that 'in one temple of Long Island, New York ... people who sit further back can thus receive the illusion that the first two rows in the congregation are almost participating in the service'.[18] Almost – but not quite; and the irony is unintended! Similar numinous effects are also desired of the building which must 'emphasize the finite stature of man as he confronts God' by its 'strong vertical accents',[19] and 'be capable of arousing the deepest emotions ... of awe, respect, humility, and the closeness of man with his Creator... a greater emotional response from those who enter than from any other type of building...'.[20] We are already familiar with such statements in support of Christian churches in the *domus dei* tradition. This is also the language of modern secularized Jews who ask for a beautiful synagogue that will suggest the infinity and greatness of God and so assist them to pray once more.

Reform Judaism speaks with many accents, and there are voices that question the invasion of the numinous into the synagogue and the attempt to make the building itself eloquent of the God of the Jews; scattered attempts may be found to return to traditional forms, as with the free-standing ark or a bimah once more in the middle of the synagogue as at Carmel College, Wallingford, in England and in Louis I. Kahn's designs. The overwhelming impression, however, is of a section of Judaism that has accepted the impossibility of ever restoring the Jerusalem Temple and therefore endeavours to accomodate in its own practice the forms and values of this kind of sanctuary. Orthodoxy on the other hand has been protected from this transposition of synagogue into temple by its own adherence to the distinction between them and its sustained hope of the restoration of the one and only Temple on Mt. Zion.

14.6 REDISCOVERING THE JEWISH NORM

We have seen the reasons for the absence of a Jewish tradition of design and building and the extent to which forms have been borrowed from other religions and cultures, especially in the modern period of Jewish emancipation. At the same time, and despite the varying emphasis from meeting house to temple in modern Jewry, there has been sufficient continuity to enable the identification of the synagogue from early to modern times. This may be said with even greater force of the mosques of Islam but not of Christian churches, which exhibit much greater diversity across the centuries. It is possible, therefore, that with the new architectural freedom provided by twentieth century ideas and techniques Judaism may be able to abandon the eclecticism of its past and discover a distinctively Jewish mode of synagogue architecture by 'construction from the inside out... that is organic, that permits the form to be a pure expression of the content'.[21] These and similar general principles, which are so congenial to modern architecture, are being enunciated in Jewish quarters and applied in some newer building. Attempts to make the building symbolic in itself especially in its plan are rejected; rather should it be unselfconscious and modest. Half a century ago Lewis Mumford suggested the dome-on-cube basis as a most suitable synagogue form, as it has been for mosques in Islam and as it was worked out in so many variations in Eastern Christianity. Without emphasizing its potential for cosmic symbolism this form can provide a suitable meeting place and has been used with success in the form of a dome upon various polygonal bases over the past century. It serves well the unity of the worshipping community, so important to Judaism, but is perhaps too reminiscent of its Christian use and not sufficiently in tune with modern architecture to be adopted as Mumford had hoped.[22]

Probably the most important statements relevant to synagogue design are those which remind us of the central importance in Judaism of both the individual and of the community. Some have taken this emphasis one stage further, in a way that resembles the New Testament teaching of the temple being now personalized. 'Use your architectural forms', says one scholar, 'to heighten the worshipper's awareness that *he* is potentially the real temple of the Lord'; and again, varying the reference; 'a human being is potentially the Ark and the emphasis must somehow be shown in that way.'[23] Others have revived the tabernacle as a model for the synagogue which 'is more likely to resemble the biblical tent of meeting than Notre Dame or Jerusalem's sacred precincts ... tentlike because of its relative impermanence'.[24] Even Meir Ben Uri, a highly orthodox synagogue designer in Israel, returns to the desert tabernacle model with its smallness and simplicity, and its emphasis on divine presence rather than sacred building, as a token of Israel's permanent architectural contribution.[25] If the radical significance of these principles for synagogue architecture can be grasped and maintained, for they are congruent with the deepest understanding in the Hebrew Scriptures, then the norm for the Jewish place of worship will be fixed firmly within the tradition of the non-sacral *domus ecclesiae*.

EPILOGUE: THE SEMITIC EXPERIENCE

The layman, but not the biologist, may be surprised to find the bat, the lion and the whale classified together as mammals because of the importance of their common characteristics and despite their striking differences.[26] We trust that the reader who has persevered to this point will now have the professional eye to identify the synagogue, the church and the mosque as members of the same species, the *domus ecclesiae*. It is this kinship which helps to explain the many influences these forms have had, the one upon the other, both in general architectural styles and at various points in their internal arrangements, as well as the similarities that have emerged even when there has been no particular influence from the other forms. The fourteenth century Spanish churches with their bimah-like pulpits in the middle of the worshippers, the great Sancta Sophia in Constantinople with its original central structure under the cupola for the ministers, and the lessons and preaching, the earlier basilican churches with a similar arrangement projecting into the midst of the congregation, and the Quaker meeting house with its benches around a central table are following the same principles as the classic forms of the Jewish synagogue.

This family resemblance also explains why there has been a great deal of interchange of buildings for worship during the history of the three Semitic faiths. Churches have been bought for use as synagogues, especially in the United States where the dominant ethnic group in a locality may have changed; and this writer has conducted a service for a Methodist congregation rendered homeless by fire in a synagogue lent by the Jewish community — there is no bar to the selling or lending of synagogues to the Gentiles. A new form that represents this easy interchangeability is found in the interfaith type of chapel used by Catholics, Protestants and Jews at different times, perhaps with ingenious arrangements whereby a high altar, a communion table or an ark can be brought into use by a revolving platform.

The same resemblance is illustrated where churches in the Byzantine area were turned into mosques, or even shared by the two faiths, and in Spain where the opposite chances of history saw mosques converted into churches. Among the Muslims of Mindanao in the Philippines Frank Laubach built 'a house of prayer' open to Muslims and Christians alike, and in Muslim lands in modern times Christian churches have been modelled on mosques: the Armenian cathedral at Julfa (1663), All Saints Memorial Church at Peshawar (1883), and the Church of St. Simon The Zealot at Shiraz in Iran; the small courtyard mosque has also been recommended as a suitable form for churches in India and Pakistan. In the southern Sudan experiments have been made with open air chapels on local Islamic models, and in western Nigeria large mosques and churches may be almost indistinguishable except for insignia such as crescents and crosses. Interestingly enough, the courtyard plan developed quite independently of Muslim associations in the mission churches of the mendicant orders among the American Indians of New Spain in the sixteenth century; here a large walled courtyard with a cross in the centre had an open chapel across one end corresponding to the *haram* of a mosque; at times the town square served as a still larger courtyard.[27]

The interaction of mosque and synagogue has already been demonstrated at Baghdad and Aleppo, and in the Spain of the Moors. As a modern example we may instance the synagogue at the Hebrew University, Jerusalem (1957), which is strikingly similar to the university mosque in Ibadan, Nigeria (1963). Like synagogues, many modern churches have approximated to Protestant church styles based on a single space without pillars. These similarities are reflected in the fact that according to the original traditions of each faith members of the other faiths could be admitted without defilement of synagogue, church or mosque, since none was consecrated or sacralized, although a minority of Muslims and some Christians would now object to 'infidels' in their own places of worship. Likewise, with little or even no rearrangement each could conduct its own worship in the place of the others, with the exception of the multi-cell churches and cathedrals that have been so clearly in the temple mode.

Besides these similarities in form there are the important parallels we have traced in their histories. The place of worship for all three faiths had humble and domestic beginnings, made a radical break from earlier forms, and established itself in the *domus ecclesiae* tradition. Each has had at least one major opportunity for rapid expansion with new resources: Christianity in the fourth century, Islam from the eighth, and Judaism in the nineteenth century. In all cases the new opportunity has been marked by a spectrum of forms showing the return of the *domus dei* as well as the survival of the meeting house principle.

All these resemblances have their roots in the common features of the three Semitic faiths – the new united community based on revelation from the one true God conveyed in sacred scriptures. The emphasis on historic revelation to a community has replaced that given through sacred places and shrines. When, however, we compare the interpretation of this community with the history of places of worship in each of the three faiths some paradoxical results emerge. It would appear that the most radical departure from the temple tradition occurred when Jesus-in-community was established as the 'new temple' in the first Christian century: here was a new holy people deriving its holiness from identification with the divine incarnation in Jesus. Equally radical in principle although somewhat more tentative in assertion and in means of achievement was the self-understanding of the Jewish community as the holy people of God which appears through their whole history; this also was a new and personalized form of temple. For Islam, on the other hand, while the Ka'bah was reformed and all other temples abandoned there was no explicit transmutation of this form into personal and communal terms, no theory of the new temple at all comparable to the other two developments.

It might be expected that these degrees in which physical temple had been replaced by personalized forms would be reflected in the history of the three faiths by corresponding degrees of allegiance to the new *domus ecclesiae* form, or of clarity in detecting the return of the temple traditions. The historical facts, however, seem to indicate exactly the reverse. Our survey would suggest that it is Islam that has been most consistent in adhering to its new mosque form, that Judaism has seen the increasing influence of temple forms, especially in modern times, and that Christianity has been most repeatedly and extensively drawn back into the orbit of the *domus dei*. Some limited explanation appears when we remember that it was Islam that made a complete break with any overt form of sacrifice in the content of its worship (whatever has been retained in other ancillary ways), that Judaism through most of its history has remained loyal both to sacrifices and to the Temple where they belonged even though unable to implement this loyalty, and that Christianity gave the sacrifice of Christ a central place in its worship and expressed this through visible elements at an altar-table. It would almost seem that the replacement of temple worship by the liturgical actions of Jesus-in-community has been too explicit; for this very reason it could readily be transposed back into the temple manner and accommodated in a building to suit.

However we interpret this paradox the history of churches as compared with synagogues and mosques remains a somewhat incongruous aspect of the Christian story. If one accepts the Christian alternative to the temple as the most radical of all the Semitic positions then it becomes ironical to realize that many synagogues and mosques would in fact make better churches than many of the buildings erected for Christian worship.

PART THREE

Theological Synthesis

15

Theological Issues
in Twentieth Century Church Building

We have now completed the application of our typology of places of worship to their history in the three Semitic religions, and so used the tools of phenomenology for the analysis of religious history and the comparison of different religious traditions, both with one another and with what would appear to be their own normative forms. In this third part of our study we turn to more theological questions and confine ourselves first to the theological issues that have arisen in the building of Christian churches in the present century. Then, from a theological standpoint, we reconsider the relevance of each of our two basic forms to the Christian place of worship and seek to establish a theological relationship between them; this will lead to an important modification of our criteria for an acceptable Christian form of building. Finally, we shall move from our extended case study of this one basic religious phenomenon, the place of worship, to a general discussion of the relations between phenomenology of religions and theology within the Christian tradition.

15.1 THE SECOND GREAT AGE OF CHURCH BUILDING

For the second time in its history the Christian religion has witnessed a great age of church building, comparable to that ensuing from the fourth century peace with the Roman state. Probably more churches have been built in the twentieth century than in all earlier centuries combined and the increase in Western Christianity alone in the last fifty years exceeds that of the previous four centuries. Between 1945 and 1962 over three thousand churches must have been built in Great Britain; for the United States expenditure on new church buildings averaged about a thousand million dollars for each year in the sixties; in 1967 it was predicted that fifteen hundred new Catholic churches would be built in France in the next decade.

Considerable building has also occurred in some of the countries where Christianity has taken more recent root. This is especially true of West Africa where some half dozen major cathedrals were under construction or design in the early sixties. In one rural area of eastern Nigeria in 1965 the writer counted no fewer than a hundred and twelve churches, many of recent construction, on a fifty-four mile stretch of road; in the same rural region there were two hundred and thirty church buildings in an area of two hundred square miles.

The main reasons for this flood tide of building are readily identified: the rebuilding consequent upon the damage of two world wars, the growth of population in most countries, together with its increasing mobility and the development of new towns, the greater economic prosperity of Western and of some other countries, and the expansion of Christianity in the non-Western world and especially in Africa. It would seem that in the quarter century since World War II church building has been one of the most conspicuous social and economic enterprises in countries as different as the United States and Nigeria.

It is a commonplace to indicate the major movements in the life of the Christian church that have a bearing on this extensive exercise in church architecture. What is called the liturgical movement is the most obvious of these; interwoven with this awakening there have been biblical and theological revivals, the ecumenical movement, renewed involvements in social, economic and political problems, and other currents less readily identified. The Christian church would appear to be in a better position than ever before in its history to control its building from a biblical and theological understanding, shared across its divisions, and set against a comprehensive view of the achievements and errors in this field over some seventeen centuries. To a client thus equipped the modern architect is able to bring the results of the greatest technical revolution in the art of building since the beginning of the Church; if the Church knows what it wants the architect and builder can provide it. Even if what is required is not yet clear the current architectural emphases on honesty and function comport well with equivalent emphases in the liturgical movement and enable both parties to join in creative experiment.

15.2 LITURGICAL REVIVAL AND CURRENT CONSENSUS

The modern liturgical movement is much older and wider than is sometimes realized. For the Anglican communion it must, in a sense, go back well over a century to the Oxford movement and the Cambridge Camden Society. The Church of Scotland Church Service Society celebrated its centenary in 1965, and incorporates the work of two somewhat younger sister societies. The present liturgical society among the Reformed Christians of the Netherlands traces its origins from about 1890. Among German Lutherans the Wiesbaden Programme drawn up by pastors and architects in 1891 rejected 'Gothic as the adversary of Protestant worship', reduced the chancel to a mere recess and stressed the equal centrality of pulpit and altar. The Roman Catholic interest has emerged in the present century. At first it was essentially conservative, as in the Encyclical *Mediator Dei* of Pius XII in 1947 which continued to speak of sacred place in the *domus dei* manner. Other influences, such as the journals *Art d'Église* and *Maison-Dieu* (despite its name!), finally led to the break-through represented by the 'Constitution on the Sacred Liturgy' of the Second Vatican Council, promulgated in 1963; here we see the collapse of traditions going back to the fourth century. Even the most conservative Eastern Orthodox communion has begun to respond to the currents of liturgical reform; there are tendencies to restore the communal character of the eucharist by alterations to its chief obstacle, the iconostasis that is so distinctive of Orthodoxy but nevertheless a comparatively late development; this is now sometimes suppressed, or constructed in a lighter and more transparent manner, or, as a first step, the doors within it are left open throughout the liturgy. And in many other communions and in divers parts of the world one could trace the same liturgical reformation at work and discover the extensive effects on Christian worship and on the building of churches freed from temple implications.

Among Protestant communions 'the chief thrust of ... liturgical renewal has been to cleanse worship from the excessively individualistic, subjective, and rationalistic elements that have crept into it ... and to restore the corporate aspect, to liberate laymen from clergy-dominated services by providing more meaningful opportunities for lay participation, and to urge the more frequent celebration of the Eucharist in the manner of the early Christians'.[1] Most of this statement would also summarize the aims of the same movement in the Roman communion, except for the rediscovery of the place of the Word in worship as against the Protestant rediscovery of the sacraments. Both in theory and in practice there has been a remarkable convergence, from different starting points; the extent of the common agreement is evident in the warm welcome given by many Protestant writers to the 'Constitution on the Sacred Liturgy'. That this consensus has diffused roots and is not confined to its more recent public expressions is evident from examples of tributes to the meeting house type of church building paid by those standing outside this tradition. Thus a Dean of Canterbury Cathedral could find in the simple Quaker Meeting House at Jordans in Buckinghamshire 'a beauty akin to that of the noblest Spanish shrines'.[2] In England an old Puritan building that had been vacated for 'a more pretentious "architectural" sanctuary by a prosperous Nonconformist congregation' was bought by the Roman Catholics who, with hardly any alteration, produced a church that was preferred by their members to the local cathedral or any other church. A cardinal in the United States acknowledged that he had taken the old Congregational meeting house at Lyme, Connecticut, as the model for a new church near Chicago. This process could be traced in an increasing number of Catholic churches erected in the last generation; for example, the Church of St. Jacques in Grenoble (1959) is a simple wooden rectangle with a free-standing altar-table in the middle of one of the long sides, embraced by pews in a typical Puritan meeting house manner.

These reforms and discoveries in effect bring together 'sectist' and 'churchman', Dissent and Establishment, radical and catholic wings of the sixteenth century and their descendants, those who have worshipped in 'conventicles', 'tabernacles', or 'gospel halls' and those who have continued to build Gothic cathedrals and Byzantine churches. It is nothing short of a revolution when Christians of all allegiances come to regard themselves as a 'meeting of God's people' with their Lord and with one another, and their church as the meeting house for this purpose, the *domus ecclesiae.*

This new perspective, if retained and applied more thoroughly, transports the Christian community behind both the Middle Ages and the fourth century to the earlier years of Christian existence, anf finally leads to the nucleus of God's people meeting with their Lord in a dwelling house. Thought on the Christian place of worship is then freed from the effects of the first great failure in the history of church architecture and enabled to proceed with understanding through the later confusions.

It so happens that the rejection of the temple for what may be called the tent-house concept coincides with a similar development in modern architecture. Here there has been a reaction from the elaborate and pretentious to the simple and direct, from concern with the facade to stress on the functional. The architect today finds himself at home with a brief that requires an honest and humble, even homely building for a Christian congregation, and the clients themselves should be better prepared for a church bearing little resemblance to a classical temple, a renaissance palace, or a Gothic cathedral. It takes very little transposition to adapt to the building of churches the following directive from the new 'Constitution on the Sacred Liturgy', which speaks of reforming the rites in such a way that they 'shine with noble simplicity, be outstanding for brevity, avoid useless repetition, be accommodated to the capacity of the faithful, and, as a general rule, not require many explanations'. Thus may the shape of the liturgy be reflected in the form of the building, when the latter is regarded as the house of God's people.

There is no doubt, therefore, that many of the unfulfilled insights of the sixteenth century reformation have found expression both within and beyond the 'Reformed' traditions in our own century. Reform movements themselves, however, soon need further reform and renewal and there are signs that the liturgical revival may have reached this point, where it is in danger of settling into a new and still inadequate orthodoxy, with its main contributions turned into cliches. As John Betjeman observed it in 1940, 'the liturgical movement in nonconformity turns "chapels" into "churches", puts flowers on the table, "cathedral glass" in the windows, blue hangings and unstained oak by the pulpit, and allows the building to be open for private prayer'.[3] For others the new conventions require round or free-shaped churches, central altars or tables, and horse-shoe shaped arrangement of the congregation. If the understanding of the Christian place of worship reaches no further than these superficialities or conventions then, for the third time in its history, church architecture will have missed the bus. We propose therefore to examine briefly three areas where unsolved problems or fundamental differences remain in thinking and practice about liturgy and architecture, and then proceed to a more theoretical statement on the nature of the place of worship for the Christian tradition.

15.3 THE NATURE OF THE CHURCH: HIERARCHIES AND SANCTUARIES?

Amid the manifold twentieth century discussions of the doctrine of the church we are here concerned mainly with the fresh emphasis on the importance of the local congregation, and on its unity and priestly character as one people of God including both clergy and laity. Churches have therefore been designed to encourage a sense of communal unity and to assist lay participation by reducing the distance between the people and the centres of activity in the liturgy, by arranging the congregation on three sides round the table, by restoring their liturgical responses, simplifying the structure and language of the liturgy, and teaching them what it is all about.

Those of the Roman obedience and some other communions, while sharing in these convictions, endeavour to maintain with equal emphasis the hierarchical structure of the church, with a distinction between clergy and laity that must also be expressed in the architectural layout. As a consequence, 'a church must have two distinct parts: the sanctuary, which is the space for the priest and his ministers, and the nave, which is the space for the faithful. ... The eucharistic room must have a structural unity that reflects the unity of the community. At the same time the distinction must be sufficiently defined to keep clear the difference of office and function between priest and people.'[4] There has therefore been a reaction from circular churches and central altars, despite the example of the new Catholic cathedral in Liverpool, and in the 1960s certain Roman Catholic directives for church building in Germany and in parts of the United States made the provision for a hierarchical community mandatory.

The problem then becomes that of defining the sanctuary as the special zone within which the hierarchy operates; in the light of Christian history this appears to be an exceedingly difficult operation if the temple connotations of a holy of holies and of graded degrees of sanctity, ever hovering over the worship of the church, are to be avoided. The statement quoted above implies virtually a two-cell plan, of sanctuary and nave, but other versions suggest a sanctuary 'within' an auditorium and so retain the single-cell plan, with a sub-division of the main space visibly defined as the sanctuary.[5] There certainly must be centres for the different liturgical actions but what is meant by calling the space these occupy a 'sanctuary'? Is it necessary even on a hierarchical view of the church? Is not the hierarchy primarily indicated by actions and functions in its liturgical dialogue with the laity? In any case the liturgical action occurs throughout the space of the congregation for the hearing of the Word and the response to the preaching, the praise, the prayers, and the reception of the Supper happen where the people are.

This fact is reflected in a rather different attempt to retain the concept of a sanctuary which appears in some churches with no hierarchical structure or in modern multi-purpose church centres where the term is applied to the whole of the space specially reserved for worship. This practice is common in the church 'plants' of the United States, and, as noted above, has even been adopted for the synagogue room in the complex of buildings of the Jewish community, The word 'sanctuary' has, however, such strong sacral connotation that it seems impossible to retain it without inviting a return of the *domus dei* outlook,[6] and we suggest 'worship hall' or some equivalent as an unambiguous alternative.

To develop more fully the unity of the Church and the participation of the people requires much more than liturgies and churches designed in new ways. These are clearly necessary and have already proved of some profit, but they amount to little more than 'a better seat for the show' or increased 'audience participation' unless matched by a corresponding sharing by the one people in other aspects of the life of the church such as its rule and doctrine and its service and mission in the world. It is to link these responsibilities of service and mission with the activities of worship that the multi-purpose church centre has been developed in recent years. When such a centre is established on an ecumenical basis a further step has been taken towards discovering the whole work of the people of God, the Church in action, but even this does not remove the difficulties or resolve the problems that the concepts of hierarchies and sanctuaries impose on church buildings.

15.4 THE STRUCTURE OF WORSHIP: WORD AND SACRAMENTS

We have already noted the influence of the liturgical movement in correcting the defects of the various traditions, especially in restoring the sacraments to their place or recovering the ministry of the Word, although we must remember that there are Protestant traditions, too easily overlooked as 'sects', which have never lost a balanced ministry of Word and sacraments. The question arises, however, as to the place of the Word, the place of the sacraments, and the relationship between them. The architectural implications for lectern and pulpit, for table and altar and font, and for seeing and hearing, eating and drinking, are obviously of some importance.

There are many signs of considerable uncertainty and imbalance, coupled with a threat of a new orthodoxy, in these matters. The imbalance arises among those who have rediscovered the sacraments. In these quarters there has been much clearing of space for a 'sanctuary' at the expense of choirs and organs, a pushing out of walls to create an apse or chancel, an installation of communion tables where no decent provision existed before, together with the moving of pulpits to one side and the installation of a lectern or prayer desk or anything else that makes the church look more 'liturgical'. Something of this has been very necessary, but in the course of clearing out the organ-choir clutter or reducing the mere auditorium effect, a new clutter of 'liturgical furnishings' is liable to appear, together with a standard pattern of a central table on a platform, with a cross on the table or on the wall behind it, perhaps set against a drape or panel, or even silhouetted in a picture window; coupled with this is the side pulpit and the increased definition of a beautiful chancel or sanctuary. This standard treatment soon becomes monotonous and both the overall effect and some of the details are more suggestive of the temple holy place than of the *domus ecclesiae.*

Along with this uncertain – or even over-certain – reform there has developed a reference to the Lord's Supper as the 'chief', 'central' or 'supreme' act of worship by the Church. At this point the new Protestant emphasis virtually coincides with the current definitions of a church building common among those within a Catholic tradition; here the church is 'a building to house a congregation round an altar', a 'eucharistic room built round an altar', and therefore to be 'designed from the altar outwards'. These statements, for those who make them, often represent a great discovery – the distinction between the *domus dei* and the *domus ecclesiae*, together with a functional approach to the building of churches.

On the other hand the implications of these statements for Christian worship are considerable. They represent still unresolved differences between the various Christian traditions as to the relation between Word and sacraments, and as to the nature of the Lord's Supper; if this is celebrated round a table we are clearly conscious of the Upper Room, whereas if we gather round an altar, and this is given architectural emphasis, it is more difficult to resist the pull of the temple tradition with the altar as a sacred place or object.

In this connection the following astringent comment deserves consideration:

... whatever the early Church did, it did not lose the Word... the place of the Word in worship is clear enough to all: it is the supposed 'central act of the Church's worship' that it has recently required clever exegetes to discover.... The most regular features of worship Pliny found were hymns and solemn asseverations about abstinence from sin. And at Justin's famous Sunday service ... 'the memoirs of the apostles or the writings of the prophets are read, *as long as time permits*', and 'the president verbally instructs, and exhorts to the imitation of these good things'. Who shall say that these are less 'central' to Justin's service than the bread and wine which follow? Even in the *Apostolic Tradition* of Hyppolytus... what the worshipper is urged to do daily is to attend to the instruction in the Word, 'especially if he can read'. Is it really primitive, or Biblical, or honouring to God or profitable to men to exalt the sacrament (and only one of them, incidentally) by hiding the Word? And are the bare essentials of a church really a congregation and an altar?[7]

Certainly to agree to the latter statement would amount to unchurching a large proportion of churches in the non-Western world.

It would therefore be a serious disservice to church design and to liturgical understanding if these phrases and the architectural layout they have tended to standardize were to become a settled achievement of the liturgical movement; there are various ways of disposing altar-table and pulpit about a common longitudinal or transverse axis, which support more satisfactory views of the relation between Word and sacrament, and avoid revived suggestions of a holy place, the sanctuary.

In addition there is the further problem of the relation of baptism to the Lord's Supper and to the Word, as well as to the congregation. Already there is more architectural variation in the provision for baptism than in that for the eucharist or the Word. Arrangements vary from detached baptistries, through a font in the narthex or close inside the entrance door of the nave, to experiments with a special area to the side of the congregation or even in their midst, or to a position in front of the congregation together with pulpit and table. Where the congregation is arranged around a longitudinal central space it is possible to have the pulpit at one end of this axis, the font at the other end, and the table in between – a commendable plan that may be seen at St. Luke's, Stocking Farm, Leicester, in Christ Church and Upton Chapel, Kennington, London, and elsewhere such as in the Church of the Ascension, at St. Andrew, Jamaica.

Where thought has been given to the place for baptism there seems to be a growing consensus in favour of a more direct relation to the Church as the living community rather than as an institution represented by its officials or its buildings.[8] This means that the location is moved from the entrance to the church building (which symbolized entrance to the community) to a more visible place close to the congregation gathered for its main sessions of worship. Such a change of emphasis and of location are entirely congruent with the shift from *domus dei* to *domus ecclesiae* views of the building, and this is a great advance; otherwise thought and practice on this matter are in a fluid and uncertain state.

15.5 THE PURPOSE OF THE CHURCH BUILDING

Despite the new insights we have surveyed,
  Neither theologians nor architects have made up their minds whether to express numinosity or community. This is evident in the vacillation in modern church architecture between the streamlined verticality which is the contemporary equivalent of Gothic, evocative of Divine mystery and majesty and of human aspiration, and the functional architecture stressing the ... congregation ....[9]
One of the commonest cliches has been the elongated A-section structure that otherwise attempts to be a meeting house; this has appeared in all sections of Protestantism, including those whose theology is most averse to any such emphasis, and corresponds to the similar confused response to Gothic a century earlier.

  An inadequate reform is evident even in the radical critique of cathedrals by Bishop Dwyer of Reno, Nevada, whose outburst in 1958 is something of a modern landmark. The cathedral style in church building was attacked as the expression of political and social domination, and of 'wealth, power, esteem, pride'. On the other hand, the buildings to replace them are still seen as the house of God, the gate of heaven, the house for the altar, the place for sacrifice, and 'not primarily ... to house the family of God'.[10]

  The confusion of the two types appears in the *Directives for the Building of a Church* issued by the Liturgical Commission of the German Roman Catholic bishops in 1947, the year of the conservative *Mediator Dei* encyclical. Here 'the Christian church, a house of God, is a sacred place filled with the divine presence ..., a place where the people of God assemble...'. There we have it both ways. And again, '... it is the "basilica", the palace of the King...'. The same mode of thought is applied to the parts of the church: '... the symbolism of church portals as representing the gates of heaven', 'the altar is ... the sacrificial and banquet table of the people of God', but it is also 'Christ's throne upon earth ..., the most sacred object, ... made evident by its isolated placement ... monumental ... situated in right perspective ... and surrounded by a baldachin or canopy'.[11] Ten years later Catholic thought had moved a good deal, but the *Church Building Directives* of the Roman Catholic Diocese of Superior, Wisconsin, repeats part of the German definition and stresses the altar as 'God's dwelling place among men', 'standing between heaven and earth ... the permanent sign of Christ's presence', so that 'the church edifice is the extension and complement of the altar of sacrifice'.[12] This latter directive is much less conservative than the German one, and contains many excellent statements, but continues the confusion at the vital point and to that extent is internally self-contradictory. These directives are chosen for criticism because they were among the rare attempts to codify thought on these matters.

One of the chief expressions of how the church building is understood lies in the formal provisions for the opening of a new church with a service of consecration or dedication. We have already outlined the earlier history of consecration[13] and noted the sixteenth century reformation emphasis on liturgical function and on a merely derivative holiness for the building. The Second Scottish Confession gave one of the more extreme expressions to this view when it declared: 'We detest ... that Roman Antichrist.... His... dedicating of kirks, altares, days....' In Scotland more moderate statements of the same principle may be traced subsequently, as in the nineteenth century scholar G.W. Sprott who avoided all 'house of God' references and adopted a functional view of 'a house for Thy honour and worship, the preaching of Thy Word, and the administration of Thy sacraments', 'without any inherent sacredness' but only a relative holiness.[14] In its 1940 *Book of Common Order*, however, the Church of Scotland seems to have admitted a good deal of the Old Testament imagery of the Temple to its order for the dedication of a church — this is a standing temptation to all compilers of such orders who attempt to draw upon biblical material, and the effect is hardly cancelled by the addition of New Testament references to the community as temple; this 'sanctuary of the Most High' is 'forever set apart from all profane and common uses' as 'a temple of the Living God'. In this Church's *Ordinal and Service Book* of 1954 the *domus ecclesiae* note is struck more clearly, and consecration by celebration of the Holy Communion is specified; the same can be said of another order in the same tradition, that of the Presbyterian Church in the U.S.A. of 1946.

Similar uncertain attitudes to consecration could be traced in the orders of many other churches including various sections of the Anglican communion. Even the Methodists seem to have departed from the strongly expressed views of John Wesley on the matter. He never tires of repudiating the notion of consecrating churches or burial grounds as sacred places, a practice required neither by the New Testament nor by the law of the land; it may 'be practised as a thing indifferent. But if it be done as a necessary thing, then it is flatly superstitious.' He even asks ironically 'how deep is the consecrated ground?... for if my grave be dug too deep, I may happen to get out of the consecrated ground: and who can tell what unhappy consequences may follow from this?'[15] Wesley notwithstanding, Methodist hymns for dedication of buildings rejoice in the 'hallowed walls' of 'holy places', in 'this Thy house, the gate of heaven', as much as in the 'living stones' of the community gathered in 'this house ... to learn of Thee'.

As might be expected the consecration rites of the Roman Catholic and Orthodox traditions show as yet little influence from the *domus ecclesiae* position. In the African context the Catholic Church has shown considerable liturgical boldness and yet a detailed proposal for a modern African consecration rite drawn up by a notable liturgical scholar in 1974 might almost have come from the seventh century! There is the deposition and censing of relics of the saints, consecration of the altar by censing, clothing, touching and kissing, and of the building by lustrations and censings; the church has a symbolic role that takes precedence over its functions as a house of assembly for it is a sign of God's presence before the whole world, the centre of reference and the special place of meeting between God and man. The identification with the *domus dei* as we have earlier analyzed this is complete.[16] A very similar procedure, representing the same viewpoint, was observed in the consecration of the magnificent new Greek Orthodox Church of the Annunciation in such a modern city as Atlanta, Georgia, in 1970.[17]

The analogy between the consecration of the sacramental elements and the consecration of buildings has been pointed out by J.G. Davies, who reminds us of the recognition that in the New Testament consecration at the Lord's Supper consisted of 'thankful acknowledgment of the relation of the object concerned to God the giver and blessing Him for it'.[18] This means it was functional rather than ontological. Similarly the consecration of a church building amounts to thanksgiving and acknowledgment of its relation to God and of the functions it can serve for His people; in other words it is consecrated by the appropriate use and most of the actions in traditional rites, other than the first celebration of the Supper, are positively misleading.

The inappropriate content of forms for the opening of new churches is found at many other points in Christian worship, and especially in Christian hymns which extol the qualities of the house of God where His presence dwells. The Old Testament is of course a legitimate source for liturgical materials and there seems to be a real difficulty here in maintaining the New Testament transformation into personal and spiritual terms as against the vividly concrete Temple imagery of the form that has been superseded. When worship commences with such a Scripture proclamation as 'the Lord is in his holy temple, let all the earth keep silence before him' it is the rare congregation that will feel reminded of the mystery of Jesus-in-community as the living temple of God. There are therefore both theological confusions and practical problems attendant upon the present century's shift of emphasis towards the *domus ecclesiae* form, and these can be resolved only by the more extensive theoretical and theological consideration of the issues involved to which we now turn.

16

Meeting House and Temple
in Theological Perspective

Apart from the consensus that has been achieved as to the church community, its worship and its building, and behind the remaining uncertainties on these matters there are fundamental issues still to be examined if we are to understand how the *domus ecclesiae* principle may
be expressed in buildings today, and whether there is any remaining
relationship to the contrasting temple forms.

16.1 ARE BUILDINGS REALLY NECESSARY?

When the emphasis is placed upon Jesus-in-community as temple, and
when the early history of the Christian Church is taken seriously, then
we are forced to admit 'that churches are not really necessary to Christianity.... A basic trait of the Christian religion is that it is not tied to
any sacred buildings.... Were all the churches of a country to be confiscated or destroyed, Christians would be hampered in their activities;
but they would have lost nothing essential. The mass loses nothing by
its being celebrated in an ordinary house or hall.'[1] This statement by
one who was at the time a prominent Catholic professor of dogmatics
in England corresponds to the position of those who call for a mora-
torium on church building. 'If there is one simple method of saving the
Church's mission,' says another English Catholic writer, 'it is probably
the decision to abandon church buildings' for 'they are basically unnat-
ural places ... and they do not correspond to anything which is normal
in everyday life.'[2]
    This must be understood partly as a desperate attempt to break the
continuing dominance of Western Christianity by its inherited buildings and the attitudes they engender. A similar suggestion is also found

in those who feel that a house church rather than a new building set apart as a church is the better way to commence in a new town — 'les sans toits' as they are known in France. Or again, those concerned with the integration of worship and daily activities reject a special chapel in lay or community centres and ask for discussions, meals, dancing and prayers all to be conducted in the one room.

The rejection of church buildings has been associated with Christianity in some of its more radical, dynamic or expanding forms. As already observed, it marked the radical wing of the sixteenth century reformation; today it occurs in those parts of the non-western world where there is rapid Christian growth, and, it should be added, a favourable climate. This is especially evident among some of the independent African churches. Thus the Friends of the Holy Spirit founded in Kenya in the 1940s dispensed with buildings, and say that if and when they do need them these will be called meeting places, and not churches. Johane Masowe directed his followers in the Apostolic Church of God in Rhodesia to avoid involvement in time-wasting projects such as churches and schools. In the same area the Vapostori, a very large movement, use Stephen's speech in Acts 7 in support of their belief that worship should be out of doors, on a flat rock outcrop or under a shady tree; at the same time they do have sacred open-air enclosures where admission is confined to those who have confessed their sins to prophets who 'guard the gate'. On the other hand Western traditions of splendid buildings have been transplanted only too successfully in other areas such as West Africa, where expensive showy cathedrals and massive church towers deflect resources from an underpaid ministry and Christian social services.

Rudolf Schwarz a generation ago seems to have speculated on the possibility of worship without church buildings, when 'churches may come into being solely out of the act of worship itself. At the beginning there would be no space and at the end none would be left over. The space would come into being and would sink away simultaneously with the service.... It would be only a final step to give up the fixed structural space entirely.... Then the liturgy would... be a "cathedral" in its secret structure....'[3] He concluded, however, that such an extreme position could never satisfy.

The practical necessity of some kind of building will ultimately prevail for most worshipping groups, as it did for the early Church. In Kenya, for instance, the Church of the Holy Spirit in Zion worshipped in the open from its foundation in 1926, but in 1971 erected its first church building at Meru. Groups in the modern West may reorder their religious priorities by temporarily escaping from the burden of special buildings and using other premises; but sooner or later any continuing community with distinctive activities, such as make up the Christian liturgy, will feel the need of more suitable accommodation for their particular purposes.

As Marc Spindler has put it, 'the visible church must be somewhere, no matter what new techniques of communication arise: one cannot baptize by radio or receive the bread and wine of the Supper by telephone'.[4] After all, Jesus went to some trouble to arrange for the upper room for the last supper. In the end the *ecclesia* will be found to need its *domus*.

16.2 ARE CHURCH BUILDINGS MERELY INSTRUMENTAL?

If the minimal argument for churches derives from the provision of suitable accommodation for particular purposes they have been reduced to the category of the instrumental or the strictly functional. The church then becomes merely a machine for performing the liturgy parallel to the house conceived as a machine for living. To keep this to the fore in all planning of buildings in one of the healthy emphases of modern architecture, but as the single determinative principle it is of too limited a perspective in any architectural activity. As an American statement put the issue, there is 'a division between... shelter engineering and... architecture.... There is the question of building a box and stuffing your congregants inside it; there is a possibility of expanding beyond that, into something that becomes architecture.'[5]

Even apart from what might be meant here by architecture, everything serving a function, every instrument, is also something in itself; for the humbler instruments this may be no more than its own qualities of shape and material but in the case of a building these further qualities are substantial, publicly visible, and semi-permanent. The church building continues to exist and therefore to speak even when the liturgy is concluded and the assembly has departed, and cannot be reduced to an occasional instrument for the congregation and its worship, that can be let down and stored away like a tent or inflatable building between services.

Even a building designed as a *domus ecclesiae* proclaims this very fact to the current assembly, although probably not at the level of full consciousness. This implies a specific symbolic function across time as well as a more narrowly utilitarian function on each occasion when it is used for worship. We may call the church a symbolic landscape within which the liturgical action is repeatedly renewed and by which it is supported and gently encouraged to remain true to the norms that it reflects. The size, shape, and liturgical layout, the material and even the location of the building all play a part in making it both instrument and symbol of the tradition that links the past with the present and the future, as may be seen in many a Quaker meeting house.

From this inevitable effect of church architecture there may arise the problem of the 'dead hand of the past' crippling and distorting current efforts towards a more truly Christian liturgy and life. As Rudolf Schwarz has put it, 'the meaning of architecture is permanency and not transformation. Time is taken out of the stream of events and made solid in architecture.... The art of building is not allied with the short transformations of breathing, of the act of worship, of the course of the day or year... the flowing space of the action is embedded in the immutably fixed space of the... structure... the stage remains whereas the action changes.'[6] The simpler the building, and the less expressive of any of the features of the *domus dei* with its inflexibility and finality, the more this danger is minimized. Again the Quaker meeting house serves to make the point, for many saddled with Gothic and other structures wish that they had something akin to this domestic style within which to effect their liturgical reforms, whether in a Protestant or Catholic manner.

16.3 DERIVATIVE HOLINESS BY ASSOCIATION?

Once we grant this wider functionalism we are faced with the possibility of recognizing a certain degree of holiness in the building itself derived from association with the personalized temple of Jesus-in-community. Since the Society of Friends has set itself against holy places and buildings as much as any of the Christian traditions two reports from within this community are especially significant. 'Places and things do not hallow people,' says the first report, 'but the enduring faith of people may hallow places. Where you are sitting in that calm cool place there has been unbroken prayer and worship generation after generation. In the outward and inner silences there, ... you may realise that... "we are surrounded by a great cloud of witnesses"... you cannot but "be the better for your coming here".'[7] Another personal report tells us that 'when I was a little lad I used to think that Meeting Houses smelt "holy".... Of course I became a critical "Young Friend", and threw all that nonsense on to the rubbish tip.... Nevertheless I'm still inhibited about the treatment due to Meeting Houses. I still feel guilty if I smoke while taking my turn on the cleaning rota; or at a weekday committee meeting held in the "worship area".'[8] An architect has made the same point in more general terms when he observed that
> some new churches, even when empty, suggest something of holiness, though not in the traditional shrine-sense. Perhaps... if the building functions as an unselfconscious servant of the Church, yet contributes... as an effective shell for its activities, then there will be something about the building even when empty that suggests its purpose, and that prompts us to regard it as 'more-than-ordinary'. But the same things could be said about a house which is designed for a Christian family to live in. It should reflect in some small degree, at least, the same quality of refreshingness that the house of the gathered family does in the Church.[9]

Instead of treating these impressions as either subjective and psychological effects or unfortunate survivals from the temple tradition we prefer to understand them in terms of the organic nature of human existence whereby the personal and spiritual always has physical and historical embodiment. The building then has an integral relationship to the living temple as community and even though we place the locus of holiness in people we cannot exclude the participation of the physical including especially the building from this same holiness. In this particular context we cannot say, as our argument so far might suggest, that holiness resides in persons and not in places or things. We must say that even the *domus ecclesiae* exhibits a holiness derived not from mere external association with the holy community but from intimate and organic participation in its life. It is this limited and derivative view that we have noted already in the Reformers of the sixteenth century.

By the same principle of organic relationship we must also grant an intimate association between physical temples as holy places and the effects they created in their users. In a real sense the spatio-physical *domus dei* succeeded when it so linked the worshipper and his god that he felt God-in-him, the divine power active in his own being and his affairs. This was especially true of the Jerusalem temple as it sustained the personal covenanted relationship between Jahweh and his people.[10] Only on this view can we attribute any authentic religious function and spirituality to the *domus dei*.

There is, however, a profound distinction between the divine presence, the source of holiness, residing in places or temples upon which people are dependent, or, on the other hand, located in the community itself with the place of worship dependent for its measure of holiness on the life of this community; it is this difference which supplies our basic typology of places for worship. The difference becomes evident when we remember the centrality and necessity of the sacred place in the one tradition as against the fact that places and buildings are secondary and not even necessary in the Semitic context.

16.4 REPRESENTATIVE HOLINESS BY SACRAMENTAL FUNCTION?

Even the *domus ecclesiae* then has a function extending beyond the utilitarian to the symbolic, and participates in the holiness of the sacred community. Once we recognize this participation and the organic principle upon which it is based we cannot avoid examining the relationship between the church building and its physical environment in the same terms: does the latter participate in the nature of the building, and therefore in its measure of holiness, because of the organic connection bewteen all buildings and their surrounding physical world of materials and geographical setting? Just as the church belongs to a community which to some extent it symbolizes so also it may be regarded as representing in a symbolic way the physical environment to which it belongs.

Christian theology usually explores this relationship in terms of the 'sacramental principle' whereby any particular object or place, in this case the church building, is potentially able to mediate and sustain the relationship between man and the divine. To this is added the further interpretation that the sacramental object acts in a representative capacity, and that those objects such as bread, wine, water, and now churches which regularly function in this way do so as a kind of first-fruits, foretaste, or fore-glimpse of the way in which the whole creation will serve in the final consummation.

In considering this attractive interpretation it must be remembered that the building itself has only a kind of secondary or derivative holiness, subordinate to that of a personal community, and that the extent to which it can express the holy on behalf of all creation is thereby limited by its own status. It is also profoundly limited by all the imperfections of this world – of the community itself in its own apprehension of holiness, and of its inadequate attempts to create a true *domus ecclesiae* that will avoid both the temptations of the temple tradition and the inadequacies of a mere secular shelter shed, and, further, the environment's own imperfections, its disorder, ugliness and indifference to mankind. The relationship therefore between the building, the community, and the environment remains uncertain and ambiguous; the symbolic function the building may have in each direction is never straightforward or entirely successful.

This situation, as it applies to many aspects of Christian existence, has been well expressed by J. J. Von Allmen:

Just as the proclamation of the Word becomes for every human word both a question and also a promise, and the same is true of a baptized person in relation to all men, of the Eucharistic service in relation to every meal, of Israel in relation to every nation and of the

Church in relation to all human societies, in just the same way a Christian place of worship becomes a sign of contradiction, of decay or of restoration to all space ... it poses for all that which surrounds it or resembles it a fundamental question: is ... it going to share in this consecration ... or is it going to refuse ....[11]

There is therefore a critical 'dialogue between the church building and the rest of the environment'[12] in which the latter is confronted, challenged, exposed as well as promised what it may yet become as represented by whatever order, peacefulness, beauty, and unselfconscious service the *domus ecclesiae* has been able to offer the community upon which it depends.

There are therefore very substantial limits on the extent to which the church building may represent the natural order symbolically, for it must speak to it and against it as much as for it.

16.5 CRITIQUE OF SACRAMENTAL HOLINESS AND AUTONOMOUS WITNESS

The ease with which these limits are forgotten, and the dangers of doing so, may be illustrated from the widespread desire to make the building for worship a sacramental offering to God of the best human skills and the richest natural resources. Most of the religions associated with the more sophisticated societies have exhibited this motive in their massive temples erected from the most permanent and precious materials by tremendous human effort and at great economic cost. The desire to build to the glory of God by using the best that men possess has been especially prominent in the *domus dei* tradition within the Christian religion. It appeared in the fourth century, reached an early climax in St. Sophia in Constantinople and a new peak in the mediaeval Gothic cathedrals, and an explicit theoretical formulation in Renaissance churches. The fifteenth century Alberti could declare that every part should be 'so contrived and adorned, as to fill the beholders with awe and amazement, at the consideration of so many noble and excellent things, and almost force them to cry out with astonishment: This place is certainly worthy of God'.[13] In Baroque churches we see the house of God having to excell even the splendours of the princely palace, and in the Gothic revival Pugin and others declared that nothing was too grand for God and that churches must be vaster and more beautiful buildings than those used for any other purpose.

All this effort could be justified in terms of an oversimplified understanding of the sacramental principle. Some recognition of the error in this view seems to have been reflected in the deliberate imperfections and asymmetries incorporated in both churches and temples of many religions that we have already noted. Man must indicate that even his best is not worthy of God. A similar sensitivity may be found in the fact that man's best materials and skills have sometimes been poured out in the creation of secular objects while religious images have been roughly shaped from cruder materials; as has often been observed, Greek religion was in decline when the beauty of the human form was used with superb skill to represent the gods.

There would seem to be a genuine insight in Feuerbach's declaration that 'the temple is only a manifestation of the value which man attaches to beautiful things. Temples in honour of religion are in truth temples in honour of architecture.'[14] This appears to be the ironic result of much human effort to glorify God — we are left with a monument to human achievement, to the glories of an epoch or of a culture, a symbol of human pride that overrides the original avowed intention of offering man's best to God.

A more explicitly Christian theology would point out that men do not own the world and have no 'best' to offer, that they do not even offer themselves but are offered insofar as they are incorporated in the perfect offering of Christ; as the hymn puts it, 'only look on us as found in him'. In the model presented by Christ there is a radical rejection of the 'nothing is too good for God' approach; instead it becomes apparent that nothing is too poor, too low, too ordinary to be inhabited or used, whether it be a stable for a birth, the washing of dirty feet as a service, an upper room in a poor part of Jerusalem for the institution of the Lord's Supper, or a cross on which to die. In this same Supper the sacramental elements are not brought as men's offerings, the first fruits of their labours, but are given with dominical authority for sacramental use by God in this continuing rite.[15] However appropriate as natural symbols, the bread and wine are basically historical symbols, metaphorical and to be learned in this particular tradition rather than self-evident because of their analogical features;[16] they are dependent, like the symbolism of the *domus ecclesiae* itself, upon the life and actions of Jesus-in-community.

The effect of these explicit and unambiguous New Testament models is to leave only a very modest and much qualified place for the building as a sacramental offering which is representative of the natural order; at the most it will testify to the coming consummation rather than to the present riches of the created world. As Rudolf Schwarz expressed it, in words if not in his churches, '... far beneath the exalted realms of true architecture lies that other area where... emergency buildings are the only possible accomplishments of men before God, waiting-rooms before his threshold. They confess to infinite need and they wait until God himself transforms it. This is the honourable way to build churches.'[17]

In theological terms this is to say that the church building has an eschatological witness which testifies not to its own achievements but to the shape of things to come, just as the community from which it constantly takes its cue also lives in terms of hope and promise. It has therefore no autonomous witness of its own on two counts – its dependence on the community of people and its pointing away from itself to the consummated form which it can no more than adumbrate. The *domus ecclesiae* always has to struggle against the tendency found throughout the liturgical life of the church whereby the building, the rites, the music, the art all claim an autonomous existence as cultural products in their own right, to be appreciated primarily by aesthetic or other canons rather than by their service of the worshipping and witnessing community. Even modern churches built on meeting house principles are open to this abuse and can become stops on the tourist beat. On the other hand one can recall worshipping in new churches of interesting materials and contemporary design where the action of the congregation in its liturgy was so absorbing that one was conscious only of the life in the meeting and took for granted the house in which it was occurring.[18]

16.6 SURVIVAL OF THE NUMINOUS HOUSE OF GOD

These considerations have clarified the nature of the *domus ecclesiae* form by setting forth a wider functionalism that includes a limited symbolism, a measure of participation in the holiness of the temple-as-community, and some representative relationship to the physical universe when this is interpreted eschatologically. At the same time the distinction from the *domus dei* has been emphasized by the rejection of all tendencies to pass over the boundary in that direction. This position would appear to have much in common with many of the emphases current in Western Christianity since the late 1950s, even if not as radical as some of these. We refer to the notions of 'secular Christianity', of 'religionless Christianity' (traced, rightly or wrongly, to Dietrich Bonhoeffer), of the 'death of God' theology, and of the assertions that modern man has completely demythologized the natural and social spheres and no longer has any sense of or interest in numinous manifestations of the transcendent or of the sanctity of places and buildings. It seems, therefore, that the *domus ecclesiae*, shorn even of the somewhat wider symbolic functions we have allowed it, is the form of the church for modern men.

This apparent congruence of viewpoints may prove very deceptive, just as many of these assertions themselves are of doubtful value, coming as they do almost entirely from sophisticated sections of Western societies with no extensive experience of other cultures where the religious dimension is very much in evidence and 'modern man' exists in other modes. It could be claimed that no century before the twentieth has seen a greater range of new religious movements across all the cultures of the world, including our own Western culture, which some sociologists and historians of religion assert is not as secular as it may seem. One thinks of the tendency to remythologize both nature in the ecology movement, and society in the communes, as well as the renewed search for the transcendent in counter-cultural and Eastern mystic forms. In addition there is concern with religious experience that includes a distinctive dimension as manifest in the charismatic movement, in reports collected by the Religious Experience Research Unit at Oxford, and in the continuing interest by students in Rudolf

Otto and the revived interest in Schleiermacher.

It is not surprising, therefore, that in 'the contemporary struggle between church architects who stand for the principle of numinosity and symbolism and those who emphasize the principle of community-feeling and functionalism',[19] even churches built within the influence of the liturgical movement often exhibit numinous features. This may be by avowed intent, as when the architect of the University of Keele chapel declares that 'every endeavour has been made to produce an interior which has something of the character of the numinous, and to do this by the simplest and most direct means, shunning all contrived excitement'.[20] Simplicity of means is certainly in the modern mood, and commonly consists of such effects as those derived from a soaring white wall behind the altar (as in Rudolf Schwarz's earlier work), or the flooding of the sanctuary space by natural light from heaven as against the subdued lighting of the congregational space. Other methods include internal changes of height or light, scale or decoration, elevated altars with implications of the sacred mountain, or vertical accents expressed through towers, spires, or more commonly the narrow A-frame structure. The Episcopal Church of St. Clement built in Alexandria, Virginia, in the 1950s went so far as to dispense with all windows and to produce an interior whose numinous darkness is broken only by shafts of light where actually needed for the liturgical action. There have also been renewed defences of the chancel as retaining a sense of the mystery and transcendence of God, for 'it is precisely the chancel, empty except for its symbolical furniture... which can bring home to the congregation, by its emptiness, the wholly "other" dimension of the word of God'.[21]

These emphases amount to a richer symbolic and sacramental function for the building and therefore strengthen its own autonomous witness; to this extent they lead away from the *domus ecclesiae* as we have identified it and soon arrive at *domus dei* forms. Peter Hammond, who argued for the numinous features of the temple tradition to be continued in churches, also recognized that 'the function of Christian symbolism is more specific. The catholic faith is not just a vague theism. A church must express far more than the otherness' of man's earlier temples. This distinctively Christian feature, however, depends for support upon a vital Christian faith, for, as Hammond also points out, decline in living Christianity coincides with greater emphasis on piety, on false Christian art, and on religiosity in the buildings and their contents; these now attempt to say what the Christian community itself is no longer able to proclaim: 'The cult of mystery, in the popular as distinct from the Christian sense of the word, always goes hand in hand with a diminished sense of responsibility on the part of the ordinary citizen.'[22]

All this suggests that there is an inverse relationship between the movement from the *domus ecclesiae* to the *domus dei* position and the vitality of a distinctively Christian position. The equivalent tendency has been commented on in North American Jewry, where the demand for the temple-like synagogue is liable to come from the more secularized members of the community. We may identify two factors affecting this shift in emphasis. Firstly, the size of the group: the larger the community and the more popular the worship, including civic or public occasions on behalf of a nominally Christian population, the greater the appreciation of the sacred place as a numinous house of God. On the other hand, the smaller the group, with greater integration and a more specifically Christocentric life, the greater the likelihood that they will look for the numinous Presence in Jesus-in-community. It would not be difficult to illustrate this from the history of the smaller 'sect-sized' groups such as the Quakers, the Brethren of various kinds and numerous independent evangelicals where the meeting house form has been chiefly located. Likewise as these groups have moved along the continuum from 'sect' to 'denomination' so they have tended to erect buildings less like a meeting house and more 'like a church'; thus the Seventh Day Adventists opened a gothic-arched 'new cathedral-type chapel' in Nashville, Tennessee, in 1967, and we have already observed the response of such groups to the Gothic revival of the last century.

The second factor would seem to concern the relationship to some major new Christian dynamic connected with the founder and his charisma or the powers released in a movement of reformation or revival. Then even a larger Christian community shows less interest in the temple forms or indeed in buildings of any kind; but as the originating impulse declines so will the concern with the church building as such be found to increase. For one illustration we may refer to our earlier mention of the Chicago Unitarian twentieth century enthusiast for Gothic churches, Van Ogden Vogt. At the same time it must be remembered that there are many other factors at work and the two we have identified will often be overridden by counter influences.

16.7 TEMPLES FOR CIVIL RELIGION

The distinctions we have been making suggest that there may be a case for the temple-like church to serve the religious needs of the wider populace on the margins of or outside the specifically Christian community, a place for the activities of civil religion, as it is sometimes called. This was recognized in the report of a recent French discussion which supported the *domus ecclesiae* principle but also gave qualified acceptance to the need for sacred buildings even in the modern secularized West. Most Frenchmen, it declares, for very diverse and complex reasons, favour the building of such churches so that where in practice the public want and will support the monumental type of building, even a cathedral, this is not excluded.[23] From the United States there is a similar claim, '... that people with the least formal faith seem willing to make relatively large sacrifices to construct religious structures. I think it is wrong to regard this as simply... the desire to create one's own monument.... People spend money on what they need psychologically if not materially. People need religious structures in order to share and celebrate the decisive times and seasons in the calendar of their lives.'[24] Similar arguments have been used to justify the erection of large new cathedrals in modern Western cities, as at Coventry and Liverpool, but the argument applies at all levels.

It also applies even to the church erected in a more distinctively Christian manner; the congregation cannot protect it

> from the sacredness with which even a semi-Christian 'tribal' religion may invest it.... As a kind of 'tribal' sanctuary, hallowed by personal memories and associations and group aspirations and loyalties.... Further, its potency as a symbol and focus of this sort of devotion has little to do with its use for worship; it will often happen that

many people who feel the strongest devotion to the structure as such rarely attend services in it.[25]
Both the exterior and the interior of the church therefore have a part to play in this civil religion, even though for the meeting house type it is the interior that has the greater importance. Even in a secularized society men retain some response to a building that suggests the more-than-ordinary dimensions of life and that stands out from the so obviously utilitarian structures around them. As a modern town-planner has expressed it, '... the Church wins a belief-inspiring identity as well as ... the opportunity to become a true point of crystallization in the so often formless sea of houses which make up your residential area'.[26] While the church is seldom the focal gathering place in the life of the urban community, unless it is also built and operated as a multi-purpose community centre, there are other more subtle functions still to be performed in modern society; something of the temple form is needed to sustain even an intangible civil religion which cannot enter into the distinctives of the Christian tradition with its meeting house principles.

The Christian community cannot avoid these involuntary functions of its building although it can seldom accord them high priority. If it does so it may produce no more than a status symbol, as when the visitors' guide sponsored by the Chamber of Commerce of an American city declared that 'the present handsome building on Chippewa Square, designed after the Parthenon in Athens, is evidence of the foothold this religion has in the community'.[27] It is doubtful whether the church building can make positive public proclamation of the Christian faith without moving into the temple mode that pre-dates this faith; at least it may be able to avoid suggestions that its faith is merely old-fashioned, dowdy, queer, presumptuous, or pretentious; at best it may be able to arouse enquiry as to what lies behind a building whose functions are not self-evident to those whose religion is of the civil variety.

A notable example of the attempt to provide a modern sanctuary for civil religion is to be found in the Meditation Room, as it had to be called, at the United Nations Headquarters in New York. This is no place for communal assembly or varied liturgical action, but a small, highly symbolic and numinous sanctuary which presents its own witness to the individual who enters for meditation. Dag Hammarskjöld, one of its main sponsors, interpreted the symbolism when it was opened in 1957. He described it as

a room of stillness with perhaps one very simple symbol, the light striking on stone... in the centre of the room there is this great block of iron ore, shimmering like ice in the shaft of light from above... a meeting of the light of the sky and the earth.... In this case it is an empty altar... because God is worshipped in so many forms. The stone in the centre symbolizes an altar to God of all...this massive altar to give the impression of something more than temporary. We also had another idea... that the material to represent the earth... should be iron ore, the material out of which swords have been made and... homes for man are also built. It is a material which represents the very paradox of human life... used either for construction or for destruction... the choice between the ploughshare and the sword.[28]

The full text of his speech, as represented by these extracts, provides an excellent modern statement of the *domus dei* principle, and the Room itself, albeit on such small scale, supplies an exemplar for the needs of contemporary civil religion at its more sophisticated and international levels. It would be foolish for Christian opinion not to appreciate this Room in its own quite authentic terms, and to look for the *domus ecclesiae* in this context; anything in the latter form would fail to meet the needs of the people the Room is meant to serve.

16.8 *DOMUS DEI ET ECCLESIAE?*

It seems therefore that some inevitable relation remains between the two types of place of worship — the church built as a *domus ecclesiae* cannot avoid interpretation and use as a *domus dei*, if not by its own congregation then by others in the surrounding community.

We must now face the question whether the needs not only of civil religion but also of the Christian community as it in fact exists in history can in practice be met by strict and exclusive adherence to the normative form. This is not to question the norm itself, but rather the capacity of an average congregation to assume all the functions of the temple in their transposed personalized forms as Jesus-in-community, and therefore to need no more than a meeting house for their place of worship. In other words, do the realities of the situation suggest the need for a more mixed form, a *domus dei et ecclesiae*?

This possibility has been raised in various places. Thus H. G. Hageman asserts that the meeting house concept has fallen into disrepute since only the horizontal dimension has been retained, and the vertical, which was included as a primary dimension in earlier forms, has been neglected. The former supports a strong sense of community, but the latter must be strongly accented to indicate the other dimension of meeting, that between God and his people; then the place of worship is a *domus dei et ecclesiae suae*. Hageman then withdraws from exploring what this might mean in concrete terms and is content to emphasize that this form will exist only when the building is so used and not in the building itself.[29]

S. Smalley also employs this dual concept, of 'the house of God for the people of God', and claims that there is a close link between the two.[30] Not having defined or analyzed either of these forms he does not explore what this link might be. A similar notion may be found in G. Cope's suggestion, already noted, for a sanctuary within an auditorium. Rudolf Schwarz is more explicit in proposing 'that both ways of building be cultivated at once... buildings which would contain both elements, the shining, manifest "field of action" and the dark hidden "shrine", the passage and the permanence of grace'. In one form there would be two separate spaces for these two purposes; in the form he preferred the table of the communal meal and the altar as the holy of holies would be 'built into each other'.[31]

Still more explicitly, W. M. Zucker declared that 'every new church, being determined by the mysterious tension between the *Domus Ecclesiae* and the *Domus Domini,* is a risky undertaking which easily falls into some heretical fallacy'. To deny the divine character of the building, i. e. its temple principles, is a lapse into Arianism, while to overlook the human nature of the building because of its inherent unworthiness amounts to a docetic or Apollinarian position. The church must be both at once for its Christian quality depends on being modelled on the dual nature of Christ as equally divine and human.[32] On the other hand, J. Dahinden is content to replace the 'pretentious confusing "sacrality" of past cultures and attempt the much more difficult task' of 'elucidation (and not symbolization) of a restrained, refined and yet strongly expressed religiousness'.[33]

Rationales of various kinds may be presented in support of the church building as a mixed form. It may be pointed out that all religious traditions are themselves mixed forms in the sense that there is a disparity between their phenomenological and historical development and their professed teachings or models as revealed or theologically formulated. There is a tension or dialectic between facts and norms in the Christian religion as in all others, and in this area the tension is manifest between the two types of place of worship each of which has found acceptance within the Christian community.

This same distinction is given positive Christian theological statement in terms of a community that is on pilgrimage from this world, the world of the religions where the church still pursues its sinful stumbling way, to the world of hope and promise, the Divine Kingdom or New Jerusalem where religion is transcended and temples are superfluous. As citizens of this world, immature and still sinful, they need the assistance of temple forms; but as already a colony of heaven with a foretaste of the consummation, and to that extent able to enter upon the transposed sanctuary as Jesus-in-community, they need the meeting house for this new dimension of their existence. To claim only the latter form of existence would amount to perfectionism; to ignore it would be to lose the Christian distinctives; and yet it can be claimed only in an eschatological sense that recognizes the tension between the two forms.[34]

It could be said that we should have established the theological relationship between the two types before entering upon the long historical analysis of Christian church buildings, and so used this in the understanding of Christian history. By so doing our analysis would have avoided the kind of oversimplification that has been revealed by the more complex and adequate position now reached.

Ideally speaking this may be true, but in practice all study involves temporary isolation of its field from the organic whole of reality, together with subsequent correction of the more significant distortions that have resulted. Our limited minds, faced with the infinite complexities about us, can do no other.

In this study of the place of worship we have first used phenomeno-logical analysis to establish the *domus ecclesiae* as the Christian norm, simply by studying the definitive Christian materials themselves (including their own theological positions), and in the same way as we gave briefer study to the Jewish and Islamic materials. The phenomeno-logical method, however, could not take account of the further complex considerations by which the two types have now been related to one another, considerations concerning the religious development and historical situation of the worshippers in any particular building. The initial over-simplification has now been corrected, but only by the introduction of a theological framework and method; and yet to have taken account of the further factors so revealed throughout our analysis of the Christian centuries would have been a nigh impossible task. Any critique of the position now reached in this study must be made in terms of further or alternative theological considerations, or, more radically, by an alternative initial phenomenological analysis. In the concluding chapter we shall attempt a more detailed examination of the relation between the phenomenological and theological methods that is beginning to appear in this extended case study.

16.9 THE FUNCTION OF THE CHRISTIAN NORM

It might seem that we have returned to an idea envisaged in the intro-duction to this work of a continuum of forms with our two basic types at the polar extremities and in between a series of mixed forms. This then would represent the actual situation of most Christian communi-ties and also allow for the variations from Quaker meeting house to Catholic or Orthodox cathedrals. If so, what then is the function of the *domus ecclesiae* as Christian norm?

In its concrete manifestations or its more notional forms it is there to represent the kind of place of worship where the transposition from the physical temple mode to the personalized temple-as-community is encouraged. It stands at the point of tension and transition between these two forms as a kind of midwife for the emergence of the one from the other. It is here that the central problem of church architecture emerges and the greatest sensitivity to the nature of the congregation using the building is required. If this is a Society of Friends or similar small and highly personalized community with distinctively Christian ethos then a meeting house akin to those of the past is readily provided. If, on the other hand, many in the congregation possess more of a civil religion the *domus ecclesiae* may add more of the features of the temple; but these must be controlled and constantly subordinated to the normative principle to allow for the emergence of the personalized temple form. The functions of the temple as such do not change but are taken up in the new transposed form of the community as temple; the functions of the building itself cease to be those of central and dominant witness to the presence of the holy and become those appropriate to an ancillary or servant of the community. The paradox and problem exist where the building must perform something of the former role while resisting its fuller expression and at the same time move into its new role as meeting place for the holy community.

We may illustrate the issue of the survival of numinous features in new churches that we observed earlier in this chapter. The place and function of these in the temple tradition is sufficiently clear but in the normative Christian position the building would appear to claim no more than a relative numinosity derived from its association with the life of the community-as-temple. The numinous is now located in persons and their actions; firstly in the person of Jesus Christ, the image and glory of God, who now manifests the immanent-transcendent presence of the temple in his own person and, as Rudolf Otto's study of the New Testament materials has reminded us, sometimes in a most numinous manner.[35]

Consequently and in dependence on the presence of Jesus in his community, the church congregation also reveals something of the numinous presence in its life and actions. This may appear during the solemn celebration of a Catholic mass, for the few at an early morning Anglican Holy Communion, in the sense of anticipation at a seasonal celebration of the Lord's Supper in a Reformed tradition after a preparatory service the evening before, or in the eloquent silences of the simplest form of the Breaking of the Bread, or of a Quaker service without visible sacraments. It is also to be found in authentic preaching of the

Word, especially under a prophetic ministry, or in a moving testimony to a trans-human Power at an evangelistic or Salvation Army meeting, and in a Pentecostal service when the presence of the Spirit in power overcomes the inhibitions and conventions of culture and of temperament to produce a more spontaneous worship in joy and freedom.

In these forms of community action, at least on their more authentic occasions, even the casual visitor might begin to sense a 'plus factor' that he can neither escape nor define, something 'there' which begins to stir in him a sense of awe and fascination and represents an embryonic apprehension of the numinous. As he might put it, 'these people seem to have got something'. The same experience may occur in encounter with individuals – the simple saintly person through whom shines another world, or who 'has been far ben' (to use the Scottish highlands term), the charismatic individual endued with more than human qualities, or the dynamic man of mana driven by supra-human powers, as in Lord Reith the founder of the British Broadcasting Corporation with his sense of predestination, or Lord Lugard the great colonial servant under compulsion from an inescapable sense of duty, which J. H. Oldman was forced to describe in terms of the presence of the numinous.[36] The fact the Lugard was neither orthodox Christian nor professed churchman, but a god-fearing man whose religion was more of the 'civil' variety, reminds us that the manifestation of the numinous in individuals is not a phenomenon peculiar to the Christian religion, but occurs throughout the religions in the form of charismatic powers, manifest inspiration, or possession behaviour.

However much individuals may be transparent to a transcendent holiness the normative centre remains that of Jesus-in-community. The Christian congregation possesses a liturgical life which localizes the numinous presence in the personal dimensions of community worship in a way not found elsewhere. As Titus Burckhardt recognized, 'a Muslim's awareness of the Divine Presence is based on a feeling of limitlessness; he rejects all objectivation of the Divine ...whereas Christian piety is eager to concentrate on a concrete centre – since the "Incarnate Word" is a centre, both in space and time, and since the Eucharist sacrament is no less a centre...'.[37] The normative location of the numinous and holy presence is therefore neither in the individual saint nor in the sacred place with its temple but in the congregation gathered by Christ around the Word and sacraments; it is in the service of this, the new temple, that the *domus ecclesiae* finds its proper function, even while it may continue to represent something of the old temple in certain aspects of its structure.

16.10 THE PRACTICAL CONSEQUENCES IN THE BUILDING

The more specific features of the meeting house type of church building have been so often and so excellently presented that there is no need to explore them here in any detail. Even if not explicitly derived from a sufficiently basic theory most of these exhortations cohere with all that has been said in these pages and serve to delineate the *domus ecclesiae* as we have sought to define it.

Since religions are concerned with reality, and the Christian religion claims that ultimate reality both as to man and to God was disclosed in Christ and is proclaimed through his community, the church building must strike the notes of honesty and authenticity in design and materials. Against the disorder of the world it must show coherence; against wordly strife and confusion, it must be a place of peacefulness and rest; to strident and disruptive affluence it must present the challenge of simplicity and austerity. In order truly to serve people it must be unobtrusive and humble, neither impressing nor oppressing them by its own features but taking its modest and efficient place in the scheme of things; it will therefore be local and human in scale and thus hospitable as a place where people can feel at home. It will encourage the sense of community by bringing people into visual and auditory relationship with one another and with the minister, and assisting their participation in all the action of the liturgy. At the same time it will not define these relationships or this participation in any fixed or final way, but leave room for both individual choice in the present and for new forms in the future. It will remember its relation to the public, its place in the local landscape, and the wider service it may offer beyond the needs of the congregation for a place of worship. Nor will it hesitate to remain somewhat of a mystery to those beyond its own worshipping fellowship, and perhaps even a scandal to those who resent what they cannot understand.

Perhaps an architect may be allowed the concluding word at this point: 'In this design there is no analogical symbolism. The space is designed entirely around a theology of the people of God. It is not primarily a eucharistic room; it is not primarily a preaching room; it is a space where people meet, and the mode of their meeting is expressed in the form of the room. They meet as a group of friends who enjoy fellowship, and above all claim the fellowship of Christ who presides at their meeting.'[38]

17

The Wider Implications
for Phenomenology and Theology

This study has now run its course from the phenomenology of the simplest places of worship to the theology of the Christian form. It remains to examine our procedures, both phenomenological and theological, and discuss the relations between them in the light of the specific religious form that we have studied; it is to be hoped that this firm anchorage will benefit a discussion that is too often conducted in terms of generalitites divorced from the actual manifestations of religion.

17.1 THE PHENOMENOLOGICAL AND HISTORICAL PROCEDURES

We have chosen one of the most basic, universal and concrete of all religious phenomena, the place of worship, and proposed a phenomenological analysis in the form of five characteristic features: the divine origin and the four religious functions. From this study there emerged a typology of two basic forms, the temple and the meeting house, and in the case of the Christian tradition the further radical transposition of the temple form from the physical to the personal mode. These working terms and categories were tested across the religions and proved capable of giving order and meaning to a vast array of forms connected with places of worship, and of revealing the structures and functions common to all religions at this point.

Special attention was given to the biblical tradition and the Semitic religions where the two types of worship place have been chiefly exhibited, where the meeting house type would appear to be normative, and where there have been confusion and tension between the two forms. This involved historical exploration of these traditions in order to analyse their particular developments with the aid of our phenomenological categories and types, thus demonstrating the interdependence of the phenomenological and historical procedures.

It was in the course of this historical exploration that we reached the particular New Testament development where the radical transposition of the phenomenological form of worship place occurred. Accepting this as the new Christian norm we then pursued the subsequent history of the interaction of the old and the new modes in the Christian tradition, describing and evaluating this history in terms of its approximation to its own new standard. Parallel but briefer phenomenological-historical studies of the Islamic and Jewish traditions revealed situations closely analogous to the Christian experience.

A similar historical exploration of other major and long-established traditions such as the Hindu and Buddhist might have discovered any departures from or transpositions of their dominant temple forms, using the phenomenological base we have established. Something of the congregational mode would have been located in certain sectarian or monastic communities of a traditional nature and still more in modern reforming movements that have been open to outside, especially to Christian, influences. We have not pursued these, partly because of our self-imposed limits, and partly because these forms have never achieved a dominant position or normative status in the major tradition to which they belong. We have been content therefore to leave these and other non-Semitic traditions associated primarily with the *domus dei* form. If this should be firmly established by more thorough study then our two-class typology also serves as the basis for a classification of religions in terms of the predominant or distinctive forms of their places of worship.

17.2 PROCEDURAL ASSUMPTIONS

It is important to be clear as to the basic assumptions or convictions implicit in the procedures described above, since not everyone would accept them, and yet without them it is impossible to pursue the course we have taken.

17.2.1 *Religions as authentic phenomena*

The first conviction is that all religious traditions are to be accepted for what they seem to be until proved otherwise, and are to be taken seriously as to some extent authentically religious and therefore referring to some transcendent and ultimate reality or dimension. We cannot proceed as we have done if religious phenomena are reduced to no more than epiphenomena of some other human activity or concern, be it psychological, social, political, or if they are initially divided as belonging to religions that are true (i.e. one's own) or false (e.g. the products of human fantasy, ignorance or error, or of deceit by evil spirits). We must credit all religions with being authentic (rather than 'true') in the sense of possessing the intention to relate to a transhuman reality which provides the meaning for these religious activities and for human life itself, and not least at their places of worship. A personal theological position, for example, that regarded all religions other than the Christian as the product of men's sinful servitude to the Devil could not support the study in which we have engaged; at every point it would reinterpret the data in a manner so diametrically opposed to the meaning held by the practitioners of the religion concerned that it would cease to be a scientific study controlled by the data and become instead a polemical exercise directed by its own prejudgment.

17.2.2 *Religion as universal phenomenon*

The second assumption or conviction is that religious concern and activities are shared by men of all races, cultures and ages so that the religious phenomena can be explored across time and space with the expectation that they will reveal something in common by way of forms, meanings and intentions. Further, what is shared is discovered not only by the phenomenologist but at another level by religious men themselves; when the most authentic representatives of different traditions meet they tend to recognize each other, for 'deep calls unto deep' at the level where the basic religious intention of communion with and service of the divine is held in common. We have set forth the common features of places of worship as understood by the student of religions; we would also expect the devout adherents of one tradition, apart from any such study, to have some positive feeling for what was happening at the place of worship of another religion. This conviction about some inner unity across all religions is also incompatible with certain theological positions; it is tenable only where one is prepared to allow for some authentic revelation of the divine, or some contact with ultimate reality in all religious traditions – in other words, that religions are not merely man-made cultural creations but are in fact the product of interaction with a transhuman realm. In this way the second conviction amounts to a variation upon the first.

17.2.3 *Religions as both ideal and actual*

The third conviction necessary for our methods is that all religions tend to be aware of the difference between belief and practice, what should be done and what is achieved, between the ideal and the actuality within their own tradition. Individuals vary in their degree of satisfaction with their own religious performance, but the more sensitive and in this way more authentically religious are often vividly aware of how far they have failed to meet the requirements or to reach the full potentiality of their own tradition. In most religions something ideal or normative may be identified and this provides at least a potential basis for self-criticism. It is in this area of the tension between fact and ideal that much of the religious life usually occurs. To understand religious phenomena it is therefore necessary to take account both of actual achievement and of the less tangible forms. In describing the divine origins and the several functions of the *domus dei* we have at the same time identified the norms concerned; this is how temples or shrines ought to be founded and designed and how they should operate; in the Semitic religions the normative forms again have their own bases and characteristics. It would be impossible to give a full phenomenological account without this attention to religious norms which in a sense are more important than actual practice.

17.3 PERSONAL STANCE

The procedures based on these assumptions are open to any phenomenologist and historian of religions, be he of any living faith or (with
certain qualifications) of none. In principle a Muslim, Buddhist, or any
other believer could have conducted this particular study, not excluding the biblical and Christian material where its own professed norms
and primary forms were used to provide a critique of the later history
of churches. A good Buddhist scholar should be able to test Christianity by its own public standards and with results that must be taken
seriously by Christian scholars; likewise this author as a Christian is still
able to offer to Muslims and Jews the studies made above of their own
places of worship, not excluding the critique drawn from their own
sources.

   This dealing with norms is not the same as doing theology, even when
one is treating the norms of one's own religion. In our case we have
asked what is an orthodox Christian interpretation[1] of the New Testament material about Jesus and the early church in relation to places
of worship; both this material and the Christian interpretations are
publicly accessible to all, including Hindu, Jewish, etc., scholars, and a
general consensus on the facts of the matter should be possible in spite
of personal allegiances, and apart from the question as to whether the
Christian interpretation is also true or false. Even if this interpretation
of Jesus is mistaken (as Jewish, Hindu, etc., scholars may personally
believe) it is a mistaken interpretation that has in fact occurred and
had its own consequences. The only value judgment required of all
scholars in this field is that here we are dealing with an authentically
and intentionally religious interpretation of some historical importance, not that it is also in fact a true interpretation.

   To discuss the latter issue is to do theology, and it is possible for the
believing phenomenologist to suspend this activity and the kind of
involvement and commitment that go with it while he adopts the phenomenological viewpoint for the time being and studies the norms of
his own religion as part of the data in much the same way as a non-
believer. The procedures of the two scholars operating from these different positions can be sufficiently similar for them to share a common

enterprise, but never completely identical, and for three reasons. The believing scholar will possess a further distinctive incentive insofar as his commitment includes the obligation to seek a fuller grasp of his religion by all possible means, and at this point by the use of phenomenological-historical study in its own authentic way. He will, further, have a more intimate knowledge of the data concerned and of the meanings involved. As a consequence of his commitment and of understanding the data from the inside he will be liable to present the phenomena and history of his own religion in such an attractive way that he is virtually commending his own faith to others. Signs of this last attitude can no doubt be detected in this work as it proceeded, but we trust that such overtones do not affect the substance of what has been attempted. On the whole, therefore, the personal position of the believing student need not be an impediment, and can be an advantage in which other scholars can share if they are prepared to benefit from the deeper understanding of the believing colleague and to recognize the occasions when he may pass over the boundary into apologetics or theology, and perhaps indicate this to him.

17.4 THE INTERACTION BETWEEN PHENOMENOLOGY AND THEOLOGY

The implications of our study for the relations between the phenomenological-historical study and the theological methods can now be examined systematically. While we shall do this in terms of Christian theology the same relations exist in principle between phenomenology and the theology of any religious tradition.[2]

17.4.1 *Phenomenology's contribution to theology*

As we have already seen, theological interpretations of man, his world, the divine and the relations between them — in this case of Jesus-in-community as temple — form part of the data of phenomenology and are even more valuable when these interpretations have a central and normative status. Since phenomenology is concerned with the meanings for the believers the more explicitly and systematically their theologians expound these meanings the richer the data for phenomenological study, and the more the interaction between the actual and the ideal can be explored. In our case we have the benefit of the extensive New Testament theological interpretations of Jesus, and of the subsequent theologizing about the place of worship especially in connection with the Jerusalem Temple as model, in the Renaissance theory of churches, in the attempts to provide a theological rationale for Gothic, and in the more recent work of the liturgical movement. The theologian thus helps to lay out the material of a particular religion for phenomenological study.

Phenomenology then adds further interpretations of another kind when it takes the Christian place of worship, as found both in practice and in theory, and sets it alongside the places of worship of other religions in order to discover any common forms or meanings. This search must also be pursued through the various historical developments in the different traditions, so that the history of religions is also involved. Some religious forms and their interpretations may prove to be peculiar to their own religious tradition and here the phenomenological point of view has less to offer; but with the fundamental form we have chosen, the place of worship, it has been possible to develop our five-point analysis across the various religions and to include in these same categories the Christian theological interpretations of Jesus in relation to the temple. Theology itself cannot perform these tasks, but it needs these results for the fullest possible understanding both of its own data and of its own positions.

Whatever phenomenology does adds further dimensions for theology to consider, and may even help to define a theological position in a somewhat new way. Thus our formulation of the Christian position as 'Jesus-in-community equals temple' is a variation on the usual theological statement that derives from our five-point phenomenological analysis. Given orthodox theological understandings of Jesus and interpretations of the New Testament this is how it appears when set amid the places of worship of religions in general. The work of the theologian has been accepted as it stands, related to a larger context, and then returned enriched with new insights into the functions of Jesus and of the Christian community and new clarity about the Christian place of worship. This presumably is what Tillich meant in claiming that 'theology must apply the phenomenological approach to all its basic concepts' as a preliminary to 'discussing their truth and actuality'.[3]

This is the first phase of the interaction between the two methods and it is facilitated by the fact that although the methods and purposes are different they share many of the common basic categories of religions. Thus theology cannot do without the categories indicated by such terms as worship, prayer, altar, sacrament, sacrifice, rebirth, communion, spirit, revelation, myth and many others, even though in its own context it may interpret these in a quite distinctive way.

17.4.2 *Consequent theological reworking*

The second phase begins when theology reworks the interpretation of its own data in the light of the phenomenological account both of these data and of its own results. In our case Christology and ecclesiology must be reworked to take account of the four *domus dei* functions which phenomenology now attributes to Jesus-in-community. Theology will then endeavour to give its own version of how Christ and the Church serve as centre, as meeting point, as earthly microcosm of the heavenly, and as the place of the immanent-transcendent presence. Phenomenology has given its account in general religious terms; theology must do so through the distinctively Christian views of the divine and the human and of their relationship. It must also make its own comment on the way phenomenology has identified and defined the Christian place of worship as *domus ecclesiae*, by way of rejection, acceptance or modification and further interpretation.

If theology cannot accommodate the phenomenological contribution in its own scheme because the proffered categories or results simply will not fit, this must be declared. Then it is possible that with a fresh start on both sides, a revised phenomenology and a fresh theological interpretation of its own data will prove to be mutually compatible with consequent profit to theology in the ways we have suggested. If, on the other hand, the phenomenological results remain unassimilable theology will have gained nothing as yet, and phenomenology will have encountered another form of the theological phenomenon which it will have to try to study. In our case this has not happened for theology can assimilate to its benefit the results of this study, as we have indicated in Chapter 16. It can even apply them beyond the areas of Christology, ecclesiology and liturgics by using them in the service of a theology of religions, and to this latter possibility we shall shortly revert.

17.4.3 *Feedback for phenomenological reworking*

Something of the second stage, that of theological reworking, has been implicit in the later portions of this study, but there is also a potential third stage in the interaction between the two methods. This emerges when theology hands back its revised views on Christ, the Church, liturgics and on other religions to phenomenology and history of religions as part of the ongoing history of the Christian religion, for that is what such revisions are. Phenomenology must then examine whether the revised forms can be accommodated in its existing categories and analyses or whether they are so different that further phenomenological development will be required to deal with such new data. Thus phenomenology would be stimulated by the feed-back from its own effects on theology.

In our case the first of these possibilities seems to apply. The original phenomenological categories have proved adequate to accomodate the seemingly so different Christian data, to cover the radical transposition of the sacred place into a unique form, and to be taken up and used by theology itself. This confirms confidence in these categories as basic phenomenological instruments in this area, at the same time as the categories themselves receive fuller and clearer meaning from their use in such a different context.

17.4.4 *Beyond phenomenology to commitment*

These three phases of interaction may be regarded by all phenomenologists as acceptable features of their own proper procedure in relation to theology. From the last of these features, however, there emerges what we may call a fourth and optional phase of the interaction. An orthodox Christian position may regard Jesus-in-community, the revised formulation of what it means by temple, to be a definitive form which reveals all other physical forms of temple as now outmoded, as only temporary and shadowy manifestations of the reality of temple that has now appeared in history. This is to distinguish among the data of phenomenology with an evaluation that has a theological judgment as its basis. The phenomenologist may merely register this claim to be definitive and note the support that Christians find for it, just as he accepts and understands the meanings of all religious phenomena for the adherents concerned. On the other hand, the claim to be definitive is a truth claim that bears upon the phenomenologist as a man involved like other men in establishing his own right relationship with ultimate reality. He may therefore decide to explore this claim for himself by tracing it to its roots in the person of Jesus and seeing if he can share the interpretations upon which it is based. At this point he ceases to do phenomenology and commences to do theology, and the motives are personal and religious rather than professional and academic.

In one sense the phenomenologist is faced with definitive claims and religious absolutes at many points across the religious spectrum, for most religions in the last resort claim a certain ultimacy for their own interpretations; to survive as a phenomenologist he has to relativize them all for his working purposes. At the same time 'he ought not simply on methodological grounds resist the *possibility* that ... this same methodology could lead to the conclusion that at this point in the history of religions', whether it be in the Christian community as temple, in the Muslim mosque in its normative form, or in any other temple, 'the ever debatable reality of the divine power in its infinity, which manifests itself in the tranformations that take place in the history of religions, appears in a definitive way and becomes revealed'.[4] As a phenomenologist he cannot rule out the occurrence of a truly definitive form, but neither could he explore and decide upon its truth without becoming something of a theologian and therefore an adherent of the tradition within which this form has appeared. This fourth phase therefore cannot be included within the procedures of phenomenology although these may well lead into it. Whether the phenomenologist can take this step and retain his integrity as a phenomenologist will depend a good deal upon whether the religious tradition concerned is able to relate its definitive form in a sufficiently positive way to the forms in other religions which it now relativizes; in other words, on whether it has a theology of religions that allows for the continuing contributions of phenomenology in the appreciations of these religions.

The interactions between theology and phenomenology therefore form an ongoing dialectical process of mutual disclosure and mutual stimulation in which each performs essential instrumental, regulative and critical functions towards the other. Phenomenology, indeed, would seem to possess a special affinity with theology insofar as they both deal with the 'essence' of religion, albeit in their own different ways. At the same time the relationship remains an open one for neither is forced to adopt the stance of the other, but merely to respect it and learn from it; nor, on the other hand, is it forbidden to cross the boundary and take up the role of the other party, or on occasion even to adopt both roles in the one enquiry as we have done at times in this work.

17.5 A THEOLOGY OF OTHER RELIGIONS

Our brief references to the need for a theological understanding of the existence, nature and value of other religions must now be pursued further. This is a modern problem, for the New Testament was written in a milieu that knew none of the universal religions, except Judaism which was in a special position, and was familiar chiefly with the religions of Greece and Rome in their decline and with the esoteric and now defunct cults of the Levant. Hence there is no New Testament doctrine of the other religions, and no more than peripheral references to them that are both positive and negative in tone and that scarcely provide support for a systematic statement. Throughout the expansion and missionary activities of Christianity the predominant attitude of hostility or indifference to other faiths has not been conducive to the development of a theological interpretation of their presence, other than the summary verdict that they represented the results of human ignorance, error or sinfulness, or of being led astray by the deceits of the Devil. Only in more recent times have some of the prerequisites for a theology of religions become available, especially the willingness to take them seriously as religions in their own right with impressive cultural histories, to study them intensively with the aid of the explosion of information about them that has been proceeding since the eighteenth century, and to accept the systematic assistance of the phenomenology and history of religions and other sections of the religious sciences. Despite the Ramon Lulls and other individual exceptions the real meeting between Christianity and the religions of the world, and by the same tokens their meeting with one another, have only begun.

Since there cannot be a theology of something that is not intimately known and thoroughly understood by the theologian, it is unlikely that satisfactory theologies of religions will arise within the confines of Western culture, and by deduction from dogmatic systems, even though their authors be of the stature of a Barth or a Rahner. The task belongs rather to the theologian living as a member of his own believing community in living interaction with the individuals of believing communities in another tradition; a theology of religion will be worked out in the situation of mission or encounter where there is a living plurality of faiths, and will proceed both deductively and inductively.

Here, however, our prime concern is with the relation of phenomenology, and especially the phenomenology of the place of worship, to this theological enterprise. The first contribution from this quarter has already been examined — the emphasis upon a positive approach to all religions as authentic endeavours to relate the human and the divine or the transcendent, at least in intention if not in achievement. A theology of religions must approach men's places of worship, as all other phenomena, in this spirit.

17.5.1 *A common language of discourse*

Given this basic attitude we may identify three further contributions from the side of phenomenology. The first is the provision of a common set of forms or categories within which religions may recognize one another as religions and by means of which they may hold converse together. For a Christian theologian this means the discovery that the relation between his religion and that of other men does not commence with his own efforts but has already been established, and established, as he must conclude, by God. Given this relationship and a common language of discourse, inter-religious ecumenical activities such as the modern meetings for mutual understanding by dialogue between the faiths become possible. The same equipment also facilitates inter-religious missionary effort, which shows signs of becoming multi-directional, and no longer the unilateral Christian action it has usually been. In the more concrete terms of this study the phenomenological understanding of one another's places of worship can contribute to both ecumenical and missionary relationships between the religions; it is an ill-equipped theologian of religions who lacks these experiences, and especially the missionary approach of another faith towards him, so that he too feels drawn to leave his 'Sandals at the Mosque'.

17.5.2 *Increased self-understanding for Christians*

A second contribution lies in the way a phenomenological analysis of the religions enables these to contribute to Christianity's self-understanding. Just as the Church once used Greek philosophy to develop her theology, so today it is possible to learn from the insights of many religious traditions concerning the mystery of the divine-human relationship and to incorporate these into Christian theology without abandoning its own distinctive anchorage. As already indicated, a Christology is still further developed when it understands Jesus-in-community as temple and reaches this understanding through a study of the sanctuaries of all religious traditions. The Egyptian, the Inca, the Hindu and all the others have then contributed to the theologian's understanding of the functions of Jesus Christ and of his relevance to other faiths, at least in this particular dimension. Theological conviction as to this relevance then has a new strength, for 'the genuine universality of a religion is first attained where this religion, in its message of salvation, establishes a positive relationship with ... the general history of religion from its earliest stages'.[5]

Such support for the theological understanding of the universal relevance and hence the uniqueness of Christ can be discovered in several different ways. It may derive from historical study of the peculiar place of Jesus and of Christianity within the general history of religions, as with A.Th. van Leeuwen, or from its phenomenological distinctiveness when set amid the forms and typologies of religions, as with Mircea Eliade and Paul Tillich, and in this work. It may result from a negative evaluation of all other histories and phenomena, as when Karl Barth recognizes the similarities across the religions but asserts that these are theologically irrelevant, or at most of negative value as providential signs of the difference between the true revelation in Christ and these other religions. We present the contribution of other religions in a more positive way where both the similarities and the differences are important. We have discovered the meaning of the personal mode of temple as Jesus-in-community only by asserting the continuing identity of functions within the differences of mode. It is therefore a case of identity-in-difference where the identity is discovered from the phenomenology of religions and the difference of formulation from a phenomenological study of the Christian religion. The theological understanding now owes something of substance to the contribution from the other religions; as Pannenberg would put it, a theology of religions need neither deny its Christian perspective nor use its Christian presuppositions as arguments, but can appeal to observable phenomena across all the religions including its own.[6]

17.5.3 Self-understanding in all religions

The final contribution from the phenomenology of religions is seen in the way the Christian self-understanding we have been discussing can in return assist the self-understanding of the other religions. Firstly, each religion can be stimulated by the Christian example to develop its own distinctive theology of other religions and of its relationship to them. Practical attitudes, of course, already exist from one to another, whether peacable or polemical, but there are few signs of a systematic attempt to reach an understanding of the existence and content of other faiths in terms of one's own. Christian attempts at a theology of religions, recent as they are, may encourage others to follow in their own ways, and as they do so their own self-understanding will undoubtedly benefit.[7]

This understanding will benefit further when each religion comes to consider the distinctive Christian forms within the common categories that apply to them all. The very fact that the temple form in the Christian mode presents a strikingly new version of the underlying identities shared across the religions should enable other faiths to understand 'temple' in a fresh light, to see more clearly what temples have been trying to do in the religious situation, and whether they have been successful in their endeavours. The other Semitic religions have the opportunity to understand better their own places of worship, their synagogues and mosques, after study of the Christian norm of the *domus ecclesiae*, a norm which they themselves can, as we have seen, also help to clarify. These two religions will also have to ask themselves whether the functions of the *domus dei* are permanently necessary in religions, and if so how they are fulfilled in their own case.

A Christian theology of religions will be involved in all these complex interactions and will both stimulate them and benefit from them. At the same time it will be concerned with its own distinctives, especially its understanding of the universality and the uniqueness of Jesus Christ, and to this issue we must give some separate attention.

17.6 THE CHRISTIAN NORM IN A THEOLOGY OF RELIGIONS

By phenomenological and historical methods we have interpreted the normative Christian version of the sacred place as Jesus-in-community and this coheres with the necessary christological basis for a Christian dogmatics, and for a Christian theology of religions. One of the tasks of the latter is to define the relation of Christ to all other religions in a way that preserves his centrality and finality for the Christian faith; we now examine the bearing on this task of our study of the relation between Jesus-in-community and the place of worship in other religions.

The central and final position of Christ in the Christian view excludes any theology of religions that suggests either indifference to one another or mere co-existence in peaceful plurality; the concepts or models used have therefore taken either negative or positive forms. On the one hand Christ has been regarded as judging and condemning all other religions as false; these are then to be replaced by the true faith represented by the Church. On the other hand there are many models proposed whereby judgment amounts to a purging preparatory to the tradition concerned being 'taken possession of' by Christ, 'baptized' and 'renewed'. Other models again seek the relationship in terms of fulfilment and interpret this concept in many ways. An evolutionary version, for example, views Christianity as the spiritual, rational, or ethical high point in the long historical development of religions, or, in a slightly different sense, as the crown of man's religious search across all the faiths; these views have been further developed with the aid of the notion of Christ as implicit, latent, or incognito in the other religious traditions, but made manifest in the Christian revelation. Other versions again find the fulfilment not in relation to the past but in eschatological terms whereby the promised consummation is manifest in the present only in sign or foretaste, and the relation of Christ to the religions remains a matter of hope and faith.

Our study of this relationship in the particular area of places of worship suggests the following Christology for a theology of religions. It seems necessary to retain the notion of fulfilment in some real sense if we are not to abandon our analysis of Jesus-in-community as exhibiting the essentials of the temple form. On the other hand, 'there is much in all religion, including Christianity as historically known, which is *not* fulfilled *in* Christ, but totally condemned by Christ'.[8] It is clear that men's sanctuaries have supported false religious hopes and deceitful, unspiritual priesthoods, have sanctioned inhuman cruelties and immoral practices, have exhibited cultural and imperial pride and economic waste, and been an agent in political intrigues and struggles for power. None of these things, however, enters into the essential functions and forms of the *domus dei* or represents the ultimate intentions and needs of the worshippers, a communion between man and the divine. We therefore retain the notion of selective, or rather, essential fulfilment of the deeper and distinctively religious dimensions of other faiths. This view recognizes some real continuity between the Christian and other religions, which is certainly supported in our study of the temple form; it would also seem congruent with the new attitudes to the 'non-Christian' religions expressed at the Second Vatican Council.

On the other hand our survey of places of worship has revealed sharp discontinuities both between the *domus dei* and the *domus ecclesiae* in their forms and purposes, and between the physical and the transposed personal-communal modes of the temple type. There is therefore no simple continuity of an evolutionary kind whereby this essential fulfilment occurs. It takes place in the course of a radical transposition or transformation from a physical to a personal focus in the course of which one form dies and the new form emerges.[9] This new-life-through-death is of course a basic motif in many religious traditions, and not least in the Christian, so that when the Christian form claims to both replace and also fulfil other forms it is still operating within a familiar religious category: he that loses his life — or his temple — shall find it. The essential meaning of this category is that real fulfilment and the continuity this implies are to be achieved only through the discontinuities of sacrifice and death. It is at this point that a Christian theology of religions is able to make its statements about the uniqueness and finality of Christ as the definitive fulfilment of the temple form.

We also found it necessary to qualify our statements about the actual historical forms of churches by the introduction of the eschatological dimension, and this also must be included in any theology of religions. The essential fulfilment effected by Christ, and achieved only through a radical transposition of the old to the new, appears in history and experience only in foretaste, now here, now there, now more, now less, but always with faith in the promised consummation at the time of the end. This was the principle exhibited in our consideration of the mixed form, the *domus dei et ecclesiae* when we pointed out that it is possible to achieve no more than varying degress of approximation to the pure forms of Jesus-in-community and of its accompanying meeting house. The full effect of the radical transposition and hence of the ultimate fulfilment is not yet manifest empirically and in history but, as the Revelation of St. John expresses it, awaits the advent of the new heavens and the new earth, where all physical temples are no more.

In summary statement, the guiding principle of a Christian theology of religions (including Christianity as a religion) will be to find in Christ their essential fulfilment through radical but eschatological transformation.

17.7 THEOLOGICAL DEFINITION OF THE SACRED PLACE

As our final consideration we shall revert to our presentation of the Christian version of the sacred place as an illustration of this guiding principle, and to bring into sharper theological focus the definitive nature of Jesus-in-community and its significance for the phenomenological understanding of 'temple'. This issue has hovered over our discussion at a number of places and we have been content to describe it as belonging to the fourth and optional phase in the interactions between phenomenology and theology, a phase which would involve the phenomenologist in also doing theology.

17.7.1 *Ontological-Christological definition of temple*

The theologian who has reached this theological definition of 'temple', and done so with the phenomenological assistance we have employed, will then be in a position to claim that the 'essence' of the holy place in religious history will be discovered not by further explorations across the religions but rather by attending to the fulfilment exhibited in the person and work of Jesus Christ-in-community. If he really is the point of reference for the understanding and the management of life, as the sacred place has always sought to be, then the holy place itself including its climax in the temple will best be comprehended in terms of what Christ has done and still does in his community. In other words, having approached the problem of the Christian place of worship through the general phenomenology of religion, as we have done in this essay, the Christian theologian must then reverse the procedure and apply the Christian norm to his understanding of this feature of man's general religious history.

The theologian is saying that Jesus-in-community *is* temple in an ontological and not merely an analogical sense; he is not referring to the physical temple having some analogy with the Christian form whereby the latter may be illustrated up to a certain point; he is reversing the analogy and claiming that physical temples are to a certain degree comparable to the definitive Christian form. A specific example based on a particular feature will show the difference more clearly. The function of temples as meeting points between the human and the divine, standing at the transition from the earthly to the heavenly realm, has been exemplified in the phenomena of doors, entrances, arches, porticoes, vestibules and other means of marking entry into the place of the divine presence.Here the door really and ontologically *was* the door to the divine, the gate of heaven, and effected the transition of the worshippers from the one realm to the other. If we were to call the door a symbol of this transition it would only be with the full meaning of a religious symbol whereby the symbol effects what it symbolizes.When, therefore, the New Testament reports Jesus' saying, 'I am the door', it is not using a vivid illustration based on metaphor or analogy but making a definitive statement: he *is* the door now in a way that fulfils all the functions of temple entrances, for he effects the entry from the earthly to the heavenly realm. Henceforth all physical arrangements for entry to the place of the divine presence, including church doorways, are seen as no more than approximations to a final and radically personalized form. The theological error of the Gothic revivalists lay in reversing this relationship and in finding the ultimate forms and symbols in the physical features of the Gothic church building.

To apply the notion of Jesus-in-community as temple to specific phenomenological features of the temple such as entrances and doors reveals how radical and comprehensive this ontological claim has become.There is, however, no new theological principle involved for temple is but another example of a very wide range of terms which, for the theologian, receive ontological form and final definition in Christ. The New Testament gives similar meaning to the terms life, truth, Logos, and in somewhat more complex manner to the notions of sonship and husbandhood. In such cases, as John McIntyre has put it, 'there is an identity of content between them and the very nature of Christ.... To say so is not to deny either that when Christ first used these terms of himself or was so described by St. John ... there was then an element of analogy in them; or that we may use these terms today in reference to other qualities than Christ.What is meant is that now we know that Christ is the key to what these terms signify, for he is each one, and that other applications are declensions from that absolute meaning, secondary and derivative applications.'[10]

17.7.2 *The two analogies: models for, and models of*

This statement indicates the dual senses in which such terms continue to be used, both as models for (the definitive and ontological theological sense) and as models of (the analogical or comparative phenomenological sense) the reality concerned. Thus Jesus-in-community is one model among others of the temple type, a particular example within a certain cultural and historical milieu with its own flexible and dynamic features but to be understood from its similarities with other temple forms and their functions. This represents the approach made in this work, and this procedure retains many kinds of priority – phenomenological, historical, pedagogical and psychological. On the other hand the definitive Christian theological understanding of Jesus-in-community as the ultimate form, function and meaning of temple provides a model for all other temples with a priority that is both logical and theological.

This dual way in which the temple model operates corresponds to the two basic procedures in all religious understanding. Men may seek to understand the divine in terms of its analogy with human experiences and forms: 'Like as a father pitieth his children, so the Lord pitieth them that fear him' (Psalm 103:13); this is known as the analogy of being, as distinguished from the 'analogy of faith (or of Christ)' where the human is interpreted in terms of its analogies with the divine. Both procedures seem to be involved in all religious knowledge. Knowledge of the divine or ultimate is not reached by infinitely extending human scales of goodness or justice, or projecting human experiences of fatherhood – or of temple – into some ideal form; and yet by proceeding along these scales and making these idealizations on the basis of phenomenological and historical experience we come to a situation where 'the penny drops' and all past forms are seen in a wholly new light. Then the human experiences that have led up to this point are seen as poor approximations, distorted forms, or finite derivatives from the divine and ultimate reality which henceforth supplies the true forms and meanings. A closely analogous process is found in the scientist whose patient experimentation in terms of known forms and theories leads him to the point where the sudden flash of inspiration introduces a whole new insight that transforms previous facts and theories through a new and better model for the phenomena of his field.

It is never possible to dispense with phenomenological and historical study of places of worship and of all forms across the religions of mankind, preparatory though this study may prove to be for the theologian; nor is it easy to stop short of theological study of whatever consummatory forms of temple or of other religious features men may find revealed to them. We have sought to demonstrate this, starting from the human and historical side. We may conclude our study with the statement that the phenomenological approach and the theological interpretation are each indispensible to and inseparable from the other, and that phenomenology may gain a new dimension of meaning when set within a theological context.

Notes

NOTES TO CHAPTER 1: 'METHODS OF APPROACH'

1. Clements, R.E. (1965), *God and Temple* (Oxford, Blackwell).
Cole, A. (1950), *The New Temple* (London, Tyndale Press).
Congar, Y. (1962), *The Mystery of the Temple* (London, Burns & Oates); Eng. transl. of French original: *Le Mystère du Temple*, 1958.
Davies, W.D. (1974), *The Gospel and the Land* (Berkeley, University of California Press).
Gärtner, B. (1965), *The Temple and the Community in Qumran and the New Testament* (Cambridge, Cambridge University Press).
Gaston, L. (1970), *No Stone on Another* (Leiden, E.J. Brill).
Lohmeyer, E. (1961), *Lord of the Temple* (Edinburgh, Oliver & Boyd); Eng. transl. of German original: *Kultus und Evangelium*, 1942.
McKelvey, R.J. (1969), *The New Temple* (London, Oxford University Press).
Freedman, D. N., & Wright, G. E., Eds. (1961), *The Biblical Archaeologist Reader* (Garden City, N.Y., Doubleday).
Besides those mentioned see especially the various works of W.B. Kristensen, Gerardus van der Leeuw, and Mircea Eliade as background to much of this study.
2. Spindler, M. (1968), *Pour une théologie de l'espace* (Neuchâtel, Delachaux et Niestlé).
Torrance, T.F. (1969), *Space, Time and Incarnation* (London, Oxford University Press); see also his *Space, Time and Resurrection* (Edinburgh, Handsel Press, 1977).
3. Smith, J.Z. (1969), 'Earth and Gods', *The Journal of Religion*, 49 (2): 103-127, especially 106-108.
For an even more serious lacuna in Islamics see Adams, C.J., in Kitagawa, J.M. (1967), *The History of Religions* (Chicago, University of Chicago Press), ch. 8.
4. Butler, J.F. (1964), 'Presuppositions in Modern Theologies of the Place of Worship', *Studia Liturgica*, 3 (4): 216.
5. Davies, J.G. (1968), *The Secular Use of Church Buildings* (London, S.C.M. Press), p. 205.

NOTES TO CHAPTER 2: 'THE SACRED PLACE'

1. Cassirer, E. (1955), *The Philosophy of Symbolic Forms* (New Haven, Yale University Press), Vol. 2, p. 103.
2. Kristensen, W.B. (1960), *The Meaning of Religion* (The Hague, M. Nijhoff), p. 359, quoting Seneca, *Epistle* xli, 3, from Kern; also ch. 19 *passim*.
   Parrinder, E.G. (1961), *West African Religion* (London, Epworth Press), p. 61ff.
3. Pedersen, J. (1953), *Israel* (London, Oxford University Press), Vol. 3, pp. 203-214 on consecration legends.
   Also Eichrodt, W. (1961), *Theology of the Old Testament* (London, S.C.M. Press), Vol. 1, pp. 102-107.
4. Reymond, Eve A.E. (1969), *The Mythical Origin of the Egyptian Temple* (Manchester, Manchester University Press), pp. 251-255.
5. Brown, J.E. (1971), *The Sacred Pipe* (Baltimore, Penguin Books), pp. 88-90.
6. Reymond (1969), *Op. cit.*, p. 327.
7. Patai, R. (1967), *Man and Temple in Ancient Jewish Myth and Ritual* (New York, Ktav Publishing House), p. 85.
8. Goodenough, E.R. (1954), *Jewish Symbols in the Greco-Roman Period* (New York, Pantheon Books), Vol. 4, ch. 5, §§ B, C, and p. 210.
9. Eliade, M. (1958), *Patterns in Comparative Religion* (London, Sheed & Ward), pp. 102-108, and Bibliography, p. 122; also his *The Sacred and the Profane* (New York, Harper & Row, 1961), pp. 32-36, and ch. 1.
10. Mirsky, J. (1965), *Houses of God* (London, Constable), p. 45, and *passim*.
11. On above see Lord Raglan (1964), *The Temple and the House* (London, Routledge & Kegan Paul), pp. 147-153.
12. Bouyer, L. (1963), *Rite and Man* (London, Burns & Oates), pp. 155-156.
13. Kristensen (1960), *Op. cit.*, p. 53.
14. Burckhardt, T. (1967), *Sacred Art in East and West* (Bedfont, Middlesex, Perennial Books), pp. 32-33.
    Examples may be multiplied, for they were common in the Middle Ages (the towers of Chartres, the portals of Notre Dame in Paris, King's College chapel in Aberdeen) and are widely found in many other cultural activities (Navaho women weaving imperfections into their rugs and Maoris painting irregularities into their repetitive designs).
15. Charles, R.H., translation, quoted by Eliade (1961), *The Sacred and the Profane*, p. 61.
16. Van der Kroef, J.M. (1959), 'Javanese Messianic Expectations', *Comparative Studies in Society and History*, 1 (4): 301-302.
17. See Baynes, N.H. (1925), *The Byzantine Empire* (London, Williams & Norgate), chs. 2-4 for the working out of this correspondence.
18. See Nelson, H.H., in Freedman, D.N. & Wright, G.E., Eds. (1961), *The Biblical Archaeologist Reader* (New York, Doubleday), pp. 152-154.
    Some primal religions may carry this emphasis even further, as with the Nuer of the Sudan who build no sanctuaries since Kwoth (the ultimate Spirit) is found everywhere.
19. Clements, R.E. (1965), *God and Temple* (Oxford, Blackwell), p. 63, as against G. von Rad's disjunction between theophany-temples and dwelling-temples.

NOTES TO CHAPTER 3: 'THE TEMPLE TYPE'

1. Speck, F.G. (1931), 'A Study of the Delaware Indian Big House ceremony...', *Publications of Pennsylvania Historical Commission*, Vol. 2, p. 22.
2. See Lord Raglan (1964), *The Temple and the House* (London, Routledge & Kegan Paul).
3. Monod-Herzen, G.E. (1953-54), 'Evolution and Significance of the Hindu Temple', *Asia* 3: 249.
4. Hiroa, Te Rangi (1962), *The Coming of the Maori* (Wellington, Whitcombe & Tombs), pp. 477-484.
5. Monod-Herzen (1953-54), *Op. cit.*, p. 258.
6. Oppenheim, A.L., in Freedman, D.N. & Wright, G.E., Eds. (1961), *The Biblical Archaeologist Reader* (New York, Doubleday), p. 165.
7. Oppenheim (1961), *Op. cit.*, pp. 161, 168.
8. Glueck, N. (1966), *Deities and Dolphins: the Story of the Nabataeans* (London, Cassell), p. 64.
9. See Thompson, L.C. (1969), *Chinese Religion: an Introduction* (Belmont, California, Dickenson Publishing Co.), pp. 60-61.
10. Boston, J. (1959), 'Alosi Shrines', *Nigeria Magazine*, 61: 161.
11. Ezeanya, S.N. (1966), 'The "sacred place" in the traditional religion of the Igbo people...', *West African Religion* (Nsukka), 6:1-9.
12. Mbanefo, F. (1962), 'The Iba House of Onitsha', *Nigeria Magazine*, 72: 18-19.
13. Swithenbank, M. (1969), *Ashanti Fetish Houses* (Accra, Ghana University Press), *passim*.

NOTES TO CHAPTER 4: 'THE TEMPLE IN JERUSALEM'

1. See Wright, G.E., in Freedman, D.N. & Wright, G.E., Eds. (1961), *The Biblical Archaeologist Reader* (New York, Doubleday), p. 174.
2. De Vaux, R. (1961), *Ancient Israel* (New York, McGraw-Hill), p. 310.
3. As Clements, R.E. (1965), *God and Temple* (Oxford, Blackwell), p. 61.
4. Clements (1965), *Op. cit.*, pp. 55, 59.
5. Congar, Y. (1962), *The Mystery of the Temple* (London, Burns & Oates), pp. 49-51.
6. For this theme in the sources see McKelvey, R.J. (1969), *The New Temple* (London, Oxford University Press), pp. 15-20.
7. Quoted by McKelvey (1969), *Op. cit.*, p. 189, and see his Appendix A, *passim*.
8. Patai, R. (1967), *Man and Temple...* (New York, Ktav Publishing House), p. 85, with the Hebrew terms transliterated.
9. Wright (1961), *Op. cit.*, p. 180.
10. De Vaux (1961), *Op. cit.*, pp. 328-329.
11. Daniélou, J. (1957), 'Le Symbolisme du Temple de Jérusalem chez Philon et Josèphe', in *Le Symbolisme cosmique des Monuments Religieux* (Rome, Istituto Italiano per il Medio et Extremo Oriente), pp. 83-90.
12. Quoted from Rabbi Pinhas ben Ya'ir by Patai (1967), *Op. cit.*, pp. 108-109.
13. Josephus is summarized in Patai (1967), *Op. cit.*, pp. 112-113.

14. E.g., Nelson, H.H. (1961), in *The Biblical Archaeologist Reader*, pp. 150-151; Wright, G.E. (1961), in *Idem*, p. 170.
15. Clements (1965), *Op. cit.*, p. 67, and see his whole discussion.
16. Clements (1965), *Op. cit.*, p. 106. n. 3.
17. Ahlstrom, G.W. (1963), *Aspects of Syncretism in Israelite Religion* (Lund, Gleerup), p. 46.
18. Clements (1965), *Op. cit.*, ch. 3 surveys the whole question of ark and throne, and we follow his conclusions.
19. See Pedersen, J. (1953), *Israel*, Vol. 3, p. 280; also, pp. 254ff., 280f..
20. Clements (1965), *Op. cit.*, p. 94.
21. Clements (1965), *Op. cit.*, pp. 64, 79.
22. Clements (1965), *Op. cit.*, p. 117, n. 3.
23. See McKelvey (1969), *Op. cit.*, ch. 3.

NOTES TO CHAPTER 5: 'THE PROBLEM OF THE JERUSALEM TEMPLE'

1. Clements (1965), *Op. cit.*, p. 93, and see ch. 6 *passim*.
2. Clements (1965), *Op. cit.*, p. 118, and see pp. 109-122.
3. Simon, M. (1952), 'La prophétie de Nathan et le Temple', *Revue d'Histoire et de Philosophie Religieuse*, 32: 41-58; also his 'St Stephen and the Jerusalem Temple', *Journal of Ecclesiastical History* (1951), 2 (2): 127-142.
4. Both quotations given in McKelvey's discussion (1968), *The New Temple* (London, Oxford University Press), pp. 53-54: Seneca, *Epistles*, 41: 1; Philo, *De Sobrietate*, 62.
5. Gärtner (1965), *Op. cit.*, pp. 14, 16, 18, 19.
6. Filson, F.V., in Freedman, D.N. & Wright, G.E., Eds. (1961), *The Biblical Archaeologist Reader* (New York, Doubleday), p. 185.
7. Clements (1965), *Op. cit.*, p. 62.
8. Van Leeuwen, A.T. (1964), *Christianity in World History* (London, Edinburgh House Press), pp. 81-82.
9. Van Leeuwen (1964), *Op. cit.*, p. 81.
10. Clements (1965), *Op. cit.*, pp. 61-62.
11. Kaufmann, Y. (1961), *The Religion of Israel* (London, George Allen & Unwin), p. 269, and see pp. 267-268, 289-290, 303-305 for his whole argument.
    Other efforts to resolve the apparent tension are found in M. Haran, a pupil of Kaufmann, who argues that there was little conflict between *domus dei* and covenant ideas — see his 'The divine presence in the Israelite cult and the cultic institutions', *Biblica* (1969), 70: 251-267. Harran's important work (1978), *Temples and Temple-Service in Ancient Israel* (Oxford, Clarendon Press), appeared too late to be used in this study.
12. Kaufmann (1961), *Op. cit.*, p. 290.
13. Childs, B.S. (1960), *Myth and reality in the Old Testament* (London, S.C.M. Press), pp. 90-94.
14. Childs (1960), *Op. cit.*, p. 92.
15. Kaufmann (1961), *Op. cit.*, p. 290.
16. Childs (1960), *Op. cit.*, p. 91.

17. Eichrodt,W. (1961), *Theology of the Old Testament* (London, S.C.M. Press), Vol.1, p.270.
18. Kaufmann (1961), *Op. cit.*, p.290; this would seem to be exemplified in the synagogue.
19. As example of a radical critique of the sacred place from an apparently unsophisticated quarter we may quote the gross imitation of coitus by two clowns right in the sacred shrine of the Hopi Indian people in Arizona, as recorded at the turn of this century. See Tedlocks, D. & B. (1975), *Teachings from the American Earth* (New York, Liveright), p.115.

NOTES TO CHAPTER 6: 'NEW FORMS: TABERNACLE AND SYNAGOGUE'

1. We follow the reconstruction of Davies, G.H. (1962), in *The Interpreter's Dictionary of the Bible* (Nashville & New York, Abingdon Press), Vol. 4, pp.504aff.; for a similar position see Cross, F.M.Jr. (1947), 'The Priestly Tabernacle', *Biblical Archaeologist*, 10 (3): 45-68, reprinted in *The Biblical Archaeologist Reader* (1961), pp.201-228.
2. See Cross (1947), *Op. cit.*, pp.217-219, and De Vaux, R. (1961), *Ancient Israel* (New York, McGraw-Hill), pp.294-297, on this tent.
3. M. Haran in various Hebrew publications and a dissertation; in English, see his 'The Nature of the "'Ohel Mo'edh" in Pentateuchal Sources', *Journal of Semitic Studies* (1960), 5 (1): 50-65.
4. See Rylaarsdam, J.C. (1951), in *The Interpreter's Dictionary of the Bible* (Nashville & New York, Abingdon Press), Vol.1, pp.844-846, 1027-1028.
5. Haran (1960), *Op. cit.*, pp.53-56.
6. Ahlstrom, G.W. (1963), *Aspects of Syncretism in Israelite Religion* (Lund, Gleerup), p.30, n.2.
7. Cross (1947), *Op. cit.*, p.227.
8. Kaufmann, Y. (1961), *The Religion of Israel* (London, George Allen & Unwin), p.184.
9. Kraus, H.-J. (1966), *Worship in Israel* (Oxford, Blackwell), pp.128-134.
10. Louvel, F. (1963), 'Le mystère de nos églises', *La Maison-Dieu*, 63 (3) [Printed (4)]: 8 (our translation).
11. Stevenson, F.R. (1961), 'Architecture and Liturgy', *Scottish Journal of Theology*, 14 (4): 394, *et passim*. The same model has also been suggested for modern synagogues: see Rubinstein, R.L., in Hunt, R.L., Ed. (1969), *Revolution, Place and Symbol* (No place, International Congress on Religion, Architecture and the Visual Arts), p.151 – a 'tent-like, impermanent structure'.
12. Chapman, P. & Lake, C. (1959), 'Towards a theology of architecture', *Motive* (Nashville), 19 (8): 32.
13. Moore, G.F. (1962), *Judaism in the First Centuries of the Christian Era* (Cambridge, Mass., Harvard University Press), Vol.1, pp.31ff.
14. Moore (1962), *Op. cit.*, Vol.1, pp.281-287, 306-307.
15. Moore (1962), *Op. cit.*, Vol.2, p.12.
16. May, H.G. (1944), 'Synagogues in Palestine', *Biblical Archaeologist*, 7 (1): 1-20; reprinted in *The Biblical Archaeologist Reader* (1961), pp.229-250,

traces further temple influences in later synagogues; see also Sonne, I. (1962), 'Synagogues', in *The Interpreter's Dictionary of the Bible*, Vol. 4, pp. 476 ff.
17. Moore (1962), *Op. cit.*, Vol. 1, p. 436, with other examples.
18. Filson, F.V. (1961), in *The Biblical Archaeologist Reader*, pp. 192-193.
19. It is true that some temple-type sacred places provided for an assembly of the worshippers; we have named two Greek temples large enough for this, also the temples of the mystery cults of antiquity, and even open-air sanctuaries such as Stonehenge or other large stone circles might have enclosed a congregation; such uses, however, are incidental to the main purposes and features of the sanctuary which retains the typical characteristics of a house of God or sacred place.
20. See Rutschman, L.A. (1962), *Altar and Sacrifice in the Old Testament Nomadic Period with Relation to Sacred Space and Sacred Time* (Southern California School of Theology Th.D. dissertation), as in *Dissertation Abstracts* (1963), 24 (3): 1266, from which we extract the following: '... sacred space, although reinterpreted, was retained. Sacred time, however, was greatly modified to permit a linear view which leaves room for the prophetic thrust of promise and fulfillment.'

NOTES TO CHAPTER 7: 'THE NEW TEMPLE OF THE NEW TESTAMENT'

1. McKelvey, R.J. (1968), *The New Temple* (London, Oxford University Press), pp. 179, 180.
2. Congar, Y. (1962), *The Mystery of the Temple* (London, Burns & Oates), p. 117.
3. Todd, A.S. (1963), 'Our Standards and Traditions in Worship', *Church Service Society Annual*, 33: 9.
4. See Cole, A. (1950), *The New Temple* (London, Tyndale Press), pp. 18-26, 53-54 for these conclusions. The more recent massive study of Gaston, L. (1970), *No Stone on Another* (Leiden, Brill) argues that Jesus could not have uttered the first part of the statement in Mark 14:58, which goes back to Stephen, but that the second part is clearly authentic; see his Summary, pp. 242-243. Should this be so our discussion is not greatly affected since it is the second half that is more integral to our position. See further on Stephen below.
5. McKelvey (1968), *Op. cit.*, pp. 71-72.
6. Moule, C.F.D. (1950), 'Sanctuary and Sacrifice in the Church of the New Testament', *Journal of Theological Studies*, n.s., 1 (1): 34; also *passim*, on the views we present, especially the full significance of the term 'body'; Congar (1962), *Op. cit.*, pp. 132-150 surveys the whole question.
7. Eichrodt, W. (1961), *Theology of the Old Testament* (London, S.C.M. Press), Vol. 1, p. 107.
8. Cole (1950), *Op. cit.*, p. 42. It is still possible that the explanation is simply that all New Testament documents were written before A.D. 70, as has been recently argued again by Robinson, J.A.T. (1976), *Re-dating the New Testament* (London, S.C.M. Press). Yet another explanation might lie in the continuation of the sacrificial ritual until A.D. 135, as has been discussed by Clark, K.W. (1960), 'Worship in Jerusalem Temple after A.D. 70', *New Testament Studies*, 6: 269-280.

9. Cole (1950), *Op. cit.*, p. 42.
10. On Stephen, see especially, Simon, M. (1958), *St. Stephen and the Hellenists in the Primitive Church* (London, Longmans); or more briefly in his *Jewish Sects at the Time of Jesus* (Philadelphia, Fortress Press, 1967), pp. 96-105; also his articles cited in *Op. cit.* (1958), ch. 5, n. 3. We follow Simon's interpretations, except for his view of Stephen as more a reformer of Judaism than the apostle of the gospel that he appears to have been for the early Church. Gaston (1970), *Op. cit.*, pp. 154-161, presents Stephen as representing the climax of growing opposition to the temple among various groups within Judaism, and so agrees with Simon. It is quite possible that Stephen was an extremist on this issue and at variance here with the early Church, which otherwise held him in high regard (Acts 6: 5-10).
11. McKelvey (1968), *Op. cit.*, p. 98; we are indebted throughout to his expositions of the New Testament epistles in his chs. 7-9.
12. Congar (1962), *Op. cit.*, pp. 153-154, 161.
13. Quoted with other passages by Shaw, R. D. (1903), *The Pauline Epistles* (Edinburgh, T. & T. Clark), pp. 223-224.
14. Creedon, J. (1965), *The Sacred Place – Some New Testament Evidence* (Seminar Papers 5, Department of Religion, University of Nigeria), p. 4, drawing on Lyonnet, S. (1960), *De peccato et redemptione* (Rome), pp. 112-113, and Moraldi, L. (1956), *Expiazione sacrificale e riti expiatorii...* (Rome), ch. 5.
15. Stibbs, A. M. (1959), *The First Epistle General of Peter: A Commentary* (London, Tyndale Press), p. 100.
16. We follow here Balzer, K. (1965), 'The Meaning of the Temple in the Lukan Writings', *Harvard Theological Review*, 58 (3): 263-277, who in turn draws on Conzelmann, H. (1960), *The Theology of St. Luke* (London, Faber & Faber); see also Laurentin, R. (1966), *Jésus au Temple...* (Paris, J. Gabalda & Cie), showing Luke's view of the intimate relation between Jesus and the temple at all stages of his life.
17. For a good account of the temple in this epistle, and especially of the influence upon it of Stephen's individualistic position, see Manson, W. (1951), *The Epistle to the Hebrews* (London, Hodder & Stoughton).
18. McKelvey (1968), *Op. cit.*, p. 173, and see also his whole treatment, pp. 155-178.
19. McKelvey (1968), *Op. cit.*, p. 176. Note also how in Ezekiel's vision the new Jerusalem is called 'The Lord is there' (48:35).

NOTES TO CHAPTER 8: 'PHENOMENOLOGICAL ANALYSIS OF NEW TESTAMENT CONTRIBUTIONS'

1. Congar, Y. (1962), *The Mystery of the Temple* (London, Burns & Oates), p. 51, n. 9 draws a like contrast between 'the useless efforts of the prophets of Baal' and 'the simple prayer' of Elijah, upon which 'the fire of the Lord fell' (I Kings 18:19ff.).
2. On the Johannine material we are indebted to McKelvey, J. R. (1969), *The New Temple* (London, Oxford University Press), pp. 75-84.

3. Spindler, M. (1969), *Pour une Théologie de l'Espace* (Neuchâtel, Delachaux et Niestlé), pp. 56f.
4. See Lohmeyer, E. (1961), *Lord of the Temple* (Edinburgh, Oliver & Boyd), p. 85; also Cullman, O. (1959), 'L'Opposition contre le Temple de Jérusalem...', *New Testament Studies*, 5 (3): 166-167, on Bo Reicke's (1959) demonstration in *Glaube und Leben der Urgemeinde*, pp. 136ff., that Stephen's survey of Israel's history in Acts 7 was to show how the essential revelations of God had been given outside Canaan; also Von Allmen, J.J. (1958) in his *Vocabulary of the Bible* (London, Lutterworth), pp. 284-285, and especially Davies, W.D. (1974), *The Gospel and the Land* (Berkeley, University of California Press). Davies presents an extensive discussion of the temple, pp. 150-154, of Paul, pp. 185-194, and of John's Gospel, pp. 289-296, that supports our own position on the de-sacralization of temple, Jerusalem and the land of Israel.
5. See Eliade, M. (1961), *Images and Symbols* (London, Harvill), pp. 39-40.
6. Eliade (1961), *Op. cit.*, pp. 42-43, 161-163; also his *Patterns in Comparative Religion* (London, Sheed & Ward, 1958), pp. 292-294, 375-379; De Lubac, H. (1953), *Aspects of Buddhism* (London & New York, Sheed & Ward), ch. 2.
7. Eliade, M. (1961), *The Sacred and the Profane* (New York, Harper & Row), p. 64.
8. Congar (1962), *Op. cit.*, p. 134, quoting Cullman, O. (1951), *Les Sacraments dans L'Évangile johannique...* (Paris), p. 43.
9. Levy, R. (1963), *Religious Conceptions of the Stone Age* (New York, Harper & Row), pp. 134-135.
10. Senft, C., in Von Allmen, J.J., Ed. (1958), *Op. cit.*, p. 180.
11. *Idem.*
12. Eliade, M. (1961), *The Sacred and the Profane*, pp. 172-178.
13. Patai, R. (1967), *Man and Temple...* (New York, Ktav Publishing House), pp. 113-115.
14. Balzer, K. (1965), 'The Meaning of the Temple in the Lukan Writings', *Harvard Theological Review*, 58 (3): 276, suggests that Luke's singular 'cloud' in Acts 1:9, as against 'clouds' elsewhere, links with the Ezekiel tradition (1:4, etc.) of the cloud as the Presence.
15. Eliade, M. (1961), *Images and Symbols*, p. 170; we think the term 'theophany' could be misleadingly inadequate.
16. Congar (1962), *Op. cit.*, p. 209.
17. Von Rad, G. (1966), *The Problem of the Hexateuch* (Edinburgh, Oliver & Boyd), p. 124, and referring especially to John 1:14; II Corinthians 12:9; Hebrews 8:2,9,11; Revelation 7:15; 15:5; 21:3.
18. See Louvel, F. (1963), 'Le Mystère de nos églises', *La Maison-Dieu*, 63 (3) [printed as (4)]: 17.
19. Davies, G.H., in *The Interpreter's Dictionary of the Bible* (Nashville & New York, Abingdon Press), Vol. 4, p. 506b.
20. McKelvey (1969), *Op. cit.*, p. 73, and also p. 150; cf. S.G.F. Brandon's interpretation as Mark's apologia to the Romans, *Jesus and the Zealots* (Manchester, Manchester University Press, 1967), pp. 227-230.
21. Cf. the legend of the Buddha showing how a stupa was to be built: see De Lubac, H. (1953), *Op. cit.*, p. 147, n. 9, quoting from Focillon, H. (1921), *L'Art bouddhique* (Paris), pp. 33-34.

22. Todd, A.S. (1963), 'Our Standards and Traditions in Worship', *Church Service Society Annual*, 33: 10, summarizing Brunner, P., 'Zum Lehre vom Gottesdienst', in *Leiturgia* Lieferung 2 (Greek transliterated).
23. Eliade, M. (1961), *Images and Symbols*, p. 168.
24. Cox, Harvey (1965), 'The Restoration of a Sense of Place', *The Living Light* (Fall, mimeo reprint by National Council of Churches of Christ in the U.S.A.), p. 4.
25. This congruence is illustrated by Maertens, T. (1970), *Assembly for Christ* (London, Darton, Longman & Todd), p. 70, with discussion of some eight situations where the gospel writers contrast the private house with the temple.

NOTES TO CHAPTER 9: 'CHURCHES IN THE EARLY CHRISTIAN CENTURIES'

1. Cardinal Lercaro (1957), in *Documents in Sacred Architecture* (Collegeville, The Liturgical Press), p. 5.
2. Acts 1:13, 2:46, 20:7-8; Romans 16:3,5; Colossians 4:5; Philemon 2.
3. Lewis, M.J.T. (1966), *Temples in Roman Britain* (Cambridge, Cambridge University Press), p. 108, also pp. 112-113; for fullest account see Painter, K.S. (1969), 'The Lullingstone Wall Plaster: An Aspect of Christianity in Roman Britain', *British Museum Quarterly*, 33 (3-4): 131-150.
4. Sources and fuller accounts on these points and on the theme of this chapter in Krautheimer, R. (1965), *Early Christian and Byzantine Architecture* (Harmondsworth, Penguin Books), especially parts I and II; also, Davies, J.G. (1952), *The Origin and Development of Early Christian Architecture* (London), or his (1968) *The Secular Use of Church Buildings* (London, S.C.M. Press), pp. 1-17 for useful summary.
5. For vivid description of the new situation see Dix, G. (1945), *The Shape of the Liturgy* (London, Dacre Press), pp. 306-312.
6. Krautheimer (1965), *Op. cit.*, p. 19.
7. Davies (1952), *Op. cit.*, ch. 2.
8. Krautheimer (1965), *Op. cit.*, p. 44.
9. Davies (1952), *Op. cit.*, pp. 26-30.
10. Davies (1952), *Op. cit.*, p. 80.
11. Davies (1952), *Op. cit.*, p. 120.
12. See Davies (1952), *Op. cit.*, ch. 5, and Davies (1968), *Op. cit.*, p. 12.
13. Krautheimer (1965), *Op. cit.*, pp. xxiii-xxiv.
14. Mbiti, J.S. (1969), *African Religions and Philosophy* (London, Heinemann), pp. 154-155.
15. James, E.O. (1965), *From Cave to Cathedral* (London, Thames & Hudson), pp. 100-103, 118, for illustrated account of the development of the pyramid with mortuary temple from royal burials.
16. Snyder, G.F. (1969), 'Survey and "new" thesis on the bones of Peter', *Biblical Archaeologist*, 32 (1): 15.
17. Butler, J.F. (1959), 'Further thoughts on Church architecture in India', *Indian Journal of Theology*, 8 (4): 137.
18. See Krautheimer (1965), *Op. cit.*, pp. 30-38, and Snyder (1969), *Op. cit.*, *passim*.

19. Wightman, E.M. (1970), *Roman Trier and the Treveri* (London, Rupert Hart-Davis), pp. 230-231.
20. The term 'pagan' is not used pejoratively but merely as the most convenient term for religions outside the Judaeo-Christian tradition.
21. See Harnack, A. (1961), *History of Dogma* (New York, Dover Publications & London, Constable), Vol. 4, ch. 4, p. 314.
22. Snyder (1969), *Op. cit.*, p. 22.
23. Congar (1962), *The Mystery of the Temple*, p. 203, and quoting the 14th century Nicholas Cabasalis, *La Vie en Jésus Christ* (Fr. transl., n.d.), pp. 142, 147.
24. Harnack (1961), *Op. cit.*, p. 314; for early rites see Duchesne, L. (1919), *Christian Worship...* (London, S.P.C.K.), ch. 2, especially, pp. 405-407.
25. Bouyer, L. (1963), *Rite and Man* (London, Burns & Oates), p. 187.
26. See Davies (1968), *Op. cit.*, pp. 18-21, 141-144, with sources.
27. Hammond, P. (1960), *Liturgy and Architecture* (London, Barrie & Rockliff), p. 160.
28. Davies (1952), *Op. cit.*, p. 115.
29. Fiddes, V. (1961), *The Architectural Requirements of Protestant Worship* (Toronto, Ryerson Press), p. 36, quoting MacGregor, W.M. (1945), *The Making of a Preacher* (London, S.C.M. Press), p. 16. On the iconostasis being a later Byzantine rather than a primitive development in Eastern Orthodoxy, see Walter, J. (1971), 'The origins of the iconostasis', *Eastern Churches Review*, 30 (3): 251-267.
30. Lercaro (1957), *Op. cit.*, pp. 5-6. The Cardinal was appointed to lead the Liturgical Commission that was to implement Vatican II's 'Constitution on the Sacred Liturgy' of 1963.
31. Eliade, M. (1961), *The Sacred and the Profane*, p. 62; also Krautheimer (1965), *Op. cit.*, pp. 212-213; for convenient summary of the impact of paganism see Jungmann, J.A. (1960), *The Early Liturgy to the Time of Gregory the Great* (London, Darton, Longman & Todd), ch. 11.
32. See Hastings, J., Ed. (1908), *Encyclopaedia of Religion and Ethics* (Edinburgh, T. & T. Clark), Vol. 1: pp. 171b-172a.
33. Dix, G. (1945), *Op. cit.*, pp. 387-396 for a fair account of the 4th century, and Krautheimer (1965), *Op. cit.*, pp. 64-65, 127, for the delayed adoption of 'classicism' in buildings.

NOTES TO CHAPTER 10: 'A THOUSAND YEARS OF THE *DOMUS DEI*'

1. Following the analysis of Krautheimer, R. (1942), 'Introduction to an "Iconography" of mediaeval architecture', *Journal of the Warburg and Courtauld Institutes*, 5: 20-33.
2. Quoted from Migne *PL* CLXXII, Vol. 2 (1929), p. 168, by Knowles in: Knowles, D. & Obolensky, D. (1969), *The Middle Ages* (London, Dartman, Longman & Todd), p. 394.
3. As quoted from Chabot, J.B. (1903), *Synodicum orientale: Receuil des synodes nestoriens*, pp. 408, 441 in: Hastings, J., Ed. (1918), *Encyclopaedia of Religion and Ethics* (Edinburgh, T. & T. Clark), Vol. 10, p. 216.

4. See Krautheimer (1942), *Op. cit.*, pp. 2-20, which we follow.
5. Krautheimer (1942), *Op. cit.*, p. 11.
6. Krautheimer (1942), *Op. cit.*, pp. 19, 16.
7. Addleshaw, G.W.O. & Etchells, F. (1948), *The Architectural Setting of Anglican Worship* (London, Faber & Faber), pp. 16-17.
8. Gutton, A. (1956), *Conversations sur l'architecture* (Paris), Vol. 3A, p. 127, as quoted by Biéler, A. (1965), *Architecture in Worship* (Edinburgh, Oliver & Boyd), p. 37.
9. Sherrard, P., in: Allchin, A.M., Ed. (1967), *Sacrament and Image* (London, Fellowship of St. Alban and St. Sergius), p. 63.
10. Following the version of Sherrard (1967), *Op. cit.*, pp. 60-61.
11. Rice, D.T. (1954), *Byzantine Art* (London, Penguin Books), p. 65.
12. James, E.O. (1958), *The Beginnings of Religion* (London, Hutchinson), p. 144.
13. From Book I, ch. 4 of Durandus as in: Neale, J.M. & Webb, B. (1843), *The Symbolism of Churches and Church Ornaments: A Translation of the First Book of the Rationale Divinorum Officiorum, written by William Durandus sometime Bishop of Mende* (Leeds, T.W. Green), pp. 88-92. The *Rationale* was the 'first work from the pen of an uninspired writer ever printed' – in 1459; its influence is indicated by some thirty-eight different editions or printings before 1515 held by the British Museum.
14. Krautheimer (1942), *Op. cit.*, p. 1.
15. Forsyth, P.T. (1911), *Christ on Parnassus* (London, Hodder & Stoughton; repr. London, Independent Press, 1959), pp. 183-184.
16. Drummond, A.L. (1934), *The Church Architecture of Protestantism* (Edinburgh, T. & T. Clark), p. 257.
17. Forsyth (1911), *Op. cit.*, p. 184.
18. Drummond (1934), *Op. cit.*, p. 257.
19. *Idem.*
20. Drummond (1934), *Op. cit.*, p. 329, n. 4, quoting A.C. McGiffert Jr..
21. Drummond (1934), *Op. cit.*, p. 258.
22. Otto, R. (1957), *Mysticism East and West* (New York, Meridian Books), pp. 185-187.
23. Forsyth (1911), *Op. cit.*, pp. 183f.
24. Von Simson, O. (1956), *The Gothic Cathedral* (London, Routledge & Kegan Paul; New York, Pantheon Books) as expounded in Fiddes, V. (1961), *The Architectural Requirements of Protestant Worship* (Toronto, Ryerson Press), pp. 38-39.
25. Cram, R.A. (1924), *Church Building: A Study of the Principles of Architecture in their Relation to the Church* (Boston, Jones, Marshall Co.), p. 89 – a much-quoted passage.
26. Davies, J.G. (1962), 'Architecture and Theology', *Expository Times*, 73 (8): 232-233.
27. Wittkower, R. (1962), *Architectural Principles of the Age of Humanism* (London, A. Tiranti), pp. 8, 9. We are indebted to this excellent account throughout this section.
28. Pollio, Vitruvius (1961), *De Architectura*, I, 2; English transl. *Ten Books on*

Architecture (London, Constable), see I, 1: 72-75, for the analogy between
the temple and the body.
29. Wittkower (1962), *Op. cit.*, pp. 14, 16.
30. Palladio, *Quattro Libri dell'Architectura*, Vol. 4, p. 2, as quoted by Wittkower,
(1962), *Op. cit.*, p. 23.
31. Wittkower (1962), *Op. cit.*, p. 27.
32. Drummond (1934), *Op. cit.*, p. 16.
33. See Addleshaw & Etchells (1948), *Op. cit.*, pp. 19-22, with plans.
34. Bucher, F. (1960), 'Cistercian Architectural Purism', *Comparative Studies in
Society and History*, 3 (1): 93; see also Bilson, J. (1909), 'The Architecture
of the Cistercians with Special Reference to ... England', *The Archaeological
Journal*, 66: 185-280.
35. Sources collected by Wakefield, W.L. & Evans, A.P. (1969), *Heresies of the
Middle Ages* (New York & London, Columbia University Press), see Index,
'church buildings'.
36. See further, Ullendorf, E. (1956), 'Hebraic-Jewish Elements in Abyssinian
(Monophysite) Christianity', *Journal of Semitic Studies*, 1 (3): 216-256, especially pp. 233-236; also Pawlikowski, J.T. (1972), *Journal of Religion in
Africa*, 4 (3): 178-199.

NOTES TO CHAPTER 11: 'REFORMATIONS AND THEIR AFTERMATHS'

1. Brion, M. (1960), 'Ces palais où Dieu habite', *L'Architecture religieuse de 1400
à 1800* (Paris), p. 47, quoted by Biéler, A. (1965), *Architecture in Worship*
(Edinburgh, Oliver & Boyd), p. 68.
2. Davies, J.G. (1968), *The Secular Use of Church Buildings* (London, S.C.M.
Press), pp. 119-121, 135.
3. By Senn, O.H. (1962), 'Church Building and Liturgy in the Protestant Church',
in: *Lucerne International Joint Conference on Church Architecture...* (New
York, National Council of Churches of Christ in the U.S.A.), p. 8.
4. *Ibid.*
5. Calvin, *Institutes*, IV, i: 5.
6. *Idem*, III, xx: 30.
7. *Idem*, IV, ii: 3.
8. *Idem*, III, xx: 30.
9. *Idem*, Prefatory Address to King Francis I ..., 6, quoting Hilary of Poitiers,
Against the Arians..., p. xii.
10. 'Sermon on Deut. 16: 13-17', quoted by Biéler (1965), *Op. cit.*, p. 49.
11. Section XV, 'For Reparation of Churches'.
12. *Scripta Anglicana* (Basel, 1577), p. 457, as translated by Evans, E. in: Addleshaw, G.W.O. & Etchells, F. (1948), *The Architectural Setting of Anglican
Worship* (London, Faber & Faber), pp. 245-246.
13. Ch. XXII, 'Of holy and ecclesiastic meetings', as translated by Leith, J.H., Ed.,
(1963), *The Creeds of the Churches* (Garden City, N.Y., Doubleday & Co.),
pp. 176-177.
14. As quoted by Von Allmen, J.J. (1964), 'A Short Theology of the Place of Worship', *Studia Liturgica*, 3 (3): 161, 166.

15. *Certain Sermons or Homilies appointed to be read in Churches in the Time of the Late Queen Elizabeth* (Oxford, University Press, 1844), pp. 243, 307, 157.
16. *Of the Laws of Ecclesiastical Polity*, V, xv: 3; see also xvi: 1.
17. *Idem*, V, xii: 2.
18. *Idem*, V, xiv.
19. *Idem*, V, xvi: 1.
20. *Idem*, V, xvii: 6.
21. *Idem*, V, xv: 3; see also xi: 2.
22. *Idem*, V, xiv.
23. *Idem*, V, xvii: 6; see also 1-5.
24. *Idem*, V, xvi: 2.
25. Short, E.H. (1951), *A History of Religious Architecture* (London, Eyre & Spottiswoode), p. 277.
26. For examples, see Langley Chapel, Shropshire, and Hailes, Gloucestershire, as in Addleshaw & Etchells (1948), *Op. cit.*, pp. 111-112, also Pl. VI, and the full discussion, pp. 22-24.
27. Bruggink, D.J. & Droppers, C.H. (1965), *Christ and Architecture* (Grand Rapids, Eerdmans), pp. 82-89, with photos.
28. *Reformatio Ecclesiarum Hassiae* as translated by Senn, O.H. (1962), *Op. cit.*, p. 5.
29. Addleshaw & Etchells (1948), *Op. cit.*, pp. 24-25, 109 n. 9.
30. Short, H.L. (1945), 'The Architecture of the Old Meeting Houses', *Transactions of the Unitarian Historical Society*, 8 (3): 105.
31. Sprott, G.W. (1882), *Worship and Offices of the Church of Scotland* (Edinburgh, Wm. Blackwood & Sons), p. 232.
32. Garvan, A. (1950), 'The Protestant Plain Style before 1630', *Journal of the Society of Architectural Historians*, 9 (3): 11; this is an excellent survey of little-known history.
33. Short (1945), *Op. cit.*, p. 101.
34. See Biéler (1965), *Op. cit.*, pp. 58-59, for sketches of adaptations in Switzerland.
35. Addleshaw & Etchells (1948), *Op. cit.*, pp. 126 n. 2, 130, 132; also *The Cathedral Church of St. Martin* (Gloucester, 1965), pp. 17-18, 20.
36. Hammond, P. (1960), *Liturgy and Architecture* (London, Barrie & Rockliff), pp. 139-149.
37. Senn (1962), *Op. cit.*, pp. 8-9.
38. Drummond, A.L. (1934), *The Church Architecture of Protestantism* (Edinburgh, T. & T. Clark), p. 33 and footnotes; also Biéler (1965), *Op. cit.*, pp. 62-67, with sketches of Huguenot and other churches; and Garvan (1950), *Op. cit.*, pp. 6-7, figs. 4, 5, and references.
39. Senn, O.H. (1958), 'La construction d'églises contemporaines', *Bulletin du Centre Protestant d'Études*, juin, pp. 6, 8, as quoted in translation by Biéler (1965), *Op. cit.*, p. 63.
40. Garvan (1950), *Op. cit.*, p. 6.
41. Garvan (1950), *Op. cit.*, p. 5.
42. Senn (1961), *Op. cit.*, p. 10.

43. On Scotland see Hay, G. (1957), *The Architecture of Scottish Post-Reformation Churches 1560-1843* (Oxford, Clarendon Press); and Lindsay, I. G. (1960), *The Scottish Parish Kirk* (Edinburgh, St. Andrew Press).
44. Garvan (1950), *Op. cit.*, pp. 11-12, with illustrations.
45. Garvan (1950), *Op. cit.*, p. 12.
46. We draw upon the following convenient sources: Williams, G.H. (1962), *The Radical Reformation* (Philadelphia, Westminster Press); and especially *The Mennonite Encyclopaedia* (Hallsboro, Kansas, Mennonite Brethren Publishing House, 1955), Vol. 1, pp. 146-151, also Plates I-XIII, and III, article 'Meeting Houses'.
47. Williams (1962), *Op. cit.*, p. 644.
48. Lercaro (1957), in *Documents for Sacred Architecture* (Collegeville, Minn., Liturgical Press), p. 7.

NOTES TO CHAPTER 12: 'ADVANCES AND RETREATS'

1. *Confession of Faith*, ch. 1: 6.
2. *Idem*, ch. 21: 6.
3. See Davies, J.G. (1968), *The Secular Use of Church Buildings* (London, S.C.M. Press), pp. 106-108, 113-119, for a selection of these.
4. *Dispute Against the English Popish Ceremonies obtruded upon the Church of Scotland* (1637), p. 123, quoted by Davies, H. (1948), *The Worship of the English Puritans* (London, Dacre Press), p. 269.
5. *The Journal of George Fox* (Rev. ed.: Cambridge, Cambridge University Press, 1952), pp. 85, 125; see also pp. 107, 109, 500. That Fox could be equally concerned with the suitability of a building for use as a meeting house see his careful directions for converting a barn in his letter of 28 February 1687 to Thomas Lower, quoted from the Tuke Papers of the Borthwick Institute, York, in Chedburn, Olive S. (1976), *Theology and Architecture in the Tradition of the Meeting House* (University of St. Andrews, B.Phil. thesis), pp. 179-180.
6. See Banton, A.E. (1964), *Horningsham Chapel. The Story of England's Oldest Free Church* (Chapmanslade, Westbury, Wiltshire, Dryer's Printing Works) — used by Chedburn (1976), *Op. cit.* in note 5 above, pp. 107-112 in an extended account. See also, Short, H. Lismer (1945), 'The Architecture of the Old Meeting Houses', *Transactions of the Unitarian Historical Society* (1945), 8 (3): 98-112.
7. Quoted by Davies (1948), *Op. cit.*, p. 106; and see pp. 103-108 for a full account of Caroline studies.
8. A recent study emphasises the influence upon Laud of Continental Baroque culture, rather than mediaeval nostalgia or Tridentine theology — see Clark, D.L. (1967), 'The Altar Controversy in Early Stuart England' (Harvard University, Th.D. dissertation), as in *Harvard Theological Review*, 60 (4): 486.
9. Ross, M. (1961), *Architectural Form and Christian Doctrine* (Toronto University, School of Architecture dissertation), p. 15.
10. See Addleshaw, G.W.O. & Etchells, F. (1956), *The Architectural Setting of Anglican Worship* (London, Faber & Faber).

11. See Drummond, A.L. (1934), *The Church Architecture of Protestantism* (Edinburgh, T. & T. Clark), p. 31.
12. Davies (1968), *Op. cit.*, p. 127.
13. Brion, Marcel (1960), *L'Architecture religieuse de 1400 à 1800* (Paris), p. 72, quoted by Biéler, A. (1965), *Architecture in Worship* (Edinburgh, Oliver & Boyd), p. 53.
14. See Sinnot, Edmund W. (1963), *Meetinghouse and Church in Early New England* (New York, McGraw-Hill).
15. Short (1945), *Op. cit.*, p. 112; see also his 'The Evolution of the Unitarian Church Building', *Transactions of the Unitarian Historical Society*, 12 (1949): 146-153. See also, Routley, E. (1961), *The Story of Congregationalism* (London, Independent Press), pp. 128 ff., for the identification of three phases in the history of their churches — Family (to 1750), Audience (1750-1900), and Community (1900-).
16. For a devastating account of Scottish auditoria between 1870 and 1900 see Lindsay, Ian G. (1960), *The Scottish Parish Kirk* (Edinburgh, St. Andrew Press), p. 78.
17. Drummond, A.L. (1932-33), 'Contrasting Tendencies in Protestant Church Architecture', *Church Service Society Annual*, 5: 42.
18. *First and Last Loves* (London, John Murray, 1952), pp. 101-102.
19. The phrases are Pugin's, in *An Apology for the Revival of Pointed Architecture in England* (London, J. Weale, 1843), p. 7.
20. Quotations from Neale, J.M. & Webb, B. (1843), *The Symbolism of Churches and Church Ornaments: A Translation of the First Book of the Rationale Divinorum Officiorum, written by William Durandus sometime Bishop of Mende* (Leeds, T.W. Green), Introductory Essay, pp. xxi, xxii, xxiii.
21. Neale & Webb (1843), *Op. cit.*, p. liv.
22. Neale & Webb (1843), *Op. cit.*, p. lxii.
23. Neale & Webb (1843), *Op. cit.*, p. lxx, quoting a poem of St. Gregory Nazianzum.
24. Pugin (1851), *A Treatise on Chancel Screens and Rood Lofts, their Antiquity, Use, and Symbolic Signification* (London, Charles Dolman), *passim*.
25. Pugin (1841), *The True Principles of Pointed or Christian Architecture* (London, John Weale), pp. 44, 42; reprinted Oxford, St. Barnabas Press, 1969.
26. See p. 188 above.
27. Neale & Webb (1843), *Op. cit.*, pp. cxxi-cxxiii.
28. Neale & Webb (1843), *Op. cit.*, pp. lv-lvi.
29. Clark, Kenneth (1950), *The Gothic Revival: An Essay in the History of Taste* (Rev. ed., London, Constable), p. 238.
30. Short (1949), *Op. cit.*, p. 151; see also Davies, Horton (1962), *Worship and Theology in England* (Princeton, Princeton University Press), Vol. 4, pp. 63-64, for the successive steps by which Elder-Yard Meeting House, Chesterfield, was transformed into a so-called liturgical building between 1818 and 1927.
31. Forsyth, P.T. (1911), *Christ on Parnassus* (London, Hodder & Stoughton; repr. London, Independent Press, 1959), ch. 7: Architecture, *passim*. Another attempt to both accept and reject Gothic is seen in the work of two Nonconformist architects, Crouch, J., and Butler, E. (1901), *Churches, Mission Halls*

and Schools for Nonconformists (Birmingham, Buckler and Webb). 'Palladian was insincere', and meeting houses and full Gothic both unsuitable, hence a 'modified Gothic' was recommended.

32. Murray, K. & Hammond, P., Eds. (1962), *Towards a Church Architecture* (London, Architectural Press), pp. 89-90.
33. Hagemann, H.G. (1963), 'Liturgical Place', *Princeton Seminary Bulletin*, 56 (2): 31.
34. On the Continental revival see Drummond (1934), *Op. cit.*, pp. 62-64.
35. On Hopkins, see White, J.F. (1963), 'Theology and Architecture in America: A Study of Three Leaders', in Henry, S.C., Ed., *A Miscellany of American Christianity* (Durham, N.C., Duke University Press), pp. 362-371.
36. See Brown, B. (1968), *Quest for the Temple: the New York Ecclesiological Society, 1848-55* (General Theological Seminary, New York, S.T.M. dissertation), and summary in *Bulletin, General Theological Seminary* (1968), 54 (4): 10-11.
37. Quoted by White (1963), *Op. cit.*, p. 375.
38. White (1963), *Op. cit.*, p. 379.
39. White (1963), *Op. cit.*, p. 381.
40. White (1963), *Op. cit.*, pp. 367, 377; see also quotations from Cram on pp. 208-209 above.
41. Van Ogden Vogt (1929), *Art and Religion* (New Haven, Yale University Press), p. 189, quoted by White (1963), *Op. cit.*, p. 389.
42. See Drummond (1934), *Op. cit.*, pp. 108-109, and Plate XIX.
43. Conover, E.M. (1928), *Building the House of God* (New York, Methodist Book Concern).
44. As a recent example among many, at the opening of the new hall for the Faith Mission in Fort William, Scotland, the acting-Superintendent for the Highlands said 'Our prayer is that the building may be a temple where the Holy Spirit will be delighted to dwell....' See *Life Indeed*, August 1975, p. 153.
45. Senn, O.H. (1962), 'Church Building and Liturgy in the Protestant Church', in *Lucerne International Joint Conference on Church Architecture...* (New York, National Council of Churches of Christ in the U.S.A.), p. 14.

NOTES TO CHAPTER 13: 'THE EXPERIENCE OF OTHER TRADITIONS: ISLAM'

1. Those who regard this Sura as late Meccan strengthen the point here made.
2. Obermann, J., in Bainton, R.H., *et al.*, Eds. (1955), *The Idea of History in the Ancient Near East* (New Haven, Yale University Press), p. 278.
3. Dickie, J. (1965), 'The development of the mosque form in relation to the needs of the Muslim liturgy', *The Islamic Review*, 53 (9-10): 14. Dr. Dickie's fuller and most admirable statement analysing the liturgical nature of mosques, etc., appeared too late for use in this chapter: 'Allah and eternity: mosques, madrasas and tombs', in Michel, G., Ed. (1978), *Architecture of the Islamic World* (London, Thames and Hudson), pp. 15-47.
4. Dickie, J. (1972), 'The Iconography of the Prayer Rug', *Oriental Art*, N.S., 18 (1): 5.

5. Kuban, D. (1974), *Muslim Religious Architecture* (Leiden, E.J. Brill), Part 1, p. 14; the whole is an excellent brief account relevant to our theme. See also Cresswell, K.A.C. (1972), 'Islamic Architecture', *Encyclopaedia Britannica*, Vol. 12, pp. 671-676.
6. Forster, E.M. (1953), *Abinger Harvest* (London, E.Arnold), Part 4, The East: The Mosque, p. 307.
7. Muhammad Zufrallah Khan (n.d. [ca. 1970]), *Pilgrimage to the House of Allah* (London, The London Mosque), for a modern sophisticated pilgrim to the Prophet's tomb and Mecca.
8. Dickie, J. (1967), 'Modern Islamic Architecture in Alexandria', *The Islamic Quarterly*, 13 (4): 187 for the Kurayyim Mosque (1953) as an excellent example. Burckhardt, T. (1976), *Art of Islam* (London, World of Islam Festival Publishing Co.), pp. 9-14, discusses the cosmic symbolism deliberately incorporated (in the first century of Islam!) in the Dome of the Rock, which was regarded as an 'avatar' of the Ka'aba.
9. Dickie (1965), *Op. cit.*, p. 10.
10. Dickie (1965), *Op. cit.*, p. 6.
11. Burckhardt, T. (1967), *Sacred Art in East and West* (Medford, Middlesex, Perennial Books), p. 108, and quoting Vogt-Goknil, U. (1953), *Türkische Moscheen* (Zürich).
12. Doi, A.R.I. (1966), 'The Islamic Version of the Sacred Place' (University of Nigeria Seminar Paper, Department of Religion), p. 7.
13. Doi (1966), *Op. cit.*, p. 9.
14. Pedersen, J., *et al.* (1927), 'Ka'ba', *The Encyclopaedia of Islam* (Leiden, Brill & London, Luzac), Vol. 2, p. 588.
15. Guillaume, A. (1954), *Islam* (Harmondsworth, Penguin Books), p. 103.
16. I am told by Dr. James Dickie that a Wahhabi proposal to demolish the Prophet's tomb was countered by the British sending a gunboat to the Red Sea with a threat to bombard Jedda!
17. See *The Islamic Review* (1965), 53 (9-10): 20-22; and *The Straits Times Annual* (Singapore, 1966), pp. 50 ff.
18. See note 8 above.
19. Forster (1953), *Op. cit.*, p. 306; also, Burckhardt, T. (1967), 'Perennial Values in Islamic Art', *Studies in Comparative Religion*, 1 (3): 135-137 for similar interpretation.

NOTES TO CHAPTER 14: 'THE EXPERIENCE OF OTHER TRADITIONS: JUDAISM'

1. Nothing is said about the building and its position in the only rabbinic rules concerning synagogues – in *Tractate Megillah*, ch. 3; only the *Tosephta, Megillah* 4: 22-23 mentions the site and orientation.
2. Mihaly, E., in Schoens, M.E. & Lipman, E.J., Eds. (1958), *The American Synagogue: A Progress Report* (New York, Union of American Hebrew Congregations), p. 93.
3. For good historical surveys see the extensive material in *Encylopaedia Judaica*

(Jerusalem, Keter Publishing House, 1971), especially Vol. 17, the article 'Synagogue', and bibliography; also May, H.G. (1944), 'Synagogues in Palestine', *Biblical Archaeologist*, 7 (1): 1-20.

4. See Leslie, D.D. (1972), *The Survival of the Chinese Jews* (Leiden, Brill), ch. 7, with sketch by Père Domenge in 1721 (Plates 21-22).
5. See Obermann, J. (1931), 'The Sepulchre of the Maccabean Martyrs', *Journal of Biblical Literature*, 50: 250-265.
6. Goodenough, E. R. (1954), *Jewish Symbols in the Greco-Roman Period* (New York, Pantheon), Vol. 4, pp. 210-211, *et passim*.
7. Rosenau, H. (1938), 'The Early Synagogue', *Archaeological Journal* (Royal Archaeological Institute of Great Britain and Ireland), 94: 66, and references.
8. Quoted in *Encyclopaedia Judaica* (1971), Vol. 8, col. 922, from S. Pinsker, *Likkutei Kadmoniyyot*. Addenda, pp. 27ff.
9. Kaufman, J., in Schoen & Lipman (1958), *Op. cit.*, p. 6.
10. *Encyclopaedia Judaica* (1971), Vol. 17, col. 601.
11. *Encyclopaedia Judaica* (1971), Vol. 3, col. 457.
12. Kline, A., in Schoen & Lipman (1958), *Op. cit.*, pp. 138-139.
13. Mihaly, E., in Schoen & Lipman (1958), *Op. cit.*, pp. 97, 100-101.
14. Michaels, L., in Schoen & Lipman (1958), *Op. cit.*, pp. 203-204.
15. Freehof, S.B., in Blake, P., Ed. (1954), *An American Synagogue Today and Tomorrow...* (New York, Union of American Hebrew Congregations), p. 9.
16. Landsberger, F., in Kline (1958), *Op. cit.*, p. 140; also Tachau, W.G. (1926), 'The Architecture of the Synagogue', *The American Jewish Yearbook*, 28: 155-192, *illus.*
17. Freehof, S.B. (1963), *Reform Jewish Practice and its Rabbinic Background* (New York, Union of American Hebrew Congregations), Vol. 2, p. 27.
18. Feder, A.H., in Blake (1954), *Op. cit.*, pp. 218-219.
19. From the dedication booklet, Temple Emanu-El (Nuuanu Valley, Hawaii, 1960), quoted by Mulholland, J.F. (1970), *Hawaii's Religions* (Rutland, Vermont, C.E. Tuttle Co.), p. 245.
20. Michaels, L., in Schoen & Lipman (1958), *Op. cit.*, pp. 200-201.
21. Kline, A., in Blake (1954), *Op. cit.*, p. 45.
22. Mumford, L. (1925), 'Towards a Modern Synagogue Architecture', *The Menorah Journal*, 11 (3): 225-240.
23. Mihaly, E., in Schoen & Lipman (1958), *Op. cit.*, pp. 94, 154.
24. Rubenstein, R.L., in Hunt, R.L., Ed. (1969), *Revolution, Place and Symbol* (No place, International Congress on Religious Architecture and the Visual Arts), p. 151.
25. See *Christianity Today*, 12 March 1971, p. 43.
26. An analogy we owe to Yinger, J.M. (1969), in *Journal for the Scientific Study of Religion*, 8 (1): 98.
27. See Butler, J.F. (1956), 'The Theology of Church Building in India', *Indian Journal of Theology*, 5 (2): 10-15 for the Islamic models and New Spain forms. See also McClenahan, R.S. (1942), 'The Moslem's Mosque and the Christian's Church', *The Moslem World*, 32 (2): 159-166.

NOTES TO CHAPTER 15: 'THEOLOGICAL ISSUES IN TWENTIETH CENTURY CHURCH BUILDING'

1. Briner, L.A. (1964), 'A Protestant Looks at the New Constitution on the Sacred Liturgy', *McCormick Quarterly*, 17 (4): 18.
2. Drummond, A.L. (1932-33), 'Contrasting Tendencies', *Church Service Society Annual*, 20: 5.
3. Betjeman, J. (1940), 'Nonconformist Architecture', *The Architectural Review*, 88: 161-174.
4. Davis, C., in Hammond, P., Ed. (1962), *Towards a Church Architecture* (London, Architectural Press), pp. 117-118.
5. See especially Cope, G. (1963), *Ecclesiology Then and Now* (London, The Ecclesiological Society), pp. 9 ff.
6. In support, see Hammond, P. (1960), *Liturgy and Architecture* (London, Barrie & Rockliff), pp. 86-87.
7. 'Shimei' [n.d. (Oct. 1962)], in *Themelios* [2 (1)]: 31-32; also Smith, P. F. (1972), *Third Millennium Churches* (London, Galliard), pp. 38-40 on preaching as prior to ritual in Christian worship.
8. E.g., Debuyst, F. (1968), *Modern Architecture and Christian Celebration* (London, Lutterworth), p. 61.
9. Davies, H. (1966), *Worship and Theology in England 1900-1965* (Princeton, Princeton University Press), p. 441.
10. Dwyer, R.J. (1958), 'Art and Architecture for the Church in Our Age', *Liturgical Arts*, 27 (1): 2-6.
11. English translations available in Hammond (1962), *Op. cit.*, pp. 248-254; and in *Documents for Sacred Architecture* (Collegeville, Minn., The Liturgical Press, 1957), pp. 15-23.
12. Reprinted in Hammond (1962), *Op. cit.*, pp. 255-262.
13. See cult of the saints in ch. 9.4 above; good accounts also available in Davies, J.G. (1968), *The Secular Use of Church Buildings* (London, S.C.M. Press), pp. 36-38 and ch. 8; and in Bouyer, L. (1963), *Rite and Man* (London, Burns & Oates), pp. 186-188.
14. Sprott, G.W. (1882), *Worship and Offices of the Church of Scotland* (Edinburgh, Blackwood & Sons), pp. 25, 250, 257.
15. Wesley, John (1860), *Works* (fourteen vols.), Vol. 10, pp. 509-511; also his *Journal* in Vol. 5, pp. 92, 447; and his *Explanatory Notes upon the New Testament* (London, Epworth, 1952), on Acts 19:9.
16. Luykx, B. (1974), *Culte chrétienne en Afrique après Vatican II* (Immensee, Nouvelle Revue de Science Missionnaire), ch. 7.
17. Full report in *Atlanta Journal* (Atlanta, Georgia), 19 December 1970.
18. Davies (1968), *Op. cit.*, ch. 8; also G. Cope's many articles on this theme.

NOTES TO CHAPTER 16: 'MEETING HOUSE AND TEMPLE IN THEOLOGICAL PERSPECTIVE'

1. Davis, C., in Hammond, P., Ed. (1962), *Towards a Church Architecture* (London, Architectural Press), p. 113.
2. Winter, M.M. (1973), *Mission and Maintenance* (London, Darton, Longman & Todd), pp. 24ff.
3. Schwarz, R. (1958), *The Church Incarnate* (Chicago, H. Regnery & Co.), p. 198.
4. Spindler, M. (1969), *Pour une théologie de l'espace* (Neuchâtel, Delachaux et Niestlé), p. 62.
5. Goodman, P., in Schoen, M.E. & Lipman, E.J., Eds. (1958), *The American Synagogue* (New York, Union of American Hebrew Congregations), p. 88.
6. Schwarz (1958), *Op. cit.*, pp. 196-197.
7. Nicholson, F.J. (1975), 'A Hallowed Place', *The Friend*, 132 (12): 288.
8. Baily, K. (1974), 'Meeting Houses', *The Friend*, 132 (7): 149. That this is not merely a recent Quaker attitude is attested in a publication on meeting houses by William Alexander in 1820: 'The Society... does not attach any sanctity to the *building*, but everyone must, to the purpose for which it is designed' [Quoted by Chedburn, O.S. (1977), 'Theology and Architecture in the Tradition of the Meeting House', *The Friends' Quarterly*, 20 (2): 67-68].
9. D. Roller, personal communication.
10. See M. Haran's development of this in his 'The Divine Presence in the Israelite Cult...', *Biblica* (1969), 50: 251-267.
11. Von Allmen, J.J. (1964), 'A Short Theology of the Place of Worship', *Studia Liturgica*, 3 (3): 166-167.
12. Rykwerk, J. (1966), *Church Building* (London, Burns & Oates), p. 126.
13. See Alberti, L. B. (1955), *Ten Books on Architecture* (London, A. Tiranti), Book VII, pp. 3, 136.
14. Feuerbach, L. (1957), *The Essence of Christianity* (New York, Harper), p. 20.
15. Grisebrooke, W.J. (1964), 'Oblation at the Eucharist. I: The Theological Issues', *Studia Liturgica*, 3 (4): 227-239, for good critique of the semi-pelagianism of an 'offerings-theology'. Also, Butler, J.F. (1964), 'Presuppositions in Modern Theologies of the Place of Worship', *Studia Liturgica*, 3 (4): 210-226, for a radical criticism of such symbolism.
16. Smith, P.F. (1972), *Third Millennium Churches* (London, Galliard), p. 39, and ch. 12 for this distinction in relation to churches.
17. Schwarz (1958), *Op. cit.*, p. 230.
18. Church of England General Synod, Report by Standing Committee (1973), *The Use of Church Properties... in Multi-racial Areas* (London, The Synod), pp. 4-12 on 'Holiness, consecration and reverence' for good discussion of the themes of this chapter. As it has been well expressed by an architect: 'Abandon the preoccupation with symbols to allow the real symbolic function to emerge' [Quinn, P.J., 'Whither Church Building?', in Davies, J.G., Ed. (1976), *Looking to the Future* (Birmingham, Institute for the Study of Worship and Religious Architecture), p. 69].
19. Davies, H. (1966), *Worship and Theology in England 1900-1965* (Princeton, Princeton University Press), p. 4.

20. Pace, G. (1966?), 'The Chapel', *University of Keele Chapel Guide* (Keele, University Christian Society), p. 11.
21. Senn, O.H. (1962), 'Church Building and Liturgy in the Protestant Church', *Lucerne International Joint Conference on Church Architecture and Church Building* (New York, National Council of Churches of Christ in the U.S.A.), p. 5; see also Frazer, J.W. (1962), 'On Behalf of the Chancel', *Church Service Society Annual*, 32: 32-34, and a kindred plea in Turner, H.J.M. (1971), 'The Mysterious within Christianity', *Eastern Churches Review*, 3 (3): 301-305.
22. Hammond, P. (1960), *Liturgy and Architecture* (London, Barrie & Rockliff), p. 160, *et passim*.
23. See Cercle Saint Jean Baptiste, Paris (1970), *Axes: La Ville et le Sacré*, 13-14: 135, 107-108. This is akin to Bernard of Clairvaux's distinction between an austere norm for monks and more lavish forms for the general populace; see ch. 10: 5 above.
24. Rubenstein, R.L., in Hunt, R.L., Ed. (1969), *Revolution, Place and Symbol* (No place, International Congress on Religion, Architecture and the Visual Arts), pp. 152-153. Other dimensions of this need appear in N. Schweizer's statement: 'The young people are not interested in multi-purpose spaces. They want a sense of the sacred' — quoted by Quinn (1976), *Op. cit.*, p. 70, who also refers to 'the need for ritual place' (p. 71), and the increasing inability of secular institutions to supply centres of public and community enrichment (p. 50).
25. Church of England General Synod (1973), *Op. cit.*, p. 10.
26. Widtmann, in Hunt (1969), *Op. cit.*, p. 209.
27. Federal Writers' Project in Georgia (1937), *Savannah* (Savannah), p. 58, on the Baptist Church.
28. Hammarskjöld, Dag (1957), 'A Room of Stillness', *United Nations Review*, June 1957: 38-39.
29. Hageman, H.G. (1963), 'Liturgical Place', *The Princeton Seminary Bulletin*, 56 (2): 36ff.
30. Smalley, S. (1967), *Building for Worship* (London, Hodder & Stoughton), p. 85.
31. Schwarz (1958), *Op. cit.*, pp. 202-203.
32. Zucker, W.M. (1964), reported in *News and Views* (N.C.C.C.U.S. New York), 2 (2): 4.
33. Dahinden, J. (1968), *New Trends in Church Architecture* (London, Studio Vista), p. 74.
34. F. Debyst seems to support a similar limited acceptance of the *domus dei*: 'I must confess that I am still able to enjoy once in a while a monumental church. ... But churches of this kind ... should be very rare exceptions, responding to particular needs and functions'. See his 'Whither Church Building?', in Davies (1976), *Op. cit.*, p. 39. Debyst has also warned against developing 'a system, an *ideology* of the house-church', which 'if imposed or applied too strictly would in fact narrow our chances to influence or improve church buildings as a whole' (*Idem*, p. 40).
35. Otto, R. (1923), *The Idea of the Holy* (London, Oxford University Press), ch. 11; see also our earlier discussion, ch. 8.

36. See the moving incident quoted in Perham, M. (1960), *Lugard: The Years of Authority 1912-1918* (London, Collins), p. 673.
37. Burckhardt, T. (1967), *Sacred Art in East and West* (Bedfont, Middlesex, Perennial Books), p. 106.
38. Smith (1972), *Op. cit.*, p. 89.

NOTES TO CHAPTER 17: 'THE WIDER IMPLICATIONS FOR PHENOMENOLOGY AND THEOLOGY'

1. In speaking of 'an orthodox Christian interpretation' we do not forget that there is an ongoing variety of Christian theologies representing many different emphases and regional traditions within the Christian faith; the phenomenologist might therefore have to deal with these separately. In our particular subject, however, it would appear that the biblical interpretations concerning 'temple' in both Old and New Testaments are not involved in the differences but would be acceptable to a wide variety of Christian scholarship. It is probably at the level of subsequent emphasis and practical application in the various Christian traditions and cultures that the differences in this field begin to emerge.
2. It is recognized that not all religions engage in theological explication and the associated self-criticism, and that this activity is more evident in the Semitic religions and especially in Christianity where theology plays a key role. The extent to which other major traditions can or wish to do theology for their own benefit may vary, and is connected with cultural variations as to how to apprehend reality and to reach truth. In view, however, of the remarkable critical reflective capacity revealed in some of the individual thinkers reported from primal religions in North America, Africa and elsewhere, we are inclined to think that there is an undeveloped theological potential in these particular traditions that may yet develop under the stimulus of literacy and the new modes of thought that this encourages. Our own discussion clearly applies in the first instance to the Semitic traditions.
3. Tillich, P. (1951), *Systematic Theology* (Chicago, University of Chicago Press), Vol. 1, p. 118.
4. Pannenberg, W. (1971), *Basic Questions in Theology* (London, S.C.M. Press), Vol. 2, p. 116.
5. Benz, E. (1961), *Ideen zu einer Theologie der Religionsgeschichte* (Wiesbaden), p. 49, quoted in Pannenberg (1971), *Op. cit.*, p. 69.
6. Pannenberg (1971), *Op. cit.*, pp. 69-71.
7. As Professor L. G. Geering pointed out to me, some other religions in the 19th century had to face the issues raised by the invasion and power of Christianity before the latter came to take these others seriously. Indeed this new seriousness has been induced in some degree by the renewed vitality of the great Asian religions in the 20th century, a renewal which itself owes something to the influence Christianity has had on the Asian faiths. The work of Radakrishnan is a case in point. Interactions between the great religions have therefore been leading towards their various 'theologies of other religions' for some time.
8. Warren, M. A. C., memorandum 'The Uniqueness of Christ', quoted in British

Council of Churches, Final Report (1974), *The Community Orientation of the Church...* (London, British Council of Churches), p. 56.

9. Transposition is discussed in Van der Leeuw, G. (1963), *Religion in Essence and Manifestation* (New York, Harper & Row), Vol. 2, pp. 610-611. This refers to 'the variation in the significance of any phenomenon... while its form remains quite unaltered'. On the other hand the transposition of temple we describe involves a transposition of form while the significance remains essentially the same. This seems to be a more radical form of transposition.

10. McIntyre, J. (1966), *The Shape of Christology* (London, S.C.M. Press), p. 69.

Indexes

3. INDEX OF MOSQUES AND SHRINES, INDIVIDUAL

4. INDEX OF SYNAGOGUES, INDIVIDUAL

5. INDEX OF TEMPLES AND SHRINES, INDIVIDUAL

6. INDEX OF PERSONAL NAMES

RELIGION AND SOCIETY

Already published

1. M.U. Memon, *Ibn Taimiya's Struggle against Popular Religion*. 1976, XXII + 424 pages.
2. R.de Nebesky-Wojkowitz, *Tibetan Religious Dances*. 1976, VIII + 320 pages.
3. W. Grossmann, *Johann Christian Edelmann: From Orthodoxy to Enlightenment*. 1976, XII + 210 pages.
4. B.B. Lawrence, *Shahrastānī on the Indian Religions*. 1976, 300 pages.
5. M.A. Thung, *The Precarious Organisation: Sociological Explorations of the Church's Mission and Structure*. 1976, XIV + 348 pages.
6. F.W. Clothey, *The Many Faces of Murukaṇ. The History and Meaning of a South Indian God*. 1978, XVI + 252 pages.
7. W.A. Graham, *Divine Word and Prophetic Word in Early Islam. A Reconsideration of the Sources*. 1977, XVIII + 266 pages.
8. A. Jackson, *Na-khi Religion. An Analytical Appraisal of the Na-khi Ritual Texts*. 1979, XXII + 366 pages. 16 plates and 1 color plate.
10. M.Ayoub, *Redemptive Suffering in Islam. A Study of the Devotional Aspects of 'Āshūrā' in Twelver Shī'ism*. 1978, 304 pages.
11. J.H. Stewart, *American Catholic Leadership: A Decade of Turmoil, 1966-1976. A Sociological Analysis of the NFPC's*. 1978, XX + 200 pages.
13. B.L. Goff, *Symbols of Ancient Egypt in the Late Period*. 1979, XXVI + 310 pages. Many plates.
14. J.-P. Deconchy, *Orthodoxie religieuse et sciences humaines*. With a summary in English. 1979, 324 pages.
15. M. Vassallo, *From Lordship to Stewardship. Religion and Social Change in Malta*. 1979, 272 pages.
16. H.W. Turner, *From Temple to Meeting House. The Phenomenology and Theology of Places of Worship*. 1979, XIV + 404 pages.
19. *Official and Popular Religion. Analysis of a Theme for Religious Studies*, ed. by P.H. Vrijhof and J.Waardenburg. 1979, XIV + 740 pages.

In preparation:

9. J. van Kessel, *Danseurs dans le désert (en Chili). Une étude de dynamique sociale*. With a Summary in English. 1979.
12. J.Y. Lee, *Korean Shamanistic Rituals*. With photographs. 1979.
17. J.Pérez-Remon, *Self and Non-self in Early Buddhism*. 1979.
18. J. Thrower, *The Alternative Tradition. A Study of Unbelief in the Ancient World*. 1979.

MOUTON PUBLISHERS · THE HAGUE · PARIS · NEW YORK